A Perilous Imbalance

Law and Society Series
W. WESLEY PUE, GENERAL EDITOR

The Law and Society Series explores law as a socially embedded
phenomenon. It is premised on the understanding that the conventional
division of law from society creates false dichotomies in thinking, scholarship, educational practice, and social life. Books in the series treat law and
society as mutually constitutive and seek to bridge scholarship emerging
from interdisciplinary engagement of law with disciplines such as politics,
social theory, history, political economy, and gender studies.

A list of the titles in this series appears at the end of this book.

A Perilous Imbalance

The Globalization of Canadian Law and Governance

...... Stephen Clarkson and Stepan Wood

UBCPress · Vancouver · Toronto

20 19 18 17 16 15 14 13 12 11 10   5 4 3 2 1

Printed in Canada on FSC-certified ancient-forest-free paper (100% post-consumer recycled) that is processed chlorine- and acid-free.

Library and Archives Canada Cataloguing in Publication

Clarkson, Stephen
    A perilous imbalance: the globalization of Canadian law and governance / Stephen Clarkson and Stepan Wood.

(Law and society series, ISSN 1496-4953)
Includes bibliographical references and index.
ISBN 978-0-7748-1488-1 (bound); ISBN 978-0-7748-1489-8 (pbk.);
ISBN 978-0-7748-1490-4 (e-book)

    1. Law and globalization – Canada. 2. Globalization –Political aspects – Canada. 3. Globalization – Economic aspects – Canada. I. Wood, Stepan. II. Title. III. Series: Law and society series (Vancouver, B.C.)

KZ1268.C53 2009   341.0971   C2009-905205-9

Canadä

UBC Press gratefully acknowledges the financial support for its publishing program provided by the Government of Canada (through the Canada Book Fund), the Canada Council for the Arts, and the British Columbia Arts Council.

This book has been published with the help of a grant from the Canadian Federation for the Humanities and Social Sciences, through the Aid to Scholarly Publications Programme, using funds provided by the Social Sciences and Humanities Research Council of Canada.

UBC Press
The University of British Columbia
2029 West Mall
Vancouver, BC V6T 1Z2
604-822-5959 / Fax: 604-822-6083
www.ubcpress.ca

IN MEMORIAM

The Law Commission of Canada, 1997-2006
The Law Reform Commission of Canada, 1971-1992

Contents

A Perilous Imbalance ....

1

Introduction

Consider these scenarios:

- An American company restructures its Canadian operations, relocating an assembly plant to Mexico and many management functions to its US headquarters.
- A Canadian mining company is implicated in environmental and human rights abuses in an African country.
- Cheap international travel and instant global communications allow growing numbers of Canadians to forge new identities and social bonds that challenge traditional notions of national citizenship.
- Respiratory disease in China spreads rapidly via airline passengers, straining public health systems and devastating Toronto's lucrative tourism economy for months.
- Victims of torture find their way to Canada and eventually launch lawsuits in Canadian courts against the foreign government officials who allegedly tortured them.
- Canadian labour and human rights groups collaborate with civil society organizations around the world to eliminate sweatshops and promote fair trade.
- Canadian corporations entrust resolution of their disputes to international arbitrators whose decisions are giving rise to an autonomous, stateless "law merchant."
- The amorphous threat of global terrorism prompts the Canadian government to restrict certain civil liberties and tighten controls on immigration and refugees.

All of these seemingly disparate developments are both manifestations of and responses to a bewildering array of phenomena collectively referred to as globalization. Two decades after this term entered the public vocabulary, globalization remains one of the most controversial and challenging phenomena facing Canada and the world. Efforts to manage both it and its myriad effects are as controversial as globalization itself and often constitute aspects of globalization in their own right. Novel forms of governance are proliferating outside the conventional bounds of national government and domestic law in many areas, even while state power is being reasserted in others. Complex systems of multi-actor, multi-level governance are emerging in which states and their official law, though still occupying prominent roles, are being dislodged from their once unassailable pre-eminence.

This book examines the challenge of governing globalization in the context of Canada, a substantial but not dominant middle power that is strong enough to have some impact on the world beyond its borders, a world that increasingly influences what goes on within them. It canvasses historical patterns and contemporary developments to examine the role of law in a reciprocal dynamic: in the impact of global forces on Canada and in the conduct of Canadians as actors on the global stage.

Governing beyond Borders

Our consciousness of globalization as a putatively new phenomenon forces us to question not just the borders one sees on maps but a whole range of other familiar boundaries, whether they be political, social, cultural, or economic. It also makes us interrogate conceptual and institutional borders such as those associated with the state, law, public policy, sovereignty, and personal identity. These borders condition or impede the movement of people, goods, services, and ideas. They define the limits of political authority, of community, even of the self. Globalization is not simply a matter of erasing these borders. It may also shift or redefine them. In other cases, it may bring them into sharper relief or draw new borders where none existed before.

The nation-state is our prime example. Throughout most of the twentieth century, it was recognized as the primary, even the exclusive, institution for governing national societies. Its territorial borders were seen as co-extensive with those of society, so that the two formed an organic unity. The state was understood as having a monopoly over law, policy making, and the legitimate use of coercive force, a proposition captured in the notion of sovereignty. It was also seen by many as possessing a unique capacity and responsibility to promote collective prosperity, health, and welfare by intervening directly in markets and society, a vision embodied in the Keynesian welfare state after the Second World War. Numerous developments have combined to loosen the state's apparent monopoly and undermine the geopolitical and conceptual borders on which it depended. In an era of instantaneous worldwide communication, porous societies, apparently seamless global production networks, and liberalized international trade, many Canadians feel they are living in a borderless world.

National borders seem to be disappearing in some respects as states cede some functions to multilateral structures such as the United Nations (UN) or the World Trade Organization (WTO). Other governmental responsibilities are being assumed by an array of informal, flexible, private global institutions including markets, transnational corporations (TNCs), and civil society organizations (CSOs). Whether they feel victimized by global economic forces they cannot control, enjoy the cosmopolitan pleasures of international tourism, pursue professional occupations that span national borders, or identify with tsunami victims half a world away, many Canadians experience the territorial borders of the Canadian state as decreasingly relevant and governance as an increasingly transnational phenomenon.

In other respects, the borders of the nation-state appear not to be disappearing but shifting. For certain actors, effective economic and political boundaries are moving to the continental level due to such treaties as the *North American Free Trade Agreement* (NAFTA). Something similar can be discerned in post–11 September 2001 efforts to turn North America into a continental fortress via the Security and Prosperity Partnership and in efforts to create a Fortress Europe on the other side of the Atlantic. In both cases, the goal is to stop terrorists and unwanted immigrants before they enter the continental community by relocating defence perimeters and immigration controls from the national to the continental level. In other domains, effective boundaries are shifting downward as central governments devolve their responsibilities, and provincial and local governments assert their authority. Some scholars believe that subsidiarity (the principle that governance authority should rest at the level best able to address the policy problem) is "in the process of replacing the unhelpful concept of 'sovereignty' as the core idea that serves to demarcate the respective spheres of the national and international" (Kumm 2004, 920-21). Some governmental functions are still exercised within the same geographic formations but are moving "sideways" from the state to market or civil society actors. Changing combinations of CSOs, business groups, and provincial/state governments interact with their national capitals to work out transborder arrangements – to clean up the

Great Lakes, for instance. Whether formal or informal, these new kinds of politics become confusingly messy.

But that is not all. In some cases, globalization seems to reinforce existing borders or throw up new ones, as federal and provincial governments battle over jurisdictional boundaries, or Ottawa tightens immigration barriers in reaction to newly perceived threats from terrorism or disease. New psychic borders are being erected when, for instance, minority groups seek to protect their customs, values, or identity, when the earth's billion or so slum dwellers are effectively kept out of the global economy, or when the millions who lack access to telephones or the Internet are excluded from the new virtual communities made possible by the information-technology revolution.

In short, drawing a sharp line between the domestic and the international neither reflects contemporary realities nor addresses the needs of Canadian and global societies. A coherent analysis of globalization must look beyond received conceptual and institutional boundaries to consider the realities of how globalization and governance are experienced.

Globalization

In common parlance, "globalization" refers to the increasing breadth, intensity, and speed of worldwide interconnectedness in all aspects of social life and its consequences for human conduct. In the constricted space and contracted time of the "global village," decisions made or actions occurring in one place have direct and rapid impacts on the health, prosperity, and prospects of individuals, communities, or ecosystems halfway around the world. The term "globalization" is already something of a cliché, "the big idea which encompasses everything from global financial markets to the Internet but which delivers little substantive insight into the contemporary human condition" (Held et al. 1999, 1). Yet clichés are meaningful, because they "often capture elements of the lived experience of an epoch. In this respect, globalization reflects a widespread perception that the world is rapidly being moulded into a shared social space by economic and technological forces and that developments in one region of the world can have profound consequences for the life chances of individuals or communities on the other side of the globe" (ibid.).

Five further characteristics demonstrate the richness and complexity of the phenomenon: it is pervasive, heterogeneous, dynamic, interactive, and contested.

Globalization is *pervasive*, affecting government, business, civil society, and individuals and permeating all domains of human life. It includes

- the *globalization of consciousness:* a growing collective consciousness of humanity, the planet earth, and its ecosystems as a single community with a shared fate
- *political globalization:* the rise of transnational political regimes in which corporations, civil society organizations, and governments establish new norms for global trade, environment, and human rights
- *economic globalization:* the global spread of free trade rules and ideology, a spectacular increase in transnational investment, and a dramatic expansion of world trade in goods and services
- *societal globalization:* massive movements of peoples, transnational networks of activists, and a huge proliferation of personal interaction in cyberspace
- *technological globalization:* the instantaneous worldwide communications networks now provided by information technology, employed particularly in the industrialized world
- *legal globalization:* harmonization of national laws, proliferation of international law, the increasing use of model contracts and international arbitration by commercial actors, the incorporation of foreign and international law in domestic courts, and the worldwide transmission of American legal norms by US-based law firms as they serve the needs of large transnational corporations
- *medical globalization:* societies' increasing vulnerability to epidemics such as HIV/AIDS, SARS (severe acute respiratory syndrome), or influenza, whose devastation respects no borders
- *cultural globalization:* the increasing global domination of American (and to a lesser extent European) entertainment industries and cultural products
- *ecological globalization:* the emergence and rapid intensification of environmental change, from ozone depletion to climate change to biodiversity loss
- *criminal globalization:* the growth of networks of sex trade, drug trafficking, and terrorism, as well as the rise of white-collar corporate crime employing sophisticated tools and having transnational effects
- *military globalization:* the rise of "humanitarian intervention," the war on terror, the Iraq invasion and resulting civil strife, a burgeoning global

arms trade, and the presence of Canadian troops in Afghanistan, Haiti, and other states that have been torn apart by conflict, crime, or corruption

- *psychological globalization:* the spectre invoked by ideologues that the dire threat of irreversible competitive pressures forces politicians to make drastic cuts to government programs and requires businesses to cut jobs and reduce wages.

Irreducibly *heterogeneous,* globalization takes many different forms, involves a multiplicity of actors pursuing disparate goals, and has a wide range of contradictory effects – adverse and beneficial, creative and destructive, intended and unanticipated. It involves both integration (in continent-wide trade blocs, globally integrated production and distribution networks, transnational social movements, and universal human rights norms) and fragmentation (in separatist movements, the weakening of established social bonds, the disintegration of established states, and the increasing gulfs between rich and poor or between advanced and marginalized sectors), processes which demonstrate the intensification of transnational interactions at every geographic scale. It involves both universalization, whereby local ideas and practices are projected globally, and domestication, whereby universalized ideas and practices are received, adapted, or resisted in particular locales (for example, the adoption of Shari'a law in Ontario's Muslim communities). The benefits and costs of globalization are not evenly distributed. Some people and places bear the brunt of its negative impacts, whereas others enjoy the bulk of its gains.

Inherently *dynamic,* globalization is characterized by rapid, intense change in almost all domains of human affairs. Seemingly beyond the control of any single actor or class of actors, it appears to have a life of its own, reinforcing certain relations of power and privileging certain models of social, political, and economic organization while destabilizing, marginalizing, or eradicating others. As a result, any approach to managing globalization must be adaptive to change and ready to challenge entrenched or emerging patterns of injustice.

Globalization is also *interactive* and results in the spread of intergovernmental agreements, organizations, and regimes. One of the most significant developments of the post–Second World War period has been the proliferation of international law and organizations, which has occurred multilaterally, regionally, and bilaterally. Although some might argue that internationalization should be distinguished from globalization because it reinforces rather than challenges the state-based character of the existing world system, we believe its impact is more ambiguous, in some ways reinforcing the dominant position of states, in other ways undermining it. Besides, we want to appraise the complete picture that Canada faces in the world. Defining globalization only in terms of phenomena that undermine the existing state-based system would prejudge a question we prefer to leave open by including in our remit aspects of internationalization that have acquired new significance or surfaced in recent decades.

Finally, globalization's meaning, effects, and desirability are fundamentally *contested* – in Canadian society as elsewhere. Any analysis of globalization and any attempt to manage its processes and effects must be sensitive to the deep conflicts that are generated by efforts to facilitate, constrain, or even simply to understand its various manifestations.

In sum, "globalization" refers to a pervasive, heterogeneous, dynamic, interactive, and contested intensification of interconnectedness in all aspects of human affairs, at all geographic scales.

Lessons from History

The intensification of transnational interconnections and the reconfiguration of the borders within which we live are nothing new for Canadians. Throughout Canada's history, political and other borders have continually been erected, dismantled, and reconstructed, shifting on a continuum from porous to solid and back. From the beginning, the fit between state and society has been imperfect, with First Nations, Québécois, Hutterites, polygamous Mormon sects, and numerous ethnic minorities asserting varying degrees of autonomy vis-à-vis a dominant anglophone society.

As Neilson (2004, 5) writes, "The present stage of globalization may be in our face, so to speak, but its antecedents in law and practice have been with us for centuries." Those antecedents, in legal terms, include Roman law, canon law, the law merchant, and the law of nations. In economic and political terms, Western colonialism and the rise of a capitalist world economy were early manifestations of globalization. Born of colonial expansion, Canada from its first days was dependent for its economic well-being on its insertion into a nascent global marketplace. To understand what, if anything, is new in contemporary globalization, Canadians can draw two linked lessons from their history: Canada's destiny was shaped from the beginning by external forces, and Canada's experience of global processes has always been mediated through its relationship with an imperial or hegemonic power.

External Forces

Since Samuel de Champlain first sailed up the Gulf of St. Lawrence, the Canadian state has been constructed, then largely constrained by external influences, from the market forces driving the original cod fishery and fur trade to recent massive waves of immigration. Ever since the arrival of the Europeans, Canada's indigenous and settler populations have been affected by distant forces and actions. It was the Europeans' search for increased supplies of less perishable protein that pushed their fishermen until they discovered the Grand Banks' teeming schools of cod. The subsequent demand for furs in France and England, along with the two great powers' search for a route to the Orient, motivated their establishing permanent settlements in New France and the Maritimes. These colonial outposts of expanding European empires established the embryonic structures that were to evolve into the Canadian federation.

From prehistoric migrations across the Bering land bridge, to the influx of European settlers and the displacement of the indigenous populations, to contemporary diasporas from around the globe, Canadian history is a story of ceaseless human movement. Modern Canada is a nation of immigrants, many of whom preserved strong ties to their home cultures, languages, and communities even as they cobbled together a pan-Canadian identity. Intolerance, prejudice, and discrimination in many forms were central to this history. They were directed toward people of Aboriginal, Métis, Irish, French, Chinese, Japanese, Southern European, Eastern European, Jewish, African, and other heritages. They were embodied in discriminatory immigration policies that could at best be described as a "calculated kindness" (Folson 2004). They were also aimed at women and religious minorities. Outside the largest cities, which received the bulk of our immigrants, the population remains predominantly French in Quebec and Anglo-Saxon in the rest of Canada. Notwithstanding these facts, Canadian society has become remarkably diverse in the past six decades as it has built a deserved reputation for multiculturalism, tolerance, and respect for civil rights. Canadian society, especially its urban population, is a microcosm of global cultural diversity and home to numerous diasporas. In short, the history of Canadian demography is itself a parable of globalization.

Similar stories could be told in the realms of economy, technology, and politics. The Canadian economy has long been export oriented, responding to the demand for renewable resources and raw materials in European, American, and, increasingly, Asian markets. It has long been dependent on imports of manufactured and finished goods. As a result, it is chronically sensitive to fluctuations in international commodity prices and changes in the economic fortunes of its major trading partners. "The need and the efforts to deal with the problems posed by its insertion into the global economy are nothing new for the Canadian state," observes McBride (2001, 35): "Indeed, there is a sense in which the political history of Canada consists of little else."

In terms of scientific developments, Canadian economic and social history was driven by the same transformations that wrote the technological story of globalization: from sail to steam, from carriage to railroad, from telegraph to telephone to television, from the car to the computer, from electricity to e-mail.

On the Periphery of Empire

The second lesson from Canada's history is that its experience of globalization has always been mediated through its relationship with a single dominant power, first as an outpost of the French, then the British Empire, and, more recently, as an extension of American hegemony. Canadian politics have always been heavily oriented toward an imperial metropolis – once Paris, later Whitehall, now Washington – the chronic dependence on which has generally been counterbalanced by efforts to establish some degree of autonomy. Under French control, even as they strengthened their connections with Paris, New France's voyageurs claimed their mastery over the continent, extending their relationship with Native peoples. From the days of these first European settlers, Canada has related to its global context as a receiver, relying on investment and know-how coming from a more powerful and advanced economy, and then depending on that economy's market for selling the resulting raw materials or manufactures.

Canadians have at times felt themselves the hapless pawns of imperial conflicts going on elsewhere. By the end of the eighteenth century, the struggle among the European empires for global dominance left the territory to the north of the new United States of America in the hands of the British, whose need for timber and wheat caused their staple-producing North American colonies to burgeon. Some residents of these colonies did not fare so well in these imperial geopolitics. First Nations were steadily marginalized, despite the 1763 *Royal Proclamation*, which pledged to protect their lands and interests. The Acadians were brutally deported to Louisiana, whereas the Canadiens of New France became second-class citizens within British North America, provoking nationalist tensions that continue to define Canadian politics today. Under British rule, colonial politicians worked to consolidate an autonomous state structure, even as they tried to ensure that London maintained its troops along their impossibly long American border.

Dependence is not a one-way street. The imperial powers needed Canada's supplies of furs and fish, timber and wheat, oil and uranium for their own wealth, health, and security. Although this interdependence may always have been mutual, it has also been asymmetrical, with the weaker periphery depending more on its powerful imperial centre than the centre depended on its periphery. Furthermore, the colonial periphery was inherently vulnerable to interruptions in the supply of technology and capital from the metropolis and to fluctuations in its demand for the colonies' staples. In the nineteenth century, this vulnerability generated a desire for autonomy from Great Britain, but fear of being swallowed up by the expansionist United States tempered this impulse. Canadian politicians' efforts to extract themselves from British control evolved gradually over almost one hundred years from the 1860s until the mid-twentieth century.

After the First World War, Canada's locus of economic dependence shifted steadily from the declining British Empire to the rising colossus to the south, as American investors elbowed aside their English rivals to become the dominion's main source of capital. In this process, the United States also displaced the United Kingdom as Canada's major foreign market and its principal supplier of technology. Former US secretary of state Henry Kissinger (1999, 3) famously quipped that globalization was just a euphemism for Americanization. The prime economic indicators of globalization – development of communication technologies, the spread of TNCs, the emergence of a global capital market, the negotiation of new economic rules for global capitalism – were indeed the product of the US political economy. For Canada more than any other country, globalization has been experienced as Americanization. Since it felt the social, cultural, and economic effects of post–Second World War US power more fully than any other country, discussion of Canada's experiences of globalization must start with American hegemony.

HEGEMONY, IMPERIUM, AND AUTARCHY

Before getting deeper into the Canada-US relationship, we need to clarify our use of the term "hegemony," which describes a situation in which a dominant actor achieves its goals by generating a willing consensus with subordinate actors about how their shared system should operate (Clarkson 2008a,

17). Such a consensus may transcend social classes and include a wide range of interests (Gill 1995, 400). Subordinate actors submit consensually to the will of the dominant actor. Hegemony can be located in the middle of a continuum passing from imperium at one end to autarchy at the other. "Imperium" describes a situation in which a single dominant actor employs coercion to impose its will upon others – typically via threats of physical force or the infliction of severe economic penalties (Clarkson 2008a, 17). Such compulsion can be exercised either through law or in spite of it (Koskenniemi 2007, 13). At the other extreme, "autarchy" describes a condition in which an actor is disconnected from and unconstrained by the wills of other actors. Until the NAFTA era, Mexico's approach to economic development after its revolution was largely autarchic. The United States continues to assert autarchy in certain economic sectors.

These three categories are ideal types. In practice, the relationship between them is complex and dynamic. A particular project such as NAFTA may be experienced as hegemonic by Canadian and Mexican elites and by some workers in export-oriented industries but as imperial by those who strenuously oppose it (such as labour, environmental, and nationalist movements). Hegemony may expand and deepen over time as a dominant actor, such as the United States, extends a consensual approach to more and more areas of foreign relations, and as broader segments of subordinate societies come to believe there is no alternative. This was the trend in several North American policy arenas as the project of continental integration unfolded during the 1980s and 1990s. By the same token, if a dominant actor shifts from consensual to coercive tactics for exerting its will, we may see a move from hegemony to imperium. This is exactly what happened in North America after 11 September 2001, when the United States retreated from its previous practice of consensual governance to a more traditional variety of unilateral strong-arm tactics, using the threat of restricted access to US markets to press Canada and Mexico into enacting tougher border controls that would buttress American homeland security. This return to imperial relations with its continental periphery was accompanied by a reassertion of autarchy, as the United States unilaterally closed its borders and brought cross-border trade to a temporary standstill. The same autarchic reflex was seen again in 2003 when Washington closed its borders to Canadian cattle imports in response to a "mad cow" disease scare. Following most such autarchic episodes, the United States eventually reopened its borders and re-established hegemony, but on new and tougher terms.

NEO-CONSERVATISM

In this book, we devote substantial space to what we call the neo-conservative project of economic globalization. In the literature on globalization, there is some confusion about the terms "neo-liberalism" and "neo-conservatism," which are often used to denote the same phenomenon. Because the word "liberal" has various meanings, we use "neo-conservative" to indicate the economic orthodoxy that became dominant in the aftermath of the Keynesian policy paradigm's rejection by the political, economic, and media elites of the capitalist world following the election of Margaret Thatcher in 1979 and Ronald Reagan in 1980. Their perspective is also referred to as the "Washington Consensus," which describes the formula for prosperity offered by the World Bank Group and the International Monetary Fund (IMF) to their client states: freeing their markets by deregulating the domestic economy, privatizing state-owned firms, shrinking the public sector, reducing the social wage, and liberalizing the rules for international trade and investment.

Many writers use "neo-liberalism" in this sense, evoking nineteenth-century economic liberals who championed a reduced role for autocratic governments in order to liberate the economy's burgeoning capitalist forces. This usage can be confusing for those who associate "liberal" with generous, socially progressive policy and "conservative" with tough-love free-market policies. This is not to suggest that neo-conservatism is either monolithic or unchanging. It is neither. Although it has a certain amount of global coherence, it is marked by regional and national variations as well as disagreement on various points among its principal proponents. Reconsideration or abandonment of some elements of the Washington Consensus, along with the aggressive military unilateralism and unabashed Christian fundamentalism of the George W. Bush administration, make contemporary neo-conservatism qualitatively different from that of two decades ago. As we shall see, neo-conservatism has proved flexible and resilient, and still supplies the dominant ideational impetus to the economic dimension of globalization.

SLEEPING WITH THE ELEPHANT

It was during the Cold War standoff between the socialist and capitalist blocs from the late 1940s to the late 1980s that the US asserted its predominance as the world's most dynamic economy, ideological leader, and military power. Its decisive role in setting up, financing, and staffing the Bretton Woods institutions that restructured the capitalist order after the Second World War (the IMF, the World Bank, and, later, the *General Agreement on Tariffs and Trade*

[GATT]) and its partners' acceptance of this international system made it the unquestioned hegemon of the capitalist world. Although American hegemony may have declined in certain respects during the late twentieth century thanks to the rise of the European and Asian economies (Keohane 1984), it was revived by the collapse of Eastern European communism, which left the United States the sole global military superpower. More subtly, American actors, institutions, products, and ideas remained hegemonic economically, politically, and culturally as well (Gill 1993). Whatever might be said for the rest of the world, American influence remains the central feature of Canada's experience of globalization. Cohen (1974, 4) summarizes the situation nicely:

> No one could have foreseen in 1776 or 1783 that the new, independent English-speaking United States would grow so rapidly as to overshadow quickly the imperial remnant to the north and create by these geopolitical facts the permanent crisis in Canadian life; namely, its development beside an immense neighbour who would outstrip Canada in everything, perhaps, but the determination to achieve an integrity of its own. It is no surprise, therefore, that the long-term Canadian international experience par excellence, and the concomitant political-legal preoccupation, should have been the form and substance for managing Canadian relations with the United States; and this remains true to the present day.

Well before the word "globalization" was invented, Canada's autonomy was already limited by the fact that substantial parts of its economy, including the most modern sectors such as the petroleum, chemical, automotive, electrical machinery, and computer industries, were owned by American companies and thus controlled from south of the border, where the best management jobs and most important research and development facilities were located. With much of the country's gross national product flowing to the US through intra-firm transfers, the federal and provincial governments' capacity to regulate the domestic economy has been limited.

This branch-plant economy's pervasive dependence on the United States did not prevent considerable autonomous political evolution. Notably, in the first decades following the Second World War, Canada, along with its fellow nation-states in the industrialized world, developed a sophisticated management capacity and social infrastructure. This Keynesian welfare state had three main tasks. First, it fine-tuned the macro-economy's overall stable growth by adjusting interest rates and setting taxation levels. Second, it implemented micro-economic policies for specific economic sectors aimed to increase exports, reduce imports, and expand domestic production for the home market. Third, this import-substitution strategy was complemented by programs designed to provide a basic social wage (through pensions, unemployment insurance, and workers' compensation) along with public health care and education for all citizens. As the federal and provincial governments learned to manage these three tasks, the Canadian state achieved considerable legitimacy as the manager of a marketplace and society that were largely coterminous with its political boundaries.

Ever since Canada emerged from the blood-soaked battlefields of the Second World War as a significant actor in international affairs, its foreign policy has been cosmopolitan and internationalist. During the Cold War period, it built a reputation for itself as an honest broker in great power politics, exercising an influence seemingly beyond its material capabilities. A staunch supporter of multilateralism and international law, it played a key role in the negotiation of universal human rights instruments and was a vocal proponent of decolonization and Third World development. An eager participant in multilateral forums, it joined every international club for which it was eligible, from the Commonwealth to la Francophonie. Its avid multilateralism helped offset its asymmetrical relationship with its overwhelmingly stronger neighbour by generating multilateral political spaces in which Ottawa could manoeuvre outside Washington's bilateral influence.

In response to a nationalist surge critical of the country's deepening integration in and dependence on a bellicose America fighting an imperial war in Vietnam, the Trudeau government sought in the 1970s and early 1980s to reduce Canadian dependence on the US economy and vulnerability to US policy by forging a more independent foreign policy and a more nationally focused domestic economy. Trudeau established Petro-Canada, tried to buy back or limit foreign (read: American) investment in crucial sectors, launched the controversial National Energy Program, and espoused a foreign policy that was at times openly critical of US international stances. To think that Canada could be an autonomous state pursuing its own priorities domestically and internationally would be naive. For the four decades following 1945, Canada's tenuous, ambiguous sovereignty was primarily tied to its deep dependence on the giant next door. With globalization, Canada's relations of interdependence have become more complicated.

WHAT'S NEW?

Canada's contemporary experience of globalization differs from that of its past mainly because of economic and technological transformations in global capitalism made possible by a breakdown of the post–Second World War bargain among industrialized states (Cox 1996b; McBride 2001, 16). This bargain, which Ruggie (1982, 209) calls the compromise of "embedded liberalism," had enabled the emergence of the modern welfare state: "The task of postwar institutional reconstruction ... was to ... devise a framework which would safeguard and even aid the quest for domestic stability, without, at the same time, triggering the mutually destructive external consequences that had plagued the interwar period. This was the essence of the embedded liberalism compromise: unlike the economic nationalism of the thirties, it would be multilateral in character; unlike the liberalism of the gold standard and free trade, its multilateralism would be predicated upon domestic interventionism."

The identity between states' political boundaries and their economic space started to break down in the 1970s for a number of reasons, both internal and external. Domestically, the success of the Keynesian welfare state generated a crisis as an ever-enriched social wage and escalating labour demands for higher pay put inflationary pressures on governments, which were unwilling to tax their citizens enough to finance their generous programs. Internationally, the world economy was shaken first by the collapse of the Bretton Woods system of international currency controls in 1971 when President Richard Nixon disconnected the US dollar from gold and then by the next decade's oil shocks, when the Organization of Petroleum Exporting Countries (OPEC) doubled, redoubled, and doubled again the price of oil on the world market. Computer technology and the intermediation of financial institutions made capital markets increasingly integrated across borders, helping TNCs to escape from government regulation and so weakening national governments' control over their economies.

These problems proved to be more than the old formula of Keynesian welfarism could resolve. With stagflation – simultaneously high inflation and unemployment, a combination Keynesian theory had believed impossible – economists and business advocates made the case for a radical policy shift that would restrain the state in order to liberate and reinvigorate the market.

The election of Prime Minister Margaret Thatcher in 1979 and President Ronald Reagan in 1980 made neo-conservatism the dominant policy paradigm in the capitalist world. As Canada lost more control over its markets and found it was competing with other countries to lure foreign investors, it came under pressure to cut back the social wage and restrict such regulations as those designed to achieve environmental sustainability.

Finding it increasingly difficult to resolve problems on their own, governments started cooperating more extensively with their neighbours. With the European Community in the lead, regional groupings of states emerged as common markets or free trade areas, permitting their corporations to cut their costs (via lowered tariffs) and achieve greater competitive efficiency (via economies of scale). The economic trade-off was straightforward: in return for their increased access to other markets, domestic firms received less protection from foreign competition. The social trade-off was less obvious. Reduced protectionism spelled job losses in beleaguered industrial sectors. Since investment tended to follow trade, enlarged access to foreign markets meant more jobs created abroad than at home by successful TNCs. The result: further downward pressure on the social wage without compensating salary increases.

By the late 1970s, Canadian business had abandoned its historical support for the import-substitution industrialization that had kept the home market largely to itself. With tariff protection falling as a result of the continual negotiating rounds at the GATT, the business community was losing control of what was in any case a relatively small home market. Unable to survive by producing for the domestic market, Canadian entrepreneurs decided their best hope lay in selling to and investing in the huge market next door. At the same time, American business was lobbying for Washington to break down other countries' economic development programs that fostered domestic corporations by discriminating in their favour. Claiming they faced unfair discrimination abroad, American TNCs promoted an ambitious agenda centred on the ability to operate freely in all economies. Giant firms in the entertainment, biotechnology, and computer sectors wanted their intellectual property rights protected around the world. Corporations in the energy, courier, education, and health sectors argued that other countries' public-sector provision of these services amounted to unfair protectionism and should be deregulated and privatized to allow them to compete there.

Incorporating these demands in a sophisticated dual strategy, the US government pressed its global counterparts for major changes in the rules governing the GATT. Finding multilateral resistance to this vision from major industrialized players such as the European Community and Japan as well as from rising Third World powers such as Brazil and India, Washington also pursued a bilateral approach, twisting the arms of its more compliant trade partners to make concessions that could be used as precedents in the ongoing multilateral negotiations. It enjoyed its first major success with the 1987 *Canada-US Free Trade Agreement* (CUFTA). The year 1994 saw the implementation of the *North American Free Trade Agreement* (NAFTA), which expanded the bilateral deal to Mexico and provided corporate investors with unprecedented rights and powers to overturn regulations issued by the governments of the three member states. That same year saw the conclusion of the GATT's Uruguay Round, which launched the World Trade Organization, effectively universalizing American-inspired norms of international trade liberalization.

Opinions differ regarding the beneficial or harmful impact of these free trade arrangements, but all agree that they have fundamentally changed the balance between states and transnational capital. Throughout this period, "an international economy made up of discrete and strongly regulated national economies trading with and investing in each other slowly became eclipsed by a world economy 'in which production and finance were being organized in cross-border networks that could very largely escape national and international regulatory powers'" (Ó Tuathail, Herod, and Roberts 1998, 2-3, quoting Cox 1996b, 22).

Although these politico-economic changes are of fundamental importance, what is new about globalization is not limited to the economic sphere and associated modifications of the administrative state. The collapse of the Soviet bloc, the end of bipolar geopolitics, and the emergence of the United States as the only superpower have had profound effects, including newfound instability and uncertainty in the former Third World, a massive ideological boost to agendas for the global spread of capitalism and liberal democracy, and the transformation of global military conflict from a relatively stable nuclear stalemate to unstable, largely localized, yet persistent warfare. We are witnessing a global "rights revolution" in which new and old states are emerging from the yoke of totalitarianism and embracing greater democracy, human rights, and personal freedoms (Schneiderman 2004). We have also seen the rise of Islamist extremism, Christian fundamentalism, and other nominally religious transnational movements. The experience of catastrophic environmental change in the last thirty years, from ozone depletion to climate warming, shows for the first time that human activity can impair ecological functioning at a planetary scale and intensifies the urgency for cooperative action to forestall disaster. The Internet and other information technologies make possible an unprecedented density and velocity of personal connections across borders, instantaneous communication concerning events around the world, and new forms of social solidarity and personal identity, at least for those with access to them. The list goes on. Suffice it to say that, though the roots of globalization are old, some of its manifestations and implications are substantially new in the contemporary period.

Although debate continues whether the current characteristics of globalization differ in degree or in kind from the interdependencies that existed in the past, it is increasingly clear that contemporary developments fundamentally challenge our received understandings of how we govern and are governed, whether in Canada or abroad.

BRINGING THE STATES BACK IN[1]

Many Canadians perceive no connection between their country's role on the global stage and its relationship with the United States. In terms of Canada-US relations, they understand Canada as a generally loyal geopolitical ally and economic extension of the global superpower, its room for manoeuvre perennially constrained by the need not to antagonize the behemoth for fear of being crushed underfoot. But in relation to the rest of the world, they see Canada as an independent force, punching above its weight as it brokers solutions to international conflicts, advances world peace, and pursues its own national interest. This compartmentalized outlook needs to be corrected by understanding how Canada's position on the global stage is inseparable from its relationship with American hegemony.

Many proponents of a robust, independent Canadian foreign policy become so caught up in their visions of Canada as a potential force for good in the world that they underestimate the extent to which Canada's connection with the United States restricts its possibilities for action abroad (Byers 2007; Welsh 2004). The highly asymmetrical Canada-US relationship is a constitutive condition of Canada's role in world affairs. Middle powers such as Canada understandably favour multilateralism because working in international organizations with many partners can enhance their room for manoeuvre and can compensate for the limitation they feel in their unequal dealings with a dominant neighbour. Yet this same asymmetry makes multilateralism problematic since it can induce Canada to take actions such as committing troops to an unwinnable war in Afghanistan just to ingratiate itself with Washington. A belief in an independent foreign policy may lead many to ignore their federal and provincial governments' considerable dependence on actions taken in government offices and corporate headquarters south of the forty-ninth parallel.

Nevertheless, Canada is neither as helpless in its bilateral relationship nor as autonomous in its international endeavours as many may assume. Indeed, its bilateral relationship sets the main parameters for its international possibilities, which in turn help orient its relations with Washington. After 1945, Canada experienced the dilemmas of interdependence mainly through its complex political, economic, social, and cultural relationships with the United States; however, the forces of globalization now expose it to different dynamics, which open prospects for new types of engagement.

CANADIANS AS AGENTS AND OBJECTS OF GLOBALIZATION

Canadians as individuals and the Canadian state as a set of institutions are both agents and objects of globalized governance. Given their history, it is not surprising that Canadians tend to feel they are *objects* of globalization, either as winners or losers. The happy winners find themselves the beneficiaries of global forces, enjoying an increasingly multicultural Canadian society, the World Wide Web, cheap international telephone calls, an amplified variety of consumer goods and cultural products from all over the world, better job opportunities in some sectors, affordable international travel, almost instant worldwide e-communication, rapid transmission of ideas across borders, and growing understanding of the "outside" world. Others see themselves as victims of globalization, pointing to more job insecurity, the Canadian economy's vulnerability to external shocks, worsening social tensions, a loss of national identity, the homogenization of cultural and consumer products, growing disparities between rich and poor, deteriorating environmental quality, and a spread of transnational criminal activity, disease, and terrorism. They feel their destiny controlled by decisions made outside the country by actors and institutions that are neither transparent nor accountable. Whether lucky victors or unhappy sufferers, citizens feel themselves to be passive objects of external forces.

But this is only part of the picture, because Canada and Canadians are also *agents*, shaping globalization by acting on the world stage. Consider the following:

- The Canadian government early became adept at parlaying its sheltered position in the global hierarchy of power into unusual, if limited, influence in global politics, punching above its weight diplomatically, earning a reputation as an honest broker, and championing multilateralism and international peace. From Lester Pearson to Maurice Strong to Louise Arbour, individual Canadians have been leading figures in the development and implementation of international law and policy in a wide range of fields, such as peacekeeping, environmental protection, human rights, and global criminal law.

- Federal and provincial governments have been active champions, not just passive objects, of many of the changes associated with neo-conservative globalization, from government downsizing and privatization to negotiating trade agreements that deliberately reduced their own powers.

- Many Canadian businesses operate abroad, bringing jobs, technology, and industrial best practices to host communities, while others bring social dislocation, human rights abuses, and environmental devastation. Some industry self-regulatory initiatives developed in Canada have spread globally, such as the chemical industry's Responsible Care program.

- CSOs are also global players. Greenpeace began as a small group of environmental activists in Vancouver. Canadian CSOs were instrumental in securing the adoption of a global treaty to ban anti-personnel land mines. Canadian Native peoples are influential advocates of indigenous rights and self-government in Australia, Chiapas, and the circumpolar region.

- As tourists, Canadians influence other societies and economies through their choice of destinations, activities, accommodations, meals, and souvenirs. A Canadian tourist who engages in child-sex tourism has very different impacts on the world, and different implications for legal governance, than one who travels to ski, hike, or visit art museums. At home, the choices Canadians make as consumers and investors affect health, prosperity, ecosystems, and life prospects half a world away, sometimes supporting unsustainable systems of production, sometimes pressuring firms to be more socially and environmentally responsible.

- Canada is often itself a model for the world. Its health care system; social programs; *Charter of Rights and Freedoms*; laws and policies regarding multiculturalism, indigenous rights, women's equality, and sexual diversity; the relatively successful coexistence of Quebec in the Canadian federation; and most recently Ottawa's banking regulations are held up for emulation around the world (Welsh 2004, 190) – or occasionally for derision by those who mock "Canuckistan" as a socialist perversion (Trickey 2002).

In sum, when thinking about globalization, we must simultaneously consider its impact on Canada and Canadians' impact on it, because these inward and outward dynamics are dialectically inseparable sides of the same coin. Canadians experience their engagement with the world as a double movement. Not only do they feel the effect of external forces on them, they also have impacts on the world outside Canada's borders. They are concerned about the fate of communities in other countries and want to know what they, as Canadians, can do as cosmopolitan citizens of the world to ameliorate that fate.

Canada's relationship with the United States is similarly dual. Canadian governments promoted US hegemony when they subscribed to the entrenchment of neo-conservative economic norms in NAFTA and the WTO but also when they negotiated bilateral trade and investment agreements with other countries (discussed in Chapter 3). Sometimes Canada resists the United States. As we explain in Chapter 4, Ottawa backed the UNESCO *Convention on the Protection and Promotion of the Diversity of Cultural Expressions* as a reaction against the WTO *Sports Illustrated* ruling, through which the United States threatened the Canadian magazine industry. Canada's championing of the International Criminal Court (ICC) despite sustained American opposition provided another example of principled resistance.

Rethinking Our Concepts

For all these reasons, globalization requires us to rethink four of the key terms of contemporary political order: governance, law, sovereignty, and legitimacy.

GOVERNANCE

Globalization prompts us to interrogate the meaning of governance. How are societies governed under conditions of globalization? How and by whom is authority to govern distributed and exercised? We can no longer accept the conventional assumption that formally elected governments wield the ultimate authority in Canadian society. Other institutions and actors, from NAFTA to transnational corporations, coexist in a complex tapestry of power relations that may substantially constrain governments' autonomy to direct Canadian society according to their own priorities.

For most of the last two centuries, "governing" was viewed as an activity undertaken by "the government" – that is, the formal apparatus of the state: legislatures, executive bodies, bureaucracies, courts, and the coercive agencies of the police and the Armed Forces. Many believe that this way of looking at governance is now obsolete because the conventional institutions of the nation-state are ill-suited to deal with problems that transcend borders or those for which other actors such as business associations are better equipped to address. From private corporations to international organizations, from local social movements to transnational networks of scientists, countless institutions play important, even decisive, roles in contemporary governance.

Many analysts employ the term "governance" to describe the confusing situation created by the emergence of multiple decision-making centres. Formerly restricted to a few specialized areas, the term has recently spread to almost all domains of human endeavour. People now talk about the governance of health care and education, prisons and pension funds, non-governmental organizations (NGOs), and even families – and, in our case, the global governance of world affairs through the UN, the WTO, or other international regimes. Indeed, it is now almost impossible to speak about how to conduct human affairs without mentioning governance, although little agreement exists regarding what the word means.

This does not mean that national governments have become irrelevant. Whether acting through the international organizations and regimes to be discussed in Part 1 of this book or through the reconfigured instrumentalities of the nation-state described in Chapter 6, governments remain at the centre of efforts both to promote and respond to globalization. Yet, as we argue in relation to the economic supraconstitution in Chapter 3 and to governance "beyond the state" in Chapter 7, it is also important to recognize that a wide range of non-governmental actors and institutions is involved in governance, from TNCs to non-profit aid organizations.

Despite the proliferation of forms of governance beyond the state, many decision makers, stakeholders, and journalists continue to connect governance with the government, defined in terms of the nation-state, territorial sovereignty, and formal law, thus perpetuating the old sharp distinction between the domestic and international spheres. Rejecting this approach as outmoded, and cognizant of the myriad ways in which people are actually affected by public and private regulations, we adopt a broader definition of governance in order to examine state and non-state governance arrangements alongside one another.

All governance arrangements are not created equal. Some have more muscle than others and some more legitimacy. In the past, the term "government" was understood to designate those institutions that had ultimate constitutional authority in any given territory with a monopoly over law making and the legitimate use of force. Government actions and pronouncements were seen as having a binding authority that those emanating from other actors and institutions could not claim. If this picture was ever accurate, globalization has made it obsolete. Today, certain non-governmental actors and institutions may, and in some cases clearly do, have more effective and binding authority than some governments. Giant transnational corporations, international organizations (such as the IMF); credit-rating agencies, and the rules of the world trading system have greater clout than many domestic authorities. Because they exert effective authority over their own affairs, it would even be consistent to apply the term "government" to these institutions and to acknowledge that they stand alongside (or are even superior to) some national governments in terms of their power and authority. Regardless of terminology, it is important when exploring the numerous forms of governance in a globalized world to consider the relative muscularity of different governing authorities and institutions.

This brings us to a further question about the relationship between globalization and governance: can globalization itself be governed? In practice, attempts to manage globalization are made in a piecemeal, incoherent, sometimes conflicting manner by a range of forces including the needs and demands of global capital, the geopolitical priorities of the major states, the set of quasi-constitutional rules and institutions underpinning the world economic system, and, to a much lesser extent, the actions of transnational civil society. Some critics refer to this heterogeneous organizational hodge-podge as global "dysgovernance" (Latham 1999). Our question for Canadians is less whether globalization can be managed as how it can be managed in ways that respect and enhance equity, justice, human development, ecological sustainability, and democratic legitimacy. Even after much heated debate everywhere in the world, the answer is not yet clear (Falk 1999; Bhagwati 2004). But it is certainly worthwhile, indeed imperative, for us to strive to achieve a satisfactory answer.

LAW

Because governance extends well beyond government, globalization also invites us to challenge the conventional conception of law as a formal product of the state and to consider a range of unofficial and transnational normative orders as elements of a broader, pluralistic set of legal systems that govern our lives in various ways and to varying degrees. Legal pluralism, at its simplest, refers to "a situation in which two or more legal systems coexist in the same social field" (Merry 1988, 871). Such is the case in Quebec, for instance, where the common and civil law systems coexist. Canadian law interacts increasingly with international law, Aboriginal law, and a range of unofficial or informal legal orders such as cyber-law, corporate codes of ethics, fair trade labelling schemes, workers' rights certification programs, the *lex mercatoria* (a body of private rules designed to facilitate transnational business dealings), Torah, and Shari'a.

Legal pluralism is more than just a description of coexisting or overlapping legal orders. It is a normative project to embrace and foster the diversity of normative orders, to enable their coexistence, and to reject the dominant tradition of "legal centrism" in which official state law remains at the apex of a hierarchical pyramid of normative authority (Sinha 1995; Tie 1999). Legal pluralism implies focusing on the "living law" (the real patterns of regularized conduct in society) rather than law "on the books." It also implies a conception of law that is not restricted to official statutes, administrative rules, and court decisions but is defined in terms of all the ways people actually experience authority and rule in their own lives. Of course, the formal legal system features prominently in these experiences for most people, but other normative orders work alongside or in place of this official law.

Why should we use the term "law" to describe these unofficial rule systems? Without rehearsing long-standing debates about the definition of law, we offer the simple reason that the term carries with it certain expectations of transparency, democratic accountability, fairness, and justice that facilitate an inquiry into the legitimacy of governance in a globalized environment. These aspirations are often unrealized in practice, but as Szablowski (2007, 288) says, "to leave law tied to the state when the state's myths of authority and competence are so visibly eroded is to abandon one of our most powerful metaphors – one which combines a concern for accountability, legitimacy, and justice":

> The modern concept of state law may be said by many measures to have failed to live up to expectations, but it has left us with at least one vital legacy, that of its aspirations. Disillusionment with the emancipatory capacities of the state may be widespread, [but]

the aspirations of effective and democratic governance have if anything increased their resonance around the globe. The task of re-
imagining what law should mean in a globalizing world should
be guided by these aspirations. (Szablowski 2004, 20)

Taking a broader view of law also prompts us to be realistic about the
potential that official law-making institutions could play in bringing about
legal and social change. Although they are central to conventional accounts
of law, legislatures and courts play only small roles in the day-to-day operation
of law as it is lived in this broader pluralist conception, which understands
"law" to be made and applied in a multitude of arenas, from union halls to
corporate boardrooms, commercial arbitral tribunals, religious councils,
community organizations, and Internet chat rooms. To appreciate how all
these varieties of law operate in lived experience requires us to "turn away
from the canonical texts and the privileged sites of legal reason, and turn
towards the minor, the mundane, the grey, meticulous, and detailed work of
regulatory apparatuses, of the control of streets, of the government of trans-
port, of the law of health and hygiene, of the operation of quasi-legal mechanisms for the regulation of relations between men and women, parents and
children ... of all the places where ... laws, rules, and standards shape our ways
of going on, and all the little judges of conduct exercise their petty powers of
adjudication and enforcement" (Rose and Valverde 1998, 546).

Similarly, we should recognize that projects to reform state law play
limited roles in social change. In the pluralist understanding of law advanced
here, "law reform" occurs in the imperceptible evolution of normative structures through daily social interaction, in marketplace arrangements invented
by imaginative business people and civil society groups, in innovative grassroots political action, and in other social institutions and practices. If official
law reform is to have any substantial influence on legal and social change, it
must be acutely sensitive to these social practices.

SOVEREIGNTY

Globalization also challenges received conceptions of sovereignty, which,
along with the complicated sets of social practices that constitute it, has lain
at the heart of conventional understandings of law's international context.
It has been at the foundation of the modern world order since the peace of
Westphalia in 1648. Sovereignty denoted complete, exclusive, and independent authority over a defined territory and its permanent human population,

along with security from intervention in its internal affairs by other sovereigns. So understood, sovereignty implied the absence of any higher authority capable of binding a sovereign against its will. Hence, all international obligations, whether arising by customary law or treaty, were dependent, in theory, upon the consent of the affected sovereign, freely given on the basis of formal equality.

Inherent in the image of the modern nation-state is

> the idea not only that political systems have to be hierarchically organized but also that this system should have a final arbiter of law – a sovereign – over which no other authorities can decide. This historical image of the European nation state has, however, been transformed from an empirical fact that shaped life in Europe from the Thirty Years War onwards to an ontological claim on which modern theorizing is based ... The result is that we have a tremendously hard time conceiving of political systems where territory, identity, and power are separated, functionally and/or spatially. (Wind 2003, 124)

New forms of governance challenge the traditional conception of sovereignty upon which the nation-state, its legal order, and the whole structure of international law are based. They throw the continuing meaning and relevance of sovereignty into question, seemingly weakening the sovereign authority of many states, casting doubt over the adequacy of a purely territorial model of sovereignty, increasing the kind and numbers of entities claiming some form of sovereignty, and inviting us to reconsider what sovereignty entails in the contemporary world. Toward the end of the twentieth century, this conception of sovereignty as a nation-state's territorially bounded and exclusive authority over a specific geographic space came under increasing pressure from many sources at once, including market globalization, transnational interdependence, neo-conservative political and economic ideology, global ecological changes, the retreat of the welfare state, and the collapse of communism. As a result, sovereignty is no longer what we once thought it was.

For some observers, sovereignty is dead, overwhelmed – for better or worse – by the advance of a now worldwide capitalism, global environmental crises, universal human rights, armed humanitarian intervention, and newly intrusive international treaties. For others, sovereignty still exists but has been fundamentally transformed so that, far from denoting a state's freedom to act as it chooses, it signifies the state's capacity to participate in the international regulatory regimes that make up international life and increasingly constrains unilateral action. In Abram and Antonia Chayes' (1995, 26-27) famous formulation, "for all but a few self-isolated nations, sovereignty no longer consists in the freedom of states to act independently, in their perceived self-interest, but in membership in reasonably good standing in the regimes that make up the substance of international life."

This brings into focus the old dispute over whether international agreements detract from state sovereignty. On the one hand, we can view signing international treaties or joining international organizations as limiting Canadian sovereignty because they effectively restrict the autonomy of national, provincial, or local governments to regulate as they see fit the business firms or other actors within their own territorial boundaries. Such restrictions are found, to varying degrees, in many policy fields, from foreign investment (for instance, in NAFTA) to biodiversity protection. Something like one-third of the laws adopted by the federal Parliament derive from the domestic implementation of international agreements. For these reasons, many observers view international treaties and organizations as limitations on Canadian sovereignty.

By negotiating international agreements and joining international organizations, Canada can also be seen as exercising its sovereignty and extending its capacity to act beyond its borders. In this view, treaty making is how Canada exercises its sovereign will on the international level. Ottawa enters only those arrangements it deems in the national interest, and treaties contain provisions that allow it to exercise its sovereign prerogative to register exceptions to or withdraw from those arrangements that do not meet its needs. Granted, many international treaties restrict Canada's freedom of action, but, like a contract between private individuals, such limitations are (in theory) assumed freely and voluntarily. This is so even when Canada "binds itself to the mast" of an intrusive international regime (see, for example, Wood 2002-03). In this view, if international arrangements curtail the regulatory autonomy of Canadian governments to a greater extent than initially anticipated, this is more a failure of informed consent than an invasion of Canadian sovereignty.

Still others believe that contemporary developments challenge our conceptions of sovereignty on an even more fundamental level, requiring recognition that sovereignty lies with people (or peoples), not states. This is

manifested in, for example, the emerging recognition of a right to democratic governance and the assertion of sovereignty by national minorities
around the globe. Many of these claims are asserted over territories that are
not coterminous with existing sovereign states or are based on factors other
than territory. The result is that, more and more, we may be living in a world
of multiple, overlapping, and even deterritorialized sovereignties.

Sovereignty nonetheless remains a powerful rhetorical device in struggles
for governance authority. In Canada, the Québécois and First Nations assert
the sovereign right to govern themselves and participate in the international
domain. In many developing countries, state sovereignty is widely seen as an
indispensable defence against "Northern" impositions. In powerful countries
such as the United States, sovereignty is routinely invoked to justify everything
from high import duties to rejection of the International Criminal Court's
jurisdiction or non-compliance with an unfavourable ruling by a NAFTA
dispute settlement panel.

The concept of sovereignty is bound together with the ability of a political collectivity (usually a nation-state) to determine and achieve its own
goals. The ability of Canadian governments to set their own goals and achieve
them, both domestically and internationally, is shaped by Canada's relationship with the United States and the world beyond. We find it useful to distinguish between two aspects of this ability. We use "autonomy" to refer to
a state's authority to do what it wants within its own territory. It may be
limited by the influence of powerful external actors such as states, international organizations, or transnational corporations. It may be constrained
by supranational norms and institutions. It may be restricted internally by
powerful domestic actors or by constitutional constraints such as federalism
and a bill of rights. Major states, such as the United States or China, have
more success in retaining their autonomy because they are relatively un-
inhibited by the threat of retribution for violating their international obligations. Less powerful states, such as many developing countries, often find
they have little or no autonomy in domestic affairs, although they may enhance it by making common cause with like-minded states. Canada, as a
mid-size advanced industrialized country, finds its autonomy constrained
mainly by its relationship with its huge southern neighbour.

We use "capacity" to refer to a state's ability to achieve its objectives outside its own territory. By entering into international agreements, a state and
its constituents may lose autonomy domestically but gain capacity to achieve
their goals beyond their borders. Canadians' enthusiasm for multilateralism

and for "rules-based" continental and global free trade regimes reflects their desire to enhance their country's capacity in international affairs. Sometimes capacity is gained at the expense of autonomy, because, during negotiations, a state may give up some of its powers in order to win concessions that increase its capacity in the other states' economies. But capacity and autonomy do not necessarily vary inversely with each other. Sometimes, after a country emerges victorious from a conflict, the two may be enhanced simultaneously. In the aftermath of a severe currency crisis when it becomes a ward of the international community, a state may find both its internal autonomy and external capacity shrinking at the same time.

"Sovereignty," in short, remains a central term of political and legal discourse, even as its meaning is increasingly problematized by globalization.

LEGITIMACY

Globalization also complicates the age-old problem of legitimacy – the popular approbation that comes when decisions affecting people are made by appropriate authorities, in acceptable ways, with acceptable results. Systems for legitimation have not kept pace with recent changes in the locus and operation of political authority (Bernstein 2004). Conflicts between the proponents and opponents of economic globalization are, at bottom, struggles over the legitimation of international political authority:

> Mainstream economists now routinely express their puzzlement at the rise and rapid expansion of "anti-globalization" protest movements around the world. If the protestors would only learn some basic economics and a little Riccardian trade theory, we often hear, they would realize that the costs of international interdependence and even deepening integration are overwhelmed by the benefits. It is, however, becoming very hard to believe that simple ignorance is driving a spreading reaction to global change. Mass demonstrations sweeping through relatively prosperous cities like Seattle, Washington, DC, Quebec City, and Genoa in the early years of the twenty-first century reflected broad agenda-defining coalitions among a variety of not necessarily convergent interests. But they also suggested something deeper. Certainly protestors commonly claimed that corporate power and vested interests were usurping public space and dictating the agenda for public policy, that elected governments actually charged with

making policy were becoming powerless, and that an ideology of free market individualism was eroding social cohesion around the world. At the systemic level, their concerns seemed to centre on what we might call the constitution of international political authority. Who makes the rules at the systemic level? Whose interests are most effectively served? Who pays the price? (Pauly 2002, 76)

Globalization first prompts us to rethink the question of legitimacy by casting doubt on the tendency to identify legitimate governance authority exclusively with the state. Until recently, legitimate political authority was understood, in the liberal democracies at least, to rest primarily with the governmental institutions of the nation-state. Their legitimacy was based on their representation of and ultimate accountability to citizens, as well as the existence and more or less consistent observation of constraints on their authority in the form of constitutionally mandated divisions of powers, civil rights, judicial review, the rule of law, and the like. The legitimacy of international governance rested, in turn, on state sovereignty: international laws derived their legitimacy primarily from the consent of sovereign states, freely given when treaties were signed on the basis of sovereign equality. Although these traditional sources of legitimacy were already under strain domestically and internationally (Habermas 1975; Chayes and Chayes 1995), globalization has sometimes stretched them beyond the breaking point.

The problem of legitimacy is found wherever humans govern or are governed. Every would-be state or non-state authority is compelled to justify itself in some way: "to govern, one could say, is to be condemned to seek an authority for one's authority" (Rose 1999, 27; see also Weber 1968, 3:953). Legitimacy is "another name for the willingness and capacity of individuals to submit to the necessities" of collective authority; as such, it lies ultimately with, and must be conferred by, those over whom it is exercised (Ruggie 1998, 61, quoting Barnard 1938).

This paradox leads to a second problem. If authority is ultimately conferred by those over whom it is exercised, its legitimacy is not just a question for normative analysis and prescription: it is also a sociological issue. Legitimacy – the esteem in which an institutional order is held by stakeholders – is the contingent outcome of social interactions among "rule makers" and "rule takers." Legitimation – processes that generate legitimacy – is one of the central strategies used by both state and non-state rule makers to establish and maintain their authority, whereas opponents may engage in efforts at delegitimation to undermine the same authority.

Legitimation involves deliberate strategic efforts by rule makers to establish the appropriateness and authoritativeness of their status and decisions as rule makers (that is, legitimacy), which is achieved when the relevant communities accept the rule maker as "appropriately engaged in the task at hand" (Bernstein 2004, 4). This does not mean that rule takers necessarily agree with the rule maker or its rules, only that they perceive them to be binding and authoritative (Weber 1947). Diverse audiences may have differing perceptions of legitimacy. These perceptions may vary over time, space, and subject matter. Depending on the context, a rule maker's legitimacy may be grounded in any number of sources, including appeals to truth, justice, fairness, neutrality, objectivity, expertise, ethnic identity, tradition, consent, the will of the people, and the dictates of God. Legitimacy may depend on characterizing the rule maker's authority as public or private, technical or political, religious or secular, and so on.

Legitimation simultaneously disguises and puts limits upon the exercise of power. It may mask unequal power relations by shrouding them in the guise of authority, such as when a repressive government uses the label "constitution" to cloak its acts of domination in the inauthentic robes and mystifying aura of legitimate authority (Walker 2003, 32). Yet, in order to be successful in the long run, legitimation processes must have some demonstrated effectiveness at curbing that power (Szablowski 2007, 19, citing Thompson 1975, 265). It is thus no coincidence that all legitimation strategies share one characteristic: "they seek to justify the exercise of power by claiming to set certain constraints upon its exercise" (Szablowski 2007, 18). Governments, for example, might claim to respect the autonomy of a "private" sphere or to respect due process and the rule of law. Technical experts might claim to stay away from "political" questions (Wood 2003a, 2005). For legitimation to function, rule takers must believe that these constraints are, for the most part, actually observed (Szablowski 2007, 19).

Rule takers who are well organized, attentive to rule-making activities, capable of posing a threat to rule makers' authority, and who command substantial material resources typically receive special attention from rule makers and are likely to have their legitimacy expectations taken seriously. The opposite is true of disorganized categories of rule takers who are less vigilant, more easily demobilized, and less able to threaten rule makers' authority (*ibid.*,

20). Hence well-organized and well-funded business lobbies typically receive more attention from governments and international organizations than do less disciplined, poorly funded anti-poverty or environmental activists. This discrepancy has particular significance for transnational relations, in which some sets of rule takers are fragmented and dispersed, whereas others are highly organized and easily able to mobilize resources across borders.

The legitimacy or illegitimacy of a given actor, institution, norm, or decision is the contingent outcome of interacting legitimation and delegitimation efforts in a particular social field. The result is that, though we can take a principled approach to the question of legitimacy, we must remember that "legitimacy in global governance is not conducive to formulaic lists of requirements ... [but is] highly contextual, based on historical understandings of legitimacy and the shared norms of the particular community granting authority" (Bernstein 2004, 18). When considering established and new forms of governance in an era of globalization, we should ask not just "Are they legitimate?" as if legitimacy were an objective reality, but "*How* are they legitimated or delegitimated?" Having understood that legitimacy is socially constructed, it is important to be clear about the normative criteria we are using to evaluate the competing authority claims made on behalf of different forms of governance under conditions of globalization.

Legitimacy as Emancipatory Potential

From a normative point of view, legitimacy ought to be judged ultimately by the extent to which the governance arrangement in question advances or hinders the goal of emancipation – freedom from the legal, social, and political restraints that keep people in positions of subjugation and oppression. This is a noble concept. One of the central goals of Western political philosophy since the Enlightenment has been to free people everywhere from oppression, injustice, violence, social exclusion, ignorance, poverty, disease, and premature death. The project of emancipation remains vital to progressive political practice and, even if they do not use the word, central to the aspirations of most Canadians. The goal of emancipation is not mere survival but the flourishing and enfranchisement of individuals, communities, and, increasingly, the ecosystems on which life depends.

Furthermore, as Santos (2002, 2) explains, emancipation requires breaking the bond between experience and expectations. Guaranteeing the stability of expectations for transnational corporations is a key ingredient of neo-conservatism's global agenda. The most obvious example is the insistence by the World Bank Group, transnational corporations, and developed states that the security of property and contract rights and the stability of reasonable investment-backed expectations are crucial for good governance and economic development. In advanced industrialized countries, people demand stability of their hard-won achievements of good health care, shelter, decent jobs, prosperity, cheap and plentiful food, and security against arbitrary violence. These demands have, understandably, intensified in the current economic downturn as the realization of these expectations has been jeopardized for millions of (formerly) well-off people.

Billions of people do not share in or benefit from this stability of high expectations. The price of achieving or preserving stability for some is increased instability and misery for others. For this impoverished majority, low expectations follow predictably from grim experience, as they have for generations. Maintaining these low expectations is one of the main goals of those who benefit most from current forms of globalization.

Emancipation requires breaking and re-establishing the link between experience and expectations by confronting and delegitimizing the norms, institutions, and practices that perpetuate the production of oppression and the maintenance of hopelessness. Admittedly, this is risky for those struggling to break free of oppression and threatening to those clinging to received advantages. But it is also promising, especially for those with the least to lose and the most to gain from it. Emancipation does not necessarily mean fighting to destabilize existing legal systems. In some cases, it may involve using them – for instance, by invoking the citizen complaint mechanisms of the NAFTA environmental or labour side agreements to campaign for more effective enforcement of existing laws. In others, it may mean struggling for deeper social transformation (Santos 2002, 470).

Who, then, are we talking about when we speak of those needing emancipation? We mean those people who are effectively excluded from the social contract. On a global scale, this means the "majority world" – the majority of the human population living in chronic and pervasive poverty, disease, violence, drought, or pollution. In advanced liberal democracies such as Canada, it means the inhabitants of "internal Third Worlds" such as Aboriginal peoples, the rural poor, and the homeless.

From a normative perspective, legitimacy can thus be reconceptualized in terms of emancipatory potential – the capacity of a given governance actor, institution, norm, or decision to advance social inclusion, human rights, human welfare, individual and collective self-realization, and ecological sustainability. Legitimacy is usually analyzed in terms of the processes by which decisions are made ("process legitimacy") or the outcomes of such decisions ("outcome legitimacy"). Emancipatory potential is a function of both.

Process Legitimacy

A decision may be legitimate if it was made by a decision maker who is perceived as legitimate, through processes that are recognized by the relevant audience to be appropriate in the circumstances (Franck 1990; Chayes and Chayes 1995, 127; Szablowski 2007). Put in other words, process legitimacy is a function of both the status of the decision maker and the role of those affected by the decision.

Whether a decision was made by a proper authority raises several subsidiary issues, including the distribution of competences between authorities of different kinds and across different topics (for example, ecclesiastical matters should be decided by religious officials, purely local questions should be decided by town councils), whether the issue in question falls within the scope of the rule maker's authority (is this bishop's ruling really about an ecclesiastical matter?), what limitations exist on the rule maker's authority, whether they have been observed, and whether the authority has followed the internal rules and procedures that prescribe its own behaviour (Szablowski 2007, 20-21).

Process legitimacy typically raises such questions of accountability as "Is the rule maker's authority open to challenge and by whom?" or "Can the rule makers be held to account democratically for their actions, and how?" Process legitimacy also invokes such questions of technical expertise as "Is the issue in question properly characterized as a 'technical' matter over which specialized experts should have authority?" or "How should technical matters be distinguished from 'political' ones?" and "How should expert authorities be held accountable (is peer review adequate)?" Related questions of subsidiarity and centralization ask, "Should authority be centralized, or should it be located as close as possible to the affected people and places?"[2] Finally, process legitimacy entails questions about "private" and "public" domains, because in many places, including Canada, perceptions of legitimacy depend partly on whether the matter in question is understood as falling within a private or public sphere. Within the former, the individuals and groups are widely considered to have the freedom to govern their own affairs as they see fit within the limits established by law and civic responsibilities, and public authorities have a duty to protect and foster the autonomy of this private sphere (*ibid.*, 21). This leads to the difficult question of what is private and what is not, a question to which there is no a priori answer and the resolution of which varies from one audience to another.

The second question is whether all those subject to or affected by a decision have a say in decision making. Most perceptions of legitimacy are based on the assumption that there should be congruence between the decision-making authority and those targeted or affected by its decisions (Conzelmann and Wolf 2008). Those affected by rules should have an effective voice in the development of the rules by which they are bound. In this view, legitimacy requires the public's participation in and access to transparent decision-making processes on matters that affect it (Bernstein 2004, 7). Many difficult questions arise here, such as who is included in the relevant "public" – neo-Nazis in Germany? Mafiosi in Sicily? – along with what form their participation should take, how transparency should be ensured, and to what extent non-state or "expert" authorities should be subject to the same requirements.

Legitimacy expectations may differ depending on whether the relevant community comes together voluntarily to address a specific issue or is a "community of fate" bound together by shared destinies (Held et al. 1999, 29-30). Legitimacy in the case of spontaneous groupings may depend only on officials explaining and defending their decisions to those directly concerned. In communities of fate, legitimacy may require broader democratic participation and deliberation. Unfortunately, it is often difficult to distinguish between voluntary, issue-driven institutions and general-purpose jurisdictions (Bernstein 2004, 9). Complex questions also crop up in relation to self-regulation, especially the self-regulation of business, with some observers emphasizing the advantages of self-determination and others warning against the dangers of allowing the foxes to guard the henhouse or permitting an actor to be the judge in its own cause. In many cases of global governance, process legitimacy issues are acute because those affected by norms that were created under conditions of diplomatic or business secrecy and implemented by unknown officials or executives in far-off cities have no sense of control over or access to these procedures or decision makers.

Outcome Legitimacy

Outcome legitimacy is a function less of means than of ends. Conventional analyses of legitimacy tend to identify three potential sources of outcome legitimacy. Perceptions of legitimacy may be based on *outcome favourability* when the outcome of the decision favours the observer's interests, on *substantive fairness* when the outcome is just according to the observer's values, or on *effectiveness* when the rule or decision in question achieves its stated goals (Szablowski 2007, 16-17; Chayes and Chayes 1995, 127; Peters 2003, 86). Outcome favourability is typically discounted as a measure of legitimacy when dealing with large heterogeneous audiences (such as one finds in many national, transnational, and international settings), since outcomes are likely to favour particular interests over others. In such circumstances, basing legitimacy on outcome favourability would be to take sides in a contestable value judgment. Similarly, substantive fairness or justice is typically discounted as a measure of outcome legitimacy on the grounds that conceptions of what is substantively fair or just are subjective and bound to differ (Franck 1990). According to this logic, legitimacy can only then be determined in terms of process, since evaluating outcomes is necessarily too fraught with subjectiv ity to be reliable (Szablowski 2007).

Nevertheless, we believe it is meaningless to discuss the legitimacy of governance beyond borders without referring to its outcomes. The content and effects of rules are just as important as where or how they are made. We argue in this book that the dominant rules governing globalization systematically (though not uniformly) favour concentrated economic interests in the global North at the expense of human welfare and global ecological sustainability. The reason for the intensity of the worldwide backlash against the rules governing economic globalization, from the Seattle WTO ministerial meeting in 1999 to the London G20 meeting in 2009, is that the outcomes they produce are viewed by many millions of people – both the relatively well-off residents of advanced liberal democracies who are experiencing unaccustomed insecurity and downward mobility, and the global majority whose long-standing immiseration endures or deepens – as disproportionately benefiting global capital at the expense of ordinary people. Despite the irreducible heterogeneity of interests and values that characterizes politics, this public condemnation of outcomes should not be ignored in assessing the legitimacy of global governance, which cannot be judged exclusively or even primarily in terms of "right process." Although competing conceptions of the just and the good will always exist, an outcome-oriented account of legitimacy allows us to acknowledge that what the winners in struggles over norm-creation see as good and just has major impacts on the health, happiness, and security of the losers.

Outcome legitimacy is, moreover, likely to acquire increasing salience as we move away from governance by democratically elected governments, since few other institutions can boast the universality of representation claimed by modern liberal-democratic states. Breadth of representation is one of the keys to process legitimacy. By contrast, whatever legitimacy most CSOs can claim is bound to rest less on the nature of their membership structures, funding sources, and decision-making processes than on their capacity to advocate substantive positions "that are recognizably in the 'global public interest,' rather than the narrow self interest" of a privileged few, and this is so even if a truly cosmopolitan set of global values remains elusive (Buchanan and Long 2002, 62).

One final caveat about outcome legitimacy: some analysts maintain that legitimacy is as much a product of the effectiveness of rules at achieving their stated goals as it is of rule-making processes (Peters 2003, 86). The relationship between legitimacy and effectiveness is complicated. Many rules and institutions are effective in achieving their goals without being legitimate (Nazi concentration camps are one example). Conversely, many may be perceived as legitimate without being particularly effective. And of course some, such as the detention facility at Guantanamo Bay, Cuba, and the 2003 Iraq invasion, are neither legitimate nor effective in achieving their stated goals. As a result, effectiveness and ineffectiveness are not reliable gauges of legitimacy, although in the long run we can expect that effective authority will need to cloak itself in legitimacy in order to remain effective, and legitimate authority will need to demonstrate some effectiveness in order to remain legitimate.

To summarize, legitimacy is normatively related to emancipatory potential. Emancipatory potential is, in turn, a function of both process and outcomes. It is an index of the extent to which the norms, actors, or institutions in question challenge the hegemonic forms of governance that perpetuate illegitimate processes and outcomes.

Legitimacy and Legality

The relationship between legitimacy and legality has long exercised analysts because legality does not guarantee legitimacy (Bernstein 2004, 11). A rule or decision may have the force of law (legality) yet lack legitimacy. Conversely, many rules and decisions recognized as legitimate in social relations lack the status of formal law. Formal law must earn its legitimacy just like any other form of authority. In some ways, it enjoys a legitimation advantage due to its close historical and ideological association with ideals of justice and fairness. In other ways, it is at a disadvantage because of its historical and continuing role as a mask for injustice and domination. Throughout history, the powerful have employed law as an instrument of repression. Beyond this, many business people view formal law as a burden on entrepreneurial innovation, and many civil society actors are disillusioned with law as a tool for social change. In short, the legitimacy of formal law should not be assumed but should be evaluated according to the same criteria as other forms of authority.

As a result, the relationship between legitimacy and the rule of law – a fundamental constitutional principle in Western liberal democracies – must be reconsidered. As typically understood in Canada, it has three elements: the equality of all before the law, the existence of a system of positive law (which embodies and preserves the more general principle of normative order), and the need for all government action to be grounded in law rather than arbitrariness (Hughes 2004). The rule of law tends to enhance the legitimacy of laws by providing a principle of constraint on arbitrary or unfairly discriminatory government action. If the rule of law is observed in practice, the process legitimacy of formal law and state action is likely to be enhanced. On the other hand, the rule of law does not itself guarantee legitimacy. From a legitimacy perspective, appeals to the rule of law will always beg the question of which law, and whose interests it serves. Efforts to promote the rule of law in a transnational setting – from trade and investment treaties to World Bank "good governance" projects, civil-society-led anti-corruption campaigns, and official development aid programs – preach a particular conception of law and the role of government in social change. Some of them advance a neoconservative agenda of economic globalization, property rights protection, free markets, and limited government that may be at odds with Canada's constitutional tradition and with the ultimate goal of social justice (*ibid.*; Schneiderman 2004).

Government, law, sovereignty, and legitimacy are not the only conceptual categories to have been exploded in a globalizing world. A whole range of received understandings about politics and law has been thrown into question. The conventional dichotomy between the domestic and international realms has disintegrated with the emergence of increasingly muscular international laws and organizations. Conceptions of the self based on citizenship and territory are giving way to new forms of identity as information technology and human migration break down old barriers. The previously sharp distinction between national security and human development is collapsing into the emerging concept of human security. The distinction between war-fighting and peacekeeping died with the Cold War. The already shaky dichotomy between commercial dealings and public regulation has been further eroded by the growth of investor-state arbitration under NAFTA Chapter 11 and bilateral investment treaties. The list could go on. Although many of these categories were contested long before globalization entered the lexicon, contemporary global transformations have intensified this contestation and exposed the inadequacies of conventional understandings of these terms.

Plan of the Book

Canadians debate whether globalization and the attendant transformations in law and governance are beneficial or harmful. Some see these developments in a positive light, welcoming freer trade, stronger international laws and institutions, harmonization of different countries' laws, innovative changes to the structure and operation of the welfare state, a burgeoning global civil society, a growing commitment by global business to sustainability and social responsibility, and the spread of Canadian constitutional values and jurisprudence to other nations. Others take a more negative view, pointing to the expanding power of unaccountable and opaque international bodies, the retreat of Canadian governments from their responsibility to protect public welfare, the increasing supremacy and continuing social and financial abuses of transnational corporations, and the questionable motives and accountability of some NGOs.

These disagreements are bound to persist because the manifestations of globalization are so diverse they are inherently controversial. But persisting controversy does not mean that taking sides on the pros and cons of globalization is inappropriate. Indeed, normative engagement with new (and old) forms of governance in a globalized world is as imperative for citizens nowadays as is their need to engage with their own domestic politics. Rather than attempting a comprehensive analysis of all forms of governance in a globalized environment, the following chapters examine selected developments in four spheres: the international system, the nation-state, the market, and civil society. Like imperium, hegemony, and autarchy, these categories are ideal types that correspond imperfectly to lived reality and overlap in complex ways. Nonetheless, these familiar categories of political and legal analysis are useful heuristic tools to help us make sense of globalization.

The international system is the subject of Part 1, in which we examine the proliferation of international law and organizations, one of the most striking aspects of the contemporary world. We investigate these developments from a constitutional perspective, arguing that certain aspects of this burgeoning international normative architecture have acquired constitutional status, effectively constraining the exercise of public authority in Canada. In Chapter 2, we explain this *supraconstitutional* perspective as a framework for analyzing international law and organizations. Chapter 3 expands on Canada's emerging economic supraconstitution in the form of international trade and investment rules and institutions. Chapter 4 then explores international social and environmental governance, while Chapter 5 takes the measure of the global supraconstitution by contrasting its economic, social, and environmental dimensions.

Whereas interaction between the domestic and international spheres is a central theme of Part 1, in Part 2 we turn our attention from the interstate system to the nation-state and the realms of non-state actors and institutions. In Chapter 6, we investigate the globalization of the Canadian state, both in terms of the localization of global ideologies and legal forms in Canada, and the role of Canada and Canadians in the exportation and globalization of law and governance. In Chapter 7, we focus on the role of market actors – especially business elites and transnational capital – in globalized law and governance. We also discuss civil society, in the form of public-interest NGOs and social movements. Developments in these arenas do not occur in isolation from each other. Indeed, interaction between and hybridization of these different spheres are defining characteristics of governance in a globalizing world. In the final chapter, we evaluate the implications of our analysis for Canadians. Throughout the book, we assess what globalization means for law and governance in a middle power that exists in the shadow of a global hegemon, and how such a country and its nationals can influence law and governance beyond their borders.

Our central thesis is that the globalization of law and governance is characterized by severe, ever-perilous imbalances between economic and social priorities, between the needs of capital and of people, between elites and the general public, between hegemonic expansion and democratic self-determination, between Canada and the United States, and between the global North and South. We maintain that these imbalances are the manifestations of a continuing neo-conservative project to remake the world to suit transnational business. We believe that if globalization is to realize its potential as a progressive and legitimate process, these imbalances must be redressed. We close by arguing that the seeds of a solution lie in the embrace of a pluralist conception of law and governance, which asserts a space for emancipatory governance projects outside the hegemonic instrumentalities of the state, the interstate system, and the market. Though acknowledging the continuing centrality of those hegemonic forms, we conclude that the need to work within and through them should be infused by the quest for just and sustainable governance, not solely for Canadians but for all humankind.

PART 1

Canada's Emerging Supraconstitution

2
The Supraconstitution: A Framework for Analysis

If you ask many interested citizens what globalization means to them, one of the first things they will point to is the massive proliferation of international organizations, agreements, and regimes within a single human lifetime – the United Nations, the World Bank, the World Trade Organization, the European Union (EU), et cetera – and the increasing impact of these international actors and arrangements on their daily lives. Since the end of the Second World War, nation-states have been embedding themselves in complex webs of international agreements, organizations, and regimes, whose number, scope, and competencies seem to have expanded almost without end. As we have already seen, we have reached a point where participation in networks of multilateral regimes – not the unhindered capacity for unilateral action – is the defining feature of sovereignty in the contemporary world (Chayes and Chayes 1995).

This aspect of globalization is found at all geographic scales, from bilateral to regional to global. Canadians – whether politicians or diplomats, scholars or commentators – have been among the most enthusiastic architects and supporters of this phenomenon of *internationalization*, especially in its multilateral forms. In turn, internationalization has had substantial impacts on Canada's society, economic structures, and state institutions. It is highly uneven over time and space, and across domains of human activity. This unevenness – this perilous imbalance – is primarily what concerns us in Part 1. International regimes are more robust in some places, regarding some domains of activity, and for some actors, than others. Their burdens and benefits are distributed highly inequitably. They are in perennial flux, moving in inconsistent directions toward contested destinations.

One of the most important if least understood dimensions of internationalization is the emergence of what we call a global *supraconstitution*. What began as the creation of interstate institutions and agreements governed by general principles of public international law has in some respects morphed into a process of constitutionalization: the appearance of supranational political formations governed by their own brand of constitutional law (Weiler 1999). Simultaneously international and domestic, the supraconstitution refers to a constitutional order arising at the international level, which at the same time transforms the domestic legal order by embedding an "external" constitution into its domestic one (Chantal Thomas 2000; Clarkson 2004).

Because the supraconstitution acts upon and is partially embedded in domestic constitutional orders, it is experienced differently in different nation-states. Canada's supraconstitution is not the same as Mexico's, let alone those of the United States or China. The processes, structures, and effects of the supraconstitution also diverge greatly by subject area, reflecting the wide variety of bilateral, regional, multilateral, and global interstate structures, and the bewildering proliferation of transnational legal arrangements "beyond the state" (Teubner 1997). Although this diversity might lead to a sense of "irreducible heterogeneity," the emerging global supraconstitution has a number of unifying features and implements a specific political agenda (Schneiderman 2000a, 83).

The supraconstitution is found neither in the *Charter of the United Nations* and the post–Second World War project of achieving world peace through world law, nor in world federalists' tired dreams of a world super-state. Rather, it springs from the rules and institutional forms of what Stephen Gill (1995, 412-13) calls the "new constitutionalism": a continuing program to restructure state and international political forms to promote market efficiency and discipline, enable free capital movement, confer privileged rights on transnational corporations, insulate key domains of the economy from state interference, and constrain democratic decision-making processes. The new constitutionalism is rooted in an interlocking network of agreements and rule-making structures intended to promote and protect transnational corporate investment and insulate it from majoritarian politics (Schneiderman 2008, 2). Its normative architecture is animated by a neo-conservative ideology and propelled by the world's most powerful state elites and corporations. The thrust of this supraconstitutional program is the international entrenchment of economic rights for transnational capital within domestic constitutional orders – often at the expense of human rights, cultural integrity, social justice, human security, environmental protection, and national political autonomy.

This venture to re-constitutionalize the world has had the sharpest impact on countries and actors – mainly in the global periphery and semi-periphery – which have had to make the most changes to conform to its norms. Since the new constitutionalism represents the continental and global projection of mainly US constitutional norms by mainly US economic and political elites, the United States has been affected the least, whereas Mexico's constitutional and legal order has been substantially transformed, and the effect on Canada's has been intermediate in comparison to these two. But Canadians are not simply passive recipients. Canadian political and business elites were and are active agents of the new constitutionalism, both at home and abroad. Having taken an active part in constructing the constitutional architecture of North American free trade and investment, Canadian state and corporate elites became champions of this same disciplinary neo-conservatism in the World Trade Organization, and they continue to re-export it by negotiating further trade and investment agreements with other countries.

This quiet transformation is proceeding without being legitimated by many affected national publics, who remain unaware of its significance. It is occurring without a corresponding supranational constitutionalization of social, environmental, cultural, or labour rights. It has significant negative consequences for social justice, human security, ecological integrity, and national autonomy. The supraconstitution, in short, is highly asymmetrical and raises important questions about legitimacy.

The Move to Constitutions in International Law

To speak of international law and organizations in constitutional terms is nothing new. Scholars have long applied concepts and terminology drawn from constitutional law to the United Nations, the European Community, the international trade system, international human rights law, international organizations, and the international legal system generally (Verdross 1926; Lauterpacht 1950, 463; Ross 1950; Opsahl 1961; Jackson 1969, 1980; Stein 1981). This trend intensified after the end of the Cold War and was especially pronounced in relation to Europe, where – despite the failure to ratify the *Treaty to Establish a Constitution in Europe* – the scholarly debate has moved past *whether* Europe has a constitution to *what kind* of constitution it should be (Weiler 1999; Weiler and Wind 2003; Avbelj 2008). Constitutional analyses of – and prescriptions for – the World Trade Organization (De Búrca and Scott 2001; Cass 2005), international economic law (Joerges and Petersmann

2006), the UN Charter (Fassbender 1998), and international law as a whole are now commonplace (Joerges, Sand, and Teubner 2004; Orrego Vicuña 2004; Macdonald and Johnston 2005; de Wet 2006; von Bogdandy 2006; Dunoff and Trachtman 2009).

This upsurge of interest in the existence of constitutions beyond the national state is a reaction to a threefold transformation occurring over the last two decades in the way that international law is experienced in the core capitalist democracies. Led by the liberalization of trade and investment rules, international law has expanded to cover subjects that were traditionally addressed as domestic concerns, from money laundering to consumer and environmental protection. In the European Community, by 1990, it was possible to say that there was simply "no nucleus of sovereignty that the Member States can invoke, as such, against the Community" (Lenaerts 1990, 220). Kumm (2004, 913) claims that the same can be said of international law today. This "comprehensive blue-print for social life" has become "a multi-faceted body of law that permeates all fields of life, wherever governments act for promoting a public purpose" (von Bogdandy 2006, 226, quoting Tomuschat 1999, 63, 70). The result is that, during the last two decades, governments in the core capitalist countries have begun to feel pervasive pressure to align their domestic policy choices with international legal rules and obligations. They are finally experiencing the same loss of autarchy that international law has always meant for the weak and poor countries of the global periphery.

Second, the core countries find themselves increasingly subject to dictates to which they did not specifically consent (Kumm 2004, 914). The link between state consent and international obligations loosens as parties to international treaties delegate more law-making, interpretation, and enforcement powers to quasi-legislative bodies, adjudicative tribunals, and international standards development organizations such as the Codex Alimentarius Commission. These bodies determine the details of states' rights and duties without obtaining the affected states' consent to the specific decisions.[1]

Third, the increasing specificity and transparency of international obligations and the proliferation of compulsory third-party dispute resolution have robbed many states of a substantial degree of flexibility to interpret their international obligations as they see fit (ibid., 914-15). Led by the European Court of Justice, which established the supremacy of European Community law and its direct effect in the domestic legal systems of member states, this constraint over states' self-determination is especially true in international economic relations (Weiler 1999, 19-20). With the establishment of the International Criminal Court (ICC) and numerous ad hoc international criminal tribunals during the last decade, international criminal law limits some state systems – if not others. Its teeth are felt much more sharply by countries of the global periphery and semi-periphery than by the core capitalist countries, as illustrated by the United States' fierce refusal to submit its own nationals to ICC prosecution, and the refusal of the chief prosecutor of the International Criminal Tribunal for the Former Yugoslavia to indict NATO leaders for alleged war crimes arising from their 1999 bombing campaign against Serbia (Cerone 2007).

Since the end of the Cold War, many countries have increasingly experienced international law as "a firmly structured normative web" that exerts "influence on national political and legal processes and often exerts pressure on nations not in compliance with its norms" (Kumm 2004, 912). To make sense of this development, international lawyers are turning to constitutional analysis, a move that has generated considerable controversy. Because the term "constitution" is strongly associated with the national state (see Hogg 2004, 1; Monahan 2002, 3), it is usually reserved for the fundamental arrangements by which governmental powers are allocated, organized, and limited in order to define the relationship between public authorities and citizens within a sovereign state. Since it is still widely assumed that only the state can supply the exclusive, systematic, and unified hierarchy of norms characteristic of a constitution, it is also thought that only within boundaries can one find the single constituent power (the "We the People") that a constitution presupposes and to which public authorities can be held accountable. Thus, to suggest the existence of a constitution at the international level strikes many not only as nonsensical but dangerous (Howse and Nicolaidis 2001). The danger is summarized by Walker (2003, 32, emphasis in original) as follows: "Constitutionalism is not just about the history of legitimate self-government, but also about the history of *illegitimate* domination – of cloaking illegitimate regimes and the illegitimate acts of sometimes legitimate regimes with the inauthentic robes and mystifying aura of legitimate authority."

Notwithstanding this concern, many commentators view international constitutionalism as a positive development, a manifestation of international law's civilizing mission (Koskenniemi 2001). The Cold War's collapse reinvigorated this project and inaugurated a burst of international institution building, driven by a renewed enthusiasm for international human rights, the rule of law, and market liberalization. Many proponents of this project were inspired, implicitly or explicitly, by the liberal-democratic capitalist version of constitutionalism that had apparently emerged victorious from the ideological struggle with communism.

This euphoria came to an end with the United States' aggressive resort to unilateralism, exceptionalism, and armed force after 11 September 2001 when the mood among many international lawyers shifted from triumphalism to anxiety (Dunoff 2006, 649).[2] Constitutionalism became less a confident project of international integration and more a defence against the perceived threats to the international order posed by the Bush doctrine of pre-emptive self-defence, the Anglo-American invasion of Iraq, the torture of terror suspects by the US and allied governments, American hostility toward international law and organizations, and other aspects of the American-led global war on terror

The upshot is that many international lawyers employ constitutional terminology loosely and in a bewildering variety of ways. Moreover, they often do so with little or no effort to clarify their analytical frameworks or acknowledge the normative presuppositions embedded in their analysis (Walker 2003, 39). An effort at clarification is therefore necessary.

CONSTITUTIONAL CONCEPTS AND TERMINOLOGY

At a general level, "constitution" refers to the system of fundamental norms by which any organization – whether a professional association, corporation, or national state – is governed (Weiler 1999, viii). As the British foreign secretary quipped during the debate over the failed European constitutional treaty, in this sense, even golf clubs have constitutions (Kumm 2006).

In the term's narrower, political sense, we can distinguish three uses of "constitution." First, the word can refer in a *formal* sense to the written text or fundamental legal act that sets forth the essential norms by which a political community is governed (Snyder 2003, 56). The norms entrenched in a constitutional instrument have the highest rank in the legal system and are subject to more burdensome amendment procedures than other norms (Kumm 2006, 508). The US constitution and the *Canadian Charter of Rights and Freedoms* qualify as constitutional documents in this sense. The UN Charter and the European Union's basic treaties do too. Many social systems, however, have fundamental norms that are not entrenched in any document, including the United Kingdom's largely unwritten constitution. A formal or textual definition is therefore inadequate.

The term "constitution" can be used in a second, *functional* sense to refer to the ensemble of fundamental norms and practices that perform certain basic roles in the establishment and organization of a polity's legal order. Such functions may include creating public institutions and political subdivisions, distributing jurisdictions among them, generating objectives to guide the use of such powers, placing constraints on their exercise, protecting fundamental rights, and enabling judicial review of the exercise of public authority (Verdross 1926; Snyder 2003, 56; Kumm 2006, 508). In this view, a constitution typically establishes guiding *principles* by which the community's collective life is to be conducted, basic *rules* that govern members' behaviour, fundamental *rights* of community members vis-à-vis governing authorities, and specific *institutions* that perform legislative, executive, and adjudicative functions (Black 1979; Constitutional Law Group 2003, 3-4; von Bogdandy 2006, 230). As fundamental elements of the legal order, these principles, rules, rights, and institutions constrain ordinary political and legal decision making; are harder to change than other principles, rules, rights, and institutions; and are rooted in a particular system of core values (Wiener 2003; von Bogdandy 2006, 231).

Finally, the term "constitution" can be employed in a *normative* sense to denote the establishment of an independent authority that structures and legitimates a political process (Kumm 2006, 509). A community may have a constitution in the formal or functional sense without having a constitution in the stronger normative sense. What is necessary to establish a constitution in this strong sense depends on which normative constitutional theory – in other words, what variety of *constitutionalism* – one subscribes to.

"Constitutionalism" refers to a position advocating constitutionalization (Trachtman 2006, 630), the historical process by which constitutions are generated, consolidated, or expanded to domains that did not previously have constitutional features (see Cass 2001, 2005). At the international level, "constitutionalization" refers to the transformation of international organizations and regimes from interstate arrangements governed by general principles of international law into supranational political formations whose structure more closely resembles that of a multi-layered polity (Weiler 1999, 12). It also refers to the corresponding transformation of domestic constitutional orders to enable or accommodate the emergence of these new entities.

Numerous varieties of constitutionalism are at play in contemporary debates about international law, each informed by its own theory of legitimate authority. Avbelj (2008), for example, counts seven different constitutional-isms in current legal discourse concerning the European Union alone. Rooted in Western liberal-democratic constitutional theory, most contemporary constitutionalisms tend to privilege the constraint of public power, the rule of law, the protection of fundamental rights and freedoms, and legitimation via democratic deliberation. Debates about whether a specific supranational entity has a constitution in the "strong" (normative) sense discussed above revolve around whether its fundamental norms, practices, and institutions, and the procedures by which they are established, conform to the observers' preferred version of constitutionalism. Such debates also consider what version of constitutionalism is appropriate at the supranational level.

With this conceptual ground-clearing in mind, we turn to the central term in our analysis of internationalization: the *supraconstitution*.

The Supraconstitution

The competence of many international institutions is expanding in sectors that were once the exclusive domain of states. Although typically established by intergovernmental agreement, an organization may take on a life of its own, with implications for its founders. While carrying out its responsibilities, an international body may introduce new rules that bind its members. When international tribunals make judgments to resolve a dispute between two states, their rulings often affect other states. When international standards-setting bodies make decisions about new issues, these can have substantial consequences for political and legal decision making in member states. For instance, decisions of the Codex Alimentarius Commission concerning the approval or labelling of genetically modified foods for human consumption will affect the fate of many countries' agricultural economies and the profitability of some of the world's largest corporations, which have invested billions to develop transgenic crops that are impervious to certain insects or plant diseases. Because of public concerns about the health implications of hormone-treated livestock and genetically modified fruits and vegetables, governments and agribusiness defend their positions at the Codex in the face of non-government organizations representing the often opposing interests of producer and consumer groups.

Neither the conventional concepts of international law and organizations nor the traditionally inward-looking perspective of constitutional law make sense of the new power arrangements in this globalizing multi-layered world. Understood functionally as the ensemble of fundamental norms and institutional practices that define the establishment, organization, and division of power in a supranational legal order, the concept of a supraconstitution bridges this gap. When we speak of Canada's supraconstitution, we refer to those norms and institutions at the international level that can be said to form part of the assemblage of fundamental practices by which Canadian society is governed and from which domestic Canadian laws and policies are not allowed to derogate.

At the level of norms, the supraconstitution can be analyzed in terms of general *principles* guiding the allocation and exercise of power, basic *rules* governing community members' behaviour, and fundamental *rights* of community members. At the level of institutional practices, it can be analyzed in terms of the *institutions* that perform – to varying degrees – legislative, executive, administrative, adjudicative, and enforcement functions within a specific legal order. But these features alone do not a supraconstitution make. The supraconstitution has another defining characteristic: it constrains domestic governmental decision making and prevails over conflicting domestic laws. We call this quality *primacy*. The supraconstitution also has both domestic and international dimensions, one implication of which is that one state's supraconstitution is not the same as another's. Finally, constitutional analysis of international norms and institutions has an unavoidable normative dimension, which must be acknowledged. We develop each of these points in turn.

PRINCIPLES, RULES, AND RIGHTS

Supraconstitutional norms take various forms, from abstract principles to concrete rules. *Principles* may range from the vague and the general (such as the aspiration for peace) to the specific (such as national treatment for goods or investments). *Rules* are typically more numerous, laying down explicit prescriptions for behaviour. They might, for example, prohibit exports of hazardous chemicals or the employment of children below a certain age. Since these rules are negotiated in a power-based system, they also reflect the interests of dominant powers at the centre of the world system. A great many of these international rules, especially in the economic domain, universalize domestic American norms. For example, the WTO's *Agreement on Trade-Related Aspects of Intellectual Property Rights* supports the interests of American, European, and Japanese "Big Pharma," entertainment, and information-technology industries even as it inhibits the development of those same industries in the emerging economies of the global South. Alongside principles and rules, *rights* may be expressed along a continuum from the general (the right to development, education, or shelter) to the specific (the right to vote, the right to a fair trial, or the right of foreign investors to compensation if their property is expropriated).

Some of these supraconstitutional norms may reinforce existing national constitutional norms; others may undermine them. Not surprisingly, controversy is most likely to erupt when supraconstitutional norms come into conflict with domestic constitutional arrangements.

INSTITUTIONS

Some international institutions are powerful, well-financed, and sophisticated, as in the case of the institutional structures created by the various treaties that built the European Union into its own constitutional order. Other international institutions are flimsy. Whether strong or weak, they can be analyzed in terms of five principal functions. Although these governmental functions overlap and may sometimes be performed by the same institutions or actors, they provide a useful starting point for analysis.

Legislature

Many international institutions perform a *legislative* function, in which the assembled members or a subset of them deliberate and enact legally binding rules for the institution and its members. Taken in its totality, the body of world institutions has a spotty and uneven legislative capacity. Legislation is the least developed of all governmental functions at the international level. The UN General Assembly is a major global debating forum, but it has very limited capacity to enact binding norms. The European Parliament's legislative capability has grown but remains inferior to the European Commission's substantial legislative capacity, which manifests itself in hundreds of directives that compel member states to take a specified action. In contrast, the NAFTA Free Trade Commission has no autonomous rule-making ability and so is unable to adapt its many rules, which were negotiated in the early 1990s, to changing conditions. Between these extremes, the World Trade Organization has a forum for making new rules in the biennial meeting of its members' trade ministers. However, the requirement that decisions be reached by consensus makes it extremely difficult to arrive at any decision acceptable to some 150 states. As a result, new rules for the WTO are made following years-long negotiating "rounds" between the member governments.

Executive

Most international institutions have a body or bodies mandated to perform *executive* functions ranging from management of routine day-to-day operations to making momentous decisions such as the UN Security Council's determination whether to endorse a pre-emptive war against Iraq. On the whole, the executive function is weakly developed at the international level because nation-states have been reluctant to allow international institutions much autonomous decision-making authority. The WTO has no executive to speak of, whereas NAFTA's merely consists of periodic meetings of the three countries' trade ministers.

Administration

A more extensively developed function performed in typical international institutions is *administration*, because an administrative staff is needed to implement decisions and deliver the action for which the institution is mandated. The Organisation for Economic Co-operation and Development (OECD) and the UN have personnel in the thousands. Many others have very small secretariats, limited to organizing meetings and facilitating communication among their member states. Aggregating them all would reveal a considerable – but heterogeneous and disconnected – international civil service, many elements of which are supranational in the sense that these bureaucrats' careers are independent of their member governments' control. The WTO has an extremely lean administration: just five hundred people operate this globally crucial institution. NAFTA has no central administration at all. Each of its three signatory states merely maintains a small office to keep track of NAFTA-related paperwork, and each federal government assigns civil servants to staff a few working groups that deal with some of NAFTA's minor outstanding business.

Adjudication

Norms and rules are subject to diverse interpretations. No organization can operate for long without having to resolve conflicts generated by its own mandate and mechanisms. *Adjudication* is thus the fourth function that may be performed by international institutions. International dispute settlement mechanisms vary from the highly structured European Court of Justice, whose rulings have direct effect in each member state, to the deliberately ineffectual arbitration processes established in the *North American Agreement on Environmental Cooperation*. They range in formality and complexity from informal consultations to one-off arbitrations (such as that for the Canada-US *Trail Smelter* dispute); specialized international tribunals (such as the WTO Appellate Body, the ICC, the Rwandan and Yugoslav criminal tribunals, and the International Tribunal for the Law of the Sea); private international commercial arbitral panels (such as those used for NAFTA Chapter 11 investor-state disputes); and the venerable International Court of Justice.

Enforcement

Finally, international institutions have very uneven *enforcement* capacities. NATO has the capacity to enforce its decisions through a command structure that can mobilize the armed forces of its members to fight a hostile regime or intervene militarily to keep the peace in a failed state. In fact, many NATO members ultimately find ways to minimize their contributions to military missions that are unpopular at home, as evidenced by the reluctance of most governments to undertake combat missions in the post-2001 occupation of Afghanistan. The European Commission's directives can be enforced through the rulings of the European Court of Justice. By contrast, the enforcement of international human rights, environmental agreements, and labour conventions is weak. Compliance with the WTO's dispute settlement rulings tends to be high, in part because its rules permit economic retaliation by a successful state against a defendant who does not comply with its judgment. WTO rulings are also effective largely because members perceive that conforming to an adverse judgment is in their own interest because they expect a counterpart to comply when they win a ruling against it.

To summarize, we can analyze the supraconstitution in terms of the existence of supranational principles, rules, and rights, and the performance of these five institutional functions. But the mere presence of these norms and institutions does not, on its own, create a supraconstitution. Supraconstitutional norms and institutions are also fundamental to the legal and political order. They effectively constrain political and legal decision making. This quality is captured in the concept of *primacy*.

PRIMACY

We use the prefix "supra" ("above") not just to indicate that the supraconstitution spans multiple nation-states but to denote the primacy of the supraconstitution within the domestic orders of participating nation-states. Supraconstitutional norms and decisions take precedence over domestic laws and constitutional provisions when the first conflict with the second. This feature of the supraconstitution is one of the most difficult to define. In the European Union, where supraconstitutionalization is most advanced, primacy is expressed most often in the doctrine of *direct effect,* which means that Community legal norms become the law of each land (Weiler 1999, 19) by creating enforceable legal obligations not just among member states or between individuals and their governments, but among individuals themselves. These norms may be invoked by individuals before national courts, and national courts must provide adequate remedies for their violation just as if they had been enacted by national legislatures.

Direct effect on its own does not distinguish supraconstitutional from ordinary international law, however. In some nation-states, international treaties are automatically received into the domestic legal order. Some provisions of international treaties are recognized as self-executing (that is, directly effective) in the domestic legal order. Canadian law generally subscribes to the opposing view that international treaties are not incorporated automatically but must be "received" via implementing legislation in order to take effect within the domestic legal system. Hundreds of international treaties have been received into Canadian federal and provincial law in this manner. When we speak of supraconstitutional primacy, we are not talking about the reception of international treaties via domestic legislation. Primacy refers to international norms taking effect in the domestic legal system in the absence of domestic legislation or even in the face of conflicting domestic legislation, not by virtue of it. Canadian reception of customary international law, which consists of customs rooted in widespread state practice and recognized as binding by states in their relations with each other, comes closer to what we are talking about because, in theory, it is automatically received into Canadian law as part of the common law (Kindred 2006). When customary international law is received automatically as part of the common law, this is an example of direct effect. But direct effect is so rarely operationalized in general international law that it falls below whatever threshold is required for most observers to liken it to constitutional law (Weiler 1999, 25). More importantly, direct effect alone does not qualify a norm as supraconstitutional. Even in Europe, where direct effect is widespread and presumptive, it is the combination of direct effect and the doctrine of *supremacy* that makes Community law supraconstitutional (*ibid.,* 20).

The doctrine of supremacy in EU law holds that, within the Community's sphere of competence, any Community norm, from a treaty article right down to a "minuscule administrative regulation enacted by the Commission, 'trumps' conflicting national law whether enacted before or after the Community norm" (*ibid.*, 20-21).[3] Crucially, the Community's own judicial organ, the European Court of Justice, has the "*Kompetenz-Kompetenz*" – that is, the competence to determine the Community's sphere of competence and hence the matters on which Community law is supreme (*ibid.*, 21). International law also boasts supremacy over national law, in theory: in a dispute between states, national law is no defence to a violation of international law. But supremacy in international law is not the same thing as supremacy in constitutional law.

Even if the reception of customary international law into domestic Canadian law is an example of direct effect, it is not an example of primacy. A norm of customary international law that is received as part of the common law would not prevail over conflicting domestic legislation because legislation "trumps" common law. Moreover, whereas legislation is presumed to be consistent with Canada's international legal obligations, it prevails over international law in the event of a conflict (Van Ert 2002, 99-136; Kindred 2006, 19-21).

EU-style direct effect and supremacy represent the fullest expression of supraconstitutional primacy in the contemporary world and distinguish the European legal order from other supranational orders. Nevertheless, international norms and institutions may be supraconstitutional without reaching the European standard. Here we part company with those who insist that only Europe has a supraconstitution (Weiler 1999). But we do not go as far as Johnston (2005), Macdonald (2005), Fassbender (2005), or Tomuschat (1999), who see a supranational constitution in the supposed paramountcy of the UN Charter, the operation of certain basic principles of intersovereign relations, and the existence of an ethical core of international human rights norms. In our logic, international norms and institutions are supraconstitutional if they establish constraints on the authority of governments that are legally binding, practically effective, and difficult to amend. Outside the EU, the leading form of supraconstitutionality is the international trade and investment regime, which provides the main normative and institutional architecture of neo-conservative globalization.

The main purpose of international trade and investment disciplines is to prevail over domestic legal and constitutional arrangements by placing on government authority legally binding limits that are difficult to revise and are designed to bind states far into the future (Schneiderman 2008, 4-6).

These limits are enforced through robust international dispute settlement mechanisms, the outcomes of which are made effective domestically via enforcement proceedings in domestic courts (in the case of investor-state disputes under investment treaties) or via trade sanctions (in the case of WTO dispute settlement rulings). Like domestic constitutional provisions, they represent a form of precommitment strategy in which their proponents seek to constrain decision-making far into the future (*ibid.*, 3). Ratifying governments must change their laws and regulations in a context that makes them practically irreversible. Unlike normal alterations to statutes made by national or subnational legislatures, which can further amend or revoke their acts in response to changing circumstances, revisions to statutory enactments incorporating international trade norms are valid only if the external regime changes its rules by international agreement. A perfectly legitimate democratic government action could subject a state to severe sanctions or penalties if it were deemed by the relevant international dispute settlement body to violate the international agreement in question.

Any consideration of the emerging global constitutional order must pre-emptively recognize its fragmentary, disconnected, imbalanced, heterogeneous, and multi-faceted nature. As we have seen, international organizations and regimes range in their territorial scope from bilateral to regional to global and in their size from tiny to huge. Some are relatively autonomous; others are little more than agents of their member states. Some are of marginal significance, whereas others exercise substantial influence over world developments as well as national governments. They vary from relatively informal secretariats to bricks-and-mortar organizations with their own buildings, permanent civil service, insignia, and even flags. They include ad hoc arrangements for cooperation in specific functional areas (such as international fisheries management regimes) and general-purpose political structures complete with all the organs of government, such as the United Nations.

This order is "post-national" or "post-statal" in several senses (Walker 2003). It reconfigures and in important ways constrains or diminishes the nation-state. Non-state, substate, and transnational actors and structures play important roles in this new order and create their own constitutional orders "without the state" (Teubner 1997, 2004; Schepel 2005). Supranational entities do not reproduce the national state at the supranational level. Some may exhibit state-like features, but they are not states. Notwithstanding these realities, the state has not disappeared from this new constitutional order. It remains central to it. The supraconstitution may run roughshod over the national sovereignty of many states, but it does not obliterate them: rather, it reconstitutionalizes them.

INESCAPABLE NORMATIVE DIMENSIONS

By calling certain rules and institutions supraconstitutional, we advance a descriptive claim. Our goal is to describe how, under contemporary conditions of globalization, public powers are established, organized, and constrained, and how fundamental rights are allocated and protected. At the same time, we recognize that any analysis of what constitutionalization means or even whether it exists is irreducibly normative, grounded in a particular vision of constitutionalism. To describe something as a constitution is always to make a normative claim.

For critics of supranational constitutional analysis, describing international arrangements as constitutional is dangerous because it has the unwarranted effect of legitimizing them. In their view, the very language of constitutionalism may confer legitimacy by presupposing democratic self-government, popular validation, the rule of law, and effective protection of individual human rights, the first two of which are completely absent and the latter two patently weak at the international level (Howse and Nicolaidis 2001; Cass 2005). Invoking constitutional discourse "may be a rhetorical strategy designed to invest international law with the power and authority that domestic constitutional structures and norms possess" (Dunoff 2006, 649). Critics also point to the danger that constitutional language will demobilize opposition to undesirable international arrangements by making them appear natural, inevitable, or immutable. To call international trade and investment rules supraconstitutional "might appear to establish economic globalization as an irreversible 'fact,' furnishing the convenient alibi to political and other global actors that there are no alternatives in sight" (Schneiderman 2008, 5). Constitutional discourse may have the intended or unintended effect of suppressing ambiguity and political contestation (Dunoff 2006).

Although these dangers are real, constitutional analysis does not necessarily reinforce the existing global status quo. Constitutionalism may challenge as well as support existing arrangements, having a long history as a *"critique of rule,* as a vocabulary of rights, accountability and transparency" (Koskenniemi 2005, 17, emphasis in original). Our account of the supraconstitution is presented in this critical evaluative mode. We employ constitutional terminology precisely because of its normative power. By characterizing certain international norms and institutions as forming part of the basic ensemble of practices by which contemporary societies are governed alongside national constitutions, we hope to alert readers to the fundamental significance of these arrangements and the serious normative issues they raise. Our intent is to challenge the choices embedded in NAFTA, the WTO, and other aspects of the institutional and normative architecture of neo-conservative globalization, not to legitimize them. Constitutional concepts and terminology provide potent tools to accomplish this:

> The discourse of constitutionalism is a powerful one and can
> equally rouse citizens into action as it can immobilize them. It has
> the advantage of assessing the new terrain of economic globaliza-
> tion from a perspective different from that in which it was con-
> ceived and so can engage critically with the dominant discourses
> of [neo-conservatism] ... Constitutionalism, in this way, performs
> a double role: both as descriptor and as normative guide to the
> current scene. (Schneiderman 2008, 5)

Canada's Supraconstitution: Where to Begin?

Choosing the time period at which to begin an account of Canada's supraconstitution is somewhat arbitrary. Canada has experienced two supraconstitutional phases in its history (Clarkson 2008b). During the colonial era, it was explicitly embedded in an imperial constitutional order, which was dismantled over more than a century as democratic self-government and foreign policy autonomy were established gradually in the Canadian dominion. By the second half of the twentieth century, Canada enjoyed substantial independence from Britain in domestic and foreign policy matters, but it was not until the 1982 repatriation of the constitution that the last vestiges of the imperial supraconstitution were erased (although even now the British monarch remains Canada's head of state).

Throughout the decline of the imperial supraconstitutional order, a second supraconstitutional order centred on the United States was emerging, whose loosely interrelated elements had complicated effects on Canadian autonomy and capacity. One aspect was Canada's position as a generally loyal junior partner in the American Cold War alliance. Canadians performed, with considerable success, a somewhat schizophrenic role as good Cold Warriors and simultaneously strong advocates of multilateral arrangements outside the Cold War framework (Whitaker 2006). On the foreign policy front, Canada's role as Cold War ally constrained it from openly criticizing American foreign policy, but the quid pro quo was substantial Canadian independence to pursue its liberal internationalist foreign policy and to undertake certain missions the Western bloc leader would not or could not take on itself.

In defence policy, the limitations were more severe. Ottawa was in effect obliged to establish defence forces and doctrines to the Pentagon's satisfaction. If Canada did not finance the military structures and adopt the tactical orientation deemed necessary in Washington, American forces would do the job themselves. Although generations of Canadian politicians have insisted on Canadian defence sovereignty at a rhetorical level (as they must, for political survival), the reality is that Ottawa's resistance to this arrangement has been rare and short-lived, whether in relation to BOMARC nuclear missile deployment during the 1960s or cruise missile testing in the 1980s. In 2005, Ottawa refused to support the US Ballistic Missile Defense program. Whether this latest act of resistance will be sustained, dropped, or made irrelevant by new efforts to construct a "Fortress North America" as part of the US war on terror has yet to be seen. Canada's lop-sided defence relationship with the United States was formalized in the North American Air Defense Command (NORAD, established 1957), a prototype for North America's asymmetrical institutions, in which a real reduction in autonomy for the periphery was nominally offset by increased capacity to affect American policies via Canadian participation in NORAD's joint command. This trade-off between domestic autonomy and nominally enhanced capacity to be heard in Washington was replicated across a range of policy arenas, as we will see.

A second element of the nascent supraconstitutional order was Canada's semi-peripheral position in an American-dominated continental and global economic system. Canada's resource-oriented economy, its asymmetrical dependence on trade with the US, and its high level of American foreign direct investment imposed limits on Canadian domestic autonomy and foreign affairs capacity. When, for instance, the Progressive Conservative government of John Diefenbaker set up a commission to design a national strategy for the petroleum industry, the major American oil companies along with the US Department of State participated directly in the advisory process and effectively wrote the Diefenbaker government's National Oil Policy of 1961. The 1965 *Canada-US Automotive Products Agreement* (Auto Pact) was not the first bilateral economic integration agreement to introduce an externally controlling element in a Canadian policy area, but it was economically the most consequential because it transformed one of Canada's biggest tariff-protected industries into a continentally rationalized sector that guaranteed a minimum level of Canadian production in US-owned assembly plants. President Nixon's unilateral 1971 detachment of the US dollar from the price of gold and imposition of a surcharge on all imports produced shockwaves around the world, but closer to home it was seen as a cataclysm. Previously, the bilateral relationship had been governed by a norm of "quiet diplomacy" in which Canadian-American disagreements were to be mediated to the extent feasible by bureaucrats behind closed doors in order to keep political tensions at bay (Merchant and Heeney 1965). Nixon unilaterally amended the parameters of this informally constituted relationship, simultaneously reducing Ottawa's capacity to influence American decision makers and increasing America's autonomy over its own affairs.

In the global economic context, Canada was a semi-peripheral player in a post–Second World War international economic system characterized by the "compromise of embedded liberalism," which combined an agenda of trade liberalization at the international level with a commitment to state intervention to moderate the adverse impacts of this liberalization at the domestic level (Ruggie 1982). The main objective of the 1947 *General Agreement on Tariffs and Trade* (GATT) was to promote economic growth and prosperity by limiting the power of national governments to impede the movement of goods across borders. The GATT was born out of a belief that excessive protectionism had contributed to the calamity of the Great Depression and that freer trade would spur a rising tide of prosperity that would lift all boats. The quid pro quo, however, was agreement to embed the international trade liberalization agenda in the fabric of the West's emerging Keynesian welfare states. National states would use their armament of fiscal, monetary, and social policy to moderate the impacts of trade liberalization and to promote employment, economic development, education, health, and welfare.

In these ways, elements of a new external constitution began to materialize for Canada during the latter half of the twentieth century, displacing its colonial one. But they remained rudimentary, disconnected, and largely informal, allowing Canada a considerable degree of autonomy domestically and independence in foreign policy. This relative freedom found expression in Canada's post-war prominence in multilateral diplomacy and peacekeeping, its friendly policy toward Cuba, its decision to sit out the Vietnam conflict, and its development of socialized medicine, old age security, unemployment insurance, and other features of the Canadian welfare state. This situation was transformed rapidly starting in the 1980s, when Canada's fragmentary supraconstitution was shaped into a more coherent and intrusive form by an aggressive transnational political program.

Ironically, this neo-conservative supraconstitutional project arose at the very time that the last remnants of Canada's imperial supraconstitution were being dismantled. This was not entirely coincidental. Just as the final demise of the colonial supraconstitution was the result of Prime Minister Trudeau's successful effort to repatriate control over Canada's constitution from Britain, so the new supraconstitution sprang, in part, from his unsuccessful effort to repatriate control over Canadian oil and gas resources from American TNCs. The federal Liberal government's notorious National Energy Program (NEP) of 1980 was the first major effort by a Canadian government to restructure a crucial foreign-controlled industry. It sought to achieve energy self sufficiency, increase Canadian ownership and control of the industry, substantially enhance federal influence over the sector, and secure a greater share of petroleum wealth for federal coffers (Clarkson 1985, ch. 3). American transnational petroleum firms and their Canadian subsidiaries protested that their property rights had been expropriated. They found allies in the government and citizens of oil-rich Alberta, who saw the NEP as an outrageous ploy by Ottawa to overstep its jurisdiction and steal their riches; in the federal Conservatives, who saw the NEP as a socialist plot to expand an already bloated state, stifle private enterprise, and cripple economic prosperity; and in the newly installed Reagan administration, which pressured Ottawa to abolish the NEP on the grounds that, due to their very presence in the Canadian economy, US corporations had acquired rights not to have the value of their assets diminished by government action. On the other side, the NEP and its theme of "Canadianization" were popular among many citizens outside Alberta and among some traditional critics of the Liberal Party on the political left.

The NEP was ultimately derailed by an unanticipated decline in world oil prices in 1982, but it was one of several factors precipitating a crisis from which a new supraconstitutional project emanated. Others included the oil shocks of the 1970s, rising unemployment and inflation, increasing foreign competition in the Canadian marketplace, ballooning public deficits and debt, and the rapid expansion of environmental regulation of business. By the late 1970s, Canadian big business had abandoned its traditional protectionist stance and concluded that greater economic access to the US market was its only hope. In 1985, the Macdonald Commission, headed by a former

Liberal Cabinet minister, concluded that the Canadian regulatory and welfare state was broken and in need of fundamental reform. The same trends were experienced, to varying degrees, throughout the industrialized democracies. Similar crises gripped the Third World, from the Latin American debt crisis to the Northern backlash against post-colonial states' efforts at economic nationalism and their proposals for a New International Economic Order. The modern Keynesian welfare state was in crisis in the North, as was the national developmentalist state in the South. The compromise of embedded liberalism was unravelling.

This predicament provided an opening for the appearance of a new transnational political project. Incubated in Milton Friedman's Chicago School of Economics during the 1960s and given its first field test in Pinochet's Chile in the 1970s, neo-conservatism came into ascendancy in the capitalist world with the elections of Margaret Thatcher and Ronald Reagan. This transnational neo-conservative political project built upon the supraconstitutional foundations laid during the earlier post–Second World War period, but it differed from these antecedents in important respects. Rejecting the interventionist welfare state as ideologically bankrupt and practically counterproductive, it proposed a radical policy shift that would restrain the state in order to liberate the market. Discarding the compromise of embedded liberalism, it promoted aggressive liberalization of international trade and investment as well as a major reduction of state intervention in markets and society (except to protect private property, contracts, and free enterprise). It advocated a restructuring of the state in the advanced industrialized economies, the developing economies of the Third World, and later the communist bloc, around a set of "free market" prescriptions that could be tailored to varying circumstances. This recipe for reorganization included deep tax and government spending cuts, deficit reduction, downsizing of the public sector, business deregulation, strict cost-benefit analysis of proposed regulations, privatization of government enterprises and public service delivery, elimination of wage and price controls, and free movement of goods and investment across borders. Coupled with this restructuring of the nation-state was the promotion of international norms and institutions dedicated to advancing and entrenching this ambitious agenda. Paradoxically, this supraconstitutional project combined a commitment to the worldwide propagation of liberal democracy with a concerted effort to insulate key aspects of the economy from national democratic control. A central feature of the new constitutionalism was the imposition of lasting constraints on democratic politics "to prevent national interference with the property rights and entry and exit options of holders of mobile capital with regard to particular political jurisdictions" (Gill 1995, 413).

The triumph of this agenda marked a break from past supraconstitutional projects. Although neo-conservatism was a complete political program, its main supraconstitutional thrust was in the economic realm. We therefore continue our account in Chapter 3 with the genesis of Canada's economic supraconstitution in the 1980s.

3
Making the World Safe
for Transnational Capital:
The Economic Supraconstitution

Free trade with the United States and a neo-conservative restructuring of the Canadian political system became centrepieces of federal policy in the mid-1980s, after the election of Prime Minister Brian Mulroney's Progressive Conservative government. This reorientation did not happen without external persuasion. American big business aggressively promoted its agenda of global trade liberalization and limited government in the United States, at international venues, and among Canadian economic and political elites. Espousing its corporate citizens' cause but encountering European and Japanese resistance to its efforts to remake the multilateral trade regime, Washington pursued the dual multilateral-bilateral strategy described in Chapter 1 by pressuring its more compliant trading partners into signing agreements that embodied the norms it desired for the global level. Its first major breakthrough came with the *Canada-US Free Trade Agreement* (CUFTA), which became the first step toward a new global regime that would effectively constitutionalize international corporate rights.[1]

NAFTA continentalized CUFTA's bilateral regime by incorporating Mexico into its toughened set of rules.[2] Driven by Washington's demands that its two neighbours further open up their economies by cutting back their governments' control, NAFTA strengthened CUFTA's investment provisions, extended its rules on services, and added powerful intellectual property rights, which were of particular importance to American Big Pharma.

With the conclusion of the Uruguay Round of GATT negotiations a year after NAFTA had established a continental economic regime, the WTO Agreement transformed international governance by entrenching at the global level the trade rules that the core capitalist countries wanted for their TNCs.[3]

These regimes' main thrust is to liberate transnational capital from the limitations of majoritarian politics. Through global, regional, and bilateral

agreements, states commit themselves to dismantling barriers to the movement of goods, services, and capital (but generally not labour, except for some
affluent professionals and highly skilled workers in the case of NAFTA) across
borders; revoking policies that favour domestic over foreign producers, goods,
or services; and eliminating all forms of government intervention that distort
market competition. All of this is done in the hope that the economy will
reap the benefits of comparative advantage, more efficient production, lower
prices, wider choice of goods and services, and greater capacity for Canadian
companies in international economic affairs.

Throughout this process, Canadian elites willingly consented to US
dominance. For them, neo-conservatism was a hegemonic rather than an
imperial project since they embraced its agenda as their own, turning it to
their advantage where they could. Senior Canadian officials, for instance, were
the original proponents of the new WTO dispute settlement mechanism.
Believing that greater economic openness was critical to Canada's economic
survival, they pressed for clear, enforceable rules to temper the overwhelming
power of their massive southern neighbour and other dominant trading
partners. As they were to discover, however, the rules they agreed to impose
on themselves did not necessarily constrain their American counterpart to
the same extent.

In this chapter, we examine the extent to which these continental and
global regimes for trade and investment have established a supraconstitution
for Canada. Using the framework set out in Chapter 2, we will examine this
supraconstitution in terms of its *principles* guiding the allocation and exercise
of power, its *rules* governing members' behaviour, the fundamental *rights* of
its community members, and its *institutions* for the exercise of adjudicative
and enforcement functions.

Canada's Economic Supraconstitution

PRINCIPLES

The WTO and NAFTA established general principles to guide the behaviour
of member states. These international trade regimes' fundamental policy is
non-discrimination, which is expressed in two principles: *national treatment*
and *most favoured nation* (MFN). The former obliges states not to discriminate
between domestic and foreign goods or investors.[4] The latter prohibits discrimination between goods or investors from different foreign countries.[5]
Goods or investments coming from one foreign country must be treated as
favourably as those from any other foreign country. These two principles rule

out discriminating between trading partners on the basis of poor social or environmental policies in the places where goods are produced or investors are based.[6]

National treatment and MFN are supraconstitutional norms because they have been incorporated as a superior legal order that effectively binds Canadian legislatures in their exercise of regulatory authority. There is no Canadian law stating that federal or provincial governments must treat foreign-owned furniture companies at least as well as they treat Canadian-owned equivalents. Likewise, no Canadian law prohibits Canadian governments from barring the import or sale in Canada of goods made in factories with labour or environmental practices that would be illegal in Canada. But since CUFTA and NAFTA extended the national treatment and MFN principles from goods to investment and even to services, if any level of government discriminates in favour of a Canadian-owned firm – even on the basis that the foreign producer, investor, or service provider does not meet minimal standards for labour, human rights, or environmental practices in its foreign operations – the government of Canada is liable to legal attack by another party to NAFTA or the WTO that deems one of its companies to have suffered from unequal or discriminatory treatment at the hands of Ottawa, a province, or even a Canadian municipality.

The impact of these supraconstitutional norms on member state autonomy is growing, because the interpretation of GATT 1994 principles by WTO dispute settlement tribunals has proven more expansive than that of identical norms under the earlier GATT. Even when government measures are formally neutral with respect to nationality, the WTO may strike them down if in practice they bias the competitive conditions in favour of domestic service providers (national treatment) or of particular foreign providers (most favoured nation) over others (S. Sinclair 2000, 44).

It must be noted that these supraconstitutional norms may work to the advantage of Canadian governments and firms. As a constituent of the global constitution, Canada also enjoys rights with its economic partners who are themselves constrained supraconstitutionally. In the *Embraer* case, for example, Canada successfully sued Brazil for its WTO-illegal subsidization of its aircraft exports.[7] But when Canada sued France for restricting the import of asbestos mined in Quebec, it lost its case because the WTO Appellate Body acknowledged the validity of the French government's health concerns about the carcinogenic properties of asbestos.[8]

RULES

When we speak of Canada's supraconstitution, we also refer to those rules at the international level that can be said to form part of the collection of fundamental practices by which Canadian society is governed. Identifying all such rules would be a monumental task, given the thousands of international commitments Ottawa has signed, but certain rules of economic globalization are clear candidates for this status. We focus here on the rules of CUFTA, NAFTA, and the WTO.

Canada and Mexico paid for greater access to the US market with diminished political autonomy. Although CUFTA and NAFTA reduced American tariffs for Canadian exporters, the price Ottawa had to pay for a partial opening of the US market was to accept constraints on the legislative and regulatory capacity of Canadian governments. Ottawa was no longer allowed to manage a two-price system that supplied petroleum products for domestic industry and consumers at a price lower than their export price to American importers. No new cultural policies could negatively affect the commercial interests in Canada of American entertainment corporations. CUFTA also introduced rules reducing the capacity of Canadian governments to regulate investments, whether foreign or domestically owned. CUFTA and later NAFTA went beyond goods and investment to lay down rules for cross-border trade in services, which include an enormous range of activities, from those traditionally in the private sector (such as banking, advertising, engineering, entertainment, and tourism) to those provided by governments as public goods (such as education, health care, policing, and public utilities). Even if not provided directly by governments, many of these services are closely regulated by them (including competition, environmental, labour, health, safety, and consumer protection) and may fall under international rules for services if they have any commercial characteristics that make them competitive with foreign private-sector providers of the same service.

By signing CUFTA, Canada undertook to make immediate changes in a wide range of legislation and regulations. For example, in the case of foreign takeovers, CUFTA's investment chapter raised the exemption from review from $5 million to $150 million, requiring changes to the *Investment Canada Act*. CUFTA was highly controversial, but it had some process legitimacy because, though carried out in secret, the negotiations were the subject of intense media concern, public interest, and ultimately an election campaign that was a virtual referendum. Once the agreement was published, fierce debate over its various provisions continued for months, reaching a climax in the 1988 federal election campaign whose results – a majority of seats (if only a minority of the popular vote) for Prime Minister Brian Mulroney's Progressive Conservative government – gave the accord a degree of parliamentary legitimacy. Conversely, CUFTA's outcome – the loss of hundreds of thousands of industrial jobs in the Canadian economy's manufacturing centres – left it highly unpopular among labour unions and civil society organizations, which continue to deem "free trade" illegitimate.

The WTO and NAFTA rules are so comprehensive that their members had to change hundreds of existing laws in their implementing legislation. Because the negotiation process through which these rules were produced benefited from much less public debate and information than CUFTA, their process legitimacy remains dubious. Their outcome legitimacy is difficult to assess, since their effects may take years to become evident – apart from specific dispute settlement rulings highlighted in the media. When the WTO Appellate Body agreed with Brazil's case against Ottawa's subsidization of Bombardier regional jet export sales by declaring the federal industry department's Technology Partnership Fund to be GATT-illegal, it invalidated a whole generation of industrial development strategies based on federal and provincial support programs for domestic enterprise.[9] When it also struck down much of Canada's magazine policy in favour of Time Warner's split run magazine *Sports Illustrated Canada*, it suddenly became clear that the country's new external constitution had very sharp teeth even in the cultural policy domain, which had been declared exempt by Ottawa's trade negotiators.[10]

Within their domestic legal orders, governments change laws and regulations according to the institutional and legal framework established by their internal constitutions and in response to demands from the electorate or specific functional constituencies. What makes NAFTA supraconstitutional is not that the signatory governments revised their laws and regulations to implement their treaty obligations. International rules are supraconstitutional when they enjoy primacy in the domestic legal system even in the face of conflicting legislation. NAFTA rules are incorporated into Canadian law in a context that makes them effectively irreversible. As we saw, unlike normal amendments to statutes enacted by domestic legislatures, which can further amend or revoke their acts in response to evolving considerations, amendments to statutes incorporating international trade norms are valid only if the external regime changes its rules by international agreement.

In this respect, the Canadian legal order has been altered by accepting statutory and regulatory modifications over which Parliament or the provinces no longer exercise ultimate control. This higher power over domestic politics is what the champions of free trade alluded to when they described NAFTA as "locking in" neo-conservatism – despite the fact that this paradigm was and is no closer to being accepted as a sustainable societal contract in Canada than it is elsewhere (Clark 1997). Even if political parties that reject this neo-conservative model were to win power, they would find their hands tied by an internationally negotiated and domestically implemented supraconstitution to which their predecessors had committed them – unless they were willing to violate or withdraw from it and pay the resulting costs involved in their trading partners' commercial or political retaliation.

In theory, states may withdraw at any time from international trade and investment agreements. A party may withdraw from the WTO and its multilateral trade agreements upon six months' notice.[11] Similarly, Canada, Mexico, or the US may withdraw from NAFTA upon six months' notice to the other parties.[12] This prospect was publicly mooted by then-Senators Barrack Obama and Hillary Clinton during the 2008 race for the Democratic presidential nomination.

The world trading system consists of more than NAFTA and the WTO: it is interlaced with thousands of bilateral investment treaties (BITs), the number of which is growing dramatically. Canada is party to dozens of BITs. Unlike the processes for withdrawing from NAFTA and the WTO agreements, termination of BITs is often permitted only after ten years (although most of Canada's recent BITs do not have this restriction), and their rules continue in force for a further ten to twenty years for investments made during the period of the BIT (the default for Canadian BITs is fifteen years).

Even if possible in theory, exit is not a feasible option for Canada in practice, let alone for economically weaker countries (Schneiderman 2000b, 771; Unger 1998, 82-84). Moreover, the network of international trade and investment agreements is so extensive, entrenched, and interwoven that fundamental renegotiation of its terms is not a feasible option for disgruntled individual governments. The international trade and investment regime subjects nation-states' exercise of public regulatory authority to an unusual degree of external control (Van Harten and Loughlin 2006). The infeasibility of exit or renegotiation means that this external control is unlikely to relax in the short or even the medium term.

Paradoxically, though the international trade and investment regime is based on a general principle of non-discrimination, some NAFTA and BIT rules require member governments to discriminate *in favour* of foreign capital. One such rule is the prohibition against imposing performance requirements as a condition for the establishment, management, conduct, or operation of foreign investments.[13] Formerly, governments might have obliged foreign investors to make export commitments, use local suppliers, transfer technology to domestic partners, or guarantee certain levels of employment (Chang 1998).[14] Canadian governments may still impose such conditions on Canadian investors. Indeed, such conditions are commonly imposed in large projects to ensure benefits to the local community and economy. The result is that investors from other NAFTA parties are accorded more generous treatment than are Canadian firms.

To be precise, these rules do not actually *prevent* governments from imposing performance requirements on foreign investors or subsidizing domestic firms. But any federal, provincial, or municipal government action that violates these NAFTA, BIT, or WTO norms is vulnerable to international legal action that could result in a damages award enforceable in Canadian courts or in economic sanctions to compensate for the harm that successful foreign plaintiffs claim to have suffered.

As with internal constitutions, the supraconstitution's rule book is never finalized. A chronic state of flux results from the continual negotiation of global rules by governments and the recurrent interpretation of these rules by international tribunals. At the WTO's Doha Round, for instance, Canada came under pressure from countries trying to obtain better access to the Canadian market for their agricultural products. As a result, Ottawa's negotiators agreed they would ultimately have to abandon both the marketing boards (which guarantee protection from foreign competitors for chicken, dairy, and egg farmers in central Canada) and the Canadian Wheat Board (which gets western grain farmers the best price on the world market for their wheat by selling it collectively). Canada is also under constant pressure from the United States, in the context of the *General Agreement on Trade in Services*, to allow the entry of transnational corporations into its public health and education systems. This impetus to make further concessions creates an instability that puts the supraconstitution's legitimacy in continual jeopardy. Although Ontario or Quebec farmers may not realize that Ottawa cannot forever protect the marketing boards on which their entrepreneurial calculations depend, their way of life and the already marginal economic viability of the Canadian family farm are in danger.

Rights

The corollary of a limit on government may be a right for the citizenry. Whereas the treaties establishing the European Union confer important civil, political, economic, and social rights directly upon all citizens of member states and allow them to sue their own governments before the European Court of Justice, the only beneficiaries of expanded rights in Canada under CUFTA were American (and in theory under NAFTA, Mexican) investors. Chapter 11 of NAFTA conferred four important rights on investors from the other NAFTA countries: national treatment (Article 1102), most favoured nation treatment (Article 1103), fair and equitable treatment in accordance with an international minimum standard (Article 1105), and freedom from expropriation or measures "tantamount to expropriation" (Article 1110). Like Article 1605 of CUFTA before it, NAFTA Article 1110 provides that no party government "may directly or indirectly nationalize or expropriate an investment of an investor of another Party in its territory or take a measure tantamount to nationalization or expropriation of such an investment," except for a public purpose, on a non-discriminatory basis, in accordance with due process of law and minimum standards of treatment, and on payment of compensation. "Investment" is defined expansively to cover almost any form of business asset, actual or anticipated, tangible or intangible, including future contracts arising from an investor's enterprise.[15] Chapter 11 tribunal decisions even suggest that "market access" and "market share" may constitute protected investments.[16]

Similar rights are included in the bilateral investment treaties Canada has negotiated with other countries. The impact of these NAFTA Chapter 11 rights and similar provisions in BITs upon Canadian public law and policy is uncertain and has yet to be fully felt. It is already clear that, in important and potentially disturbing ways, they have modified the domestic constitutions of the states that are subject to them. There are three reasons to be concerned about these provisions:

- On their face, they are inconsistent with the limited protection afforded to private property rights in Canadian law.
- They are enjoyed only by foreign investors (for all intents and purposes, transnational corporations).
- They are very difficult to amend or repeal.

Inconsistency with Canadian Constitutional and Legal Norms

NAFTA provides by far the most extensive protection of private property rights in Canada. Its rights for foreign investors are unprecedented in Canadian law and inconsistent with the treatment of private property in the Canadian constitution, which gives no protection against the taking of private property. Property rights were deliberately excluded from Canada's *Charter of Rights and Freedoms* in 1982, because they would excessively enhance corporate power, which was thought to be adequately protected by the common law and ordinary legislation. Notwithstanding this purposeful democratic choice, just a few years later CUFTA introduced into Canada's legal system a guarantee of property rights for foreign investors modelled after the takings clause of the US constitution.[17] Soon afterward, NAFTA reconfirmed and extended these rights to Mexican investors. The effect of these provisions, as Been and Beauvais (2003, 143) conclude, is not merely to "internationalize" the US takings clause but to "extend the scope of potential regulatory takings claims in significant respects." This was understood at the time neither (apparently) by the Canadian government nor (certainly) by the public.

It is true that the Canadian constitution protects some aspects of property rights, including security against unreasonable search and seizure, freedom to use one's property for expressive purposes, freedom to trade on the Sabbath, protection against racially motivated confiscations such as those inflicted on Japanese Canadians in the Second World War, and protection of Aboriginal property rights. But there is no constitutional protection against deprivation of private property and no constitutional requirement for compensation in the event of a taking. The contrast between NAFTA and the Canadian constitution in this respect is stark.

On its face, NAFTA also goes well beyond the protection accorded to private property rights by ordinary Canadian law. Contrary to NAFTA Article 1110, common law rules of statutory interpretation provide that legislation may validly deprive citizens of property without compensation if the statutory language clearly dictates this result.[18] In practice, provincial and federal expropriation laws provide for procedural due process and compensation, but there are exceptions, and in any event these rules can be amended or repealed by the legislatures that enacted them. Canadian courts usually grant minimal compensation for expropriation, whereas NAFTA Article 1110 requires compensation to be prompt, fully realizable, freely transferable, and equivalent to fair market value immediately before the expropriation (Schwartz and Bueckert 2006). Although human rights legislation such as the *Canadian Bill of Rights* and some provincial statutes contain provisions protecting private property rights, courts have generally interpreted them narrowly and been reluctant to apply them to invalidate laws.[19] Finally, Canadian courts have shied away from the American notion of "regulatory takings" implicit in the NAFTA reference to measures "tantamount to expropriation."

This latter point is crucial to understanding NAFTA's significance for Canadian public law and policy. According to the US regulatory takings concept, government regulation that falls short of direct expropriation can nevertheless amount to an illegal taking. As Justice Oliver Wendell Holmes wrote in 1922, "while property may be regulated to a certain extent, if regulation goes too far it will be recognized as a taking."[20] In the United States, the concept of regulatory takings has been invoked to challenge all kinds of regulation. Since the 1980s, "property-rights advocates have turned in increasing numbers to 'takings' arguments as a way to galvanize public support and roll back what they argue to be oppressive governmental interference with the rights of private property" (Underkuffler-Freund 1996, 162; see also Epstein 1985). They have won important victories in state and federal courts, and have succeeded in enacting ballot measures and statutes in several states requiring compensation for reductions in property value resulting from land-use regulation.

After decades of confusion, some clarity has finally been achieved in the US Supreme Court's regulatory takings jurisprudence (M.B. Kent 2008). Compensation may be required for either total or partial regulatory takings (Meltz 2007).[21] A total regulatory taking occurs when regulation deprives the owner of all economically beneficial uses of the property and renders it economically idle. Thus, in the *Lucas* case, a local council in South Carolina designated a beachfront area as unavailable for development under a state statute for the protection of ecologically sensitive seacoast property, thus prohibiting the owner of affected beachfront lots from erecting any permanent structures on his land. The US Supreme Court held this to be a taking.[22]

When government action falls short of total deprivation of the property's economic use or value, a partial regulatory taking may still be found if the impugned regulation is "functionally equivalent" to direct appropriation or ouster.[23] This will depend on the severity of the economic impact on the property owner, the degree of interference with the owner's reasonable investment-backed expectations, and the character of the government action.[24]

The intent of the takings clause, according to the court, is to prevent the government "from forcing some people alone to bear public burdens that, in all fairness and justice, should be borne by the public as a whole."[25] Thus, requiring landowners to dedicate a public greenway over a portion of their property or to allow public access to a privately owned beach as a condition for issuing a building permit has been held a taking, as has an interim ordinance prohibiting construction of any structures in a flood zone.[26] Even regulations that predate the plaintiff's acquisition of title may qualify as takings.[27] In general, the purpose behind the regulations (environmental protection, public health, and so on) is not considered relevant.[28]

On the other hand, the US Supreme Court has dismissed many regulatory takings claims, including challenges to rent control regulation, restrictions on surface mining of prime farmlands, requirements to restore original slope contours after surface mining, temporary land development moratoria, and the use of historical landmark designation to prevent construction of a skyscraper atop a historic building.[29] The court has recognized fairly wide scope for government regulation, holding that "government hardly could go on if to some extent values incident to property could not be diminished without paying for every such change in the general law," and that deprivation of a property's most profitable use is not, in itself, a taking.[30] As a result, regulatory takings claims remain a "difficult sell" in the United States (Meltz 2007, 371).

They are an even harder sell in Canada. Two requirements must be met to prove a de facto taking necessitating compensation in Canada: first, an acquisition by the Crown of an interest in the property or flowing from it and, second, deprivation of all reasonable uses of the property.[31] Not even a "total" taking of the kind found in *Lucas* would normally be considered a de facto expropriation in Canada. In circumstances similar to those in *Lucas,* the Nova Scotia Court of Appeal in *Mariner Real Estate* upheld a provincial government prohibition of beachfront development.[32] The government had designated the plaintiffs' beachfront lots in Kingsburg, Nova Scotia, as a beach under the *Beaches Act.*[33] Once this occurred, all development on such lands – from trails to fences to buildings – was prohibited unless authorized by the minister. The plaintiffs applied for permission to build single-family residences on their lots. An environmental study commissioned by the government concluded that the houses should not be constructed, due to the sensitive nature of the dune landforms and the probable damage to the houses themselves from the breakdown of the dune system. The provincial government refused the applications. The plaintiffs sued, claiming that their lands had, in effect, been expropriated and that they were entitled to compensation under the provincial expropriation statute. The trial judge agreed, but the Court of Appeal reversed the decision.

The Court of Appeal concluded that "US constitutional law has, on this issue, taken a fundamentally different path than has Canadian law."[34] It held that regulatory takings claims in Canada were constrained by two governing principles: "The first is that valid legislation ... or action taken lawfully with legislative authority may very significantly restrict an owner's enjoyment of private land. The second is that the Courts may order compensation for such restriction only where authorized to do so by legislation ... In short, the bundle of rights associated with ownership carries with it the possibility of stringent ... regulation."[35]

The question posed in US takings cases is therefore fundamentally different from that before a Canadian court. Although deprivation of economically beneficial or productive use qualifies as a taking of land in the United States, it does not in Canada, even when the deprivation is drastic. The appropriate question, rather, is whether the effect of regulation is to eliminate "virtually all rights associated with ownership."[36] This is a considerably higher threshold. In *Mariner*, the court held that "preclusion of residential development ... particularly on lands of this environmental sensitivity, is not, of itself, the extinguishment of virtually all rights associated with ownership."[37] The plaintiffs had not shown that other traditional or reasonable uses were precluded, such as walking, camping, taking pictures, gardening, horseback riding, or grazing livestock. Nor had they shown that they were precluded from forms of development that were more environmentally appropriate than houses built on standard concrete foundations. They therefore retained some of the normal rights and incidents of ownership, precluding a finding of de facto expropriation. In contrast, the fact that the *Lucas* plaintiff could still engage in camping on his beachfront property did not prevent the US Supreme Court from finding a taking in that case.

Mariner also highlighted a second major difference between American and Canadian takings law. In the United States, a plaintiff need not prove that the state acquires any interest in the land regulated; in Canada, de facto expropriation will be recognized only if there is an acquisition of an interest in land by the Crown. The court in *Mariner* held that the development freeze and strict environmental regulation of beachfront property did not confer any interest in the land on the province. Even if the measures enhanced the value of publicly owned property (for example, the public portion of the beach), the court held that regulation enhancing the worth of public property was not an acquisition of an interest in land.[38]

Mariner was recently endorsed by the Supreme Court of Canada in a decision that further underlined the contrast between Canadian and US regulatory takings law. The US Supreme Court has found regulatory takings where the government required private owners to grant public beach access or create a public greenway over a portion of their property as a condition for issuance of a building permit.[39] By contrast, when the City of Vancouver amended its Official Plan to require an *entire* privately owned property – a discontinued Canadian Pacific Railway (CPR) rail corridor – to be used only as a public thoroughfare for transportation or greenways, the Supreme Court of Canada upheld this as valid regulatory action notwithstanding the fact that the effect of the by-law was to "freeze the redevelopment potential of the corridor and to confine CPR to uneconomic uses of the land."[40] The court held that neither of the two requirements for a regulatory taking was satisfied. It rejected CPR's argument that the City had in effect acquired a public park, concluding that the City "has gained nothing more than some assurance that the land will be used or developed in accordance with its vision, without even precluding the historical or current use of the land."[41] Furthermore, the court held that the by-law did not remove all reasonable uses of the land, noting that it did not prevent CPR from operating a railway there, maintaining the track, leasing the site for use in conformity with the by-law, or developing public-private partnerships. Finally, the court held that, even if the facts could support the inference of a de facto taking, that inference had been conclusively negated by a section in a provincial statute providing that the City was not liable to compensate landowners for loss as a result of by-law restrictions and that property affected by a by-law was deemed not to have been "taken" by the City. As the court noted, the legislature has the power to alter the common law, and by providing that the effects of the by-law cannot amount to a taking, "it has rendered inapplicable the common law *de facto* taking remedy upon which CPR relies."[42] This reinforces a crucial difference between takings law in Canada and the United States: because protection against takings is not constitutionally entrenched in Canada, it can be modified or removed by legislation.

What does all of this tell us about NAFTA's investor protections? The phrase "measure tantamount to nationalization or expropriation" is not defined in NAFTA, and only a few tribunal decisions have interpreted it. We discuss those decisions below, in the section on adjudication. But it is clear that the rights incorporated into NAFTA – national treatment, most favoured nation treatment, protection against expropriation, no performance requirements, minimum international standard of treatment – are on their face inconsistent with the Canadian constitution and other Canadian laws. They are much more closely aligned with American law than with either Canadian or, as we will see shortly, Mexican law (Schneiderman 1996; Starner 2002). It is also evident that Chapter 11 "adopts wholesale" the rights that American TNCs had long demanded in their dealings abroad and that the US government had advocated on their behalf (Afilalo 2001). The formula for compensation adopted in NAFTA – prompt, adequate (that is, fair market value), effective, fully realizable, and freely transferable – was the same one called for by the US government and industry in bilateral and multilateral forums, especially in relation to nationalizations by developing states in the Third World. The US has long argued that this stringent compensation formula is the standard required by international law. Thus are NAFTA's investor rights more in line with American legal norms than with those of the two other continental trade partners.

We can go further. Investors' rights under Chapter 11 may be more expansive even than in American law. As Echeverria (2006, 984) points out, the language of NAFTA Article 1110 is quite different from that of the US takings clause, and the rulings of NAFTA tribunals are essentially unreviewable in Canadian or US courts, "practically ensuring that the international law of takings will evolve along a separate and independent path from domestic takings law." At the very least, the contrast between the Canadian and American law of takings, and the decades of confusion within US regulatory takings jurisprudence, indicates that the line between valid public welfare regulation and actions "tantamount to expropriation" can be drawn in very different places.

A discussion of NAFTA's investor rights would be incomplete without considering their implications for NAFTA's third partner, Mexico. If NAFTA Chapter 11 represents a "minimal shift" in US takings law and a "significant shift" for Canadian takings law, it embodies a major departure from Mexico's highly interventionist constitutional takings tradition (Starner 2002, 428, 431). Experience in Mexico and some other Latin American countries that have signed Chapter 11–like investment treaties indicates that, if investment treaties contradict domestic constitutional rules, so much the worse for the constitution. The modern constitutions of Mexico and other post-colonial countries were substantially shaped by those countries' experiences with and reactions against transnational, especially British and American, capital. Like those of many other developing and less developed states, the Mexican constitution vested in the state a monopoly over certain key economic sectors along with authority to intervene in the market to steer economic development, redistribute wealth, and resist foreign influence.

Article 27 of Mexico's constitution contains a version of the famous "Calvo Clause," commonly traced to the writings of nineteenth-century Argentinian jurist Carlos Calvo.[43] As Schneiderman (2000a, 89) explains, "Based on the dismal Latin American experience with interventionist international capital, Calvo argued that the countries of Latin America were entitled to the same degree of respect for their internal sovereignty as the United States of America and the countries of Europe. Among Calvo's precepts is the proposition that states should be free, within reason, from interference in the conduct of their domestic policy." This doctrine contained two basic principles: absolute equality of treatment of aliens and nationals, and non-intervention by the home state in the event of a dispute between an alien investor and the host country (Starner 2002). First, foreign investors who chose to establish themselves within the territory of the host state had no greater protection from state action (including expropriation) than did nationals, were entitled to pursue domestic remedies only, and were prohibited from seeking diplomatic intervention by their home state, in some cases on pain of forfeiture of their property rights. Home states were prohibited against intervening, diplomatically or otherwise, to enforce their citizens' rights in the face of nationalization or expropriation of their property. The intent was for government action, including nationalization, to be judged by domestic standards in domestic courts, not by "international" standards dictated by the major capital-exporting nations.

The Mexican constitution also establishes national sovereignty over and state ownership of natural resources, limits foreign ownership, permits expropriation of private property for public use (subject to payment of indemnity), and authorizes the regulation of private property and natural resources for the collective good, "to ensure a more equitable distribution of public wealth, to conserve them, to achieve the well-balanced development of the country and the improvement of the living conditions of the rural and urban population."[44] Such regulation does not give rise to a right to compensation, even though it may drastically diminish the value of private property or eliminate almost all rights of ownership (Starner 2002, 414).

These constitutional provisions reflected a distinct Latin American brand of constitutionalism (Cox 1996a) called "state capitalism," which emerged as an alternative to both Western capitalist imperialism and Soviet socialism. State capitalism emphasized public control of key economic sectors, intervention in the market to redistribute wealth, and insulation from external economic and political pressures. It was never accepted by the United States and the capital-exporting countries of Europe, although some of its principles were included in UN General Assembly resolutions associated with the proposed New International Economic Order in the 1970s. By the 1990s, state capitalism was in disfavour, pushed aside by its main post–Cold War rival, the neo-conservative constitutionalism we described in Chapter 2. Developing countries in Latin America and elsewhere began to implement massive constitutional reforms to relinquish state control of the commanding heights of the economy, reduce or eliminate limits on foreign ownership and control, and roll back the state's central role in redistributing wealth and directing economic and social development.

In Mexico, some thirty constitutional provisions that gave expression to the Calvo Doctrine and the state-capitalist model of constitutionalism were amended in the lead-up to NAFTA. One of these amendments precipitated the Zapatista armed uprising in Chiapas, by authorizing the redistribution of "underused" collective rural land to campesinos (Schneiderman 2000b, 766). Although the Calvo Clause remained formally intact, it was implicitly erased, at least as regards NAFTA parties, by a series of non-constitutional and legislative edicts (*ibid.*; Flores 2005). In effect, the Mexican constitution was amended to submit to NAFTA discipline.

This phenomenon is not restricted to Mexico. Governments in Latin America and elsewhere that once pursued a state-capitalist development path have increasingly become parties to BITs and regional free trade agreements that incorporate NAFTA-style investor rights. When such arrangements conflict with domestic constitutional arrangements, the latter have often been jettisoned. The Colombia–United Kingdom BIT of 1994 contained the usual provisions concerning national treatment, most favoured nation treatment, and prohibition against expropriation except for a public purpose and upon payment of prompt, adequate, and effective compensation that is fully realizable and transferable. When the legislation implementing the BIT was presented to the Colombian Constitutional Court for certification, as required by the constitution, the court held that the BIT violated the Colombian constitution of 1991 in two ways. First, by guaranteeing compensation for expropriation, it contradicted a provision that authorized expropriation without compensation for reasons of equity. Second, by granting British investors preferential treatment that was not available to Colombian nationals, it violated the equality provisions of the constitution. The response of the Colombian government was to amend the constitution in 1999 to prohibit expropriation without compensation. As Schneiderman (2000a, 106-8) concludes, "Here is a clear instance of [neo-conservative] constitutionalism disciplining a domestic constitutional text: Interference with private property and investment rights simply is beyond the bounds of acceptability."

Enjoyed Only by Foreign Corporations

This example brings us to the second reason for concern about the rights conferred on foreign investors by NAFTA and BITs: they are enjoyed only by foreign investors, not by nationals. Unlike rights in Canada's internal constitution, investor rights in NAFTA and BITs are not available to Canadian investors in Canada. They are enjoyed only by American (and, theoretically, Mexican) investors. For practical purposes, this means transnational corporations. The more that citizens' groups understood that foreign transnationals had been given rights to nullify domestic legislation that were not just beyond recourse in domestic courts but were unavailable to Canadian enterprise, the more NAFTA's Chapter 11 became delegitimized. Moreover, these enhanced rights are not accompanied by any corresponding obligations. The new justiciable empowerment accorded by trade agreements to transnational corporations subjects them to no balancing obligations enforced by continental-level institutions with the clout to regulate, tax, or monitor transnational business in the newly created continental market (Blank and Krajewski 1995). Chapter 11 expanded the scope of investment rights with no corresponding requirements for TNCs to promote the public interest by, for example, protecting the environment or public health. Some commentators suggest that the solution to the disparate treatment of foreign investors and nationals instituted by NAFTA and BITs is to extend similar rights and privileges to nationals. "Ideally," one article predicts hopefully, "better remedies for 'regulatory takings' under international law will pressure Canadian authorities to adopt a more generous compensatory approach for their own citizens" (Schwartz and Bueckert 2006, 485). The economic supraconstitution itself thus becomes a tool to advance a neo-conservative project to transform domestic constitutions, laws, and public policies.

Difficult to Change

These rights are difficult to amend or repeal. Unlike domestic laws, the investor rights conferred by NAFTA and BITs cannot be amended unilaterally by any one state. As we have already established, withdrawal from or renegotiation of NAFTA or BITs would be difficult at best. As BITs with NAFTA-style investment rights proliferate, the difficulty of exit or renegotiation increases. From this perspective, the failure of the *Multilateral Agreement on Investment* (MAI) can now be seen as a victory for neo-conservative constitutionalism, since renegotiating a single multilateral investment treaty would probably be easier than revising the thousands of BITs that took its place. This imperviousness to change is an important part of what makes these rights supraconstitutional. As Schwartz and Bueckert (*ibid.*, 483) assert, "because it would be politically and economically difficult for Canada to withdraw from NAFTA, the treaty provisions have quasi-constitutional force."

Beyond Investor Rights: Corporate Rights in the WTO System

The WTO agreements also contain rights for transnational corporations but none for citizens per se. The WTO *Agreement on Trade-Related Investment Measures* (TRIMs) created rights for all corporations based in states belonging to the WTO but not for their citizens. Its *Agreement on Trade-Related Aspects of Intellectual Property Rights* (TRIPS) required that all member states amend their intellectual property legislation and change their judicial procedures in conformity with the stipulated norms (C. Kent 1994).[45] That these rights possess supraconstitutional quality can be seen in the fact that they accorded transatlantic pharmaceutical firms the legal justification to have the EU successfully take a case against Ottawa to the WTO, on the grounds that Canada's drug legislation did not give European Big Pharma the full patent benefits that it claimed were now its due.[46] Unlike NAFTA, the TRIPS Agreement recognizes the need to balance rights with obligations. But as the United Nations Commission on Human Rights (2001, 8) concluded,

> It gives no guidance on how to achieve this balance. On the one
> hand, the Agreement sets out in considerable detail the content
> of intellectual property rights – the requirements for the grant of

rights, the duration of protection, the modes of enforcement. On the other hand, the Agreement only alludes to the responsibilities of intellectual property holders that should balance those rights in accordance with its own objectives ... But unlike the rights it sets out, the Agreement does not establish the content of these responsibilities, or how they should be implemented.

ADJUDICATION

A supraconstitution also consists of institutionalized practices for the performance of legislative, executive, administrative, adjudicative, and enforcement functions. We saw in Chapter 2 that the legislative, executive, and administrative institutions of the economic supraconstitution are weakly developed. The most remarkable feature of Canada's economic supraconstitution from an institutional perspective is its institutions for the adjudication of disputes.[47]

Global environmental, human rights, and labour governance is notably bereft of adjudicative weight. The strength of global economic norms, rules, and rights, on the other hand, is due largely to the power of the WTO dispute settlement mechanisms and the investor-state adjudication instruments in NAFTA and BITs. Whereas the WTO was endowed with an impressive apparatus for adjudicating intergovernmental disputes, NAFTA was created without a supranational judiciary. Instead, North American governance is distinguished by various dispute settlement processes whose supraconstitutional impacts range from minor (for general disputes between member states) to negligible (for trade disputes between exporting and importing states) to substantial (for Chapter 11 disputes between transnational corporations and host states).

NAFTA Chapter 20 General Disputes

Continental dispute settlement was meant to depoliticize conflicts between the three governments by having their differences resolved by neutral arbitrators applying common rules. In this spirit, NAFTA's Chapter 20 provides for binational panels to be struck when the member states have been unable to resolve disputes related to issues generated by the agreement. Although "Chapter 20" dispute settlement was considered expeditious at first (Davey 1996, 65), later decisions have proven unable to settle conflicts without resort to power politics (Loungnarath and Stehly 2000, 43). For example, when it lost a panel decision to Canada in a wheat case, Washington responded by

threatening to launch an investigation into Canadian wheat exports.[48] Closure was achieved only when US pressure caused the Canadian government
to give way by agreeing to limit its 1994-95 wheat exports to 1.5 million tons
(Davey 1996, 56). If Chapter 20 rulings are unable to constrain US power,
submitting general issues to NAFTA arbitration becomes futile. Continental
governance then loses legitimacy, being unable to deliver for its weaker members the rights for which they "paid" when negotiating the original compact.
In this respect, the general judicial function of NAFTA is faulty as an aspect
of North American governance because it fails to have supraconstitutional
effect in the US legal order.

NAFTA Chapter 19 Trade Disputes

Had NAFTA created a true free trade area, its members would have abandoned
their right to impose anti-dumping (AD) or countervailing duties (CVD) on
imports coming from their partners' economies. Instead, it would have dealt
with problems of predatory corporate behaviour by establishing continent-
wide anti-trust and competition policies. The United States refused such a
real levelling of national trade barriers, which would have created a single
continental market. It simply agreed to cede appeals of its protectionist rulings to binational panels, which were restricted to investigating whether the
administration's AD or CVD determinations properly applied *domestic* trade
law (Trakman 1997, 277).

Written into CUFTA's Chapter 19, this putatively binding judicial expedi-
ent turned out to be almost as disappointing as its critics had predicted. When
the US CVD action against Canadian softwood lumber exports was remanded
for incorrectly applying the notion of subsidy as defined in American law,
Congress simply changed its definition of subsidy to apply to the Canadian
situation. Excepting softwood lumber's long-lasting fiasco (Howse 1998, 15),
Canada has not had a satisfactory experience in using Chapter 19 to appeal
American trade determinations. In 1993, for instance, there were multiple
remands in five cases, which led the panels to surpass their deadlines significantly. Furthermore, problems have arisen regarding the lack of consistency
in Chapter 19 panel decisions, which have shown differing degrees of deference to agency decisions (Trebilcock and Howse 1999, 83).

Although AD and CVD jurisprudence may have been ineffective in helping the peripheral North American states constrain the United States, the
opposite is not necessarily true. Canadian trade agencies have had to become
more attentive to American interpretations of the standards they apply in AD

or CVD determinations out of a concern for what the binational panels, which necessarily include American jurists, may later decide on appeal.

Thus, Chapter 19 confirms the experience of Chapter 20, that NAFTA's judicial function has asymmetrical impacts. On the one hand, it does not have supraconstitutional clout over the hegemon's behaviour. On the other, it is used to enforce NAFTA rules in the periphery where it has some limiting effect on Canadian administrative justice. When these processes do not satisfy Washington, it can still exercise coercive power to achieve its objectives.

NAFTA Chapter 11 Investor-State Disputes

In relation to host states, Chapter 11 of NAFTA and similar provisions in many bilateral free trade and investment treaties confer expansive rights on foreign investors. Through NAFTA and dozens of BITs to which Canada is party, Canada constricted its own legislative, executive, and judicial autonomy by accepting the jurisdiction of private international arbitration when investors from other party states claim that action (or inaction) by a federal, provincial, or municipal government violates these rights. It did so, presumably, in the hope of gaining greater capacity for itself and Canadian business in the economic affairs of other countries. Although barely noticed when NAFTA was debated before its ratification, this dispute settlement mechanism has established a powerful new zone of adjudication to enforce corporate rights. Under NAFTA Chapter 11, American or Mexican investors have the right to challenge such regulations as those designed to secure public health and safety or to protect the environment, by taking member governments to compulsory international adjudication (Levin and Marin 1996, 90). These investor-state disputes are taken for arbitration before an international panel operating by rules established under the aegis of the World Bank's *International Convention on the Settlement of Investment Disputes between States and Nationals of Other States* (ICSID) or the United Nations Commission on International Trade Law (UNCITRAL) for settling transnational commercial disputes (Horlick and DeBusk 1993).

There are three reasons to be concerned about the system of private adjudication established to interpret, apply, and enforce these rights:

* The meaning of these rights and the validity of government actions that allegedly restrict them are determined by private commercial arbitrators outside the constraints of national democratic institutions such as legislatures and courts.

- The resulting determinations are effective and enforceable in the domestic legal system without the need for – indeed, despite – government legislative action.
- These rights are intended to limit governments in the exercise of their public regulatory authority and may have a chilling effect on government action to protect and promote public welfare.

Privatization of Public Disputes

Chapter 11's investor-state dispute system represents an almost unprecedented privatization of public law adjudication (Dunberry 2001). Rather than challenging government action in domestic courts or before administrative tribunals, disgruntled investors may take the offending government to private international commercial arbitration where trade law experts will determine the validity of the government's exercise of public power. This is a most unusual way to challenge states' exercise of their public authority to regulate business. For example, in the Chapter 11 case of *Metalclad*, the tribunal held that, as a matter of Mexican law, a municipal government had no constitutional authority to authorize or prohibit construction of a hazardous waste dump that had been authorized by the federal government – a judgment that hitherto only the Mexican courts had the power to make *(ibid.)*.

Historically, international commercial arbitration developed as a means to resolve transnational business disputes between commercial parties. Its norms of confidentiality (according to which, the existence, nature, and outcome of disputes remain secret unless the parties agree otherwise) and party autonomy (according to which, parties have complete freedom to choose the laws by which their disputes will be governed, the forum in which they will be decided, and the judges who will adjudicate them) may facilitate transnational commerce, but they are deeply at odds with contemporary norms for challenging government exercises of public authority in democratic societies.

Public transparency and participation were the first casualties of Chapter 11. One of the most significant and hard-won developments in public administration in the past generation has been the establishment of the public's right to transparency of and participation in government decision making. Previously, closed-door negotiations between government authorities and regulated industries were the norm for the development, implementation, and enforcement of regulatory standards. Legislative hearings were unintelligible or inaccessible to many citizens and civil society organizations. The development of rules and regulations was secretive and mysterious except to governments and the affected industries. Only directly affected parties were entitled to receive notice of proposed administrative decisions or to challenge government actions in court. Members of the public were mere supplicants before unanswerable bureaucracies (Sax 1971).

Now, in Canada, the United States, and many other countries, the public has enforceable legal rights to receive notice of, and comment on, a wide variety of proposed administrative rules and decisions, obtain information held by governments, and challenge government action and inaction in courts and administrative tribunals (see Richardson and Razzaque 2006). Not just industry but concerned citizens and public-interest groups have standing to challenge government decision making. Courts and tribunals are more liberal in allowing public-interest groups to intervene as *amici curiae* (friends of the court) to make submissions on the validity of public law and policy. Increasingly, citizens themselves may go to court to enforce laws when governments fail to do so. And the proceedings before and decisions of these official courts and tribunals are almost always public. Although behind-closed-doors bargaining between government and industry still characterizes public policy making on some issues in some places (including environmental regulation in Canada; Boyd 2003), the clear trend has been toward increasing public transparency, accountability, and participation.

Chapter 11 reversed this trend, going against twenty years of enlarged public participation, access to information, and access to justice in American public law, just at a time when Canadian governments and courts were finally taking similar steps themselves. As originally adopted, NAFTA envisaged that investor-state arbitrations would be conducted entirely in private. Arbitral decisions, and even the existence of suits, would be made public only at the discretion of the disputing parties. Tribunals could appoint experts to report on relevant matters only with the consent of the contending parties. The proceedings themselves would be held in secret. No one but the disputing parties and other NAFTA parties had a right to be present. In theory, tribunals could accept written (but not oral) *amicus curiae* submissions, but this was completely alien to commercial arbitration practice and unheard of in the early years of Chapter 11 disputes. Chapter 11 thus allowed disgruntled foreign investors to circumvent the transparency and accountability guarantees that trammelled their Canadian counterparts and to return to the good old days of one-on-one closed-door bargaining with government over matters of public policy, with one crucial difference: even the adjudication of their disputes would take place in secret instead of in open court.

The NAFTA governments finally bowed to public pressure and modified this secretive process in 2001 so that the existence of suits is now published, most documents are made public except for confidential business information, and decisions are published.[49] Observers have been permitted to attend some hearings. In 2003, the NAFTA governments adopted procedures for the submission of amicus curiae briefs.[50] But still, there is no central repository of information and documents, the official websites maintained by the three governments can be inconsistent, and each tribunal may decide whether to allow amicus briefs.[51] Despite these lingering problems, Chapter 11 arbitrations are more open now than NAFTA originally contemplated. As one Canadian environmental campaigner put it, "the three NAFTA governments have accepted the public interest arguments that lawsuits against our governments involving large sums of public money, which also concern public regulations and government decisions, may not be treated the same, procedurally, as truly private merely commercial disputes between corporate actors" (Swenarchuk 2003, 5).

The second casualty of NAFTA Chapter 11 was national democratic sovereignty. The meaning of the quasi-constitutional rights granted to foreign investors and the validity of local, provincial, and federal governments' exercises of their public authority to regulate business are determined entirely outside national democratic institutions, with very limited oversight by domestic courts. Removing disputes from allegedly biased domestic courts and majoritarian politics was one of the central goals of international commercial arbitration from the start and a long-standing objective of transnational capital.

In most international law disputes, investors are required to exhaust local remedies before bringing an international claim. This is not the case for NAFTA investors. Their claims about the effects and validity of exercises of public legislative and regulatory authority need not be tested in the legislative, executive, or judicial institutions of the host country before being brought to a private arbitral panel for decision. When they consider themselves to have been subject to abuse in a NAFTA country, they can avoid having to make their case in domestic tribunals where the pleadings would be more transparent and the rulings subject to appeal before superior courts. Furthermore, unlike others who claim mistreatment at the hands of a foreign government, NAFTA investors are not required to convince their home government to espouse their case. They themselves have standing to bring international claims against the offending state. Since they need not wait for their government to initiate proceedings on their behalf, they gain the ability to short-circuit what may be lengthy diplomatic negotiations.

When the arbitral panel has made its decision, the award is insulated from review by domestic courts. In Canada, the US, and many other countries, courts have abandoned their traditional hostility to arbitration and embraced the enforcement of foreign arbitral awards with alacrity. The reason is straight-forward. As the Ontario Court of Appeal put it, "predictability in the enforce-ment of dispute resolution provisions is an indispensable precondition to any international business transaction and facilitates and encourages the pursuit of freer trade on an international scale."[52] Courts will review awards only on very narrow grounds, such as where the tribunal decided matters beyond the scope of the dispute, violated due process, or issued a decision that conflicts with the public policy of the reviewing jurisdiction. All these grounds are narrowly construed, with a strong presumption in favour of enforcing the award.

An award will be set aside on public policy grounds only if its enforce-ment would violate the most basic norms of morality and justice in the legal system of the country where it is invoked, such as where it is tainted by fraud, bribery, corruption, perjury, breach of rules of natural justice, or failure of due process.[53] An award will not be considered contrary to public policy merely because it got the facts or the law wrong, or is inconsistent with the political positions manifested in legislation, regulations, or judicial decisions – which is how the term "public policy" is ordinarily understood.[54] As the Federal Court of Canada said when asked to review the *S.D. Myers* Chapter 11 award, "public policy does not refer to a political position, it refers to 'fundamental notions and principles of justice.'"[55] Given this narrow interpretation, public policy rarely succeeds as a ground to invalidate international arbitral awards.

This narrow approach to public policy may be appropriate for purely commercial disputes between private parties, but it is hard to see how it could be appropriate for arbitral awards deciding the legality of sovereign governments' exercises of public authority to regulate business. Yet investor-state arbitral awards are handled in exactly the same manner as is the arbi-tration of commercial disputes between private parties. This extraordinary deference to private transnational adjudication is not mandated by NAFTA itself. The rules constraining judicial review of international arbitral awards in domestic courts are found in domestic commercial arbitration statutes, most of which are based on the 1958 *New York Convention on the Recognition and Enforcement of Foreign Arbitral Awards* or the UNCITRAL *Model Law on*

International Commercial Arbitration.[56] These instruments and their implementing legislation were designed for arbitration of commercial disputes, not disagreements concerning the validity of sovereign exercises of public authority. This argument has not been accepted by the courts, however. Mexico sought judicial review of the *Metalclad* award in a British Columbia court because Vancouver had been designated the place of arbitration. Mexico argued that the courts should be less deferential toward Chapter 11 decisions than to other foreign arbitral awards because the relationship between the investor and host state was regulatory, not commercial. The judge disagreed, holding that the relationship was one of "investing" and that the applicable legislation defined this as a commercial association. The court therefore applied the usual highly deferential approach to arbitral awards.[57]

The third casualty of NAFTA Chapter 11 was the rule of law. Most legal systems are governed by the principle that courts are bound by their prior decisions. This norm guarantees a minimum level of consistency and predictability for disputing parties. There is no such rule in international commercial arbitration, including NAFTA Chapter 11 disputes.

Furthermore, NAFTA Chapter 11 disputes are not decided by impartial judges. Each party chooses one arbitrator, and these select a third arbitrator to preside over the panel. If, as is often the case, the party-appointed arbitrators are unable to agree on a president, most arbitral rules provide for the president to be appointed by the International Chamber of Commerce or another business group. The system is thus structured to favour business interests. Although the arbitrators are formally independent of the parties, the parties have an obvious incentive to pick an arbitrator they expect to be sympathetic to their position, based on nationality, past decisions, published writings, or other information. They pay the arbitrators for their services. Unlike a tenured independent judiciary, the arbitrators lack security of tenure, have a commercial interest in repeat business, and are not precluded from engaging in activities incompatible with impartiality. Van Harten and Loughlin (2006, 147-48) summarize this disturbing situation as follows:

> Although able to determine the legality and cost of the exercise of
> public authority with limited supervision by domestic courts, arbitrators are not themselves members of a tenured judiciary. In most
> cases, arbitrators are practising lawyers or academics who compete
> for appointments in a market for adjudicative services. Unlike

judges, arbitrators have a commercial interest to provide "an efficacious and economically valuable service for clients," and are not barred from political or professional activities incompatible with their independence and impartiality. It is not uncommon for a prominent figure in investment arbitration simultaneously to be sitting as an arbitrator in one case, representing an investor or state in another, and generally advising other clients on investment law. Arbitrators are therefore more susceptible than judges to influence by concerns about their reputation and by the need to secure future business. Simply put, the business opportunities of arbitrators are tied to the popularity of investment arbitration: the greater the utility of investment arbitration to investors, the greater the number of claims will be filed, the greater the demand for arbitrators. Privately-appointed arbitrators are therefore more likely to favour the expansion of the scope and remedial power of investment arbitration, and will have commercial incentives to interpret the jurisdiction of investment tribunals expansively. No matter how well arbitrators do their job, an award will always be open to an apprehension of an institutional bias against the respondent state, given that expansive treaty interpretations and the heightened prospect of state liability promote investment arbitration as a commercial venture.

Furthermore, party-selected arbitrators may come under direct pressure from appointing governments or investors to rule in their favour. One American appellate court judge who was appointed to a Chapter 11 tribunal reports being instructed by a US political official on the outcome the United States preferred in the case to protect NAFTA against political attack (Echeverria 2006, 984-85). As Echeverria (*ibid.*, 985) concludes, "for those of us who value the tradition of judicial independence, with NAFTA in place we're certainly not in Kansas any more, as Dorothy would say." In short, conflicts between investor interests and public regulation are judged by private arbitrators who are dependent on the parties for repeat business, who face structural incentives to interpret their jurisdiction broadly, whose professional expertise is focused on facilitating trade and investment rather than protecting public welfare, and whose decisions about the legality of the exercise of public authority are insulated from supervision by domestic courts.

Domestic Effect without or despite Legislative Action

The second reason for concern regarding investment arbitration awards is that their interpretations of investor rights and their rulings on the legality of government exercises of public authority take effect directly in the domestic legal order, without the need for domestic legislative action. By virtue of the ubiquitous international commercial arbitration statutes mentioned above, investor-state arbitration awards are enforceable in the domestic legal system as if they were awards of a domestic court. As we have seen, they are shielded against challenge in domestic courts. NAFTA investor rights thus take effect in the Canadian legal system without the need for the intervening step of enacting or amending domestic legislation or constitutions. Indeed, since the whole point of many Chapter 11 claims is to invalidate existing legislative measures, they take effect despite conflicting legislative or consti-tutional provisions — one of the hallmarks of supraconstitutional norms.

Constraining Public Welfare Regulation

The final reason for apprehension about the investor rights enshrined in NAFTA and other international investment treaties is that transnational corporations invoke them frequently, aggressively, and with some effect to reverse or chill public welfare regulation. The powerful private enforcement machinery of international investment treaties has been invoked by numer-ous transnational corporations to assail environmental protection laws, water export controls, and decisions to re-establish public-sector water services when privatization deals have gone sour (Shrybman 2002). Even though the respondent governments win most Chapter 11 arbitrations, the panels have taken a broad view of what can count as measures "tantamount to expro-priation," going well beyond what is considered an impermissible taking in Canadian law and effectively restricting governments' ability to regulate TNC activities in what they see as the public interest.

Early Chapter 11 decisions stoked critics' fears. The *Ethyl* case showed that the threat of an adverse Chapter 11 ruling may be enough to prompt Canadian governments to repeal offending laws without waiting for a deci-sion on the merits of the investor's claim. In *Ethyl*, Canada banned importa-tion and interprovincial trade of MMT, a highly toxic gasoline additive and suspected neurotoxin. MMT had been used in Canada since 1976 to increase the octane rating of unleaded gasoline and to reduce engine "knocking" (Michalos 2008, 72). It had been the subject of concern for years because of its suspected tendency to interfere with emission control systems and cause harmful air emissions. The scientific evidence on these points was and remains mixed. Nonetheless, public concern was high, and the Canadian government banned international and interprovincial trade in MMT. The US manufacturer brought a Chapter 11 suit claiming the ban violated the national treatment principle, imposed performance requirements, and constituted a measure tantamount to expropriation. The actions by which it claimed to have been harmed included the introduction of legislation in Parliament, its passage, and public statements about the legislation by parliamentarians and government ministers – in other words, "routine activities of elected members of parliament" (*ibid.*, 225). As Michalos *(ibid.)* remarks,

> The mere introduction and debate about proposed legislation in
> properly constituted legislative bodies ... are challenged as harms
> demanding material compensation. It is difficult to imagine a
> more egregious attack on democracy and democratic process.

After Canada failed, in 1998, to have the case dismissed on jurisdictional grounds, it settled the claim for US$13 million, rescinded the ban, and issued a statement that it had no evidentiary basis.[58] Curiously, in 2004, most major oil companies in Canada voluntarily discontinued the use of MMT, even though a long-awaited independent review of the substance ordered by the Canadian government had not yet started (*ibid.*, 73).

Metalclad concerned a US company that acquired a property near the Mexican city of Guadalcazar, planning to operate it as a hazardous waste dump.[59] The site was owned by a Mexican company called Coterin, which was authorized to operate it as a hazardous waste transfer station only. Instead, in just over a year of operation, Coterin dumped twenty thousand tons of toxic waste on the site without treatment or containment. Reacting to local outrage, the Mexican federal government shut down the facility in 1991. Coterin then applied to the City of Guadalcazar for a permit to construct a hazardous waste landfill on the site. Its application was refused. The federal and state governments were more accommodating, however, and granted the company permits to proceed with the project. Thus began a jurisdictional turf war between the three levels of government over the fate of the site.

In 1993, Metalclad (the US investor) purchased Coterin on condition that it secure the municipal construction permit or a court judgment ruling that the permit was unnecessary. Metalclad dropped these conditions after federal officials, eager to secure the foreign investment, assured it that Coterin had all the authorization it needed to undertake the project. Now owning Coterin and through it the site, Metalclad started building the landfill without a municipal construction permit. It received a further permit from the federal government authorizing the final phase of construction, but the City issued a stop-work order for lack of a permit. The company applied for the municipal permit but continued construction, which was completed before the application was decided. An opening ceremony in March 1995 was disrupted by protesters, and the landfill did not open. The federal government then entered an agreement with Metalclad authorizing it to operate the landfill for five years, requiring it to clean up the existing contamination, and increasing the capacity of the dump tenfold to 360,000 tons per year. Ten days later, the City rejected the application for a municipal construction permit on the basis that it had been denied once before, that the company had commenced construction before applying for a permit and had finished it while the application was still pending, that there were environmental concerns about the facility, and that many local residents opposed the dump. The City went to court to challenge Metalclad's agreement with the federal government, and Metalclad went to court to challenge the City's denial of a permit. After some abortive negotiations, Metalclad initiated a Chapter 11 arbitration. After the arbitration was under way but before the hearing, the state governor issued an ecological decree declaring an area of almost 200,000 hectares within the municipality, including the dump site, an ecological preserve.

The tribunal ruled in favour of Metalclad and awarded it US$16.7 million. It found that the City's refusal of a construction permit, the federal government's failure to ensure a transparent and predictable framework for Metalclad's business planning, and the state government's last-minute about-face amounted to unfair and inequitable treatment in violation of Article 1105. It also found Mexico guilty of indirectly expropriating Metalclad's investment. It held that expropriation under NAFTA "includes not only open, deliberate and acknowledged takings of property, such as outright seizure or formal or obligatory transfer of title in favour of the host state, but also covert or incidental interference with the use of property which has the effect of depriving the owner, in whole or in significant part, of the use or reasonably-to-be-expected benefit of property even if not necessarily to the obvious benefit of the host state."[60] Applying this broad test to the facts, the tribunal held that the City's denial of a construction permit, its efforts to block the dump in the courts, and the federal government's failure to ensure a transparent and predictable framework amounted to indirect expropriation by effectively depriving Metalclad of the right to operate the landfill. It also held that the state's ecological decree was tantamount to expropriation because it had the legal effect of forever barring operation of the landfill. The tribunal rejected the Mexican lawyers' arguments about the City's constitutional powers and the legal effect of the ecological decree, instead issuing its own interpretation of Mexican law.

When Mexico challenged the award, the Canadian court set it aside in part, but not because it applied an extraordinarily broad definition of expropriation, violated public policy, or took upon itself to interpret and apply Mexican constitutional and domestic law. It did so only on the basis that the tribunal had exceeded the scope of the dispute submitted to it. The court ruled that the tribunal had gone beyond the scope of Chapter 11 by importing NAFTA's general transparency obligations into Articles 1105 and 1110. It therefore set aside the findings that Mexico had violated Article 1105 and that the events before the ecological decree amounted to an expropriation. As for the ecological decree itself, the court acknowledged that the tribunal's definition of expropriation was "extremely broad": "This definition is sufficiently broad to include a legitimate rezoning of property by a municipality or other zoning authority. However, the definition of expropriation is a question of law with which this Court is not entitled to interfere."[61] As a result, the court held that there was no ground to set aside the tribunal's finding that the decree was an act tantamount to expropriation. It upheld the award to that extent, although it somewhat reduced the amount of damages.

In the *S.D. Myers* case, an American waste treatment company wished to export polychlorinated biphenyls (PCBs) from Canada to Ohio for treatment and disposal. PCBs are notorious carcinogens, which many countries have tried to phase out and clean up for years. Canada banned exports of PCBs to the US, foiling S.D. Myers' plans. As a party to the Basel Convention on the transboundary movement of hazardous wastes, Canada had an international legal obligation not to export hazardous wastes to non-parties – and the United States was not a party to the convention.[62] In any event, for all but a few months during which Canada's export ban was in effect, Washington had its own ban on imports of PCBs.

Notwithstanding these legal obstacles, S.D. Myers brought a Chapter 11 suit against Canada, and won. The tribunal held that the ban had no legitimate environmental purpose and was intended to protect the Canadian hazardous waste treatment industry. Finding that Canada had violated Articles 1102 (national treatment) and 1105 (fair and equitable treatment in accordance with an international minimum standard), it ordered Ottawa to pay $6 million in compensation.[63] The Federal Court of Canada dismissed Canada's application for judicial review, remarking that the award was not contrary to public policy, because it did not breach fundamental notions and principles of justice. The court also refused to interfere with the tribunal's characterization of the purpose of the ban, because findings of fact or law cannot be judicially reviewed so long as they are within the scope of the submission to arbitration.[64]

The *Methanex* decision of 2005 quelled some of the worst fears about Chapter 11 investor rights running amok but still left room for anxiety.[65] The case concerned California's ban on the sale of gasoline containing the additive methyl tertiary-butyl ether (MTBE). Like MMT, MTBE was originally seen as a solution to an environmental and public health problem MMT had been introduced in the mid 1970s to replace lead as an octane enhancer. MTBE was introduced during the 1990s to reduce toxic automobile exhaust emissions. It is one of several ingredients, known as oxygenates, that can be used to boost the oxygen content of gasoline, promoting more complete combustion and reducing toxic air emissions. Gasoline containing these oxygenates is known as reformulated gasoline. MTBE was by far the most common oxygenate in reformulated gasoline in the United States. Widespread use of reformulated gasoline had the beneficial effect of reducing emissions of various air pollutants including the known carcinogen benzene.

This beneficial effect was short-lived, however, because MTBE and other oxygenates do not significantly reduce exhaust emissions from newer vehicles with advanced emissions control technology. Furthermore, MTBE has a dark side. It is highly water-soluble, leading to a risk of widespread contamination of groundwater from leaking underground storage tanks and pipelines, and contamination of surface waters due to discharges from motorboats. By the late 1990s, MTBE had been detected in several California drinking water systems. Contamination was found in both groundwater wells and surface reservoirs. A major study commissioned by the State of California found that the state's water resources were being placed at risk by the use of MTBE and that the cost of treatment of MTBE-contaminated drinking water supplies could be enormous.

As with MMT, the scientific evidence surrounding MTBE's health and environmental risks was controversial, and the California government chose to take precautionary action to limit the use of a potentially dangerous substance in the absence of full scientific certainty about the nature and degree of those risks. It decided that use of MTBE posed a significant risk to human health or the environment. It based this conclusion upon a statutorily mandated, peer-reviewed, five-volume, sixty-author, six-hundred-page University of California report and widespread public consultations. On the strength of this conclusion, it first required warning labels on gasoline pumps and then, after a phase-out period, banned the sale of gasoline containing MTBE.

The Canadian company Methanex challenged these measures under NAFTA. Methanex was and remains the world's largest producer of methanol, which is a feedstock for MTBE. Methanex argued that the measures were discriminatory, tantamount to expropriation of its US investments, in violation of the minimum standard of fair and equitable treatment, and the product of an illicit conspiracy between California and one of Methanex's American competitors. The panel rejected all of Methanex's claims. It ruled that "a non-discriminatory regulation for a public purpose, which is enacted in accordance with due process and, which affects ... a foreign investor or investment is not deemed expropriatory and compensable unless specific commitments had been given by the regulating government to the then putative foreign investor contemplating investment that the government would refrain from such regulation."[66] No such assurances had been given to Methanex. On the contrary, "Methanex entered a political economy in which it was widely known, if not notorious, that governmental environmental and health protection institutions at the federal and state level, operating under the vigilant eyes of the media, interested corporations, non-governmental organizations and a politically active electorate, continuously monitored the use and impact of chemical compounds and commonly prohibited or restricted the use of some of those compounds for environmental and/or health reasons."[67]

The tribunal found that California had acted carefully and reasonably with a view to protecting the environmental interests of Californians, not with the intent of harming foreign methanol producers: "Faced with widespread and potentially serious MTBE contamination of its water resources, California ordered a careful assessment of the problem and thereafter responded reasonably to independent findings that large volumes of the state's ground and surface water had become polluted by MTBE and that preventative measures were called for. The evidential record establishes no ill will towards Methanex or methanol."[68]

The tribunal did not stop there. It held that the ban on MTBE was not even covered by Chapter 11 in the first place. Chapter 11 applies only to government measures "relating to" an investor or investment.[69] The tribunal concluded that the MTBE ban was not a measure "relating to" Methanex or its US investments: "Having concluded ... that no illicit pretext underlay California's conduct and that Methanex has failed to establish that the US measures were intended to harm foreign methanol producers (including Methanex) or benefit domestic ethanol producers ..., it follows ... that ... the US measures do not 'relate to' Methanex or its investments as required by Article 1101(1)."[70] The tribunal dismissed the case and ordered Methanex to pay the US government US$4 million in attorneys' fees and other costs.

There is still room for concern in the wake of *Methanex*. First, the *Methanex* decision is not binding on subsequent tribunals. Although *Methanex* ruled that non-discriminatory regulation of general application does not amount to expropriation unless the regulating government gave the investor a commitment not to regulate, other Chapter 11 tribunals have held that Article 1110 "does cover nondiscriminatory regulation that might be said to fall within an exercise of a state's so-called police powers."[71] It is still up to each tribunal to characterize the intent and effect of regulatory measures, and several tribunals have held environmental and public health measures to be arbitrary, unfair, discriminatory, or protectionist. These findings are immune from judicial review.

Second, TNCs continue to use Chapter 11 as a weapon against public welfare regulation. They commonly employ the threat of NAFTA litigation to "chill" proposed regulation, from the Canadian government's "plain packaging" proposal for cigarettes in the early days of NAFTA to its planned ban on advertising "light" or "mild" cigarettes a few years ago. After introducing the latter measure to much public fanfare, Ottawa quietly abandoned it shortly after the Philip Morris Company threatened a Chapter 11 claim for regulatory expropriation of its trademarks. TNCs also continue to make frequent use of Chapter 11 to challenge existing public health and environmental regulations. For example,

- In 2008, Dow Agroscience launched a Chapter 11 claim challenging Quebec's ban on lawn care products containing the pesticide 2,4-D, one of the main ingredients in the notorious Agent Orange used by the American Air Force to defoliate Vietcong strongholds during the Vietnam war.
- In the same year, the American company Bilcon, a major supplier of aggregates and cement to the massive eastern seaboard construction business, launched a Chapter 11 claim challenging Nova Scotia's refusal to approve a Cape Breton basalt quarry after an extensive environmental

impact assessment concluded the quarry would have significant adverse environmental effects.

* In 2001, Crompton Corporation (now Chemtura Corporation), the US manufacturer of the pesticide lindane, launched a Chapter 11 claim challenging Canada's decision to phase out the use of lindane as an agricultural pesticide by 2004 due to its adverse effects on the health of ecosystems, wildlife, and people. In 2008, lindane was proposed for addition to the list of outlawed chemicals under the *Stockholm Convention on Persistent Organic Pollutants.*[72]

Environmental regulation has borne the brunt of Chapter 11 litigation. Half of all Chapter 11 claims instigated to date – twenty-five of the forty-eight claims for which we could discern the subject matter – have involved attacks on environmental or natural resource regulations. A further five targeted measures related to health, including pharmaceutical products.[73] Even if the success rate of Chapter 11 claims and the ratio of damages awarded to damages claimed remain low, the respondent governments must nonetheless defend the claims, at a high cost to taxpayers.

Some positive modifications at the margins of the investment arbitration regime have occurred thanks to concerns in the US Congress that NAFTA's Chapter 11 compromised American sovereignty by giving Mexican and Canadian TNCs greater rights than US corporations in challenging US government measures. While not proposing to renegotiate NAFTA, the US *Bipartisan Trade Promotion Authority Act of 2002* required that new trade agreements not give foreign investors more substantive rights in the United States than American investors enjoyed – a home-grown version of the Calvo Clause that American multinationals had fought for decades to remove in Latin America.[74] This resulted in an alteration to the wording of some new American investment treaties. Following suit, Canada made a similar adjustment in its own bilateral investment treaty negotiations so that the 2006 Canada-Peru BIT provides,

> except in rare circumstances, such as when a measure or series of measures is so severe in the light of its purpose that it cannot be reasonably viewed as having been adopted and applied in good faith, non-discriminatory measures of a Party that are designed and applied to protect legitimate public welfare objectives, such as health, safety and the environment, do not constitute indirect expropriation.[75]

Some commentators have called for a similar amendment to NAFTA Chapter 11 (Canadian Environmental Law Association 2008), but the prospects for such a reform remain dim.

In short, there is a substantial basis for critics' concerns that Chapter 11 can undermine efforts to enact new laws and regulations in the public interest, in particular to protect the environment and human health, and that it can require governments to pay compensation to polluters for ceasing to pollute, even if their activities have an adverse impact on public health and welfare (Mann and Von Moltke 2001, 13). With its intrusive judicial institutions, NAFTA's continental economic regime creates new levels of uncertainty for governments, whose elected officials cannot be sure how measures they propose to implement might be judged by some future arbitral tribunal. As Been and Beauvais (2003, 134) conclude, "the uncertainty over how far NAFTA can be pushed to provide protection for property owners, coupled with federal, state, and local regulators' unfamiliarity with NAFTA ... and regulators' concerns about both the expense of defending against NAFTA claims and about their potential liability for compensation awards, at the very least make NAFTA a useful threat for those who oppose environmental and land use regulation."

The World Trade Organization

In contrast with NAFTA's judicial processes, which are weak at the governmental level and strong at the corporate level, the WTO dispute settlement body excludes corporations from using its services directly but gives governments a powerful tool with which to enforce the global regime's economic rules even against the most powerful non-compliant state. Indeed, the key to the WTO's unprecedented importance lies in the power and neutrality of its dispute settlement mechanisms. Unlike members of NAFTA Chapter 19 and Chapter 20 panels, WTO panellists are chosen from countries other than those involved in a particular dispute. Their rulings are not based on the contenders' own laws, as they are in NAFTA anti-dumping and countervailing duties cases, but on the WTO's own international rules, interpreted in the light of the international public law developed by prior GATT jurisprudence.

The composition of dispute panels promotes a tendency toward legalistic rigidity (Weiler 2001, 194). Panellists adjudicating WTO disputes are either trade lawyers and professors of international law, who tend to stick very close to the black letter of the legal texts they are interpreting, or middle-level diplomats, who take their cues from the secretariat's legal staff. In either case, they know that their judgment will probably be appealed by the losing side and that the judges on the WTO Appellate Body will be responding to highly refined legal reasoning (Bhala 1999, 847; Palmeter and Mavroidis 1998, 405).

Although WTO Appellate Body rulings are not, formally speaking, precedent setting, it is generally recognized that the logic of one panel's decision can be carried over from case to case as the situation dictates. Palmeter and Mavroidis *(ibid.)* also note that the appellate body "operates on a 'collegial' basis." Although only three of the seven members sit on any one "division" to hear a particular appeal, and the division retains full authority to decide the case, views on the issues are shared with the other Appellate Body members before a decision is reached. Consequently, members of the Appellate Body, in confronting prior decisions, are far more likely to be encountering their own decisions, or those of their close colleagues, than are WTO panellists. Under these conditions, "soft" arguments defending cultural autonomy or environmental sustainability hold little weight against the "hard" logic of the WTO's own rules.

Although the WTO rules create new supraconstitutional norms for member states to accept, their meaning cannot be anticipated with any certainty. In referring to one contentious concept in trade law, the WTO Appellate Body in the *Japan–Alcoholic Beverages* case memorably compared the notion of "likeness" to an accordion, which may be stretched wide or squeezed tight as the case requires (Howse 2007, 99).[76] This indeterminacy did not guarantee cultural sensitivity, as Canadians discovered when the WTO ruled that the US-written *Time* magazine was "like" Canadian-written *Maclean's* magazine.[77] This ruling invalidated several key policy instruments that had successfully promoted a Canadian magazine industry for many decades (Schwanen 1998). Because national policy makers live with the permanent threat that their policies can be challenged at the WTO, they can be sure of one thing only – until a trade dispute concerning those policies is heard, they will never know what this supreme court of commercial law will decide (Howse and Regan 2000, 268).

As any student of federalism knows, a system containing more than one order of government creates the potential for conflict between the different orders. Whether the supraconstitutional superiority of WTO rulings over domestic constitutional norms will be accepted by Canadian courts remains to be seen. No case has yet been brought to Canada's Supreme Court to test whether a ruling by a global or continental dispute panel takes precedence over a Canadian norm.[78] The introduction of a supraconstitution with judicial muscle suggests that continuing clashes between the external and internal constitutional orders must be expected.

Conflict can also be anticipated between the global and continental orders. A case in point is the WTO agreement on agriculture, whereby member states committed themselves to transform such quantitative restrictions as import quotas on foodstuffs into tariffs, which were then to be reduced. Canada duly proceeded to "tariffy" its protective regulations for farmers in central Canada. The United States then challenged Canada's tariffication of its agricultural quotas as a violation of its NAFTA obligations not to raise tariffs (Trebilcock and Howse 1999, 267). The NAFTA panel ruled that the WTO tariffication imperative prevailed.[79] Other conflicts between the two regimes' norms are bound to occur, complicating their constitutionalizing impact on their members.

The WTO dispute settlement system may be superior to that of NAFTA in many respects, but multilateralism does not necessarily present Canada with a real escape from US pressure. Indeed, much of the constraint that the WTO imposed on the Canadian state in the first few years of its existence was an application of US-driven demands that Canada comply with US-inspired WTO rules on behalf of US-based pharmaceutical and entertainment oligopolies.

The judicialization of trade rules has affected international cooperation on regulation in other areas, such as the environment. Before 1990, many governments, including Canada's, considered trade sanctions a legitimate tool for the enforcement of multilateral environmental agreements and pushed for their inclusion in such agreements. These governments, supported by many NGOs and business groups, wished to apply the teeth of the trade regime to the enforcement of environmental treaties. They achieved a break-through in 1987 with the Montreal Protocol on ozone-depleting substances, which allows member states to impose general trade sanctions against other member states that violate their obligations under the protocol.[80] Ten years later, when states were negotiating the Kyoto Protocol on climate change, Ottawa and many other governments had reversed their position and actively opposed the inclusion of trade sanctions in the agreement as an enforcement tool. Few governments will now openly support the use of trade sanctions in multilateral environmental agreements. The conclusion of the WTO agreements in 1994 led many governments, unwilling to take the risk of adverse trade rulings, to fear that the use of trade sanctions to enforce multilateral environmental agreements may violate their trade-law commitments. In this way, international trade rules have taken primacy over, and inhibit more robust action to enforce, international rules in other areas such as environmental protection. These other areas are thus denied the legal and political teeth reserved for the rules of economic globalization.

ENFORCEMENT

With the exception of Chapter 11 tribunal decisions, which piggyback on the enforcement machinery of the domestic court system, NAFTA has no enforcement capacity other than the parties' sense of their long-term self-interest. Like other international trade agreements, it relies on reciprocity: if one member state does not comply with the judgments of disputes that it loses, it cannot realistically expect other states to comply when it wins disputes against them. Given the extreme asymmetry prevailing between the centre and the periphery in North America, the United States is largely unhindered by such prudential considerations. Although its compliance record in less important cases is good, it is able to flout NAFTA's rules as interpreted by binational judicial processes, as Washington has defiantly done with both Canada (in the long-drawn-out softwood lumber quarrel) and Mexico (in relation to its NAFTA obligation to permit Mexican truckers to drive their loads to US destinations).

Like NAFTA, the WTO has no police service capable of implementing its judicial decisions. But the enforcement provisions supporting its dispute settlement rulings are significantly stronger than those of NAFTA. Indeed, Ostry (2001, 6) has called the WTO's dispute settlement mechanism the strongest in the history of international law. Once the final decision on a trade dispute has been handed down in which a signatory state's disputed law or regulation has been judged in violation of a WTO norm, the offending provisions are supposed to be changed or compensation paid. A noncompliant state is much more likely to be brought to "justice" by a litigant state, because failure to abide by a WTO dispute ruling gives the winning plaintiff the right to impose retaliatory trade sanctions against the disobedient defendant. This retaliation can block any exports of the guilty state. The amount of the damage inflicted by the retaliation can equal the harm caused to the complainant by the violation. This self-enforcement system works relatively well in the WTO where there is greater symmetry among the major powers (Howse 2000).

Canada Has an Economic Supraconstitution: So What?

We have argued that certain principles, rules, rights, and institutional practices of international trade and investment to which Canada has submitted have achieved a supraconstitutional status in the Canadian legal order. Before asking, in the next chapter, whether the same is true of the international social and environmental regimes to which Canada is a party, we reflect briefly on what makes this a noteworthy development.

SUPRACONSTITUTIONAL VALUES

The principles, rules, rights, and institutions that make up Canada's supraconstitution are rooted in a resilient and adaptive neo-conservative system of core values that remains ascendant despite the recent excesses and embarrassments of the George W. Bush era and appears likely to survive the current global economic crisis. These values include the liberation of transnational capital from the checks of majoritarian politics, freedom of key aspects of the economy from government interference, equality of transnational corporations with sovereign states, powerful remedies for aggrieved transnational investors, and "smart" government that does not unduly restrict profit in the name of public welfare. These values purport to spring from, but are in fact at odds with, liberal-democratic commitments to freedom, equality, and justice for all; respect for fundamental human rights and freedoms; and the vigorous pursuit of the public's welfare by governments while preserving a substantial domain of private autonomy. The way in which the supraconstitution accords expression to these values – by giving powerful rights against host states to foreign companies – is at odds with the domestic constitutional and legal norms most valued by citizens in Canada and other liberal democracies.

This supraconstitutional project is the instrument with which transnational corporations and powerful states seek to limit democratic majorities from exercising their political sovereignty. To paraphrase Koskenniemi (2004, 213), the supraconstitution is an important part of what can only be seen as a deeply unjust system of distributing material and spiritual values.

THE SUPRACONSTITUTION'S UNEVENNESS

Unevenness is a defining characteristic of the supraconstitution: it varies substantially among and within nation-states, between nationals and aliens, and over time and space. Because it acts upon and is partially embedded in domestic constitutional orders, the economic supraconstitution is experienced differently in differing nation-states. Its muscularity varies with the state's relative position in the global political economy and the strength of its domestic governance institutions. For countries in the global periphery, particularly those with a tradition of state capitalism, the economic supra-constitution represents a fundamental transformation. Mexico's supra-constitution is not the same as those of Canada or the United States. NAFTA has had a more transformative impact on Mexico than on Canada, and on Canada than on the United States. NAFTA Chapter 11 is in tension with some Canadian constitutional and legal norms, but it fundamentally re-wrote Mexico's. As we saw, domestic constitutions in Mexico, Colombia, and other formerly developmentalist states have been made to bend, for-mally or informally, to the exigencies of their new neo-conservative supra-constitutions. Their norms of internal sovereignty, state intervention in the economy, and legal equality of aliens and nationals were sacrificed on the altar of globalization.

Having well-governed financial institutions and long experience in float-ing its currency, Canada has not been subjected to the humiliation of these disciplines. It has, however, been subject to a process of external oversight that keeps its behaviour under constant international scrutiny. The United States Trade Representative's Office keeps federal and provincial policies under regular review, reporting annually to Congress about Canadian compliance with NAFTA and the WTO. The WTO's Trade Policy Review Mechanism as-sesses Canada's policies every two years. Moreover, Canada is subject to the subtler disciplines of American bond-rating agencies, which have been de-scribed as the new global "masters of capital" (T. Sinclair 2005). These sur-veillance mechanisms press governments toward ever greater transparency before the epistemic community of trade liberalizers and toward further conformity with their neo-conservative nostrums.

Canada inhabits an ambivalent middle position in the economic supraconstitution. As a high-income advanced industrialized economy, a member of the G8, and the United States' largest trading partner, it appears to occupy a position near the core of the global political economy. Yet, in relation to the United States and the economic powerhouses of Europe and Asia, it is some way down the power hierarchy in a semi-peripheral position, both an agent and an object of neo-conservatism's reconstitutionalizing project. As an object, it has been forced by WTO judicial rulings to terminate decades of successful public policy designed to bolster its magazine and aircraft industries. In terms of Canada's internal constitution, push has not yet come to shove. Colombia's experience indicates that, when the domestic constitutional provisions of subordinate partners come into conflict with the rights and rules of the international trade and investment rules regime, the latter usually prevail.

Canada is also an active agent of this supraconstitutional project. It has been one of the most aggressive promoters of trade and investment agreements incorporating NAFTA-style rights (Schneiderman 2000a). The tension between NAFTA investor rights and Canada's domestic legal norms shows the disconnection between Canada's trade-policy bureaucracy and the rest of the country's political system. It is even more remarkable, given the mounting evidence that the constitutional arrangements and policy instruments associated with state capitalism (such as performance requirements, import substitution, state monopoly of critical sectors) are, in fact, coupled with developmental success (United Nations Development Program 2002) and unlikely to have a substantial negative impact on foreign direct investment (Schneiderman 2000a).

Global and continental supraconstitutional rules also have differential impacts in various parts of Canadian society. Take the country's two geographically determined types of agriculture. Because the prairie provinces are exporters of grains and livestock, their farmers can expect to benefit from the WTO *Agreement on the Application of Sanitary and Phytosanitary Measures* (SPS Agreement), whose supraconstitutional norms limit the capacity of *other* member states to use health regulations to impede imports of Canadian produce incorporating genetically modified organisms. As illustrated by the North American dispute with the European Union over its refusal to allow imports of beef raised with a growth hormone, the SPS norms, if successfully applied, should make it easier for Canadian cattle ranchers to find export markets.[81] In contrast, farmers in central Canada, who supply a protected market of national consumers thanks to the quotas established by government-enforced marketing boards for eggs, milk, and poultry, can be expected to suffer under the WTO rules, as their quantitative barriers are turned into tariffs, which are subsequently cut to allow more competition from abroad in the once-closed Canadian market.

Another manifestation of the economic supraconstitution's uneven application to diverse segments of society is its differentiation between aliens and nationals. Despite the foundational norm of non-discrimination, some supraconstitutional rules – in particular, investor protection norms – require Canadian governments to discriminate in favour of foreign capital, guaranteeing foreign investors more favourable treatment than that afforded to nationals.

Finally, the supraconstitution is uneven over time, growing rapidly in scale and impact over the past two decades as international trade and investment regimes have proliferated and strengthened. Although we have tried to portray its dynamic character, we have merely presented a snapshot of it at a particular historical moment. It is likely to continue to change at a rapid pace.

The Supraconstitution's Legitimation Deficit

The insertion of authoritative new norms into the Canadian political order raises issues of both process and outcome legitimacy. The imposition of limitations on the governing capacity not just of the federal but also of provincial and municipal governments was the result of a process characterized by the secrecy and opacity typical of international negotiations. It was achieved with a minimum of informed public debate. Moreover, from NAFTA Chapter 11 investor-state arbitrations to WTO Appellate Body rulings, these supraconstitutional norms and institutions operate largely insulated from domestic deliberation. This absence of a democratic context for a major shift in the parameters of the political order contrasts with the extensive engagement not just by the political parties, the media, and interest groups – the normal actors in a political process – but also by the highest court of the land from 1980 to 1982 during the campaign to repatriate the domestic Canadian constitution.

If the supraconstitution has been put in place and maintained without robust democratic legitimation within Canada, neither has it enjoyed supranational democratic legitimation. At this point in history, no supranational *demos*, or *pouvoir constituant*, has emerged that is capable of generating and validating Canada's supraconstitution. If, as many scholars have observed, there is no such thing as a European demos that can act as the source of democratic legitimacy at the European level (Weiler 1999, 2003; de Wet 2006; Kumm 2004, 2006), even less can such a "We the People" be found in North America or at the global level. The only persons who can be seen as enjoying rights of citizenship at the North American level are investors of NAFTA member states. Even if NAFTA heralded the emergence of a continental capitalist class, or the WTO a global one, this would hardly amount to a demos capable of legitimizing an international constitution. Not only does the international realm lack a *pouvoir constituant* but "if such presented itself," as Koskenniemi (2005, 12) observes, "it would be empire, and the constitution it would enact would not be one of an international but an imperial realm." The economic supraconstitution in which Canada and many other nations are increasingly entrenched is the constitution of an empire that, though predominantly American in inspiration and location, is deterritorialized, with TNC head offices located in all capitalist countries including middle powers such as Canada and developing economies such as India, South Korea, Taiwan, and even Mexico.

Not only does Canada's supraconstitution lack a supraconstitutional demos, it lacks supranational institutions for democratic transparency and accountability that might make up for the lack of democratic supervision at the domestic level. There is no North American or global parliament. Some moves have been made toward transparency and participation in WTO dispute settlement processes, but they remain more inaccessible and secretive than domestic judicial proceedings. International investment arbitration under NAFTA and BITs remains even more so. The absence of a supranational demos and of supranational institutions for democratic deliberation and oversight does not mean that a supraconstitution cannot exist. On the contrary, a supraconstitution can be created and can effectively bind national constitutions and constrain domestic governments without a constitutive supranational demos and without supranational mechanisms for democratic accountability. The absence of these characteristics simply accentuates the democratic deficit at the heart of the supraconstitution.

In terms of outcome legitimacy, normative additions to the Canadian legal order from NAFTA and the WTO have consequences. National treatment for investment spelled the end to a whole generation of industrial development policies centred on the targeting of subsidies to domestic corporations or sectors to improve their competitive performance in order to boost their exports. It also called into question the capacity of the Canadian state to continue to bolster its cultural industries through favouring domestic entities in the private sector. In this way, supraconstitutional norms have had direct impacts on the domestic legislative and administrative order without most of the public – and even much of the government apparatus – understanding how this had happened.

As one example, an efficient public health system has become a defining characteristic of Canadians' sense of national identity. However, the main thrust of the *General Agreement on Trade in Services* (GATS) is deregulatory, because it attacks what are deemed "non-conforming" national government measures (Arup 2000, 96). If the privatization of publicly provided services is the outcome of NAFTA and GATS, Canadian society may risk losing a prime social institution that has played a major role in defining its identity and so sustaining its cohesion. Should the impact of continental and global trade norms cause the accelerated commercialization of health care with consequent increases in inequality of treatment between the rich and the poor, a central element of Canadian political culture will have been jeopardized. In this scenario, the supraconstitution's democratically inaccessible rule-making institutions would not just be of dubious legitimacy in themselves but would also help delegitimize Canada's own domestic political outputs.

Instead of developing its social and community cohesion, Canada appears to be polarizing into a society of those who can succeed in the globalized system and those left behind. Should this perception be linked to the norms and practices of the global and continental economic governance regimes, serious repercussions may be felt in the legitimacy of the country's own representative system (McBride and Shields 1997). If global institutions have "hollowed out" the Canadian state to the point that it risks being seen as incapable of defending its citizens' interests (Arthurs 2000), the Canadian political system will lose credibility at the same time as neo-conservative globalization loses legitimacy.

The international principles, rules, rights, and institutional practices we have described in this chapter constrict democratic governments in the exercise of their public regulatory authority. They were created and are interpreted and applied largely without democratic deliberation. They are effective in domestic legal systems without the need for – indeed, often in spite of – domestic legislative action. They form part of the conglomeration of fundamental norms and institutional practices by which Canadian society is governed. They are, in our vocabulary, supraconstitutional. In the next chapter, we consider whether the same can be said of the manifold international social and environmental regimes of which Canada is also a member.

4

Good Citizens of Planet Earth? The Weakness of Global Social and Environmental Governance

Canada is a party to thousands of bilateral, regional, and global agreements, declarations, processes, and organizations dedicated to the advancement of human rights, public health, poverty alleviation, arts, culture, natural resource conservation, environmental protection, and other goals in what we might for convenience call the social and environmental arena. For all its complexity and sophistication, however, the social and environmental side of international governance is tentative and weak in comparison with the far more muscular international trade and investment regime.

Since it is impossible to canvass the entire field of social and environmental governance, we focus our supraconstitutional perspective in this chapter on three areas. Environmental protection, public health, and human security represent general trends in global social and environmental governance. Human rights, science, or labour could have served our purpose, but our three chosen domains will suffice to illustrate both the broader implications of neo-conservative supraconstitutionalism and the possibilities for challenging, resisting, or reshaping it.

Global Environmental Governance

Despite the consensus about the urgent need for multilateral environmental cooperation, "the intergovernmental organizations created by the global community over the past century to address these issues remain fragile, fragmented, fixed in old frameworks, and thus often ineffective" (Kirton and Trebilcock 2004, 3). The weakness of global environmental structures is especially striking when compared to the strength of international trade and investment governance, which often prohibits national governments from implementing measures to protect their own domestic environments or to address global environmental problems. Our basic question is whether the international norms and institutions in these three fields form part of the ensemble of fundamental practices by which Canadian society is governed, constraining domestic governmental decision making and prevailing over conflicting domestic laws.

Principles

For a young field, international environmental law is characterized by a proliferation of overlapping and competing legal principles, most of which are so open-textured or contradictory that they impose no appreciable checks on most states. The development of the global environmental regime has been shaped by the norms enshrined in landmark multilateral environmental agreements (MEAs) and UN declarations. Among the most important of these are the Stockholm Declaration of the 1972 Conference on the Human Environment and the Rio Declaration of the 1992 Conference on Environment and Development (Wood 2003b; Broadhead 2002, 30-34). Major documents such as these have shaped the terms of the debates surrounding environmental protection by introducing or reflecting fundamental principles of international environmental law, which constitute the foundations of today's global environmental regime.

The relative simplicity of the trade and investment supraconstitution's basic principles (national treatment, most favoured nation, and protection against takings) stands in stark contrast to the complexity of international environmental law, in which a multitude of principles vie for primacy. Among the main contenders are sustainable development, sustainable utilization, equitable balancing, prevention, precaution, polluter pays, the ecosystem approach, intergenerational and intragenerational equity, state sovereignty over natural resources, the no-harm principle, good neighbourliness, common but differentiated responsibilities, common heritage of humanity, cooperation, notice and consultation, prior informed consent, environmental impact assessment, public participation, integration, and the human right to a healthful environment (Wood 2003b; Ellis and Wood 2006).

Canada is a party or signatory to many multilateral environmental agreements, declarations, and other international instruments embracing these principles. Some are legally binding treaties and may even be translated into specific binding limits, targets, and timetables. A much larger number are non-binding resolutions or guidelines. Whatever form they take, they have two general characteristics that set them apart from the economic

supraconstitution: they do not appreciably limit Canadian political autonomy, and they do not take effect directly in the domestic legal system in the
absence of legislative or other implementing action. The result is that, despite
their large number, broad scope, and lofty ambitions, they do not form part
of Canada's supraconstitution, as an examination of some of the most prominent will demonstrate.

The No-Harm Principle

According to the no-harm principle, states have the responsibility to ensure
that activities within their jurisdiction do not cause damage to the environments of other states or of areas beyond national jurisdiction. This cornerstone
of international environmental law was first expressed in the 1941 *Trail
Smelter* arbitration in which the US claimed that it suffered damage as a result
of fumes emanating from a smelter located in British Columbia.[1] The tribunal ruled against Canada, famously holding that "no State has the right to
use or permit the use of its territory in such a manner as to cause injury by
fumes in or to the territory of another or the properties or persons therein,
when the case is of serious consequence and the injury is established by clear
and convincing evidence."[2] This dictum is widely touted as customary international law binding on all states (Broadhead 2002, 34). Some scholars claim
that, by modifying a state's right to dispose of its own territory as its domestic interests dictate, the principle constrains state sovereignty (Brunnée 1993,
18). This is a stretch. Although *Trail Smelter* appeared to lay down a blanket
prohibition on transboundary environmental harm, this has never been reflected in international environmental law or state practice (Ellis and Wood
2006, 350). On the contrary, international law assumes that states must
tolerate a substantial degree of environmental harm as the price to be paid
for economic growth and industrial progress. A blanket prohibition on transboundary environmental harm is at odds with customary international law
rules of good neighbourliness, due diligence, and state responsibility, which
permit a certain degree of transboundary harm. It is also inconsistent with
most contemporary MEAs, which seek to limit rather than eliminate transboundary pollution and which focus on prevention and control rather than
ex post facto liability (*ibid.*, 357-58; Ellis 2006).

Another reason to be skeptical of the no-harm principle is that the *Trail
Smelter* decision had no substantial impact either on Canadian law and policy
or on the amount of pollution originating from the smelter in question. The

ruling required Canada to put certain pollution control measures in place and compensate American farmers downwind for serious damage that might occur despite the controls. The controls consisted simply of adjusting the timing of emissions so that weather and seasonal conditions would direct them away from the American farmers' land. Canada was not required to, and did not, impose emission limits that might reduce the smelter's production levels or its total emissions. Indeed, the smelter's owner, Cominco, did what almost all industrial polluters have done in similar circumstances. Insisting that such limits were technologically and economically impracticable, it fought them for years until it discovered a profitable way to capture and reprocess waste sulphur into fertilizer (Allum 2006). As for the requirement to compensate the farmers for future damage, in effect this conferred on Cominco an implicit power of eminent domain whereby, in return for payment of compensation, it could condemn property to permanent ecological degradation. Many such "smoke zones" were established by US and Canadian courts in the early twentieth century to facilitate industrialization. As Allum (*ibid.*, 26) argues, "far from being an expansive declaration of state liability, the Tribunal ultimately constructed an extraordinarily narrow doctrine on transnational air pollution that erased national borders to protect the sovereignty of industrial production in North America."

The no-harm principle does not exist in isolation. Like many other principles of international law, it is offset by the countervailing principle that states have permanent sovereignty over natural resources within their jurisdiction and the right to exploit them as they see fit. These contending principles are encapsulated in Principle 21 of the Stockholm Declaration, which provides that states have the sovereign right to exploit their own resources pursuant to their own environmental policies and the responsibility to ensure that activities within their jurisdiction do not damage the environment of other states or areas beyond national jurisdiction.[3] Recognition of a state's sovereign right to exploit its own resources according to its own policies was the *sine qua non* for developing-countries' participation in modern international environmental agreements and a central pillar of the Group of 77 (G-77) developing countries' campaign for a New International Economic Order in the 1960s and 1970s. Principle 21 thus expresses a tension at the heart of international environmental law, between economic development and environmental protection generally and between the global North and South in particular.

The Good Neighbour Principle

If the international legal status of the no-harm principle is uncertain, the related principle of good neighbourliness is on firmer footing. Good neighbourliness stands for the proposition that, even when a state is acting within its rights, it is obliged to take into account the rights and interests of neighbouring states (Ellis and Wood 2006, 351). The principle is often expressed in terms of a duty of prior notification and consultation regarding activities that may have transboundary effects, and an obligation to exercise due diligence to prevent the interests of other states from being harmed as a result of activities on one's territory.[4] It is also often expressed as a duty to assess the transboundary environmental impacts of proposed projects and share the resulting information with affected states.[5] In rare cases, it takes the form of a requirement for prior informed consent, but this is restricted to such specific circumstances as the transboundary movement of hazardous chemicals and wastes.[6] With the exception of this narrow class of cases, affected states do not have a veto over a neighbour's proposed activities or the right to require their modification. Prior informed consent has failed to prevent hazardous waste dumping in developing countries and remains controversial in other areas including indigenous peoples' environmental rights and the trade in genetically modified organisms (ibid., 371-73).

Like the no-harm principle and many other norms of international law, that of good neighbourliness is open-textured and indeterminate: "Because the principle ... does not tell states how the balance between their respective interests is to be struck, but rather that such a balance must be struck, states are compelled to reach agreement on the proper interpretation and application of this principle in a particular set of circumstances. What counts as a violation of this principle will vary depending on the interests and priorities of states" (ibid., 352).

The Precautionary Principle

Environmental governance faces a fundamental puzzle: how to respond to pervasive and deep uncertainty about the environmental and health impacts of various substances and activities produced by modern industrial society. The notion of precaution in the face of uncertainty has been endorsed in hundreds of international instruments and has been incorporated into domestic legislation and policy in most countries, including Canada. The most common formulation is found in Principle 15 of the Rio Declaration: "Where

there are threats of serious or irreversible damage, lack of full scientific certainty shall not be used as a reason for postponing cost-effective measures to
prevent environmental degradation."[7] This principle has been included, in
different formulations, in a large number of international instruments since
the mid-1980s, starting with the 1985 *Vienna Convention for the Protection of
the Ozone Layer* and its 1987 Montreal Protocol.[8] These agreements "required
action on the part of states [to curb chlorofluorocarbon (CFC) production
and consumption] before the causal link between ozone depletion and CFCs
had been conclusively established" (Birnie and Boyle 2002, 117). Since then,
the principle has been written into a growing number of treaties dealing with
marine pollution, international watercourses, air pollution, climate change,
trade in hazardous waste, and the protection of biodiversity.

The precautionary principle's legal status, content, and operational meaning remain highly uncertain. Although many commentators view it as an
emerging principle of customary international law, the United States insists
that it is not a legal principle at all but rather a non-binding "approach," a
position taken by the International Tribunal for the Law of the Sea in 1999.[9]
For its part, Canada has sometimes acknowledged precaution as an emerging
principle but more recently has taken the US line that it lacks legal status.

As to the principle's content, disagreement abounds regarding the level
of threat and degree of scientific certainty required to trigger it, as well as
whether and how precautionary action should be subject to a cost-effectiveness
criterion. When it comes to operational application, controversy rages over
whether it requires any change to conventional risk assessment and risk
management techniques, whether it implies a reversal of legal burdens of
proof (so that proponents of potentially risky activities must demonstrate
that they pose no unacceptable risk), and a range of other issues. On all these
points, the Canadian government has generally endorsed a watered-down
version of precaution.

In domestic Canadian law, the precautionary principle has been mentioned in a score or more of federal and provincial statutes and dozens of
court and tribunal decisions.[10] Under the federal *Pest Control Products Act*, a
proponent of a new pesticide "has the burden of persuading the Minister that
the health and environmental risks and the value of the pest control product
are acceptable."[11] Under the *Canadian Environmental Protection Act, 1999*, Ottawa has a statutory duty to "exercise its powers in a manner that ... applies
the precautionary principle," and in practice it puts a burden on industry to

establish that new substances and around two hundred high-priority existing ones are not "toxic" within the meaning of the act.[12] Dozens of Canadian municipalities and now entire provinces have banned cosmetic uses of pesticides, partially on the strength of the precautionary principle. Most recently, Ontario proposed a toxics use reduction law, which is intended to take precautionary action to reduce and eliminate the production and use of toxic substances rather than just avoiding their release into the environment. But in almost all these cases, governments have carefully drafted the legislation to avoid assuming specific enforceable obligations of precaution. They have also interpreted the principle in a way that does not depart appreciably from conventional risk assessment and risk management techniques. Moreover, Ontario's new toxics use reduction strategy – the most ambitious application of the precautionary principle in Canada – makes industry compliance voluntary. These domestic legal and policy measures have undeniably been inspired and influenced by the development of the precautionary principle in international environmental law. There is no evidence, however, that domestic legislatures and courts have felt obliged to adopt these precautionary stances because of international legal constraints or that international pronouncements of the precautionary principle have direct effect in the Canadian legal system. The principle is not experienced as an effective limitation on domestic law and policy, and its meaning remains deeply ambiguous. Though it may eventually become customary law, it remains inconsistently applied in MEAs and selectively observed by states.

The Ecosystem Approach

Although its status, content, and implications are controversial, the ecosystem approach merits attention because of Canada's role in its early development and disappointing record in fulfilling its promise. Many recent international agreements and declarations pledge to apply an ecosystem approach, but there is little agreement about what it entails beyond a general recognition that political boundaries artificially divide ecosystems; conventional management approaches artificially isolate individual activities, substances, and species from the ecosystems of which they are a part; and that environmental problems should be analyzed and managed at the level of entire ecosystems.

One of the first international agreements expressly contemplating ecosystem-based environmental management was the 1978 *Canada-US Great Lakes Water Quality Agreement* (GLWQA), whose stated purpose was "to restore and maintain the chemical, physical, and biological integrity of the waters of the Great Lakes Basin Ecosystem" by reducing to the minimum possible the discharge of pollutants into the Great Lakes ecosystem.[13] It called for zero discharge of persistent toxic substances and their virtual elimination from the ecosystem. Some progress has been made toward eliminating certain pollutants, cleaning up individual geographic areas of concern, and developing binational strategies. Nonetheless, major environmental problems remain, and there has been very little actual policy integration across political boundaries. Zero discharge and virtual elimination of persistent toxic substances seem almost as remote today as they did in 1978. The International Joint Commission, the binational body that monitors the implementation of the agreement, has repeatedly criticized the two governments for their slow progress in achieving the GLWQA's goals. On occasion, it has gone so far as to ask whether its reports serve any purpose and why it should continue to make recommendations when all previous ones have remained unimplemented (see, for example, International Joint Commission 1998).

Despite many references to ecosystem management in recent international instruments, the approach remains highly controversial for numerous reasons, including its potential to recharacterize many issues as international that were previously seen as purely domestic (hence potentially invading national sovereignty), its tendency to bring into question the adequacy of existing legal and institutional structures, and the chronic incompleteness of our understanding of many ecosystems. It is thus seen by many as a laudable goal but one that is practically unachievable in the foreseeable future.

The most prominent multilateral effort to reach concord on a more detailed elaboration of the principle was conducted by the Conference of the Parties (COP) to the *Convention on Biological Diversity* (CBD) in whose thematic program areas the ecosystem approach is a central pillar.[14] The parties have had great difficulty agreeing on what it entails. In 2000, the COP adopted a Decision on the Ecosystem Approach, which described the approach and set out twelve principles and five points for operational guidance.[15] Rather than resolving the controversy surrounding the ecosystem approach, the decision defined the approach in very flexible terms that amounted to a smorgasbord of overlapping and sometimes competing conservation techniques and objectives. Despite the CBD's attempt to elaborate the meaning of the ecosystem approach, it remains ambiguous as a matter of law and is rarely taken seriously in practice.

Common but Differentiated Responsibilities

A fourth central principle of international environmental law derives from the general notion of differential treatment, which "refers to instances where the principle of sovereign equality is sidelined to accommodate extraneous factors, such as divergences in levels of economic development or unequal capacities to tackle a given problem" (Cullet 1999, 551; Matsui 2002, 155). It is of particular interest because it represents one possible way to make transnational governance more responsive to the new challenges of globalization and "to foster substantive equality among states" (Cullet 1999, 549). "Substantive equality" refers to a situation in which states, though not sharing the same formally equal status in terms of obligations and rights, achieve a distribution of legal rights and responsibilities that produces more equitable outcomes. "In practice," writes Cullet, "this mainly includes deviations which seek to favour least favoured states" (*ibid.*, 551). The principle of differential treatment does not seek a radical transformation of the current international legal order: instead, it is one means of achieving more equitable and effective results within the existing system.

The concept of differential treatment has found some of its most progressive applications in the area of international environmental law, where many instruments recognize that states have "common but differentiated responsibilities" (CBDR) based on their historical contributions to environmental problems and their current capabilities to address them.[16] CBDR "posits that states should be held accountable in different measure according to their respective historical and current contributions to the creation of global environmental problems and their respective capacities to address these problems" (*ibid.*, 577) and is reflected in the recent trend toward differentiated standards and timetables for developed and developing countries in international environmental agreements. For instance, the Montreal Protocol allowed longer implementation periods for developing countries, for which compliance with the instruments was relatively more difficult. Similarly, the *UN Framework Convention on Climate Change* gives special attention to the situation and needs of small island countries and those with low-lying coastal areas (French 2000, 36; Saunders 1996, 280).[17] The principle of CBDR is also mirrored in the fact that developing countries did not take on quantified greenhouse gas (GHG) emission reduction commitments in the 1997 Kyoto Protocol.[18] The perceived unfairness of this arrangement was a main tenet of the United States' rejection of the protocol and the Stephen Harper government's decision not to comply with Kyoto even though Canada had ratified it. CBDR's emphasis on equity nevertheless resonates with many Canadians' political values and views on foreign and development policy. For Canada and other advanced industrialized countries, the main significance of the principle lies in the possibility that it may also create a duty to assist developing states in the fulfillment of international environmental obligations. Some MEAs include provisions for developed-country parties to provide new and additional resources to developing-country parties, but this seldom turns out to be more than a trickle. In any event, Canada and other developed countries resolutely resist recognition of such a duty as a matter of law.

CBDR is a manifestation of a broader meta-principle of international environmental law – equity – which defines rights and obligations in general and flexible terms, leaving their precise extent and implications to be negotiated in particular circumstances. In international law, equity has a long history as a principle for allocating shared resources. "Equitable sharing," "equitable utilization," and similar standards have been employed in numerous international treaties including those on ozone depletion, biodiversity, climate change, and international watercourses. International law does not usually specify how equitable allocations are to be achieved, although individual treaties or guidelines may list factors to be considered in specific situations. Actual allocations are usually left to be worked out through political negotiations, such as those leading up to the 1997 Kyoto Protocol on greenhouse gas emission reductions.

International law scholars distinguish between intragenerational and intergenerational equity. The intragenerational variety refers to equity within the current generation. It is reflected in the principle of CBDR, in calls for substantial flows of new and additional funds and technology from developed to developing countries, and in an emphasis on capacity building in developing countries targeted at both domestic scientific, technical, and governance capacity and the capacity to participate in international environmental negotiations. It has led developing countries to insist that implementation of their environmental commitments is dependent on the developed countries' implementation of their financial commitments.[19] This issue has also spawned controversies regarding access to and ownership of technology, especially in the area of biodiversity and intellectual property rights.

Intragenerational equity is not just about equity among states. It also recognizes that women, indigenous peoples, the poor, and other vulnerable communities often bear a disproportionate share of environmental burdens. This commonly leads to a focus on gender equity, human rights to a healthy environment, public participation, access to information, and access to justice. At a larger scale, the principle of intragenerational equity is concerned with the structure of the global economy. It is often associated with calls for a more open and equitable international economic system, improved international market access for the goods and services of developing countries, reduced external indebtedness, and elimination of unsustainable patterns of production and consumption in the developed countries. Like the calls for a New International Economic Order in the 1970s, however, it has made few inroads in practice.

The companion to intragenerational equity is intergenerational equity, which is often expressed as the proposition that human societies have a duty to use natural resources and the environment in a way that preserves them for the benefit of future generations. This principle has been replicated in many treaties and declarations, including the 1946 international whaling convention, the 1972 Stockholm Declaration, the 1992 Rio Declaration, and many more recent instruments. The norm is echoed in the concept of sustainable development, which was defined by the landmark Brundtland Report of 1987 as "development that meets the needs of the present without compromising the ability of future generations to meet their own needs" (World Commission on Environment and Development 1987, 43).

The idea that future generations have rights that can somehow be vindicated in the present remains vague and controversial. With the exception of a few isolated pronouncements such as the *Oposa* case in the Philippines, domestic and international law have not recognized the rights or legal standing of unborn future generations.[20] Meanwhile, the practical implications of the intergenerational equity principle remain uncertain.

These issues are among the most intractable facing humanity. Although the principle of equity affirms basic and often conflicting values, it is difficult to distinguish how it points the way toward a resolution of these problems. It is harder to see how it constrains domestic law and policy.

Sustainable Development

Sustainable development is not just a principle of international environmental law. It has emerged as a meta-principle of public policy as a whole. Until 11 September 2001 and the US-led war on terror, it showed signs of becoming the leitmotif of twenty-first-century public policy. Because it attempts to marry environmental protection, economic growth, and human development, no principle of international law is more ambiguous, open-ended, contradictory, or marked by compromise. The central trade-off is embodied in the Rio Declaration, which, on the one hand, acknowledges the "right to development" and, on the other, demands the integration of environmental protection into development.[21] The acknowledgment of the right to development was a major coup for developing countries, the price of which was the developed countries' insistence that environmental protection was an integral part of the development process and could not be considered in isolation from it. These contending priorities of developed and developing countries define the central tension between the global North's often hypocritical wish to resolve global environmental problems and the global South's desire for a just global order that will break cycles of poverty, inequity, and dependence.

Although sustainable development has become a routine concern of major institutions such as the World Bank and the European Community, the rise of the principle has not slowed humanity's acceleration toward planetary ecological disaster. The early euphoria around the Rio Declaration and its Agenda 21 action plan dissipated quickly as virtually all environmental and associated social indicators continued to worsen. In 2002, the world leaders who came together in Johannesburg for the Rio Declaration's sombre tenth birthday celebration observed that "the global environment continues to suffer. Loss of biodiversity continues, fish stocks continue to be depleted, desertification claims more and more fertile land, the adverse effects of climate change are already evident, natural disasters are more frequent and more devastating, and developing countries more vulnerable, and air, water and marine pollution continue to rob millions of a decent life."[22]

In 2005, the board of the Millennium Ecosystem Assessment was moved to issue a blunt statement that "human activity is putting such strain on the natural functions of Earth that the ability of the planet's ecosystems to sustain future generations can no longer be taken for granted."[23] The UN Environment Programme (2007, 6) was equally grim in its 2007 assessment of the environment twenty years after the Brundtland Report:

Imagine a world in which environmental change threatens
people's health, physical security, material needs, and social

cohesion. This is a world beset by increasingly intense and frequent storms and by rising sea levels. Some people experience
extensive flooding, while others endure intense droughts. Species
extinction occurs at rates never before witnessed. Safe water is increasingly limited, hindering economic activity. Land degradation
endangers the lives of millions of people. This is the world today.

The report concluded that environmental degradation threatens all aspects of
human well-being and development, and that integration of environmental
protection into development decision making has been limited (*ibid.*, 4).

Mainstream sustainable development discourse represents a distinct shift
away from the idea (which had gained currency in the 1970s) that economic development must respect unavoidable ecological limits to the idea that
environmental concerns must be balanced against social and economic pri
orities (Wood 2003b). Ecological constraints are understood not as unavoidable limits on human activities but as factors to be considered in the quest
to strike an appropriate balance between the environment and development.
In this view, economic growth and ecological life-support systems deserve to
be sustained equally. The appeal of the sustainable development principle
lies in its claim to square the circle, muting environmental science's central
lessons: there are limits to the regenerative capacities of species, ecosystems,
and planetary life-support systems; these limits are unpredictable; they cannot be altered by negotiation, balancing, or trade-offs; and persistent per-
turbations can cause entire systems to shift to new states that may be hostile
to the survival of humankind, let alone that of countless other species.

Nowhere have these lessons received more public attention recently than
in the field of global climate change. Momentum appeared to be building
toward broad public recognition that the planet is approaching a "tipping
point" with anthropogenic greenhouse gas emissions (Hansen et al. 2008),
but public attention to this problem rapidly dissipated with the current economic downturn. Whether climate consciousness will revive before the global
economy resumes its progression toward climatic disaster remains an open
question.

Supraconstitutional Impacts

The limited extent to which these legal principles restrict states' choices about
environmental policy stems from their contested legal status and open-
textured character. What distinguishes them from their trade and investment

norms is the lack of institutions empowered to issue authoritative determinations of their meaning and to enforce those rulings. With the exception
of marine environmental protection disputes under the jurisdiction of the
International Tribunal for the Law of the Sea, and the rare cases in which
states have submitted to the compulsory jurisdiction of the International
Court of Justice (ICJ), these international environmental principles are found
in such soft-law instruments as the Rio Declaration or Agenda 21 and in
treaties that lack formal dispute settlement or enforcement mechanisms.
When submitting to the compulsory jurisdiction of the ICJ, states often make
reservations in the case of environmental and natural resource management
disputes. Such a reservation by Canada prevented Spain from taking Canada
to the ICJ to challenge its seizure of a Spanish fishing trawler on the high seas
off Newfoundland during the 1990s' "Turbot War."

These principles nevertheless perform an important function by providing normative foundations and guiding ideas for international environmental governance. Their greatest practical effect may be on such "second-party
control mechanisms" as peer review and the bargaining processes that take
place between states (Chayes, Chayes, and Mitchell 1995, 77): "In this second-
party control process, international environmental norms can play a significant role by setting the terms of the debate, providing evaluative standards,
serving as a basis to criticize other states' actions, and establishing a framework
of principles within which negotiations may take place to develop more
specific norms, usually in treaties" (Bodansky 1995, 117).

In the dispute between Canada and the US over acid rain emissions in
the 1980s, for example, the no-harm principle did not directly restrain the
United States, but it provided a shared normative framework for the negotiations that led to the 1991 *US-Canada Air Quality Agreement*.

RULES

International environmental law also includes a vast number of specific, often
legally binding rules dictating proscribed or required behaviour. These directives range from international fisheries quotas to bans on particular substances, controls on trade in endangered species, and detailed notification and
consent procedures for trade in hazardous substances. The majority have been
promulgated in the context of multilateral treaties, although a substantial
number have been developed bilaterally or regionally. Many MEAs begin with
the negotiation of a framework convention establishing the fundamental
principles, purposes, and general operating parameters of an environmental

regime in a given issue area (Chayes, Chayes, and Mitchell 1995, 76). Detailed rules and regulations are often added later via protocols dealing with specific issues. Examples of the framework-protocol approach are legion. The *Vienna Convention for the Protection of the Ozone Layer* created a framework for eliminating chlorofluorocarbons, and the Montreal Protocol later set specific targets and timetables for doing so. The UN *Convention on Biological Diversity* produced a general framework for conservation of biological diversity, and the *Cartagena Protocol on Biosafety* established specific rules for biosafety. The *UN Framework Convention on Climate Change* set a general framework for avoiding dangerous anthropogenic interference with the climate system, and the Kyoto Protocol generated specific GHG emission targets and timetables.[24]

The detailed rules contained in protocols are negotiated directly by the states involved and come into force when a prescribed number of states have ratified them, and then only for the ratifying states. Other international environmental rules are not agreed in the text of the treaty or protocol itself but are developed on an ongoing basis by treaty organs on the basis of majority vote. States thus find themselves bound by an increasing number of international environmental rules to which they did not specifically consent.

Although the number, detail, and complexity of international environmental rules rival those for international trade and investment, what prevents them from achieving supraconstitutional status is their failure to constrain domestic autonomy to a significant degree. States may simply ignore a wide range of international environmental rules without suffering serious adverse consequences or may invoke provisions in many MEAs that allow them to opt out of rules adopted under the treaty (Wood 1997).

In the mid-1990s, Chayes and Chayes (1995, 26-27) argued that sovereignty had been transformed to the point that, no longer denoting a state's ability to act as it pleased, it now referred to the state's capacity to maintain its membership in reasonably good standing in the increasingly dense web of regulatory regimes that made up the substance of international life. If this is true in the environmental field, the transformation is very subtle. The consequences for ignoring, bending, or breaking international environmental obligations do not come close to those for violating the international economic supraconstitution in their immediacy or severity.

Canada's flouting of its Kyoto Protocol commitments is a case in point. Under the protocol, ratified by Canada in 2002 and entered into force in 2005, Canada agreed to reduce its GHG emissions to 6 percent below 1990 levels by the first commitment period of 2008-12. Between 1997 and 2006, the federal Liberal government did virtually nothing to ensure that Canada would meet its commitment (Commissioner of the Environment and Sustainable Development 2006; Jaccard et al. 2006; Simpson, Jaccard, and Rivers 2007). In 2006, the Conservative Party came to power condemning the Kyoto Protocol as unrealistic, unaffordable, and unfair, but it soon became the first federal government to take concrete steps toward regulating industrial greenhouse gas emissions, rolling out a plan to impose caps on industrial GHG emissions (Government of Canada 2007). Controversially, the plan called for caps on emissions intensity (emissions per unit of production) rather than on total emissions. According to independent analyses and the government's own estimates, the plan would not come close to meeting Canada's Kyoto commitment.[25] Indeed, the government had no intention of meeting the Kyoto target and made no secret of this fact. It issued a comprehensive regulatory framework in March 2008, detailing proposed industrial GHG emissions intensity targets, outlining several flexible compliance mechanisms, and promising an eventual transition to fixed emission caps in the 2020-25 period (Government of Canada 2008). But in early 2009, Ottawa announced that regulation of industrial GHG emissions would be put on hold "until Washington sets its course to tackle climate change and Canada's economic woes subside" (Woods 2009, n.p.). So even its belated action on climate change, which was obviously insufficient to comply with Kyoto, was shelved when the economic crisis and a new American administration presented an excuse for further inaction.

The main effect of this very public flouting of its Kyoto commitments has been to tarnish Canada's previously strong reputation for environmental responsibility and its credibility in international climate change negotiations. Canada is regularly singled out by environmental NGOs as a "colossal fossil" in these negotiations because of its obstructionist and retrograde position. Many states, including those of the EU and vulnerable developing countries, share the NGOs' negative view. The Kyoto Protocol has its own mechanisms for dealing with non-compliance. States that fail to meet their emission reduction targets in the first commitment period are to be penalized during the next period. They will suffer this penalty, however, only if they participate in a post-Kyoto deal. Naturally, they can be expected to hold out for as favourable a deal as they can get. The main effect of Canada's miserable record of failure is to put it in a weak position in these

post-Kyoto negotiations. Canada probably has less influence in these negotiations than had it refused to ratify Kyoto to begin with, but its credibility
has already sunk so low as a result of its persistent efforts to undermine
urgent international action on climate change that it is hard to see how it
could sink any lower.

The main consequence of Canada's violation of its Kyoto commitments
is that it will suffer some soft reputational effects. No international tribunal
is likely to evaluate domestic Canadian climate change laws and policies, find
them wanting, and order the government to change them or pay compensation, as would happen under the economic supraconstitution. What is most
likely to induce a reluctant Ottawa to adopt stringent emissions caps and to
take serious action on domestic GHG emissions is not international moral
pressure but the 2009 change of administration – and climate change policy
– in Washington. As in so many areas, pressure to meet American demands
and harmonize with American policy is the most effective check on Canadian
policy autonomy.

Rights

To the extent that international environmental governance concerns itself
with rights, it is primarily with those of nation-states in their relations with
each other. The idea of a human right to a healthful environment has received
some attention but remains highly controversial in international law. The
1972 Stockholm Declaration affirmed that "man" has the right to "freedom,
equality and adequate conditions of life, in an environment of a quality that
permits a life of dignity and well-being."[26] Numerous non-binding international declarations, reports, and resolutions have referred to a human right
to a healthy environment, but states have been unwilling – with a few exceptions – to sign legally binding treaties acknowledging such a right. Ongoing
controversies include whether this right would be individual or collective,
whether it would be procedural or substantive, and what a healthful environment actually means. To the extent they are recognized legally, environmental rights usually take the form of procedural rights of access to
information, public notice and comment on proposed environmental decisions, and access to limited forms of justice in environmental matters.[27] Far
from challenging the legal status quo in participating countries, however,
these international standards are relatively undemanding and do not come
close to what many countries are already doing as a matter of domestic law
(Richardson and Razzaque 2006).

Institutions

The global environmental regime has been shaped by the work of such formal intergovernmental organizations as the UN Environment Programme (UNEP), the UN Development Program (UNDP), the International Maritime Organization (IMO), the Food and Agriculture Organization (FAO), and the International Atomic Energy Agency (IAEA), as well as by informal treaty bodies (Birnie and Boyle 2002, 35-36). Though these forums are primarily intergovernmental, they often accord non-state actors more of a role than they would have in other areas of international governance. Leading NGOs such as the International Union for the Conservation of Nature and transnational business groups have helped to shape the global environmental regime's evolution either through direct participation or by lobbying their home governments. For instance, American protest movements of the 1960s were in large part responsible for the first major intergovernmental environmental conference, the 1972 Stockholm Conference on the Human Environment (Broadhead 2002, 31). On the other hand, the IMO and the IAEA "illustrate the influence wielded by states representing powerful and important industries," reminding us that international environmental organizations are no less immune than other bodies to "agency capture" (Birnie and Boyle 2002, 36).

Intergovernmental environmental organizations have often been criticized because, "without real law-making authority or, in most cases, the ability to take binding decisions by majority vote, they lack the necessary power to take effective action for the common good and to impose their collective will on individual states" (ibid., 37). Yet these organizations often provide forums for interaction and discussion on the issues when MEAs are being negotiated. More importantly, the secretariats of international organizations wield power through their influence over the global environmental agenda. For example, former UNEP executive director Mustafa Tolba "defined much of the environmental treaty-making agenda in the 1970s and 1980s," despite his lack of any formal authority (Chayes, Chayes, and Mitchell 1995, 87). At the same time, UNEP has been plagued by insecure funding, tiny resources compared to its counterparts such as UNDP, severe budget cuts, and running political battles between donor and developing countries over governance arrangements.

The construction of a robust regime for global environmental governance has been hindered by the deep divide between industrialized and less-developed countries (Anand 2004, 2-8, 15-17; Mickelson 1996, 239-41).

Though far from internally unified, these groups have tended to negotiate as opposing blocs. The developed countries have usually prioritized long-term environmental objectives and stressed a "global commons" conception of the environment, which represents it as a "common heritage of mankind" (Matsui 2002, 155-56; Mickelson 1996, 247). Developing countries have asserted their right to pursue economic development as they exercise sovereign control over their own natural resources and have demanded that the North take responsibility for the costs of global environmental protection commensurate with its historical contributions to environmental degradation (Matsui 2002, 154-55). Northern priorities include issues such as climate change and ozone depletion; Southern ones include those with more immediate effects and links with underdevelopment, such as desertification, clean water, and sewage disposal (Anand 2004, 6, 16-17; Saunders 1996, 266-67). Debates about states' sovereignty over natural resources and their rights to determine their own economic development strategies still centre on the North's historical contributions to environmental degradation and the South's experience of colonialism and demands for equity and justice (Mickelson 1996, 243-44; Anand 2004, 15-17).

One of the main factors explaining the failure of MEAs and international organizations to achieve meaningful results in environmental protection has been their lack of enforcement capacity or other mechanisms effectively to ensure state compliance with environment obligations (Handl 1997, 29-33). The compliance mechanisms in place lack the sophistication to address the highly specialized and technical subject matter of MEAs and are often very weak. Because compliance-control devices rarely involve sanctions for violations of MEAs, they do not create any significant costs for noncompliance beyond those originally associated with the environmental problem (ibid., 46-49).

The absence of formal dispute resolution procedures in most MEAs precludes the possibility of enforcement mechanisms on a par with those of the WTO. Moreover, the subject matter of most MEAs is incompatible with the types of enforcement procedure found in other kinds of international law. Since it is difficult to reliably attribute responsibility for transboundary air pollution to specific countries, it is not feasible to build enforcement mechanisms that target violators of pollution rules. For many agreements, strong compliance or enforcement devices would not be effective even if they were in place, because they would not address the underlying problems of low state capacity, which impedes implementation of environmental agreements, especially in developing countries (Saunders 1996, 266-68). As a result, most MEA compliance devices consist of little more than monitoring and transparency systems, and even these tend to be underused or ineffective (Handl 1997, 48-49). Most importantly, even when forceful systems for ensuring state compliance have been attempted, they have often been ineffectual (Bodansky 1995, 117). For example, in the case of the Kyoto Protocol, which included exceptionally strong compliance-control mechanisms, the United States simply withdrew when it perceived compliance as no longer in its interest, and Canada thumbed its nose at the norms without having the decency to leave the club.

The Supraconstitution and Global Health

As Canada's 2003 experience with severe acute respiratory syndrome (SARS) made clear, managing epidemics is one of the most challenging tasks of contemporary international governance. Although the achievements made in global health are significant, it is also in this area that we observe some of the most tragic failures of international governance and the sharpest dispar-ities between the developed and developing world. To some extent, inter-national health cooperation appears to have intensified since epidemics such as HIV/AIDS and SARS have shown the implications of global health for international security. Canadians are increasingly concerned about their vulnerability to transnationally communicable diseases, identifying it as one of the most serious threats to their security in the twenty-first century (Gov-ernment of Canada 2005). Such fears have helped move the goal of promo-ting international health cooperation higher on the foreign policy agendas of Canada and other countries, at least in their rhetoric. Security concerns related to transnational health have even prompted the creation of new do-mestic institutions with an international health focus, such as the Public Health Agency of Canada, which was established in 2004 in an "attempt to address the prevailing public health concerns in the face of globalization and re-emerging threats from disease."[28] Whereas promoting global health co-operation is a priority for Canada and other countries with an experience of transborder health challenges, concerted international action to establish a vigorous and legitimate global health regime has not yet taken place.

The 1948 constitution of the World Health Organization (WHO) declared health a fundamental human right, defining health broadly as "a state of complete physical, mental, and social well-being."[29] This position was reiter-ated in several international human rights instruments, including the 1948

Universal Declaration of Human Rights and the 1966 *International Covenant on Economic, Social, and Cultural Rights* (ICESCR).[30] These early declarations of principles and rights expressed the idea of health as a "global public good" – universal, non-exclusionary, and to be provided on the basis of need (Taylor 2004, 502). They also acknowledged the strong link between illness, underdevelopment, and poverty, reflecting an integrated approach to health care focused on the local provision of primary health care in the context of broader social and economic development (Thomas and Weber 2004, 191).

By the 1980s, the international health regime had undergone a transformation from the relatively open multilateral forums of the 1970s "to the formalized and narrowly defined policy environments" typical of neo-conservative global governance institutions (*ibid.*, 189). The broad-based parliamentary-style WHO lost much of its responsibility for global health issues to the more specialized and technocratic World Bank. As a result, international health goals "have been revised and are defined much more narrowly now around specific diseases and specific goals of quantifiable scope, precluding any comprehensive engagement with the issues of universal human rights and socio-economic transformation" (*ibid.*, 192). The Washington Consensus promulgated by the international financial institutions shifted health-policy priorities to the privatization potential of national health care programs and the economic productivity increases and growth potential associated with populations' improved physical well-being. The earlier social transformation agenda espoused by the WHO has thus been replaced with a view of health governance that is primarily about cutting back the state along neo-conservative lines.

This shrinkage of the state has occurred just as transboundary public health concerns are increasing in number and scale. As Taylor (2004, 500) observes,

> Infectious and non-communicable diseases, international trade in tobacco, alcohol, and other dangerous products as well as the control of the safety of health services, pharmaceuticals, and food are merely a few examples of the contemporary transnationalization of health concerns. The rapid development and diffusion of scientific and technological developments across national borders are creating new realms of international health concern, such as aspects of biomedical science, including human reproductive cloning, germline therapy, and xenotransplantation, as well as environmental

health problems, including climate change, biodiversity loss, and depletion of the ozone layer. Growth in international trade and travel, in combination with population growth, has served to increase the frequency and intensity of health concerns bypassing or spilling over sovereign boundaries.

The international response to the SARS crisis in Canada and China, "the first infectious disease epidemic since HIV/AIDS to pose a truly global threat," marked the turn to a new post-Westphalian system of global communicable disease governance, characterized by a weakening of national sovereignty, a "vertical" penetration of the state by international disease surveillance and other forms of intervention, and a new diversity of the actors involved in the process (Fidler 2003, 485; 2004, 803). For Canadians, the consequences of this form of global governance for state sovereignty were illustrated in the crippling local economic repercussions of the WHO decision to issue travel advisories during the SARS crisis (Fidler 2004, 803).

These incursions by microbes and international institutions have, at the same time, been accompanied by states' building up their national borders as they struggle to keep transnational health threats out. Many governments have reacted to threats such as the 2009 H1N1 A1 influenza virus outbreak with the same kind of fortress mentality found in the global war on terror, enhancing their health screenings at ports of entry in a showy but largely ineffective attempt to interdict germs at the border.

The new mode of global disease governance also involves a move away from the narrowly market-focused approaches to public health of the 1980s and 1990s toward a return to somewhat more integrative approaches, this time associated with such "global public goods for health" as public-private partnerships for vaccine delivery to the poor (Fidler 2003, 488). As Fidler (2004, 803) argues,

Germ governance in the wake of SARS is at a revolutionary moment. The evolution of germ governance before and during SARS, and the elevation of such governance as an element of good governance, place public health in exciting but unchartered waters. In the aftermath of SARS, public health can no longer be considered a secondary priority at any level. In the post-SARS environment, the Canadian National Advisory Committee on SARS and Public Health stressed the importance of public health in governance by quoting Benjamin Disraeli's argument that "public health was the foundation for the happiness of the people and the power of the country. The care of public health is the first duty of the statesman" ... Although germ governance has not achieved this level of importance, it has become an increasingly significant benchmark against which the health of national, international, and global governance is measured.

The original WHO-centred structures of governance have been weakened and sidelined over the years, but international health law has increasingly felt the impact of linkage with other areas of global governance, including labour, human rights, environment, security, and, most importantly, trade (Thomas and Weber 2004, 191-97). For instance, the UNDP 1994 *Human Development Report* proposed a new security framework that included a public health component as did the 2003 report of the Commission on Human Security and the *Human Security Report 2005* (United Nations Development Program 1994; Commission on Human Security 2003; Human Security Centre 2005). The 2005 report focused on the impacts of armed conflict on health, calling attention to these hidden human costs of war. Similarly, the Canadian government held a foreign policy dialogue examining the human security and health agenda in 2005. Health has also been linked to international peace and security in other contexts, including through UN Security Council resolutions explicitly addressing global health issues, such as the global HIV/AIDS pandemic and biological weapons (Fidler 2004, 802). As noted, the evolution of international health regimes has also been closely tied to the development of international instruments for the protection and promotion of human rights related to physical and mental integrity. Within the UN system, increasing attention is being paid to the interrelation between health and human rights, and tailored human rights instruments now address the rights of particular populations, such as women, children, migrant workers, refugees, and those suffering from HIV/AIDS and disabilities. Moreover, the "link between health and trade in a number of the [WTO] treaties is becoming increasingly manifest in a wide range of areas including access to medicines, food security, nutrition, infectious disease control, and biotechnology" (Taylor 2004, 501). In sum, health is becoming a central issue of multilateralism as a consequence of issue linkage and the pervasive impact of globalization.

The current global health regime is also characterized by a growing diversity of intergovernmental organizations and actors. International institutions participating in the health sector include not only the WHO and the World Bank but also many others from within the UN system, such as the UN Children's Fund, the FAO, UNEP, UNDP, and the UN Population Fund. The year 2006 marked the first time that health ministers attended a G8 Summit. Non-state actors, including a wide variety of foundations, religious groups, and other NGOs, have also come to play a much greater part (Fidler 2004).

Most important, however, has been the growth of the pharmaceutical industry's "powerful influence on international health policy, including global law-making" (Taylor 2004, 503). The emergence of international health coalitions, health research networks, public-private partnerships, and other arrangements grouping broad assortments of actors has blurred the distinction between public and private functions in global health governance, especially with respect to resource mobilization. Many have acknowledged a reallocation of power from intergovernmental organizations to private-sector actors, potentially accompanied by a redistribution of authority and legitimacy in global health governance.

The "proliferation and patchwork development of multilateral organizations with overlapping ambitions and legal authority" in global health carries the risk that international health law will develop inconsistently and weakly (*ibid.*, 503-4). Providing global public goods such as public health increasingly requires effectively coordinated international cooperation. The WHO's intensified assertiveness, demonstrated recently in moving forward the *WHO Framework Convention on Tobacco Control*, may herald "a new era in international health cooperation and, perhaps, an important step towards a new international health law leadership under the WHO" (*ibid.*, 505; Fidler 2004, 801).[31]

The WHO's revival has been celebrated by public health experts, many of whom observed the consequences for global health of the sidelining of this organization during the 1980s and '90s, when several areas of public health management in developing countries came within the purview of the paradigm promoted by the international financial institutions. Where these economic reform projects were implemented, the health care capacity of the state suffered substantially. The structural adjustment programs (SAPs) imposed on developing countries by the World Bank involved sharp reductions in public spending and large-scale privatization of public services, which often led to the dismantling of national health care programs (Lewis 2005, 6). These policy changes further exacerbated health vulnerabilities stemming from poverty and underdevelopment. Health care, especially preventive health care, was often among the first sectors to suffer from SAP-induced spending cuts, and the quality of nutrition, especially in urban areas, declined in societies that implemented these reforms. Where SAPs were carried out, populations showed rises in the incidence of preventable diseases and "irreversible health deterioration" (Peabody 1996, 823). In African countries, SAPs also undermined gains made in improving the equity of access to health care (Kanji, Kanji, and Froze 1991, 985-93). The hollowing out of the state by SAPs has been among the factors responsible for the rate of growth, extent, and duration of the HIV/AIDS pandemic in sub-Saharan Africa (Poku 2002, 114).

Canada's charismatic Stephen Lewis, who served as the UN secretary-general's special envoy for HIV/AIDS in Africa, has been among the most eloquent critics of SAPs for their adverse effects on efforts to deal with the pandemic in Africa (Lewis 2005, 5-7). The global public health governance regime has also had important consequences for the Canadian health care system. In 2000, Canada nearly lost a WTO dispute over an important piece of domestic legislation, the *Patent Act*, which the EU, supported by the US, charged was in violation of the WTO intellectual property rules under the TRIPS Agreement,[32] whose objective is to harmonize intellectual property rights among WTO member states by setting minimum levels of protection that each member state must give to the intellectual property of nationals of other member states. The WTO decision in the case represented a mixed victory for Canada. Though Canada successfully defended one of the *Patent Act* provisions, it nevertheless had to amend its legislation to remove the provision allowing generic drug companies to stockpile their product to be ready for marketing as soon as a patent expires.[33] This change has caused delays representing additional costs to individual patients and to public and private insurers. The decision worried Canadian health law experts and civil society members because it may establish a bias for subsequent interpretations of TRIPS, particularly as it applies to pharmaceutical policy, and because it does not recognize "the importance of balancing the protection of private patent rights with the public interest in promoting health and human rights" (Garmaise 2001, 11). Canadian decisions about public health care provision will henceforth have to be made within the purview of the TRIPS Agreement, or Canada will risk retaliation from other states.

The impact of the TRIPS Agreement on public health and on health policy has been even greater in developing countries. Nowhere are the drug-access problems associated with TRIPS more evident and more tragic than in the fight against the global HIV/AIDS pandemic. In his capacity as UN envoy, Lewis (2003) was a fierce critic of the restrictions imposed by the multilateral trading system on developing countries facing the HIV/AIDS crisis. The North-South health divide is starkly illustrated by the fact that, of the 40 million people worldwide living with the disease, 95 percent reside in the developing world. At the heart of the global AIDS challenge is improving access to medicines for people living with HIV/AIDS in poor countries. Despite years of debate and some concessions by pharmaceutical companies, access to treatment remains prohibitively expensive. The statistics on the gap between the North and South in access to treatment are astounding. In developed countries, the cost of one year's worth of treatment for HIV infection might correspond to the equivalent of four to six months' salary, with the majority of these costs being reimbursed by public or private health insurance programs. In the developing world, the cost of the same treatment would consume the equivalent of thirty years' income (Thomas 2002, 252).

The TRIPS Agreement has been a major obstacle to achieving improved access to HIV/AIDS treatment in developing countries. Rather than liberalize trade in pharmaceutical products to make them more accessible to developing-country patients, TRIPS has imposed "restrictive, US-style patent laws" on WTO member countries in order to protect the world's leading pharmaceutical companies in these markets, effectively creating product monopolies in the drug industry for the twenty-year duration of the TRIPS-mandated patent protection (Poku 2002, 124). Designed to safeguard the intellectual property rights of major drug companies, the TRIPS framework prohibits the production or import of much cheaper generic versions of anti-retroviral and other drugs for which these corporations hold patents. Despite provisions for parallel imports and compulsory licensing, the TRIPS Agreement strictures led in 2001 to the WTO's *Doha Declaration on the TRIPS Agreement and Public Health,* which stated that TRIPS does not and should not prevent WTO member states from taking measures to protect public health (Fidler 2004, 801). But even where the TRIPS framework allows countries facing public health emergencies to circumvent the normally severe patent rules and resort to buying or producing much cheaper copies of these drugs, the US and the EU have used their political and economic clout to prevent this from occurring. The problem is political, one of "the discrepancy between what is legal/permissible under WTO rules, and what is permissible/desirable under the terms of US trade policy" (Thomas 2002, 251). Bangladesh, Brazil, South Africa, and Thailand are among the best-known cases of countries that have come under pressure from the US and the EU to cease using the parallel imports or compulsory licensing mechanisms provided for under the WTO to acquire accessibly priced essential medicines for their citizens. As Thomas (*ibid.*, 258) concludes, "companies can and do pressure states and generic drug producers directly to persuade them to change their policies, even if they are acting in accordance with international law." This is an important reminder that, even where the robust legal instruments of the WTO appear on their face to favour the global South, they are insufficient to overcome North-South disparities in power and legal capacity. Though an integral part of the solution to global health problems, international law remains a tool at the disposition of the international system's dominant members and the domestic interests that dictate their policies.

In partnership with the world's leading pharmaceutical corporations, UNAIDS (the Joint United Nations Programme on HIV/AIDS) has implemented strategies for reducing the cost of drugs to poor AIDS-stricken countries, but the results so far have been disappointing. Many observers point to the structural conflict of interest that underlies this type of public-private partnership in health governance, a problem that is often aggravated by the exclusion of developing-country representatives from the negotiations of these arrangements. Moreover, under these hybrid forms of global health governance, patented drugs continue to be supported over cheaper alternatives. The pharmaceutical firms engaged in the process are still able to block or discourage the production of generic drugs by preventing such generic drug makers as the highly successful Indian manufacturer Cipla from entering these markets (Poku 2002, 124). The UNAIDS initiative "represents one of the clearest examples of the pharmaceutical companies' role in influencing the health governance agenda. It has deflected attention from the development of more sustainable solutions, regionally, nationally, or locally" (Thomas 2002, 261).

In response to the UNAIDS failure and the continuing crisis, Canada attempted to implement the WTO provisions allowing countries to circumvent patent law with domestic legislation. The *Jean Chrétien Pledge to Africa Act* of 2004, the first legislation of its kind in the world, amended the *Patent Act* to allow for the issuance of compulsory licences authorizing Canadian firms to manufacture specific patented pharmaceutical products, including HIV/AIDS, tuberculosis, and malaria drugs, for export to developing and least-developed countries that lack the capacity to produce the drugs themselves.[34] The legislation was enacted to implement a 2003 decision of the WTO General Council waiving certain TRIPS obligations and allowing developed countries to authorize someone other than the patent holder to manufacture a lower-cost version of a patented pharmaceutical product in order to export it to a developing country with insufficient or no pharmaceutical manufacturing capacity.[35]

The complexity of the legislation and the energy of Big Pharma have, however, robbed this law of its potential. Canadians can take little pride in it or in Canada's overall response to global HIV/AIDS, which has failed to address the crisis comprehensively by recognizing its roots in underdevelopment. As Lewis (2005, 33) points out, "the reality is that our initiatives on the pandemic are completely eclipsed by our failure on foreign aid," which continues to lag far behind the G8 goal of 0.7 percent of GDP.

As the cases of HIV/AIDS medicines and SARS illustrate, the international legal framework governing global health has simultaneously imposed heavy burdens on countries attempting to deal with their own health crises and proven itself too weak to muster effective international collaboration on problems of a global nature. In this way, it has some supraconstitutional effects on countries at the receiving end of its governance mechanisms, especially developing countries but also semi-peripheral developed countries such as Canada in the case of SARS. Yet its international governance architecture remains puny when compared to the global architecture for trade and investment that actually shapes and constrains domestic and global public health governance. While the most powerful states of the developed world continue to pursue their national interests through protectionism and promote neo-conservative restructuring of public health systems through multilateralism, "the South-North health divide continues to widen alarmingly," and the global vulnerability to transboundary health threats increases, affecting all states, both developed and developing (Aginam 2005, 14).

Global Governance and Human Security
The international community's failure to prevent a horrific genocide in Rwanda and in the former Yugoslavia changed the way we think about international security and, in particular, about post–Cold War international security

cooperation (McRae 2001a). These tragedies made it apparent that the traditional preoccupations of security specialists – mainly wars between states and nuclear proliferation – no longer presented the most deadly dangers to human safety or to international stability. The civil violence catastrophes of the 1990s following the end of the Cold War forced observers to recognize what had been true for a long time: namely that the threats that exact the greatest human cost – including famine, disease, and ethnic violence – are not necessarily the same threats that compromise conventional national security. In fact, the greatest harm often comes from within states, with the complicity of their governments. Though many of these threats had existed since the Second World War, they were often intensified by the processes of globalization and the changes associated with the end of the bipolar rivalry. It was in response to these realities that the notion of human security was developed in an attempt to conceptualize the myriad existing factors and new conditions compromising the safety of ordinary people (Paris 2001, 89). This redefinition of security was propelled by academics and members of civil society, as well as by national governments and international organizations (Wyn Jones 1999; Booth 2004). As it has evolved into a more accepted concept in international security cooperation, human security has also come to constitute a new facet of global governance.

The first and most authoritative articulation of the concept of human security appears in the UNPD's *Human Development Report 1994*, which refers to "safety from such chronic threats as hunger, disease, and repression, as well as protection from sudden and hurtful disruptions in the patterns of daily life" (United Nations Development Program 1994, 23). The report emphasizes seven main dimensions of human security: economic, food, health, environmental, personal, community, and political security, including the protection of human rights. Under this new doctrine, events previously excluded from the purview of security, such as famines, civil conflicts, and severe environmental degradation, were considered security problems because they imperil human beings, even though they do not necessarily compromise the survival of their state.

HUMAN SECURITY IN GLOBAL GOVERNANCE

Lloyd Axworthy (2004, 348), a leading champion of the idea of human security, summarized the transformation implied by this new focus on individuals instead of states:

Human security is establishing itself as a vital part of the international agenda, complementing more traditional notions of nation-based security and causing serious rethinking of many traditional precepts of statecraft. The shift of security concerns from those focused on national interests to those affecting the individual offers a different lens through which to understand and implement policy. It recognizes that in our interconnected world our own security is indivisible from that of our neighbours and that the basic rights of people – not merely the absence of military conflict between states – are fundamental to world stability.

The definition and content of human security remain contested. In its 2003 report, the Commission on Human Security linked "freedom from want, freedom from fear, and freedom to take action on one's own behalf" in an effort systematically to group the different components of human security, including the need to create "systems that give people the building blocks of survival, dignity, and livelihood" (Commission on Human Security 2003, 10).

Narrower interpretations of the concept focus exclusively on the protection of civilians in conflict zones. In the version espoused by the Canadian government during Axworthy's tenure as minister of foreign affairs, human security has three main aspects: conflict prevention, conflict resolution, and peace building. Conflict prevention involves many different strategies and operations such as mediation between potential combatants, preventive diplomacy, and early warning systems for countries at risk of conflict. Conflict resolution encompasses forms of international intervention in conflicts already occurring, which may include peacekeeping and other forms of military involvement. Peace building, which usually takes place at the conclusion of a conflict, aims to prevent a relapse into violence by supporting post-war elections and political institution building, as well as the reconstruction of schools, hospitals, and basic infrastructure. It may also involve transitional justice processes such as the prosecution of war criminals. Human security ceased to be a central pillar of Canadian foreign policy with the election of the Harper federal government. The concept hardly registers in the government's recent foreign policy pronouncements, although it persists in the Glyn Berry Program for Peace and Security, named after the Canadian diplomat killed in Afghanistan in 2006, which funds academic and other projects for the development of Canadian and international policies, laws, and institutions on human security.[36]

The breadth of the concept has made it an effective principle for mobilizing diverse civil society organizations, which have rallied around it in a number of transnationally networked campaigns (Hampson 2004, 349-50; Owen 2004, 373-76). Academics and policy makers have tended to be more skeptical about its value (Newman 2001, 242-47; Paris 2001, 89-93; 2004, 370-71). Critics consider human security too broad, a laundry list of problems in no particular order of priority that offers little guidance to policy makers or researchers. Advocates defend the breadth of the concept, arguing that security should be understood as an inherently holistic idea, one that need not be directly associated with violent conflict (Uvin 2004, 352; see also the discussion of critical security studies in Booth 2004).

HUMAN SECURITY, GOVERNANCE, AND THE NEW DIPLOMACY

McRae (2001a) argues that the paradigm shift placing human security at the centre of global agendas brings with it a need to find new forms of governance and diplomacy, because most existing international arrangements and organizations reflect processes that are largely intergovernmental and consensus based. He contends that "the norms embedded in the human security agenda, as with the norms encapsulated by human rights, implicitly limit state sovereignty by asserting that no state has the right to shield itself from international obligations to protect civilians in times of war" (ibid., 253-54). Because many states do not accept this principle or its implications, progress toward its realization in such global intergovernmental forums as the UN is difficult. The resulting "multilateral gridlock" in traditional forums encourages states interested in advancing the human security agenda to seek out alternative forums. McRae concludes, rather optimistically, that "this ad hoc approach may be temporary, symptomatic of a period of transition, and disappear altogether once the normative shift is more pervasive, and the Copernican Revolution in international relations complete" (ibid.).

Although there is little evidence that such a revolution is happening, international policy approaches to human security are converging around a consensus on which the UN secretary-general, many national governments, and a growing community of academics agree (Owen 2004, 373-87; Hubert 2004, 351). The most important of these is the downward shift of security policies to include the individual. The human security paradigm assumes that individuals' safety is the key to global security because, when individual safety is threatened, so too is international security (Hampson 2004, 350). There is also a shared recognition that globalization and the changing nature of armed conflict are creating new vulnerabilities, such as those related to the regional trade in small arms and large cross-border flows of persons displaced by war. Moreover, though the outer limits of the concept remain muddled, fundamental agreement exists among policy makers "that ensuring safety from violence is an integral part of the agenda" (Hubert 2004, 351). More controversial is the belief that human security requires a rethinking of sovereignty. The human security doctrine has evolved on this last dimension in part because intrastate threats to individual security can spill over borders and menace international security.

State sovereignty is being doubly qualified in the security sphere, where it had appeared the most likely to retain its traditional connotations. For one thing, a human security approach creates an imperative for increased international cooperation and governance since the multi-faceted problems of human security tend to be transnational in nature and are often caused or exacerbated by processes of global economic and cultural integration (McRae 2001b, 18). This dark side of globalization includes the growth of the illicit trade in small arms, narcotics, and conflict diamonds; the rise in human trafficking; international terrorism; and threats to cultural and linguistic identities stemming from the rapidly expanding global flow of cultural products. The transboundary nature of these threats to human security is such that "global institutions have a critical role to play in the process [of protecting human security], because local and even regional instruments are frequently not up to the task" (Hampson 2004, 350). A case in point is the danger to human security posed by land mines, to which a lasting solution could be found only through an international ban on states' production and use of these devices (Gwodecky and Sinclair 2001, 28-40).

A second way in which the concept of human security qualifies traditional conceptions of sovereignty is by forcing us to look at threats to individual security that originate within state borders and thereby challenge the traditional monopoly of the state over security matters in its territory. The strongest expression of this view of human security is found in *Responsibility to Protect*, a report by the Canadian-sponsored International Commission on Intervention and State Sovereignty (2001). The commission argued that, when states are unable or unwilling to address such large-scale threats to human security within their borders as ethnic cleansing or genocide, the international community has a responsibility to intervene on humanitarian grounds.

Though there are some signs that this component of the human security doctrine is gaining international acceptance, it remains controversial (Hubert 2004, 351-52).

CANADA AND HUMAN SECURITY

Canada has contributed substantially to the promotion of the human security doctrine, particularly from 1995 to 2000, while Lloyd Axworthy served as minister of foreign affairs and advocated incorporation of human security considerations into Canadian and multilateral security policies in partnership with concerned civil society actors (Axworthy 2004, 349). Canadians led the effort to address the danger to human security posed by land mines. Using the language of human security, Canadian NGOs and policy makers joined their international counterparts in a coalition to build public and political support for the ban through media and other international campaigns. These efforts were part of a complex multi-track process, involving national governments, the UN, and civil society channels, which culminated in the negotiation of the Ottawa Convention banning land mines.[37] The unprecedented speed and success of the convention was made possible by "the dynamic mix of public conscience, new actors, new partnerships, new negotiating methods, and a new approach to building security – making the safety of people a central focus of international attention and action" (Gwodecky and Sinclair 2001, 29). The convention was the first major accomplishment of Canada's human security agenda (McBride 2005, 138). The successful negotiation and ratification of the ban in a relatively short period of time proved that the human security doctrine could effectively propel international action by superimposing its conceptual framework over what had traditionally been seen as an arms-control and disarmament issue. The Ottawa process exemplified a new bottom-up approach to establishing norms of international conduct and enshrining them in international legal instruments, a participatory course widely seen as a valuable complement to traditional multilateral diplomacy. The land mines ban illustrated how ordinary Canadian citizens and civil society organizations are not only objects of, but can also be active subjects participating in, the development of new forms of global governance.

Among the most important of Canada's contributions to the promotion of the human security doctrine has been its initiative in establishing the International Criminal Court (ICC). Under Axworthy's leadership, Canada mobilized a coalition of countries to address the problem of war criminals' impunity, building international support for the negotiation of the *Rome*

Statute of the International Criminal Court, the multilateral agreement establishing the ICC.[38] When the statute came into effect in 2002, it gave force to several UN conventions prohibiting crimes against humanity, war crimes, and genocide. In the past, ensuring state compliance with these agreements was difficult because they lacked international judicial mechanisms and allowed states to invoke their sovereignty to evade their obligations. Since its establishment, the ICC has begun to address these issues (Bickerton and Tait 2006).

Capitalizing on the successes of the Ottawa Convention and the ICC, Canada took the human security agenda a step further by joining Norway in 1998 to establish the Human Security Network, a grouping of like-minded states and NGOs that maintained a dialogue on questions pertaining to human security and was the first international institution outside the UN system to make human security central to its work (Small 2001, 232).[39] Since then, the Canadian government developed the Human Security Program within Foreign Affairs Canada (now the Glyn Berry Program, as noted above) and established the Canadian Consortium on Human Security (CCHS), an academic network promoting research on human security.[40] Though these agencies and institutions have been poorly funded, and it is difficult to ascertain what they can achieve practically, they helped raise the profile of human security in Canadian foreign policy and brought the doctrine greater international visibility. Though Canada's achievements in this area are significant, they have been criticized for taking too narrow an approach. According to McBride (2005, 138), "Canada chose quite specifically to focus on the protection of civilians in conflict, to the exclusion of such considerations as 'economic security, food security, health security, environmental security' – each considered a vital part of human security by the UNDP."

Canada's later position on human security shows the intrusion of neoconservative economic values into an area traditionally viewed in humanitarian terms. This narrow conception of human security provides the Canadian government with an excuse for evading such fundamental issues as the role of Canadian corporations in the developing world. Ottawa's unwillingness to prevent Canadian companies from investing in conflict zones or in countries with questionable human rights records is at odds with promoting the doctrine of human security. The most egregious examples of this contradiction are found in Ottawa's reluctance to take any legal steps to stop the Canadian firms Petro-Canada and Ivanhoe Mines from investing in Myanmar and making payments to the country's government, despite the fact that

Canada, the European Union, and the United States, among others, had placed sanctions against Myanmar for its massive human rights violations. An even more striking example of Canada's selective adherence to the human security doctrine, even narrowly defined, was the government's failure to take action against the Canadian firm Talisman Energy for doing business in Sudan, despite substantial evidence that the firm's dealings were lending support to the Sudanese government, which was engaged in a brutal war against part of its own population. In striking a balance between the interests of corporations and the concerns of the constituency advocating support for human security in Sudan, Ottawa opted to favour the interests of capital. The declared foreign policy priority of promoting human security "was sacrificed on the altar of private sector profit and the imperatives of a global capitalist economy" (Matthews 2004, 245).

As Canada's failure to address corporate complicity in human security violations suggests, the weak political will of national governments remains a major obstacle to effective interstate cooperation in the promotion of human security. Though the new doctrine remains imperfectly practised, it may nevertheless substantially contribute to the development of global mechanisms for addressing basic human and social vulnerabilities. One important way in which this lens can improve global governance is by bringing to light the ways in which existing international structures actually affect ordinary people around the world. We do not understand how a plethora of international agreements interact and together have an impact on specific countries, including vulnerable communities and individuals. The concept of human security allows us to "focus on the actual impact of these intergovernmental agreements, where the individual is the nexus of competing and sometimes conflicting international and national laws and treaties, or even policies (the IMF or World Bank strictures)" (McRae 2001b, 19). A human security approach draws attention to the previously ignored and unintended effects on people's lives of this network of national and international instruments and can therefore help guide the development of new international instruments.

More importantly for the future of global governance, the human security doctrine has shown remarkable capacity for mobilizing civil society across borders and has been a valuable tool for civil society activists (Paris 2004, 370). Although NGOs and other civil society actors have played an important role in advancing the human security agenda, it has in turn also enabled and sustained a new form of international advocacy, which might herald the emergence of global civil society. As the process of negotiating the Ottawa Convention on land mines illustrated, this new form of global, bottom-up engagement is "what seems to be energizing the new multilateralism, a multilateralism that brings together states, international organizations, non-governmental organizations, and individuals in radically new combinations" (McRae 2001b, 20). These views are shared by others who believe in the potential for human security principles to mobilize civil society involvement in global governance (Axworthy 2004, 348-49). Human security, therefore, represents an area in which Canadians can be creators rather than merely receivers of global governance, using these new arrangements to advance international causes that resonate with their personal and political values.

GLOBAL GOVERNANCE, CULTURAL DIVERSITY, AND HUMAN CULTURAL SECURITY

As it is used in everyday language and discussions of globalization, the term "culture" has two distinct meanings. The first, which is social-scientific, refers to the whole complex of knowledge, beliefs, attitudes, and practices that is embodied in society and in its social, political, and economic arrangements. Also included in this broad conception of culture are "the customary beliefs, social forms, and material traits of a racial, religious, or social group" (Mani 2001, 3). A second connotation of culture has to do with creative agency and refers to cultural representations in communities or societies such as the creative arts, literature, media, and other such expressions that reflect and develop its values. Although they are distinct, these two dimensions of culture are related.

There is growing concern that the forces of globalization are having significant impacts on local and national cultures, understood in both the broad and narrow senses. These effects are often felt most acutely by such marginalized cultural groups as indigenous peoples. Protected by the international rules governing intellectual property, inflows of foreign investment may rob these vulnerable communities of their traditional knowledge. In some countries, indigenous knowledge, particularly related to agricultural practices or medicinal plants, has been appropriated without payment by foreign scientists or pharmaceutical firms claiming the authority of TRIPS' intellectual property rights.

Foreign news broadcasts, global entertainment industries, and even the Internet are experienced as threats to local culture and identity in many places. The effect of transnational information flows is felt most sharply on local languages. For example, in the People's Democratic Republic of Lao, the influence of Thai television in urban centres has led to the replacement of certain Lao words with their Thai equivalents. In many places across the South, global entertainment is criticized for influencing youth to adopt certain undesirable elements of Western culture. The importation of ideas about freedom of speech, democracy, and universal human rights – often associated with a tradition of liberal individualism – can be seen in its host environments as an imposition of alien values, triggering resentment against cultural imperialism. The introduction of an American-style culture of fast food, fashion, music, movies, cars, computer games, iPods, and other electronic gadgets, with their consumerist and individualistic implications, can have a corrosive effect on local cultures, diets, health, and social cohesion. Reversion to fundamentalism and ethnocentricity is an extreme manifestation of the reaction to adapt foreign values that are in sharp contrast to local ones (Mani 2001, 4). These adverse consequences of the information diffusion and trade associated with globalization have come to be understood as "cultural insecurity," which is generated by the reduction of diverse cultures to monocultures. In this process, local cultural expressions, identity, and value systems that preserve social and cultural capital – including indigenous knowledge systems – are undermined.

Cultural insecurity has direct links to political violence. From terrorism in Northern Ireland to ethnic cleansing in the former Yugoslavia, from the civil war in Sri Lanka to the genocide in the Great Lakes region of Africa, cases abound of conflict over the place of language, religion, or other aspects of culture in a society. Mani explains the link: when "ethnic groups experience the repression of their culture and/or exclusion from political debate or development initiatives, they may resort to violence in the form of subnational conflict, terrorism, and increasing crime" (ibid.). Ethnic conflicts are often fought because groups whose ethnicity or religious practices differ from those of the dominant majority have been sidelined in the political debate or have had to sacrifice their native languages for that of the dominant group. For example, the push for Bangladesh's political independence, which was ultimately achieved in 1972 after a bloody civil war, began with organized demands for the reinstatement of Bengali as the principal language in East Pakistan. For some groups, the experience of cultural insecurity leads to demands for their own culturally homogeneous state or self-governing region. Other groups seek protection and promotion of cultural diversity within existing political formations.

Though often occurring within states, these forms of ethnic or cultural conflict can have wide-ranging international security repercussions, from refugee flows into neighbouring states to (purportedly) humanitarian interventions. For these reasons, the imperative to protect local and national cultures has taken on an international security dimension. The obvious threats to civilian safety posed by ethnic conflict and the important place of cultural processes in peace-building efforts have placed cultural security on the human security agenda (Leaning 2004; Rubinstein 2005).

Cultural issues are also taking on a new importance in international affairs with the rise of "cultural diplomacy" as part of a reinvigorated foreign policy practice of "public diplomacy," or diplomatic outreach to audiences in foreign countries (Steger 2005, 229-30). In keeping with its domestic cultural policies of bilingualism and multiculturalism, Canada has made the promotion of "Canadian values" abroad a minor pillar of its foreign policy (Belanger 1999, 677), a commitment that was rhetorically reaffirmed by the Harper Conservative government, although the values it endorsed were more militaristic than peaceful. Canadian academics and civil society have also pushed for the introduction of cultural security considerations into Canadian foreign policy. Many other countries have recognized the economic and political value of promoting their national artists to foreign publics, both as a means of extending their "soft power" influence and because of the tremendous commercial opportunities associated with the rise of the global entertainment industry. These growing types of governmental and private activities in the cultural domain have converged to make culture an important new focus of global governance.

Most efforts at international governance on the cultural front have taken place within the UN system. The international community's role in the conservation of culture is acknowledged in the 1966 ICESCR and in such agreements of the UN Educational, Scientific and Cultural Organization (UNESCO) as the 2003 *Convention for the Safeguarding of Intangible Cultural Heritage*.[41] Canada was the instigator of the most important international instrument addressing cultural security to date, the *Convention on the Protection and Promotion of the Diversity of Cultural Expressions*.[42] Approved by UNESCO in October 2005, this convention affirms the right of all countries to defend their own distinct cultures, particularly through the electronic media and artistic expression. The convention defines cultural diversity as "the manifold ways in which the cultures of groups and societies find expression," and it reaffirms the sovereign right of states to "maintain, adopt and implement policies and

measures that they deem appropriate for the protection and promotion of
the diversity of cultural expressions on their territory" while respecting human
rights and fundamental freedoms.[43] The convention received broad support:
148 countries voted in favour, though the United States and Israel voted
against it, and 4 other countries abstained. Having led the negotiating process
in the face of US opposition, Canada was the first country to ratify the convention, which entered into force in March 2007.

Canada played an important role both in initiating and supporting the
process that led to the 2005 UNESCO agreement, leaning on its international partners in the International Network on Cultural Policy, la Francophonie,
and the Organization of American States. France also pushed strongly for the
affirmation of cultural sovereignty in the face of the threats of American
cultural domination, which, though not specifically identified in the document, is cited by most analysts as a key reason for the development of this
convention. Though too little time has elapsed to tell what concrete results
the convention will achieve, it represents an important step in extending
international legal norms and the global governance framework to include
the goal of safeguarding cultural diversity. This is reflected in the EU statement
that the convention fills a "legal vacuum" in world governance by establishing rights and obligations aimed at maintaining and developing cultural
diversity (European Commission 2005). According to this view, the new
instrument will serve as "a platform for debates and exchanges on cultural
diversity at the international level: it will allow the reality of cultural diversity in the world to be observed and closely monitored, and opinions, information, and best practices to be exchanged between the parties. It will also
be possible for the parties to coordinate and consult each other to promote
the Convention's objectives in the other international bodies and to strength-
en international cooperation" (*ibid.*, 2).

Undoubtedly important as these functions are, the UNESCO convention's
greatest significance lies in its potential to shield the cultural sphere from the
full impact of the WTO's powerful economic rules, which have facilitated the
global trade in cultural products at the cost of threatening to force the dismantling of national cultural programs in many countries. For now, the
convention's relationship to the trade liberalization rule book remains ambiguous. The new agreement's provision dealing with this issue, Article 20,
leaves unanswered the question of how the convention's provisions for the
protection of cultural industries would relate to existing WTO rules. International observers remain divided on this issue. Some, such as former WTO

official Joost Pauwelyn (2005), claim that the treaty "explicitly permit[s] the protection of cultural industries." The EU, on the other hand, maintains that the convention does not substantially modify existing WTO commitments by excluding cultural products. Rather, it merely requires parties "to consider the objectives of cultural diversity and the terms of the Convention when applying and interpreting their trade obligations, as well as negotiating their trade commitments" (European Commission 2005). Others hope that the new agreement will help change the WTO's treatment of cultural products by placing cultural diversity on the agenda in new rounds of negotiations. Though welcoming the convention, civil society actors concerned with cultural diversity have not been optimistic about its potential, pointing out its lack of clout in dispute resolution.

The UNESCO convention is binding only upon those countries that are parties to it. Because the US has not joined the convention, Canada would not be able to invoke its provisions to protect the Canadian magazine industry from a tide of American imports, as it tried to do when American *Sports Illustrated Canada* entered the Canadian market (Pauwelyn 2005). Yet the possibility does exist that the convention could play a role in the outcome of disputes involving non-parties such as the US and Israel. The WTO Appellate Body has made reference to outside treaties that were not ratified by all parties to a trade dispute, applying WTO rules "in the light of the contemporary concerns of the community of nations."[44] It could be argued that agreement by 148 countries on the need for and ways to protect cultural diversity amounts to an expression of such a contemporary concern of the community of nations. Even so, such multilateral treaties – whether cultural, environmental, or on some other subject – are only aids to interpret WTO rules. They will not excuse measures that are inconsistent with those rules when a trade dispute is brought by a state that is not also a party to the multilateral agreement, except in very rare cases such as where the offending country has exhausted efforts to get the complaining country to join the multilateral regime. Ultimately, because of the WTO's unusually powerful enforcement mechanism, the practical effects of non-WTO legal instruments designed to address social and cultural concerns depend entirely on the willingness of WTO panels to take these agreements into consideration in their rulings.

A NEW PRINCIPLE: HUMAN CULTURAL SECURITY

The two concepts of culture as artistic expression and as social structure have an important part to play in developing the principle of human security and in realizing its concrete goals. The principle needs to be refined with an emphasis on its social and cultural aspects, because it represents more than a condition of protected individual rights and is not restricted to alleviating individuals' fear of violence or fear of hunger. Individuals can be secure only if the communities with which they identify are secure. The quest for human security must take into account the socially embedded nature of individual citizens' security and recognize that, in order to feel genuinely secure, they require a social and cultural setting that allows them to partake fully in the social-relational aspects of human life. Human cultural security is therefore an approach that looks beyond merely securing individuals' freedom from fear for their personal physical and economic safety toward such objectives as protecting the social institutions, religious practices, languages, and cultural expressions of their communities. This conception is consistent with a view of human security proposed by those who argue that it must include not only basic material security but that "individuals must also be able to support basic psychological needs for identity, recognition, participation, and autonomy" (Leaning 2004, 354). It also builds upon recent anthropological work in security studies, which shows that feeling safe is an inherently contextual and cultural experience (Bubandt 2005).

The concept of human cultural security represents a reaffirmation of the principle of sovereignty as a means to provide people the safety to live securely within their own value systems and to guard a society's general well-being. In the same spirit, human cultural security encompasses the principles of non-interference and self-determination embodied in the UN Charter and reaffirmed in the *Responsibility to Protect* report (International Commission on Intervention and State Sovereignty 2001). Far from a restatement of cultural relativism or of absolute state sovereignty, human cultural security is grounded in a philosophy of universal human rights and freedoms, such that it recognizes the importance of protecting the autonomy of a culture up to the point that individual security is threatened.

The preservation of human cultural security can serve as a guiding principle for the conduct of culturally sensitive and locally responsive international humanitarian intervention. For instance, incorporating the promotion of human cultural security in peace-building missions in post-conflict societies would recognize that imposing westernized values on societies with different cultures may violate their human security and help ensure that post-conflict institution-building processes respect and permit the promotion of cultural diversity. Building human cultural security priorities into humanitarian intervention could also help turn our attention to the root causes of conflicts, such as the suppression of linguistic rights. Such an approach to human security would allow us to see peace building as a process of breaking down a culture of incitement to hate and building up a culture of reconciliation that is sensitive to local community. In many cases, integrating cultural considerations into peace building in a more meaningful way could also help bring greater legitimacy to foreign intervention (Rubinstein 2005, 528).

The doctrine of human cultural security also suggests some practical means of promoting the reconstruction and development of wartorn societies. Understanding culture as creative agency, we can look to the role of such artistic representations as musical performance and popular theatre in rebuilding the social fabric and social capital of communities emerging from conflict. For instance, Canada has supported music and art therapy programs for children in Kosovo. In Cambodia, victims of violence have used weapons collected in disarmament programs to produce sculptures that have been exhibited around the world (De Beer 2004). Such programs can help address the psycho-social consequences of war and promote ethnic reconciliation while also providing participants with new sources of income.

A human cultural security approach can also help in the prevention of conflict. For example, indicators of cultural repression, which can take the form of bans on performances or the incarceration of artists and religious leaders, could be built into early warning systems for detecting societies at risk of civil conflict. In short, a cultural approach to human security reveals the many ways in which cultural actors – musicians, dancers, sculptors, and poets – can contribute to communitarian and holistic peace building.

From the environment to public health to human cultural security, an increasingly wide and thick fabric of international governance is being woven over and through the webbing of national governance. The volume, depth, and complexity of supranational institutions and norms for the environment, public health, human security, human rights, labour, and other "social" dimensions of public policy have grown at a frenetic pace. They cover a wide range from soft-law to hard-law arrangements, and from informal networks to formal bricks-and-mortar organizations with flags, insignia, and permanent staffs. A few even boast robust adjudicative and enforcement institutions, such as the International Tribunal for the Law of the Sea and the International Criminal Court. To a first approximation, however, they do not form part of the ensemble of fundamental norms and institutionalized practices by which Canadian society is governed. They do not in general impose effective constraints on the decision-making powers of Canadian governments. They lack vigorous enforcement mechanisms, do not have direct effect in the Canadian legal system, and do not enjoy effective primacy over domestic norms and institutions. Canadian governments have observed or ignored their rules and decisions largely as they pleased. These norms and institutions have not, in short, achieved supraconstitutional status in the Canadian legal and political order.

This is not to say that they are inconsequential. In many cases, Canadian governments routinely accept and implement the decisions of these international institutions as beneficial for Canadian interests. This is especially true in technical areas where international coordination is desired by member states, such as civil aviation (the International Civil Aviation Organization), maritime commerce (the International Maritime Organization), telecommunications (the International Telecommunications Union), and food safety (the Codex Alimentarius Commission). Canadian governments not only participate in these domains of regulatory harmonization, but they also, perhaps more than most, go to considerable lengths to appear to respect international norms and obligations. They are much more likely to seek to justify their actions as consistent with applicable international law than to flout it openly. Engagement in this constant and iterative discourse of justification may have some effects in terms of how officials and citizens understand their identities and perform their roles as actors in international affairs, but it would be a mistake to attribute too much significance to it.

To take the measure of supranational social and environmental governance, it is useful to compare it directly with the economic supraconstitution. We now turn to a closer examination of the relationship between the supranational governance of the environment, public health, and human security and Canada's economic supraconstitution.

5
Taking the Measure of the Supraconstitution

Having examined developments in trade and investment, environment, public health, and human security in the last two chapters, we now contrast Canada's negligible social and environmental supraconstitution with its substantial and intrusive economic counterpart. The relationship between the two is – not surprisingly – asymmetrical, with international social and environmental governance playing a subordinate role in relation to the international trade and investment regime. Where social and environmental norms conflict with economic ones, the latter tend to have the upper hand. Often, however, supranational social and environmental governance is not in tension with economic governance but facilitates and supports it. International technical norms for product safety, information security, and consumer health, for example, tend to prevail despite the absence of rigorous enforcement ability because they do what Salter (1993-94) calls "the housework of capitalism": the everyday task of harmonizing norms for production and consumption. Like housework, the chore of setting these standards is "detailed, mundane, repetitive, and never completed" while "both essential and unrecognized in the constitution and reproduction of economic and class relationships" (*ibid.*, 107; Ewald 1990, 152). It is inconspicuous, occurring almost entirely out of the public eye in little-known international standards-setting bodies. It purports to tidy up production and exchange, imposing a modicum of homogeneity and predictability on the messiness of the market and facilitating the efficient running of the economy, just as housework tidies the home and facilitates the efficient running of the household (Wood 2005, 276). These international health and safety norms perform an indispensable but largely invisible supporting role in the economic supraconstitution and are structurally linked to the international trade and investment regime via the WTO's *Agreement on the Application of Sanitary and Phytosanitary Measures* and *Technical Barriers to Trade Agreement*, which elevate international technical standards to the status of international trade disciplines (Wood 2002-03, 171-72).

In this chapter, we explore two of the most prominent aspects of the conflict between the economic supraconstitution and global social and environmental governance. First, we consider the distinction between "hard" and "soft" law. Second, we explore the relationship between international trade liberalization and environmental protection in the context of global (WTO) and continental (NAFTA) trade regimes. We close this discussion with some reflections on the implications of the "perilous imbalance" we have examined in this part of the book.

Hard versus Soft Law

Traditionally, global governance regimes have been built on the foundation of international law, to which states were bound by their formal consent, whether by international treaties or by custom. Binding international legal instruments have the status of hard, formally authorized, codified law and regulation comparable in form to that which exists at the domestic level within nation-states (Kirton and Trebilcock 2004, 8). These hard-law instruments include the UN Charter, UN Security Council resolutions, international treaties and protocols, and decisions adopted by some international organizations or treaty organs. Increasingly, international actors are building new kinds of non-binding rules (Arts 2006, 177-82, 192-96; Koenig-Archibugi 2006, 1-3). This "soft law" has some of the characteristics of traditional international law but lacks its formal legally binding character and depends on voluntary forms of compliance (Kirton and Trebilcock 2004, 4, 8-9). Soft-law instruments consist primarily of voluntary standards and "the informal institutions at the international, transnational, and national levels that depend on the voluntarily supplied participation, resources, and consensual actions of their members, rather than on the formally mandated participation and regularly assessed obligatory contributions, organization, resources, and sanctions of the institution itself" (*ibid.*, 8-9). Soft-law instruments include UN General Assembly resolutions, declarations of international conferences, and many other policies and guidelines issued by international organizations. Though these mechanisms lack the enforcement component of hard-law arrangements, they may nevertheless induce compliance through other processes, such as the socialization of actors into their norms and the self-reinforcing quality of their institutions.

The hard-law soft-law distinction is at the heart of many of the central economic, environmental, and social issues of the day. The discussions about a successor to the Kyoto Protocol revolve around whether voluntary non-binding approaches or hard-binding commitments with precise targets and timetables are needed to combat climate change. Debates over genetically modified organisms revolve around whether voluntary standard setting and labelling are sufficient or whether mandatory national or regional regulation is warranted. In the global fight against infectious diseases, the policy issue centres on the choice between informal public-private partnerships and formal intergovernmental rules backed by sanctions (*ibid.*, 6).

Although hard- and soft-law approaches are found throughout the economic, social, and environmental domains of international governance, hard law plays a larger and more central role in the first. Many of the key norms and institutions of international trade and investment regimes have the binding force of hard law, which is one reason they have acquired supraconstitutional status. By contrast, hard law plays a much more limited role in social and environmental governance. Although some of the core arrangements of international social and environmental governance involve hard-law instruments such as human rights and environmental treaties, governance arrangements in social and environmental areas tend to be developed around soft-law instruments such as the Stockholm and Rio Declarations or the Millennium Development Goals. Even the hard-law instruments in these fields tend to lack robust monitoring, adjudication, and enforcement institutions.

In these domains, a patchwork of norms, principles, rules, decision-making procedures, and institutions comprising elements of both soft and hard law is evolving into a more integrated "tableau of global governance" that encompasses social, environmental, health, cultural, and other types of transnational activity (Kirton and Trebilcock 2004, 12). In building this new global order, international actors have employed a variety of instruments and arrangements, sometimes complementing and other times offsetting the influence of international trade law in global governance. Complementing the international trade and investment framework are initiatives such as the UN Global Compact and the *OECD Guidelines for Multinational Enterprises* (Organisation for Economic Co-operation and Development 2000), which provide voluntary guidelines for socially responsible corporate behaviour.[1] The compact and guidelines are intended to supplement rather than supersede international trade rules, which are largely silent on the ethical aspects of firms' conduct. The 2005 UNESCO *Convention on the Protection and Promotion of the Diversity of Cultural Expressions*, on the other hand, is a binding instrument that has been seen as potentially offsetting the WTO trade rules by sheltering print media, film, recorded music, and other cultural goods from its dominion (Pauwelyn 2005).[2]

The hard- and soft-law contrast is especially evident when we consider rights and obligations attaching directly to transnational capital. Individual firms or investors are not usually considered subjects of international law in their own right, but the emerging economic supraconstitution confers international rights directly upon foreign investors, who can sue host-state governments thanks to the investor-state dispute provisions of NAFTA and bilateral investment treaties (BITs). Recognizing individual rights is nothing new in international law. After all, individual human rights have been enshrined in numerous hard-law international instruments, from the 1966 *International Covenant on Civil and Political Rights* to the 1989 *Convention on the Rights of the Child*.[3] Like international investment rules, many human rights instruments give aggrieved individuals the right to bring complaints against national governments before international committees or tribunals. But unlike those associated with international investment rules, their adjudicative and enforcement mechanisms are toothless because the governments of both developed and developing countries have steadfastly resisted efforts to be held accountable for human rights violations or to give international human rights decisions direct effect in their legal systems. The main exception is the European *Convention for the Protection of Human Rights* and the rulings of its European Court of Human Rights, which have direct effect in the legal orders of member states and which have contributed in a substantial way to the establishment of a European supraconstitution in the social domain.[4] The remedies available to aggrieved investors under international trade and investment agreements, by contrast, are vigorous and effective.

The international rights and remedies afforded to transnational capital, whether via individual investors' rights or state-to-state trade disputes, tend to be hard and binding. On the other hand, the international obligations of transnational capital to respect or promote human rights, environmental protection, public health, workers' rights, and social development are almost all soft and voluntary. To the extent these matters are the subject of hard obligations, those obligations are borne by states, not by capital, and even then they tend to lack hard enforcement mechanisms. In this way, soft law can function as a safety valve for transnational capital, diffusing demands for regulation and accountability without imposing hard discipline on corporate conduct or capital flows. Soft social and environmental obligations thus play a crucial legitimating role for the neo-conservative supraconstitution, dissipating pressure for tougher social and environmental discipline on transnational business. In this light, it makes sense that the rights of transnational capital are protected by hard legal disciplines, whereas its obligations take the form of soft law.[5]

In short, global governance remains unbalanced, with international trade and investment the preserve of the most powerful, formal, and coherently integrated legal protections, whereas social, cultural, and environmental interests enjoy only weak protection. We now explore this imbalance further by taking on the familiar trade-environment debate at the level of multilateral regimes and then of North American continental governance.

Trade and Environment

MULTILATERAL ENVIRONMENTAL AGREEMENTS AND GLOBAL TRADE RULES

International environmental law has important trade implications, and international trade law has major environmental consequences. Though the areas of overlap between them are growing, these two bodies of law continue to differ dramatically in the degrees of compliance they inspire and in their effectiveness. About one-tenth of MEAs incorporate "restraints on the trade of particular substances or products, either between parties to the treaty and/or between parties and non-parties" (Brack 1998, 13; United Nations Environment Programme, and International Institute for Sustainable Development 2005, 14). Proportionally speaking, this number is small, but it includes some of the most important environmental agreements, such as the 1973 *Convention on International Trade in Endangered Species of Wild Fauna and Flora* (CITES), the 1987 *Montreal Protocol on Substances That Deplete the Ozone Layer*, the 1989 *Basel Convention on the Control of Transboundary Movements of Hazardous Wastes and Their Disposal* (Basel Convention), and the 2000 *Cartagena Protocol on Biosafety*. The WTO has also incorporated environmental language into its rhetoric, largely in response to public demands within its member states. Although the slogan of the 1990s was about making trade promotion and environmental protection mutually supportive, recent developments in the governance systems of both areas make it clear that they are often in tension.

Environmental lawyers often look longingly at the robust structures of the multilateral trading system and hope to see the global environmental regime develop in a similar manner. Some have tried to use the WTO framework to pursue environmental goals, but their attempts have met with little success. For instance, at the 2001 meeting to launch the Doha Development Agenda, environmental considerations were incorporated in the WTO mandate for a new round of trade negotiations. But these environmental commitments "remained partial, applied to a particular negotiation with an uncertain outcome rather than to the WTO's overall mandate and *modus operandi*, [dependent] on the overriding value ascribed to economic development and largely divorced from social concerns" (Kirton and Trebilcock 2004, 3). The subsequent failure of the Doha Round at Cancún "further eroded confidence that any swift solutions will come from within the WTO" (*ibid.*, 4). The future of global environmental protection therefore depends not on reforming the WTO to address environmental problems but on reinforcing the effectiveness of MEAs.

The WTO's objective of facilitating trade has been a major obstacle to effective environmental policy making at both the national and international levels because its trade rules have been invoked to prevent nation-states from using trade-related measures to address environmental problems of a global nature. Many states, including the United States, have sought to protect endangered environments or species by putting restrictions on the way in which products are harvested or made, such as the use of chlorine in paper manufacturing, the use of chemical pesticides in food production, the use of drift nets in high seas fishing, or the capture of dolphins in tuna fishing. These restrictions on processes and production methods (PPMs) become problematic when applied to goods in international trade, because trade law prohibits a state from discriminating between "like products" from other countries. Environmentally motivated trade restrictions based on PPMs have been invalidated under international trade rules, even when made by the WTO's most powerful members. An early example was the *Tuna-Dolphin* case, in which a GATT dispute resolution panel ruled that American measures designed to protect endangered dolphins from capture by tuna fishers outside US borders was an undue restriction on trade (Schoenbaum 1998, 36).[6] It rejected the United States' contention that the measures were permissible under Article XX of the GATT, which allows for exceptions to trade rules if the impugned measures are "necessary to protect human, animal, or plant life or health" or relate "to the conservation of exhaustible natural resources if such measures are made effective in conjunction with restrictions on domestic production or consumption."[7] The panel ruled that the norms and values enshrined in MEAs were irrelevant to the interpretation of trade agreements.

More recent WTO decisions have been more sympathetic to national and international environmental law. In the *Shrimp-Turtle* case, the WTO Appellate Body first struck down but later upheld an American law prohibiting imports of shrimp from countries that did not have measures similar to those imposed by the US on its own fishing fleet to prevent the inadvertent killing of sea turtles in shrimp nets.[8] When the dispute first came before it, the appellate body held that the US measures violated the GATT. It rejected the inward-looking approach of earlier decisions and held that WTO obligations must be interpreted in light of international law more broadly, including the principle of sustainable development that was included in the 1994 WTO Agreement. Determining from existing MEAs that "exhaustible natural resources" include living resources such as turtles, it held that the American law fell within the Article XX(g) exception for natural resource conservation. Nevertheless, the appellate body invalidated the US measure under the so-called chapeau (or opening language) of Article XX, which requires that exceptions not be "applied in a manner which would constitute a means of arbitrary or unjustifiable discrimination between countries where the same conditions prevail, or a disguised restriction on international trade."[9]

It found that the US had committed arbitrary and unjustifiable discrimination by requiring the use of a specific technology (the "turtle excluder device" or TED), giving the complaining countries less time to comply than other countries, rejecting shrimp from certain countries even if it was caught using TEDs, failing to take into account the cost of TEDs in developing countries, treating the complaining countries less favourably than other countries (in the Caribbean and Western Atlantic region) with whom it had negotiated a multilateral sea turtle conservation agreement, and failing to seek a similar multilateral agreement with the complaining countries.[10]

Rather than suspending or repealing the offending measure to comply with the decision, the United States kept it in place, made it a bit more flexible, and put intense pressure on the complaining countries to negotiate a multilateral sea turtle protection agreement with it. Negotiations were unsuccessful. Eventually, Malaysia brought a new complaint alleging that the US had failed to implement the earlier decision. This time, the appellate body upheld the US measures on the grounds that they no longer constituted a means of arbitrary or unjustifiable discrimination, because the United States had engaged the complaining countries in serious good-faith negotiations toward a multilateral agreement. Although no agreement was concluded, the effort to conclude one was enough. The United States could not "be held to have engaged in 'arbitrary or unjustifiable discrimination' under the chapeau solely because one international negotiation resulted in an agreement [the Caribbean and Western Atlantic treaty] while another did not."[11]

The appellate body also held that the changes to US law to allow imports from countries with programs "comparable in effectiveness" to the American one, rather than only from countries with "essentially the same" policies and enforcement practices, meant that the law no longer constituted a means of arbitrary and unjustifiable discrimination. Malaysia had argued that the US law still conditioned market access on compliance with policies prescribed unilaterally by the US. The appellate body held that such unilateral conditions were a common element of measures falling under the Article XX exceptions and that they were acceptable if they conditioned market access on the adoption of environmental programs comparable in effectiveness to the importing country's and were sufficiently flexible to take into account the specific conditions prevailing in the exporting country: "Authorizing an importing Member to condition market access on exporting Members putting in place regulatory programmes *comparable in effectiveness* to that of the importing Member gives sufficient latitude to the exporting Member with respect to the programme it may adopt to achieve the level of effectiveness required. It allows the exporting Member to adopt a regulatory program that is suitable to the specific conditions prevailing in its territory."[12]

The *Shrimp-Turtle* case suggests that the trade regime has a preference for resolving international environmental issues multilaterally, not unilaterally (although the conclusion of a multilateral agreement is not necessarily required provided the offending country makes serious good-faith efforts to negotiate an agreement with exporting countries). But states may impose trade restrictions designed to protect the environment or conserve natural resources beyond their borders only in narrow circumstances, namely,

- The restrictions are either necessary to protect human, animal, or plant life or health, or relate to the conservation of exhaustible natural resources and are implemented in conjunction with restrictions on domestic production or consumption.

- They condition market access on the exporting country's adoption of programs that are comparable in effectiveness to, but not necessarily essentially the same as, those of the importing country.
- They are applied in a manner that is sufficiently flexible to take into account the specific conditions prevailing in the exporting country.
- The importing country makes serious and ongoing good-faith efforts to conclude a multilateral agreement on the subject.

While it negotiates a multilateral agreement, an importing country may keep trade restrictions in place that have been judged illegal. In short, the ability of national governments to address environmental problems beyond their borders remains at the discretion of the WTO adjudicative organs, which decide whether or not their measures conform to the narrowly defined parameters of Article XX and the broad objectives of trade liberalization.

Only countries with massive resources, sophisticated expertise, and the ability to project their influence beyond their borders can take advantage of these environmental protection loopholes in international trade rules. Participating in, let alone initiating and leading, multilateral environmental negotiations is hugely expensive and time consuming. It usually takes several years to negotiate an MEA and more for it to come into force. Assessing the state of the environment or natural resources, evaluating policies and practices, and monitoring compliance with preferred standards are monumental tasks within national boundaries, let alone beyond. Few countries have the resources or expertise to do this outside their own territory. Launching or defending proceedings to vindicate these measures before international trade tribunals is itself an expensive undertaking that favours rich industrialized states. Complaining countries, especially in the developing world, are unlikely to be able to fund repeated challenges to the purportedly conservationist measures of other states. Small and developing nations are also less likely to have the resources to defend challenges to their own environmental protection measures, should they be attacked by another state. In short, environmentally motivated but trade-restrictive national laws are available effectively only to a small group of the most advanced and powerful states. Canada is on the fringes of that group at best.

Shrimp-Turtle also left some questions unanswered. We still do not know whether the conclusion of an MEA with a complaining country would be a complete defence against a WTO complaint. Some trade agreements specifically exempt certain MEAs from compliance with trade disciplines. NAFTA, for example, states that the trade obligations under certain specified MEAs, including the Basel Convention, will prevail over NAFTA, "provided that where a Party has a choice among equally effective and reasonably available means of complying with such obligations, the Party chooses the alternative that is the least inconsistent" with NAFTA.[13] When Canada raised this as a defence to its PCB export ban in the *S.D. Myers* Chapter 11 case, however, the arbitral panel held that Canada could have complied with the Basel Convention without banning PCB exports to the US, since the convention allows bilateral agreements with non-parties for hazardous waste trade and Canada had such an arrangement with the US.[14] In any event, this idea of exempting specific MEAs from trade agreements has not caught on. Only three subsequent bilateral trade agreements contain similar exemptions (United Nations Environment Programme, and International Institute for Sustainable Development 2005, 68).

The WTO rules also present obstacles to the use of trade measures in MEAs. Trade penalties have been important components of major MEAs in two respects. In some agreements, such as the *Convention on International Trade in Endangered Species of Wild Fauna and Flora* (CITES), they have been used as a means of exercising control over trade itself, where this trade has been the source of environmental damage. In other agreements, trade provisions have served "as an enforcement mechanism in order to provide an additional incentive for states to join and adhere to the MEA and also to ensure the MEA's effectiveness by preventing leakage – which is the situation where non-participants increase their emissions, or other unsustainable behaviour, as a result of the control measures taken by signatories" (Brack 1998, 14). An example of this second usage is the Montreal Protocol, which bans signatories' trade in ozone-depleting substances with non-signatories.

Such trade measures have proven valuable both for addressing environmentally threatening forms of trade and for promoting compliance with MEAs. Their value is illustrated in the success of CITES, the Montreal Protocol, and the Basel Convention, which has been attributed to their trade disciplines. However, the use of trade measures in MEAs has also been seen as a potential infringement on the rights of WTO members. It could be argued that they represent violations of Articles I and III of the GATT, which prohibit discrimination in trade. The trade measures used in major MEAs "discriminate between countries on the basis of their environmental performance, requiring parties to restrict trade to a greater extent with non-parties than they do with parties" *(ibid.)*. Indeed, such discrimination is one of the main objectives of these MEAs "since they aim to promote [environmentally] sustainable activities while punishing unsustainable behaviour" *(ibid.)*. Moreover, though GATT Article XI forbids quantitative restrictions on imports from and exports to other WTO members, quantitative restrictions are among the most commonly used trade restraints in MEAs. Thus, Articles I, III, and XI of the GATT could hinder the application of trade measures in international environmental agreements, robbing these legal instruments of their most effective – in some cases, their only – enforcement or compliance mechanisms.

In principle, the possibility exists that a trade measure in an MEA could be saved by the general exceptions clause of GATT Article XX. Though we cannot know for certain how a WTO panel would rule until a dispute involving an MEA is brought to the WTO for settlement, a number of MEAs adopted or currently under negotiation have raised objections from countries on the basis of their incompatibility with the trade rules. The potential for a dispute arising from this type of claim threatens the viability of global environmental governance in several ways, as Brack *(ibid., 18)* points out:

> The fact that it is not known for certain how a dispute panel
> would rule on a MEA trade measure creates an unstable and un-
> certain situation. On the surface, it does appear absurd that the
> operation of an important element of international law should be
> subject to a panel of three individuals deciding what they think
> the lines of printed text (the relevant sections of GATT Article XX)
> that were written fifty years ago could mean in a vastly changed
> international context. It creates the spectre of a potential challenge
> to an existing MEA, bringing the two international regimes of
> trade liberalization and environmental protection directly into
> conflict. It increases the likelihood of conflict over the negotiation
> of future MEAs with trade measures and, thus, potentially weakens
> their effectiveness – the "political chill" argument.

An analogous situation arises in domestic law, when panels of judges are asked to interpret possibly outdated legal texts and resolve conflicts between apparently compatible legal regimes. The resulting uncertainty is problematic whether it arises in international or domestic settings.

So far, discussions within the WTO have not resolved the problem, leaving global environmental governance weak. Certain principles of international environmental law constitute customary law and may form the basis for decisions by intergovernmental judicial bodies, such as the International Court of Justice or bilateral arbitration panels. But even the most established principles of customary environmental law usually impact state behaviour only in the context of MEAs. State compliance with MEAs, however, is weak and often dependent on poorly developed enforcement or compliance-control mechanisms. This leaves trade-related measures as the most effective devices for inducing state adherence to MEAs. But, within the current WTO framework, the possibility of resorting to such measures is jeopardized by rules prohibiting quantitative restrictions on trade and discrimination against foreign producers, including discrimination on the basis of the environmental sustainability of production methods. In this way, the WTO threatens to deprive international environmental law of its most effective means for correcting government behaviour causing global environmental damage.

WTO rules have also interfered with national efforts to address environmental problems. Where states have found their local or national policies challenged before the WTO dispute settlement panels and faced the ensuing risk of retaliation, their capacity to protect their environment has been undermined. The economic supraconstitution is at once powerful enough to block many national efforts at environmental protection and unable to compel states effectively to resolve environmental problems with transborder impacts.

PROTECTION OF INVESTMENT AND ENVIRONMENT IN NAFTA

In Chapter 3, we examined the powerful rights and remedies conferred by NAFTA on transnational capital and some of their implications for national governments' exercise of public authority to protect the environment and public health. These provisions confer privileged rights of citizenship on capital at the expense of democratic majorities. One minor exception to NAFTA's non-provision of rights to ordinary citizens is the Submissions on Enforcement Matters (SEM) process established under NAFTA's environmental side agreement. Citizens of NAFTA countries may submit complaints challenging any member government's failure to effectively enforce its environmental laws.[15] NAFTA itself also contains some environmental protection measures. A comparison of the continental governance regime's provisions for environmental protection with its provisions for investor protection brings the imbalance between economic and environmental matters in Canada's supraconstitution into sharp relief. The choices embodied in NAFTA and its side agreements, and their implementation in practice, reflect the differing value placed by the NAFTA parties on economic integration and environmental protection.

In comparison with NAFTA's tough rules on investor protection, its provisions on environmental protection are modest. Article 1114 includes two environmental caveats on investor protection. It affirms that member states may adopt measures to ensure that investment activity in their territory is undertaken in a manner sensitive to environmental concerns, but these measures must be consistent with the rest of Chapter 11. In other words, this article does not alter the members' investment protection obligations or give them the authority to derogate from them for environmental purposes. Article 1114 also contains an insipid anti-race-to-the-bottom provision, according to which "a Party should not waive or otherwise derogate from, or offer to waive or otherwise derogate from, [domestic health, safety, or environmental] measures as an encouragement for the establishment, acquisition, expansion or retention in its territory of an investment of an investor."[16] Unlike the investor protection obligations, this article is couched in the soft language of admonition ("should not") rather than the hard language of obligation. Moreover, the provision is toothless: if a member state believes that another party has offered such inducement, its remedy is consultation with the other party and, at most, a negotiated resolution. NAFTA also confirms the right of each member state to establish the levels of protection of human, animal, and plant life or health; the environment; or consumers that it considers appropriate and to adopt and apply technical regulations, voluntary standards, and conformity assessment procedures in pursuit of these objectives.[17] Again, such measures must be otherwise consistent with NAFTA, including the obligations of national and most favoured nation treatment.

At the insistence of then newly elected President Bill Clinton, an environmental side agreement was negotiated in 1993 before NAFTA was ratified. The *North American Agreement on Environmental Cooperation* (NAAEC) imposes some obligations on member governments in relation to their own domestic environmental laws, but unlike NAFTA it establishes no international standards for environmental protection, confers meagre rights on citizens to challenge government environmental (in)action, and provides for even weaker remedies.

Member states' basic obligations under NAAEC are modest. Each party must ensure that its laws and regulations provide for high levels of environmental protection and strive to improve those laws and regulations, but this obligation is expressly conditioned upon recognition of the right of each party to establish its own levels of domestic environmental protection and its own environmental development policies and priorities, and to adopt or modify its environmental laws and regulations.[18] Although this preserves the autonomy of domestic environmental policy, it also renders the accompanying obligation essentially hortatory. Secondly, NAAEC puts in place some modest guarantees of public participation and access to justice in environmental matters. Each party must, "to the extent possible," give members of the public notice of and the opportunity to comment on proposed environmental laws and regulations.[19] Each party must allow interested persons to request investigations of alleged environmental violations, must give such requests "due consideration," and must allow interested persons access to legal proceedings to enforce environmental laws.[20] Such proceedings must be fair, open, equitable, expeditious, and impartial, and parties must have appropriate avenues to seek review of the resulting decisions.[21] These public participation and access to justice guarantees are aimed exclusively at domestic justice systems. Unlike Chapter 11, they do not give aggrieved citizens any access to international legal proceedings. Moreover, they are modest by international standards (Richardson and Razzaque 2006) and do not even match what was already available to most American and Canadian citizens. So, at least for Canadians and Americans, they do not represent any significant new protections.

Most of the remaining NAAEC obligations are even less momentous. Member states must issue periodic state-of-the-environment reports, publish their environmental laws, promote environmental education, foster environmental research and development, assess environmental impacts as appropriate, and consider banning exports of pesticides that are proscribed in their own territory.[22] These obligations have had little or no discernible impact. Ottawa, for example, failed to issue any state of the environment reports for most of the 1990s and into the new century, with no consequences. In the mid-1990s, Ontario dismantled numerous environmental protection regulations in its efforts to cut "red tape" and make the province "open for business."

The only obligation of any substantial import is found in Article 5, which states that "each Party shall effectively enforce its environmental laws and regulations through appropriate governmental action."[23] This obligation was intentionally limited to domestic enforcement of existing domestic laws. It does not impose any requirement as to the content of those laws or the level of environmental protection to be achieved. It does not create any international environmental standards for member states' laws to meet nor forbid members from lowering their environmental standards. It simply requires them to enforce their own laws as they exist on the books. This is not to belittle the obligation: in all three NAFTA countries, a chasm separates environmental law on the books and on the ground. To achieve effective enforcement of all environmental laws and regulations would be a monumental accomplishment. The point, rather, is to highlight the contrast between this requirement and the trade and investment obligations enshrined in NAFTA, which do establish international standards and impose constraints on the content of domestic laws.

The contrast is even sharper when we consider the remedies available to private parties for violation of this obligation. Whereas NAFTA Chapter 11 gives aggrieved investors some of the most powerful judicial remedies known to international law, the NAAEC's citizen submission, or SEM procedure, is hobbled and lame. It makes no determination of legal rights and obligations, awards no remedies, and is subject to political control and interference by the member states. Under the SEM procedure, anyone residing in the territory of a member state may assert that a party to NAAEC is failing effectively to enforce its environmental law.[24] The complaint is submitted to the Secretariat of the Commission for Environmental Cooperation (CEC), the trilateral environmental watchdog agency established by NAAEC. The CEC is an international organization with headquarters in Montreal and a permanent professional staff. It plays an important role in reporting on pollution in the three countries and facilitating intergovernmental coordination and cooperation on environmental enforcement. Unlike a Chapter 11 tribunal, the secretariat is a permanent body of professional public servants who are independent of the member states, subject to formal standards of professional conduct including rules against conflicts of interest, and have no commercial interest in repeat business. International commercial arbitrators, by contrast, have no security of tenure, have a commercial interest in repeat business, and frequently engage in activities inconsistent with impartiality (Van Harten and Loughlin 2006). Another favourable contrast with Chapter 11 is the power of the secretariat to consider submissions from non-disputing NGOs and individuals, and to conduct its own studies or commission independent experts to undertake studies on its behalf, all without the disputing parties' consent. Chapter 11 tribunals have the power to accept written submissions from NGOs and other non-disputing parties, which they exercise with great restraint. They may not appoint experts without the consent of the disputing parties.

But the SEM process is far from a robust citizen enforcement tool. The main differences between Chapter 11 investor-state adjudication and the SEM process are summarized in Table 1. Unlike a Chapter 11 tribunal, the secretariat is precluded from making any legal determinations about the alleged failure to effectively enforce environmental laws. Nor may it prescribe any remedies. Its only power is to prepare a factual record, which has no legal force. Moreover, the entire process is subject to political control at crucial junctures: the CEC council, which is made up of Cabinet-level representatives of the three member governments (the very actors who are the subjects of the complaints), decides, by a two-thirds majority, whether to instruct the secretariat to develop a factual record in the first place and whether to release a final factual record to the public. The council decisions are subject to no criteria or restrictions, and no reasons need be given. The council frequently sits on files for long periods, failing to vote either on instructing the secretariat to prepare factual records or on releasing final factual records to the public. When it instructs the secretariat to prepare the records, it frequently restricts their scope in ways favourable to the respondent government. It has been repeatedly accused of political interference with the SEM process.

In 2004, the CEC's independent Ten-Year Review and Assessment Committee concluded that, though the SEM process had brought some transparency to environmental enforcement, its effectiveness was compromised by political interference and the perception that the parties were attempting to constrain it (Commission for Environmental Cooperation 2004). The issue came to a head in 2008 when a coalition of Mexican, Canadian, and American environmental groups and academics sent a letter to the council warning that the future of the entire CEC was threatened by ongoing political meddling.[25] The immediate trigger for the letter was the council's failure to vote on the preparation of two factual records that had been recommended by the secretariat almost three years earlier – two of a litany of examples of alleged interference dating back several years. Delays of a year or more in voting on whether to prepare factual records were common. Delays of several months in voting to release final factual records were also common, even though NAAEC provides that votes should normally be held within sixty days. In some cases, decisions were made only after unfavourable media coverage brought public pressure to bear. The letter complained that these chronic failures to make timely decisions subverted the objectives of the citizen-submission process and undermined public confidence in NAFTA by discouraging public participation in environmental enforcement matters, promoting public distrust, undermining the principles of accountability and transparency, and creating the potential for unfair trade advantages gained at the expense of environmental degradation continuing for years. The letter also criticized the council's practice of imposing arbitrary limitations on the scope of factual investigations (including narrowing an allegation of a nation-wide failure by the US government to enforce migratory bird protection laws into an investigation of two specific forests, converting a submission focused mainly on alleged failures to enforce Canadian logging regulations on Crown land into an investigation of logging on private land, restricting the time frames of investigations, and circumscribing the types of evidence to be considered).

With all these limitations, one might expect that the SEM process would not get much use. In fact, citizen environmental submissions have outnumbered Chapter 11 investor-state arbitration claims. From 1994 to 2008, sixty-seven SEMs were filed, compared with approximately fifty-five Chapter 11 claims.[26] During this period, fifteen final factual records and fifteen final Chapter 11 tribunal decisions were issued. At the end of 2008, there were eleven active SEM files. Of the remainder, most were rejected at an early stage for failure to meet the basic criteria for submissions or because the secretariat determined that no factual record was warranted. When the secretariat has recommended preparation of a factual record, the council has directed it to do so in all but three cases, albeit often after long delays and with a diminished scope. Once the secretariat has prepared the records, the council has never voted not to release them to the public, although it often sits on them for long periods.

The pattern of the SEM process reflects its origin as an American effort to discipline its southern neighbour. The environmental side agreement and the SEM process were introduced at American insistence. US industry already felt overburdened by environmental regulation and did not want this to place it at a disadvantage in relation to Mexican competitors. American organized labour was afraid that jobs would flee southward under free trade due to Mexico's lower legal standards. US environmental groups feared that freer trade, combined with Mexico's lax enforcement, would lead to an increase in environmental degradation across the continent. Not surprisingly, half of all SEMs have been filed against Mexico. One-third of the complaints have been filed against Canada, which is not startling when one considers that the 1990s were a decade of deep cuts to Canadian environmental ministries as the neo-conservative policy prescriptions that had swept the US

TABLE 1

NAFTA Chapter 11 claims versus NAAEC submissions on enforcement matters

	NAFTA Chapter 11 investor-state dispute	NAAEC citizen submission on enforcement matters
Who may complain?	An investor of a member state, for itself or on behalf of a subsidiary.	Any NGO or person residing or established in the territory of a member state.
Against whom?	Another member state (may not complain against own government).	Any member state (may complain against own government).
About what?	The member state's alleged violation of Chapter 11 obligations including national treatment, most favoured nation, fair and equitable treatment, international minimum standard of treatment, and protection against performance measures, expropriation, and measures tantamount to expropriation.	The member state's alleged failure to effectively enforce its environmental law.
To whom?	An international tribunal of three commercial arbitrators, two of whom are appointed by the parties to the dispute and all of whom have a commercial interest in repeat business.	The CEC secretariat, a permanent body of professional public servants who are independent of the member states, subject to standards of conduct including conflict of interest rules, and have no commercial interest in repeat business.
What law does the adjudicator apply?	NAFTA and international law.	No legal determinations are made.
Are the proceedings transparent and public?	Oral hearings are generally closed to the public, although some are open to observers. Since 2001, all documents submitted to or issued by tribunals are made public, subject to exceptions for confidential or proprietary information. No central repository of claims or decisions exists, but each member state maintains a web-based depository.	There are no oral hearings. All key documents submitted to or issued by the secretariat are publicly available in hard copy or via a central web-based registry, subject to exceptions for confidential or proprietary information. The final factual record remains secret until the council votes to make it public, but in practice the council usually does so eventually.

▶

◀ Table 1

	NAFTA Chapter 11 investor-state dispute	NAAEC citizen submission on enforcement matters
May NGOs participate?	Under procedures established by the Free Trade Commission in 2003, the tribunal may accept written submissions from non-disputing parties such as NGOs, but it is up to each tribunal whether to follow these procedures or accept submissions. With the disputing parties' consent, the tribunal may appoint experts to report on environmental or other matters.	The secretariat may consider submissions from NGOs, individuals, or the Joint Public Advisory Committee and may consider information developed by secretariat or independent experts, all without the disputing parties' consent.
Is the adjudicator independent?	Perhaps. The defendant member state appoints one of the arbitrators, but the arbitral tribunal reaches its own decision.	No. The Council of the Commission for Environmental Cooperation, which decides whether the secretariat should prepare a factual record and whether the final factual record should be made public, is made up of top government officials of each member state.
What kind of decisions and remedies may the adjudicator award?	The tribunal may order interim measures to preserve parties' rights or evidence, short of enjoining application of the impugned measure. At the end of the proceeding, the tribunal may issue a final award determining the parties' legal rights and obligations, and awarding compensatory damages, interest, restitution, and/or costs.	The secretariat may prepare a factual record but may not make any legal determination whether the party failed to effectively enforce its environmental laws and may not award any remedies.
Is the decision legally binding and enforceable?	Yes. Tribunal decisions are binding on the disputing parties and enforceable in the territory of any state party to NAFTA or the main arbitration treaties.	No.
Can the decision be appealed?	The disgruntled party may apply for judicial review in the jurisdiction designated as the place of arbitration. The court may overturn an award only on such narrow grounds as fraud or gross violation of due process.	No.

during the 1980s took hold north of the border. Environmental monitoring, inspections, investigation, and enforcement absorbed the deepest of these blows. Canadian environmental groups saw the SEM process as a last-ditch avenue for exposing and challenging the resulting widespread failures of environmental enforcement. Of the final factual records that have been released by the CEC, seven concern Mexico, seven concern Canada, and only one concerns the US.

That the SEM process has been deployed more against the continental periphery than against the superpower reflects the fact that it was motivated primarily by American apprehensions about enforcement practices in the southern periphery and that citizen environmental enforcement tools, which were already widely used in the United States, were a novelty in Canada and Mexico. The model of public participation embodied in NAAEC (notice and comment procedures, public advisory committees, and citizen enforcement) constituted a significant Americanization of Canadian and Mexican environmental law.

Even though SEMs to date slightly outnumber Chapter 11 claims, their impacts do not extend much beyond a modest public shaming function. Shortly after the 2008 letter was published, the council voted to instruct the secretariat to prepare factual records in two cases that had languished for almost three years. Initial submissions and final factual records receive some national and continental media coverage, typically prompting the embarrassed governments to belittle the findings, discredit the complainants, or obstruct the process. Due to its cost and toothless outputs, environmental groups view the SEM process at best as a secondary weapon in their arsenals.

Unlike Chapter 11 disputes, which involve an investor from one state challenging the action of another NAFTA government, the vast majority of SEMs have been launched by submitters against their own governments, mostly in relation to enforcement failures with mainly local environmental effects. Although it is therefore largely an international projection of domestic state-citizen relations, the SEM process has prompted the emergence of some transnational links. Several submissions have related to continental or binational environmental issues, such as migratory birds or coal-fired power plant emissions. One-fifth have been joint submissions by submitters from two or three member countries. Most of these have been Canada-US collaborations, and many have involved organizations with pre-existing links (such as Sierra Club–US and the Sierra Club of Canada). In one instance, complaints were filed against different governments in relation to the same issue.[27] On the whole, however, the SEM process has played only a modest role in promoting transnational cooperation among citizens and environmental groups.

The labour side agreement to NAFTA is an interesting contrast in this respect. The *North American Agreement on Labor Cooperation* (NAALC) provides for individuals, unions, employers, NGOs, or other private parties to submit complaints (called "public communications") about labour law practices.[28] These complaints are not submitted to and reviewed by the continental Commission for Labor Cooperation, which the three governments made sure would be an ineffectual stub of an institution. Instead, they are presented to the National Administrative Offices (NAOs) established within each country's labour ministry and reviewed, "as appropriate," in accordance with domestic, not international, procedures.[29] The public communication process is purely informational, not adversarial, and has proven remarkably ineffective at remedying labour law violations. Following an initial flurry of activity leading to virtually no concrete results, complaints shrank to a trickle after 1998 as trade unions in the three countries concluded that the scant results achieved by pursuing the complicated process were not worth the legal hassle and consequent expense. It has become clear to many observers that NAALC was "nothing more than window dressing to get us to accept NAFTA to begin with" (Clarkson 2008a, 106, quoting a Mexican union representative). The contrast between NAALC's soft-law hortatory approach and Chapter 11's hard-law approach is not just stark but paradoxical: "While the labour agreement's proponents asserted that its soft-law approach was necessary in order to respect sensitive domestic issues, critics pointed out that NAFTA Chapter 11's hard-law approach ... was deliberately designed to override such delicate domestic feelings" *(ibid.).*

The labour side agreement has, however, had the effect of fostering the emergence of transnational linkages among labour movements in each of the three countries (Buchanan and Chaparro 2008). Labour unions' initial reactions to NAFTA and NAALC were inward-focused and nationalistic. No coordinated multi-jurisdictional labour law complaints were filed under NAALC in the first three years of its operation. This soon began to change. Under NAFTA Chapter 11, an investor of one country sues the offending country directly; in the NAAEC SEM process, citizens bring complaints directly against their own governments. However, complaints about labour law violations in one country must be filed with another country's NAO, necessitating transnational alliances.

The year 1998 saw the instigation of coordinated campaigns in which complaints were filed in two countries against a third. Were it not for the utterly ineffectual results of the labour complaints process, this trend might have led to the creation of a genuine continental ethos in which citizens of the three countries would develop multiple conceptions of their membership in an emerging North American community (Gabriel and MacDonald 2003). The tentative transboundary and continental coalitions that have materialized in the labour and environmental complaints processes might be the first faint inklings of a transnational demos capable of conferring legitimacy on a continental supraconstitution, but this development is still a very long way off (Clarkson 2008a, 109-12).

Some supranational transparency and accountability in environmental and labour law enforcement, however weak, may be better than none at all. In practice, the SEM process is the only mechanism for enforcing the three countries' obligations under Article 5 of NAAEC to effectively implement their environmental laws. Part V of NAAEC provides for an interstate dispute settlement process where one party alleges a persistent pattern of failure by another party to enforce its environmental law, but this mechanism has never been activated and so, like similar counterparts in the labour side agreement, has proven entirely ineffectual and can be considered dead. Though the SEM process has generated the most activity of the three continental private complaint mechanisms, this probably reflects the frequency of enforcement failures and the high level of unmet demand for meaningful public participation and government accountability machinery in the continental periphery, rather than the effectiveness of the process itself.

Correcting the Imbalance

If international norms and institutions form part of the collection of fundamental practices by which a national society is governed, effectively limit national governments' exercise of public authority, prevail over conflicting domestic laws and policies, and take effect in domestic legal systems in the absence or even despite domestic legislation, we call them supraconstitutional. International negotiations engender compromises between countries with differing interests and different clout. As a result, the agreements to which Canada is a party often contain provisions inconsistent with its existing policies. Given that most such agreements have weak enforcement mechanisms, Canada's record of compliance has been mixed. But these international organizations and regimes exercise varying degrees of control over Canadian governments' exercise of public authority, and these restrictions are increasing. This may be for the better, if it results in more effective protection of the environment or human rights. In other cases, it may be problematic if, for example, it curbs Canadian governments from safeguarding health, safety, or the environment as they see fit or respecting the democratically expressed will of the Canadian public.

As we have seen, the global supraconstitution is highly uneven across subject areas, with the most muscularity in the international trade and investment regime, and much less in the social and environmental arenas. Supranational protection of the rights of transnational capital far exceeds that of individual citizens' human rights. Supraconstitutionalization of trade and investment norms and institutions is proceeding without a corresponding supraconstitutionalization of social, environmental, cultural, or labour rights and norms. In short, both the global supraconstitution and its North American variant are seriously skewed.

A supraconstitution is simultaneously a domestic and an international phenomenon. It is the constitutional order of a supranational or post-national political formation, but it also reconstitutionalizes every participating state, in varying ways and degrees, by entrenching an external constitution in its domestic one (Clarkson 2004). Because they transform and are embedded in domestic constitutional orders, supraconstitutional norms are experienced differently in different nation-states. As we saw vividly in Chapter 3 when considering supraconstitutional rights for foreign investors, Canada's supraconstitution is not the same as Mexico's, let alone that of the United States. Because our focus is on Canada, we have not pursued developing-countries' experience of the global supraconstitution. Whereas the social and environmental regimes we discussed in Chapter 4 may not have achieved supraconstitutional status for Canada, they may have done so for the developing world. Though the supraconstitution may be experienced as hegemonic in Canada (attracting consensual submission by a cross-section of Canadian society and being championed externally in Canadian relations with developing countries), it may be experienced as imperial by many developing countries. From their perspective, it may even be possible to speak of the entire array of international laws and organizations, including those focused on environment, society, and human rights, as an "imperial global state in the making" (Chimni 2004).

The supraconstitution enacts a neo-conservative agenda to entrench economic rights for transnational capital, insulate key aspects of the economy from state interference, and limit democratic decision-making processes (Gill 1995; Schneiderman 2008). It represents the continental and global projection of mainly US legal norms and forms by mainly American economic and political elites, and their entrenchment in Canadian, Mexican, and other constitutional orders.

Far from being solely the passive objects of external forces, Canadian political and business elites were and remain active agents of the new constitutionalism, both at home and abroad. Having helped construct the constitutional architecture of North American free trade and investment, Canadian state and corporate elites became champions of this same disciplinary neo-conservatism in the WTO and continue to export it with vigour to developing countries by negotiating further bilateral and regional free trade deals. A Canadian lawyer recently praised Canada's BITs as "particularly attractive to investors because they provide a mechanism to pursue damage claims directly against host states through international arbitration" (Cardwell 2008, 37). The lawyer, who helps Canadian extractive companies do business in Latin America, credited these BITs "with helping 73 companies recover more than $600 million of the $1.8 billion claimed in damages in 2007 alone – a huge improvement over recent years" and called them "a third way that allow us to sidestep the court system in those countries [and] avoid the use of diplomacy to [resolve conflicts]" *(ibid.)*. This blunt affirmation illustrates how Canadians contribute to strengthening a neo-conservative global supraconstitution in order to support Canadian transnational corporations' interests against those of developing countries.

On the other hand, Canada and Canadians have also long been proponents of the development of international law and organizations in the social, cultural, security, and environmental domains, from UN peacekeeping to the International Criminal Court. But Canada's reputation for leadership has been tarnished. In the environmental area, Canada was once admired for assuming leadership roles in the Stockholm Conference of 1972, the 1987 Brundtland Commission, and the Rio Conference of 1992, and for setting an early example of domestic policy innovation with the Berger Inquiry into the proposed Mackenzie Valley pipeline and with the federal Department of the Environment. Since the early 1990s, with neo-conservative governments commanding the political stage, Canada has abandoned its global environmental leadership. With a few exceptions, such as the 2000 *Stockholm Convention on Persistent Organic Pollutants*, Canada has been a laggard on the international environmental stage, obstructing international action on climate change and squandering decades of hard-earned social capital.

Canada may have lost relative position in the global hierarchy of states during the last few decades, declining from seventh-largest economy to battling with Brazil for ninth place, but it remains a player in the upper-middle range of semi-peripheral states that can make a difference in the shadow of the more influential countries that dominate the world's power system. During the Uruguay Round of negotiations to reform the GATT, for instance, Ottawa made the original proposal that led to equipping the new WTO with an authoritative judicial capacity. The question is whether it will use the influence it has to reform existing elements of the world order in a progressive direction and develop new components as needs arise.

As with domestic constitutions, the supraconstitution is not a fixed entity but a dynamic one, constantly evolving as new rules are negotiated and judicial decisions are made by international trade and investment dispute settlement or arbitration. This malleability raises the question of whether, as an agent of globalization, Canada should attempt to direct the supraconstitutional order through purposeful intervention in order to correct its imbalances. The answer depends both on how Canadians assess the global supraconstitution's strengths and weaknesses and how they define their interests. The global order's perverse strengths lie in its prevailing norms and institutions, which serve the interests of transnational capital, dominant states, and economic and political elites in many peripheral countries, perpetuating the vicious circles that keep the poor in poverty and denying them such public policy tools as tariffs and industrial subsidies that big powers used during the nineteenth and twentieth centuries to industrialize their own economies. The corollary weakness is to be found in the other institutions of global governance intended to advance human, labour, social, cultural, and ecological interests and rights.

The crisis of global governance centres on the processes of decision making in multilateral institutions, which remain shielded against direct input from, or accountability to, citizens. The supraconstitution suffers, in other words, from a lack of process legitimacy. Its outcome legitimacy is also deficient, as these multilateral institutions' policies and actions exacerbate inequalities between the richer countries of the North and the poorer countries of the global South. Supraconstitutional transformations are proceeding without genuine awareness on the part of many affected national publics and

in the absence of a constitutive supranational polity capable of conferring
legitimacy on them. Although most agree that the supraconstitutional order
needs to be rebalanced, there is no consensus on how to do this rebalancing
(Buchanan and Long 2002, 1).

It is useful to recall Polanyi's warning of the dangers inherent in a commitment to the "self-regulating market":

> Ultimately ... control of the economic system by the market is of
> overwhelming consequence to the whole organization of society:
> it means no less than the running of society as an adjunct to the
> market. Instead of the economy being embedded in social rela-
> tions, social relations are embedded in the economic system.
> (Polanyi 1944/1957, 57, quoted in Cohn 2003, 95)

A self-adjusting market, Polanyi (*ibid.*, 3) cautioned, "could not exist for any
length of time without annihilating the human and natural substance of
society; it would have physically destroyed man and transformed his surroundings into a wilderness."

Twenty years ago, a project similar to this one might have recommended
that the Canadian government establish an inventory of the country's international obligations to be used by its own departments as they formulated
policy, by judges reaching decisions, and for the information of the general
public. Now that NAFTA and the WTO have given international economic
agreements supraconstitutional weight, what is more urgently needed is a
clearer picture of what comprises Canada's supraconstitution. Achieving this
would be no easy task. Just as the implications of provisions in Canada's
domestic constitution cannot be known with any certainty until a case has
been taken through the country's judicial system and a definitive ruling has
been made upon appeal to the Supreme Court, so too many of the supraconstitution's norms cannot be understood until conflicts over their meaning have been resolved through dispute resolution in the WTO or through
NAFTA dispute panels. Even then, subsequent arbitration may change these
interpretations.

In any case, no catalogue of Canada's supraconstitution could ever be
definitive. It would always necessarily be provisional and contested. Just as
globalization has caused many kinds of boundaries to blur, supraconstitutionalization is characterized by a shifting of the conventionally understood

boundaries of national constitutions. As the ongoing debates about a European constitution attest, the existence and parameters of a supraconstitution will always be the subject of contestation. Nonetheless, the supraconstitution is a social reality, comprising fundamental norms that govern our society. The worth of supraconstitutional analysis lies in identifying the interests and values that have fundamental priority in our political and legal systems. It is also a normative intervention: "Constitutionalization is inseparable from discussion about it, and analysis of it. No significant study of constitutionalization can be 'innocent,' so to speak, because any such study is necessarily part of the processes by which a consensus is (or is not) generated about what constitutionalization means, and about whether or not it is occurring" (Lang 2006, 309). As we suggested in Chapter 2, our variety of supraconstitutional analysis plays a critical role rather than a celebratory one: it is a critique of power.

Canada and Canadians should strive to rebalance the supraconstitution by bringing markets back into equilibrium with society. This requires giving governance institutions responsible for implementing environmental, labour, and human rights agreements powers equal to those of the institutions of global economic governance. Weak individual rights need to be bolstered by granting them weight equivalent to the already strong economic rights accorded to transnational business. This view assumes that it is in Canada's long-term national interest to achieve global cultural security for all – that is, global justice, redistribution of income, eradication of poverty, societal stability, cultural diversity, and environmental sustainability, even if pursuing these goals is seen to contravene the short-term interests of Canadian corporations abroad and the wealth of Canadian citizens at home.

Interests are, of course, subjectively defined. What Ottawa perceives as the "national interest" during a particular international negotiation can be highly personal (the views of a particular minister), actually partisan (what will serve the election needs of the governing party), frankly popular (reflecting publicly expressed Canadian values), or narrowly sectoral (the interests of a powerful industrial grouping). Interests clash: when it adopts the neoconservative agenda of big business, Canadian foreign policy cannot reflect the more liberal attitudes of ordinary Canadians, let alone the diversity of their society.

Although decades of underfunding have left them too weakened to assume a leading role, Canadian diplomats have customarily played important, if secondary, parts in hundreds of multilateral deliberations held by such international institutions as the UN, NATO, and the Pan-American Health Organization and covering topics ranging from economic development to investment rules to standards for health care products and security measures. Along with Foreign Affairs and International Trade Canada, a number of federal departments may be involved in negotiations and agreements. Signing international agreements and participating in international organizations increases Canada's capacity abroad, because these activities give it forums where it can defend its interests and have some influence over the policies of its counterparts.

Even when Canada does manage to allocate personnel to take a significant part in treaty negotiation or an international organization's decision making, the public rarely learns about the day-to-day contributions of its representatives. Recognizing its own legitimacy problem, Ottawa has already taken steps to improve the transparency of its negotiating positions by making them available on the Internet. It also reintroduced the practice of tabling proposed treaties in Parliament for non-binding review. Its efforts to engage stakeholders in consultations are worthy, but they have not eased the suspicion that, whereas the wishes of citizen stakeholders are merely heard, the demands of corporate stakeholders are heeded. For the Canadian government to pursue a rigorous strategy devoted to correcting the injustice of the global constitution would require a fundamental transformation in Ottawa's mindset. Until then, we can expect that the federal government will continue to preach virtue at home while championing the interests of transnational capital abroad.

Whereas one of the main characteristics of the globalization of Canadian law and governance is the proliferation of international laws and organizations, some of which have supraconstitutional force, fundamental transformations are also occurring at the level of the nation-state and in the realm of non-state actors and institutions. These transformations are the focus of Part 2.

Consolidating or Confronting Hegemony? Governance within and beyond the State

6

From Retreat to Revitalization:
The Paradoxes of the Globalized State

Although the notion of Canada's new supraconstitution may be novel to some readers, the story of the retreat, shrinkage, and hollowing out of the nation-state is familiar to anyone who has followed debates about globalization with even casual interest. Central to prevailing narratives, it is nonetheless incomplete. The contemporary crisis and transformation of the state are better described not as a *retreat* but as a *globalization* of the state – that is, the globalization of certain ideas about the proper character and function of the state, and of certain forms of public administration and law. This transformation involves both the withdrawal of the state from various functions and social arenas, and, contrastingly, its forceful reassertion over others. Although this reassertion has so far been directed toward combating perceived internal or external threats such as terrorism and immigration, it contains the possibility for a more promising revitalization of the state as an instrument of human progress.

The transformation of the Keynesian welfare state began with neo-conservative offensives in the late 1970s. Following Margaret Thatcher's and Ronald Reagan's successes, neo-conservatism appropriated the centre of the political spectrum in the 1990s in the name of a reinvented social-democratic "Third Way," represented by the Clinton Democrats in the United States, Blair's New Labour in the UK, Schroeder's Social Democrats in Germany, and the Chrétien/Martin Liberals in Canada. Changes to the state during this period were even greater outside the advanced industrialized democracies. The socialist states of the former Soviet bloc collapsed under the combined influence of democratic upswellings and the unsupportable weight of their own dysfunctional, centrally planned economies, creating a political opening into which rushed, with varying degrees of success, domestic and foreign reformers – often trained in American universities – eager to install a particular brand of democracy emphasizing private property, free enterprise, trade liberalization, foreign investment, and a scaled-back state. Meanwhile, the developing states of the global South entered a period of profound turmoil under the pressures of unsustainable foreign debt, unprecedented public health crises, IMF structural adjustment requirements, World Bank good governance prescriptions, and WTO trade disciplines – all driven by the demands of Northern governments and their corporations for a more liberalized treatment of foreign investment.

These trends can be described as a globalization of the state because they were global in their geographic scope and were informed by an ideological consensus that spanned the globe. Reacting to the globalization of financial flows, production networks, and ecological degradation, the neo-conservative model itself went global as new beliefs concerning governance structures, laws, norms, and practices were articulated in the most advanced states and imitated by national legal and political systems elsewhere. The resulting changes continue to be felt around the world. As it was in the previous Keynesian paradigm, Canada is both an importer and exporter in this process.

In this chapter, we advance three arguments about the globalization of the contemporary state:

- The apparently disparate developments affecting states around the globe have been informed by a broad ideological consensus about the appropriate form and role of the state, one that Canadian governments of all stripes have embraced with varying degrees of fervour since the mid-1980s.
- The transformation of the state that has been effected in the name of this normative consensus is contradictory, combining a retreat from some areas (environmental regulation, social services, and cultural programming) with a vigorous reassertion in others (immigration and anti-terrorist security).
- Because the state has been a principal author of its own purported demise and retains a considerable power to re-establish its own role in governance, it should exercise this power in the service of hope rather than fear, human rights and freedoms rather than the suppression of dissent and difference, and cosmopolitan ideals rather than parochial self-interest.

A Global Ideology

Wherever it has occurred, the reconstruction of the state has been informed by a remarkably similar set of diagnoses and prescriptions. Although

characterized by local variation and internal heterogeneity, this set of prescriptions supplies the ideational foundations for the predominant forms
of globalization. Originating in neo-classical economic doctrine and neo-
conservative political movements in the United States and United Kingdom,
this ideology has become global in its scale and ambitions. The main features
of this "global hegemonic consensus," as Santos (2002, 314-17) calls it,
include a common set of views about the economy, the state, liberal democracy, and the rule of law.

The *economic consensus* holds that national markets are and should be
ever more global in their scope, involving global production chains and the
worldwide distribution of goods, services, and capital, and that private property, individualism, free markets, trade liberalization, export orientation, and
international competitiveness are the keys to national success in this universal space (*ibid.*, 314). Hand in hand with this proposition goes the *state
consensus*, according to which a good state is a weak one, or at any rate a
substantially smaller and less assertive one than what people in the advanced
industrialized countries were accustomed to. According to this view, state
intervention is fundamentally antithetical to the flourishing of both markets
and civil society (*ibid.*, 315).

As old as classical liberalism, this idea has enjoyed an energetic revival
in the last four decades and is reflected in numerous descriptive propositions:

- The welfare state, with its bloated bureaucracy, regulations, and social
  programs, has exceeded the cognitive, economic, technical, and political limits of its ability to effect social change and is at risk of "break[ing]
  down under its own weight" (Orts 1995, 1241).
- Governmental regulation and public service provision have become
  excessively rigid, cumbersome, complex, costly, inefficient, ineffective,
  anti-innovative, and adversarial (Bardach and Kagan 1982).
- Contemporary global developments – from expanding markets to environmental threats – increasingly escape or overwhelm the regulatory
  capacity of territorially bounded nation-states (Cohen 2004; Strange 1996).
- Though business may be the cause of some social problems, it also plays
  an essential part in their solution. Indeed, corporate environmental and
  social responsibility is not only desirable but profitable. Partnering with
  the private sector may be more important than the autonomy of regulatory agencies, since business is in a unique position to generate the
  knowledge and innovation that will contribute to a sustainable future,

and government lacks the resources and competence to dictate in detail how economic activity ought to be conducted for the social good (Schmidheiny 1992; Salter and Salter 1997; Elkington 1998).

These descriptive claims are accompanied by a series of normative prescriptions, the most important of which are that

- Governments should cut themselves back by reining in wasteful and inefficient public spending, reducing tax burdens, balancing budgets, and avoiding deficits.
- Regulation of business and individuals should be relaxed to unleash the creative potential of private enterprise, respect the autonomy of private decision making, enlist individual initiative in the service of public goals, make better use of market incentives, and eliminate unnecessary bureaucratic "red tape." What remains should be "smarter" regulation – more responsive, more flexible, more cooperative, more narrowly focused on preventing market failures, less hierarchical, and justified by cost-benefit or regulatory impact analysis (McConkey 2003).
- The state should privatize public enterprises, break up government monopolies, decouple the delivery of goods and services from policy making and contract it out, regulate access to resources primarily via private property rights, and restrict its own role in these spheres to creating and overseeing markets (O'Connor and Ilcan 2005).
- Authority should be devolved to lower levels of government, and decisions should, where practicable, be made at the level closest to the people (the principle of subsidiarity).
- Public management should emulate private-sector management ideas and practices, including efficiency, cost-effectiveness, quality assurance, stakeholder management, and an orientation toward customer service, results, and performance (Salskov-Iversen, Hansen, and Bislev 2000, 184).
- Individual liberty, autonomy, and choice should be the foundational principles of government, and individuals should increasingly take responsibility for their own choices and welfare.
- To support individual choice and responsibility, government decision making should be more transparent and accountable.

The idea that the capacity of governments to produce desirable social change by intervening directly in social systems is limited because they ultimately risk paralysis, collapse, or revolution if they overstep their proper bounds has been an element in Western political and legal philosophy since Plato (1952). Even today, few would deny its basic validity (Stone 1975; Nonet and Selznick 1978; Teubner 1983, 1993; Yeager 1991; Ayres and Braithwaite 1992; Gunningham and Grabosky 1998). What is significant is not the insight itself but the zeal with which it has been exploited by certain political elites who rose to power proclaiming a mission to remake prevailing state structures.

The *liberal-democratic consensus* holds that representative democracy is the only viable and acceptable form of government and that its global spread should be hastened by all means including diplomatic pressure, economic coercion, and (in appropriate cases) military force. Although liberal democracy is widely understood to require, at a minimum, free and fair elections, universal suffrage, freedom of conscience, expression, and association, and the right to oppose the government and stand for election, these characteristics are often treated as less important and their achievement less urgent than the agendas to cut back government and empower the market (Santos 2002, 315-16). These ideals are deemed to have been long since put into practice in the advanced capitalist countries, which have a resulting duty to export their superior models without necessarily subjecting them to critical self-examination.

The *rule of law consensus* holds that a predictable and stable framework of official law enforced impartially and effectively by an independent judiciary is critical to trade, investment, prosperity, and social welfare. Government corruption must be rooted out, property rights clearly allocated and protected – especially for foreign investors and the creators of profitable knowledge – contracts respected, regulations evenly applied, and offenders consistently punished (*ibid.*, 316-17). These ideals are also understood to have been largely realized in the advanced capitalist democracies, leaving them lacking primarily in developing countries, former socialist states, and international relations.

Although large elements of the liberal-democratic and rule of law consensus underlay the Keynesian paradigm, the main impetus behind the old paradigm's challengers was supplied by neo-conservative political movements in the United States and United Kingdom, which had been strongly influenced by neo-classical economics, the revival of classical liberal political theory in reaction to fascism and communism, and the views and interests of domestic and transnational business elites.

One of the pillars of the state's contemporary transformation was the regulatory reform movement launched originally in the United States as an attack on bureaucratic excess in the name of individual liberty and free market capitalism (Bardach and Kagan 1982). Following dramatic political successes by the radical Thatcher and Reagan administrations, the new consensus won converts in many countries. It found its keenest promoters in the World Bank, the IMF, and the OECD where, insulated from the moderating restraints of domestic political bargaining and nurtured in an isolated ideational culture focused on trade, finance, and economic growth, its adherents managed to entrench a purer neo-conservatism than they had been able to implement at the domestic level in many countries. The result was that some of the strongest ideological support for the contemporary refashioning of the state came from the World Bank and the IMF, with their structural adjustment and good governance programs, and the OECD, with its aborted *Multilateral Agreement on Investment* and proposals for regulatory reform. Of this ideological takeover, Joseph Stiglitz (2002, 12-13) wrote,

> Over the years the IMF has changed markedly. Founded on the belief that markets often work badly, it now champions market supremacy with ideological fervour. Founded on the belief that there is a need for international pressure on countries to have more expansionary economic policies – such as increasing expenditures, reducing taxes, or lowering interest rates to stimulate the economy – today the IMF typically provides funds only if countries engage in policies like cutting deficits, raising taxes, or raising interest rates that lead to contraction of the economy. Keynes would be rolling over in his grave were he to see what has happened to his child.

It would be a mistake to identify this ideological consensus solely with the neo-conservative right. By the 1990s, the consensus had permeated all but the margins of the contemporary political spectrum, as the social-democratic left shifted rightwards to embrace major elements of the new thinking while moderating its excesses (Ayres and Braithwaite 1992; Gunningham and Grabosky 1998). Social democrats adopted core elements of neo-conservativism into a New Left ideology as they sought to recoup the political losses they had suffered in the 1980s. As a result, early radical efforts to dismantle the Keynesian welfare state were displaced by more subtle agendas to "reinvent" it.

The Third Way, as it was called by its proponents (Giddens 2000), attempted to harness globalization, regulatory reform, and many of the ideas and practices associated with 1980s neo-conservatism to the social-democratic cause. It called on the state to do "more steering, less rowing"; govern not less but "smarter"; set overall directions, goals, and frameworks; leave details of implementation to be sorted out through co-regulation, negotiated agreements, and consumer activism; adopt private-sector managerial methods and entrepreneurial ethics; use markets and competition in the provision of public services; be transparent and accountable; and employ a sophisticated mix of regulatory tools that enlist non-state actors and resources in the task of regulation (Ayres and Braithwaite 1992; Osborne and Gaebler 1992; Gore 1993; United States White House 1995; Gunningham and Grabosky 1998; Giddens 2000). Whereas the us-against-them mentality of intensified social exclusion and increased disparities between "haves" and "have-nots" was explicit in the overt neo-conservatism espoused by Thatcher and Reagan, and later by George W. Bush and Stephen Harper, the social-democratic variant disguises its exclusionary and regressive tendencies in the language of humanitarianism and progress.

In sum, the contemporary consensus accommodates considerable diversity and has been adapted to such a variety of political conditions that its political affiliations are extremely complicated (Jordana and Levi-Faur 2004). It made political bedfellows of a Labour prime minister (Tony Blair) and a Republican president (George W. Bush) and varied from the "iron cage" neo-conservatism experienced by many Latin American countries to the more flexible "rubber cage" experienced by some Asian countries (Santos 2002, 314-15).

In Canada, it had its first national manifestation in Brian Mulroney's Progressive Conservative government of the 1980s; continued in a modified form in the Jean Chrétien and Paul Martin Liberal administrations of the 1990s and early 2000s; achieved a more extreme expression in the provincial governments of Mike Harris in Ontario, Ralph Klein in Alberta, and Gordon Campbell in British Columbia; and saw its best-trained exponent, the economist Stephen Harper, take power in Ottawa in 2006. Even the early 1990s' leftist New Democratic government of Bob Rae in Ontario embraced important elements of the consensus, including fiscal restraint, government downsizing, and such business-inspired prescriptions as private-public partnerships to build and manage state infrastructure. Despite their partisan differences, political parties, governments, and international institutions around the world had, by the turn of the century, adopted a loosely unified consensus about the economy, the state, democracy, and the rule of law.

The Paradoxes of the Globalized State

This dominant consensus contains a paradox: the truncated state demanded by the doctrine needs to be strong to produce and maintain its own weakness (Santos 2002, 315). States have played a central role in giving up their monopoly over governance, investing substantial public funds and creating new institutions to regulate the markets that emerged as the state retreated. For all its deregulatory rhetoric, the rise of neo-conservatism has in practice been accompanied by a substantial expansion in the number of regulatory agencies, the volume of official regulation, and the domains of activity subject to regulation (Jordana and Levi-Faur 2004). In some fields, such as crime and punishment, it has generated more government spending, even (after the 2008 crisis) budget deficits. Although states have been hollowed out in certain policy arenas such as social welfare, environment, and consumer protection, they appear fully capable of vigorously asserting themselves in others, including defence, counter-terrorism, prisons, immigration, and border control. These conundrums have important implications for the legitimacy of contemporary forms of national law and governance.

THE STATE IS DEAD

Without subscribing to exaggerated reports about the demise of the state in the face of globalization, we can discern various ways in which it has reduced its role in society and market. We focus here on the many signs of the Canadian state's shrinkage over the last twenty years: substantial downsizing of government budgets and staff; retrenchment of social programs; devolution of authority onto lower-level governments and independent or private organizations; and relaxation of social, environmental, and labour-market regulation.

Having started this process in the mid-1980s, but hitting its stride after the 1993 election of the Liberal Party, the federal government aggressively pursued balanced budgets and even surpluses by starving social programs, even though this spending had been a minor factor contributing to the budget deficits that had built up since the mid-1970s (McBride 2001, 83). Over the 1990s, federal and provincial program expenditures diminished to their lowest levels since the 1950s and resulted in massive staff cuts. In the area of environmental protection, for example, Ottawa slashed Environment Canada's budget by almost one-third in just three years: from $737 million in 1995-96 to $503 million in 1997-98; Environment Canada staff was reduced by one-quarter: 1,400 of 5,700 employees were let go (Clarkson 2002, 340). The Ontario Conservatives cut Ministry of Environment staff by more than 40 percent between 1994 and 1999 as they shrank the ministry's budget by half, in constant dollars. Its 2000 budget was less than that of 1971, the year the ministry was created by an earlier Progressive Conservative government (*ibid.*, 342).

The results of these federal and provincial government-wide cuts included the gutting or contracting out of research, testing, monitoring, inspection, and enforcement capacity in many important areas of regulation. The staff that remained were often stretched beyond their limits, sometimes given explicit or implicit messages to relax their oversight of regulated entities. Private service providers were often inadequately monitored. In Ontario, decisions by government leaders to cut regulatory capacity, privatize certain government functions without adequate oversight, and relax enforcement of existing laws led to injury, illness, or – for the inhabitants of the small town of Walkerton, who became victims of the improperly regulated local water supply – death (O'Connor 2002a, 4; 2002b, 3-5). A massive explosion at a Sunrise propane facility in Toronto during the summer of 2008 and an almost simultaneous listeriosis outbreak from contaminated sandwich meat raised questions about whether similar dynamics were at work in other domains.[1]

Devolution of governmental authority also occurred on a substantial scale. Ottawa downloaded its authority to the provinces and territories in various ways. It signed federal-provincial-territorial agreements on environmental harmonization, delegated enforcement of federal laws to the provinces, cut strings attached to federal transfer payments, granted the territories increased autonomy, and retreated from numerous social and economic arenas in which it had previously intervened extensively. In their turn, provincial governments off-loaded responsibility for the provision of many public services onto their municipalities. As many provincial, territorial, and municipal governments discovered, however, decentralization of authority was frequently accompanied by funding cuts, so that lower levels of government were saddled with substantially increased obligations at the same time as the revenues available to them for the discharge of those new duties dwindled.

A sizable share of public authority was also transferred to independent agencies and private establishments as the Canadian state hollowed itself

out. Many public enterprises such as Crown corporations and public utilities
were privatized; the delivery of many public services, from garbage collection
to employment insurance, was contracted out to private non-unionized firms;
and governments delegated policy and regulatory functions to independent
agencies (such as the Technical Standards and Safety Authority in Ontario,
responsible for regulating the Sunrise propane storage facility), whose transparency, public accountability, and freedom from industry influence were
limited (Winfield, Whorley, and Kaufman 2002).

Along with downsizing, devolution, and privatization came deregulation
– rolling back existing regulation – although, as we will shortly show, the
transformation of the state also involves an expansion of regulation in other
areas. Explicitly anti-government administrations such as those of Ralph Klein
in Alberta and Mike Harris in Ontario came to power on commitments to
"cut red tape," foster a more business- and investment friendly regulatory
climate, and pursue more cooperative, voluntary, and flexible relations with
regulated industries. They kept their promises with varying degrees of alacrity.
Environmental, labour, and social groups of all kinds have documented the
dismantling of federal and provincial regulation in fields as diverse as environmental protection, workplace safety, land-use planning, and rental
housing. Liberal and New Democratic governments also relaxed or eliminated many social, environmental, and labour regulations. For Gordon Campbell's Liberal government in British Columbia, for instance, deregulation was
an end in itself. Through its unabashedly entitled "Deregulation Initiative,"
the government surpassed its own campaign promise of reducing the volume
of provincial regulations by one-third over three years and boasted on its
website that "ministries continued to look for ways to modernize the regulatory system and make gains in regulatory reduction. From June to December
2004 a further 1,112 regulatory requirements were eliminated" (British Columbia Regulatory Reform Office 2005).

A more subtle example of deregulation is the "one-window" approach
to business regulation embraced by governments of all stripes in this period.
The effect has often been that the ministries tasked with protecting health,
safety, or the environment are subordinated to a ministry whose main mandate is to serve and promote the regulated industry.

Among the most remarkable developments has been governments' willingness to accept or impose legal restrictions on their own ability to regulate.
We have already discussed the supranational regulation of national regulation

via international trade regimes. Canadian governments have also tied their own hands domestically by implementing various restrictions on the introduction of new regulations including regulatory impact-analysis procedures, policies explicitly favouring voluntary or cooperative initiatives over regulation, and increasing sympathy for arguments that regulation constitutes a "taking" of private property. One example is the federal *Species At Risk Act*'s provision for compensating landowners whose property is subject to a critical habitat protection order (Wood 2001). As recently as 2009, the Liberal government of Dalton McGuinty was requiring Ontario's civil servants to repeal two regulations for every new regulation introduced.

Long Live the State

Although the Canadian welfare state has retreated on several fronts, it has advanced in other directions. Without recapitulating the deregulation-reregulation debate (Majone 1990; Ayres and Braithwaite 1992), we simply note that, as governments withdrew from public ownership and direct service provision, they turned their attention to regulating the markets they had thereby created. The state did not wither away but shifted from the "positive" to the "regulatory" and most recently the "post-regulatory" state (Majone 1997; C. Scott 2004). The positive state owned resources, provided goods and services directly, and employed a tax-and-spend model of public policy, all the while maintaining a unified civil service, large public enterprises, and active bureaucracies.

The regulatory state places more emphasis on the use of authority, rules, and standards, partially displacing the earlier emphasis on public ownership, subsidies, and service provision (Jordana and Levi-Faur 2004). It is characterized by the privatization of national enterprises, welfare functions, and service delivery, and by a rule-making regime featuring flexible, highly specialized, and relatively autonomous agencies. It shifts from direct service provision to the arm's-length regulation of others who provide services. In some cases, this takes the form of conventional command regulation: hierarchical regulation of firms via licensing, standards, mandatory disclosure rules, and so on. In other cases, states have moved from regulating individual firms to regulating markets for electricity, telecommunications, natural gas, and other products and services (Salter and Salter 1997).

The regulatory state also involves a new emphasis on "meta-regulation" – the regulation of regulation (Doern et al. 1999). Meta-regulation ranges from state regulation of industry self-regulation (Jordana and Levi-Faur 2004) to private or quasi-private actors' regulation of state activity (C. Scott 2002). In addition, as we have already indicated, it may take the form of state regulation of its own regulatory activity (cost-benefit analysis, regulatory impact analysis, public audits, "Charter-proofing" of proposed legislation) (Doern et al. 1999), and international regulation of national regulation (McConkey 2003).

A further shift may be under way from the regulatory to a "post-regulatory" state (C. Scott 2004). This is characterized by greater emphasis on information disclosure and less on detailed performance standards, greater use of flexible or creative law enforcement techniques, and the delegation of rule-making and rule-enforcing authority to industry or third parties (industry self-regulation, partial industry regulation, industry-government co-regulation, third-party certification, and citizen enforcement). It also entails efforts to facilitate more effective market-based regulation of behaviour including increased reliance on economic instruments (taxes, economic incentives, tradable permits); increased reliance on information, the public purse (subsidies, procurement, contracting), and capacity building (supporting regulated entities and community groups) instead of formal legal authority; and a focus on new targets of regulation including consumers and "gatekeepers" (financial institutions and third-party-certification bodies).

Many of these changes were undoubtedly positive from the point of view of democratic legitimacy and public health and welfare. Auditors general, for example, have proven their worth in holding governments accountable, not least in the case of the Liberal Party's notorious sponsorship program scandal, which embroiled and ultimately brought down Paul Martin's government, although in some issue areas (such as environmental commissioners) their ability to shame governments into behavioural change appears minimal. Innovative approaches to regulation have, on occasion, increased the protection of people and the environment, but they have frequently compromised them. Although a detailed assessment of the legitimacy and effects of all these adjustments is beyond our remit, the purported retreat of the state from direct social intervention has in many cases resulted in an expansion in the number of regulatory agencies, the volume of official regulation, and the domains of activity subject to official regulation.

A complementary explanation for the simultaneous weakening and strengthening of the state is a shift in the targets of state intervention, fuelled by anti-immigration sentiment and anti-terrorist paranoia, toward law and order, national security, and border protection. Crime, security, immigration, refugees, and terrorism have always been priorities for government action, but they have acquired new significance as borders fade, distances shrink, and the world becomes a scarier place for people accustomed to safety and security. Not since the early part of the twentieth century, with its concerns about the Yellow Peril and anarchist plots, have we seen such a strong inter-twined emphasis on crime fighting, immigration control, border protection, terrorism, and security in North American public policy. Of course, this is not without some basis in reality, as the terrorist attacks of 11 September 2001 and later in Madrid and London demonstrated. Indeed, the spectre of terror-ism came closer to Canadians in June 2006, when seventeen residents of the Greater Toronto Area were arrested and charged with planning to attack targets in southern Ontario with crude but powerful fertilizer bombs. But a legitimate concern with vulnerability to terrorist attack has been exploited to advance a "lifeboat ethic" of anti-terror security measures and immigration and refugee controls.

The newly invigorated state interventions pursued in the name of this agenda are problematic for many reasons (Daniels, Macklem, and Roach 2001). They heighten social exclusion, both globally and domestically, by targeting or disproportionately affecting Muslims, Arabs, people who appear Middle Eastern, new immigrants, and refugee claimants, especially poor members of all these groups, and by seeking to erect a national or contin-ental "fortress" against external incursions. They limit the civil rights and liberties not only of foreigners in Canada but of Canadian citizens. Detention of terror suspects in Canada without charge or trial on the basis of secret evidence, detention of a Canadian citizen by American military authorities in Guantanamo Bay, and rendition of Canadian citizens to third countries where they face torture are only the most questionable of many dubious legal and political practices.

Taken together, these governance activities foster and legitimize a culture of secrecy and paranoia rather than transparency, accountability, and respect for fundamental human rights. And there is little evidence that they actually protect us from terrorist attack. To make things worse, this terrorism/security agenda reinforces some of the more regressive elements in the Canadian political scene, including anti-immigrant sentiment and law-and-order ex-tremism. Both of these attitudes tend to be socially exclusionary not just because they are often inspired by racism and xenophobia but also because their effects tend to fall disproportionately on economically and socially marginalized populations such as immigrants, communities of colour, Aboriginal people, and the chronically un- or underemployed.

These examples highlight a continuing contradiction in transnational governance. The globalization of crime, terror, and insecurity have led Canadian and other governments to reassert their coercive power and tighten border controls against certain kinds of transnational movements (immigration, refugees, organized crime, terrorism, and communicable diseases), just as economic globalization has led them to de-emphasize their coercive capacities and dismantle border controls for other kinds of transnational movements (capital, goods, services, tourists, and information). The tension between these two responses has been most evident in the media and political attention given to long queues for Canadian trucks at US border crossings since 11 September 2001, but the fact that disruptions to transborder trade have received so much attention in the post–11 September environment emphasizes a more fundamental contradiction in contemporary responses to globalization: governments actively encourage the global movement of capital, goods, and services while actively discouraging the global movement of people, in particular, the oppressed or destitute.

For a tiny and overwhelmingly Northern elite of mobile executives, entrepreneurs, professionals, tourists, aid workers, and human rights activists, the obstacles to human migration have fallen away as a result of globalization, but this is not the case generally, even if there are a few counter-examples (such as labour mobility in the European Union). Refugees, persons displaced by conflict, and other members of the poorest, most desperate, most vulnerable, most persecuted segments of human society, those in most need of a new start in a new place, continue to face massive barriers to movement and great personal peril whether they stay put or try to migrate. The rich nations of the world have said *yes* to global capital flows but *no* to human flows. The reason is simple: the emancipatory potential of such a change for the global majority is so great, its destabilizing effect on accustomed privileges of the global minority so serious, that its possibility cannot be entertained. This is all the more reason to question whether the coercive state powers, armed interventions, and restrictions on human rights, freedoms, and movements invoked to manage these phenomena both in Canada and abroad actually do enhance security and well-being, and if so, for whom and at whose expense.

There are many other examples of paradox in the contemporary transformation of the Canadian state. In the following pages, we single out four: Ottawa's Smart Regulation initiative; the rise of transgovernmental networks; the multifarious processes of globalization of domestic law, in which Canada is both an importer and exporter; and the long-standing international campaign for "good governance" in developing countries, of which Canada has been a major supporter.

Smart Regulation

The Paul Martin government's Smart Regulation initiative, continued by the Stephen Harper administration under a different name, is the most recent of many globalized ideas about regulatory reform to take root in Canada (Wood and Johannson 2008).[2] It presents itself as a rational and progressive alternative to the unsophisticated excesses of neo-conservative assaults on the state and thus poses particularly subtle legitimation challenges. It also represents an adaptation to Canadian circumstances of a particular global agenda for regulatory reform.

The federal government established an External Advisory Committee on Smart Regulation (EACSR) in May 2003 to advise it on how it could redesign its regulatory system to protect health, safety, and the environment while promoting an innovative, dynamic, and globally competitive economy for the twenty-first century. The EACSR reported in September 2004, and Ottawa quickly endorsed its recommendations, mandating the Treasury Board to launch a whole-of-government regulatory reform initiative. According to the EACSR and the government, "smart regulation" is about simultaneously protecting health, safety, and the environment while enabling trade, investment, innovation, and competitiveness. It is about "taking into account the views of citizens and, at the same time, being attentive to, and balancing, the needs of firms and the challenges they face in an international economy" (External Advisory Committee on Smart Regulation 2004, 13).

The Smart Regulation initiative characterizes the current framework of federal regulation as unsustainable in the face of global market dynamics, increasingly complex policy issues, and rising public expectations for empowerment and accountability. It calls for amplified cooperation and harmonization between federal, provincial, and territorial governments, including more consistent environmental assessment procedures; more "timely" approval processes for drugs, medical devices, and pesticides; increased international regulatory cooperation, including, most importantly, greater harmonization of regulatory standards and product approvals with those of the United States; greater understanding and support for the needs of large industry; and less burdensome regulation of small business.

The proponents of Smart Regulation claim to be able to achieve these transformations while safeguarding the environment and public health, as well as maintaining a strong and effective regulatory system. In practice, however, the initiative prioritizes economic competitiveness and industry promotion at the expense of the government's responsibility to protect health, safety, and the environment.

The claim that the Canadian regulatory system is bloated, unsustainable, overlapping, and unduly burdensome is not supported by the facts. In the area of environmental assessment (EA), for instance, little evidence has been found of needless duplication of regulatory requirements even before a 1998 agreement to harmonize federal and provincial EA regimes (Hazell 1999). Moreover, the EACSR analysis neglects a more pressing problem – that the federal government routinely fails to apply and enforce many existing regulatory requirements. It also ignores evidence that traditional command regulation has repeatedly proved more effective than voluntary or non-regulatory approaches at changing behaviour and protecting human and environmental health. And it disregards evidence that international regulatory harmonization tends to exert downward pressure on environmental, health, and safety standards, and to hamper transparency, accountability, timeliness, and effectiveness – a subject to which we will return when discussing transgovernmental networks. In short, the Smart Regulation initiative is anything but smart, as numerous social and environmental groups argued when it was adopted (Canadian Environmental Law Association et al. 2004; West Coast Environmental Law Association 2004; Canadian Environmental Law Association 2004).

Development of the Smart Regulation program was dominated by business interests. Six of the EACSR's ten members were senior corporate executives or directors and one was the founder of the OECD's neo-conservative regulatory reform program. Only three of the ten represented environmental, consumer, or Aboriginal groups. With such disproportionate representation of business interests – the group with the most obvious incentives to seek a relaxation of regulation – it is difficult to see how this body can claim any kind of representative legitimacy. This situation is disturbingly common. It was repeated in the spring of 2009 when Ottawa announced an advisory panel almost exclusively composed of executives of large banks and business firms to recommend how to get credit flowing again (ignoring, apparently, the possibility that these same executives' earlier inclination to let credit flow too freely might have precipitated the crisis).

The solution to the problem of regulation in Canada will not be found in bowing to self-interested business calls for less regulation: instead, it must include a renewed commitment to the improvement and enforcement of existing laws designed to protect public health, safety, and the environment. Ottawa should make its Smart Regulation agenda truly intelligent by subjecting its priorities of efficiency, cooperation, and flexibility to an overriding commitment to protect ordinary Canadians' health, safety, welfare, and environmental integrity, and by recognizing that mandatory legal regulation (whether through standards, permits, taxes, or enforceable contracts) should regain its pride of place in a sophisticated mix of policy instruments.

TRANSGOVERNMENTAL NETWORKS

One of the most pervasive yet least noticed developments in contemporary governance has been the growing volume and intensity of transnational networks of government officials. These networks offer substantial promise as flexible, effective ways for domestic government agencies to get their jobs done, especially in the regulation of phenomena with transnational dimensions. But they also raise serious concerns in terms of transparency, democratic accountability, and public health and safety.

Transgovernmental networks have sprung up in myriad policy areas and involve all branches and levels of government. Although some important networks exist at the highest levels of government, including the G8 and G20 meetings, most differ from traditional intergovernmental organizations in that they operate without direct participation of – or close oversight by – foreign ministries and top government leaders. Instead, they often involve either actors who are formally independent of central governments (central bankers and provincial premiers) or bureaucrats who fly under the radar of political and media attention.

Leading examples include the Basle Committee of Central Bankers, the International Organization of Securities Commissions (IOSCO), the International Association of Insurance Supervisors, and INTERPOL, the international criminal police organization. North American examples include informal cooperation between the premiers of Ontario and Quebec and the governors of the Great Lakes states on environmental and economic policy in the Great Lakes region, formal defence cooperation through NORAD (the North American Aerospace Defense Command), trilateral environmental law enforcement cooperation under the *North American Agreement on Environmental Cooperation*, and regional initiatives to combat climate change involving US states and Canadian provinces. In addition, there are countless formal and informal transnational networks involving almost every kind of government official imaginable: judges, intelligence agencies, military personnel, taxation authorities, immigration officials, mayors, child welfare agencies, education officials, food and drug regulators, customs inspectors, public health officers, and, not least, elected legislators.

Transgovernmental networks bring government actors from different countries together in face-to-face meetings or via electronic communication to exchange information and ideas, collaborate on specific cases, and, often, develop shared goals and agendas. Usually, these networks are highly special ized, their participants sharing similar backgrounds, training, experiences, and expertise. They also tend to share similar values, priorities, and worldviews, although their national interests and objectives can clash when they interact strategically in pursuit of their own goals. The most informal of these networks may be the most dynamic and effective: ad hoc transnational task forces and networks that can mobilize transborder cooperation by a simple phone call or e-mail, thus bypassing cumbersome channels for official intergovernmental communication.

The strength of transgovernmental networks is their potential to enhance governments' ability to tackle issues with global reach, such as organized crime, money laundering, drug trafficking, the sex trade, child pornography, terrorism, weapons of mass destruction, environmental change, global information networks, global markets, global travel, and transnational child adoption. This strength is also one of their primary limitations. If "governments must have global reach" in a global age (Slaughter 2004, 4), transgovernmental networks answer this imperative only for a handful of already dominant governments. Although they may partially enhance the capacity of semi-peripheral and developing countries to govern transnational matters, their main effect is to consolidate and expand the global regulatory capacity of the main powers. They tend in particular to complement the United States' uses of traditional diplomacy and "hard" (military or economic) power, functioning unobtrusively to support such US foreign policy priorities as the war on terror in which networks of financial regulators cooperate to freeze terrorist assets, law enforcement officials collaborate to identify and detain terrorist suspects, and intelligence agents share information to identify and assess future terrorist threats (*ibid.*, 2). Canadians are all too familiar with some of the undesirable results of transgovernmental cooperation in the US-led war on terror, including the rendition of Canadian citizens to countries where they were tortured.

Another problem with transgovernmental networks – especially those of regulatory and law enforcement officials – is that they tend to be secretive. Their meetings and deliberations are hidden from the public. Typically, only members of the participating regulatory agencies are invited to take part. Civil society organizations are seldom offered a seat at the table, unless they provide some functional expertise from which the network could benefit. By meeting "off-shore" with their foreign counterparts, these actors may escape trans-parency and due-process requirements that would normally apply to them.

These networks operate in the political background and typically do not welcome media attention. Many of them are technocratic and elitist, portraying their work as apolitical and downplaying the contestable ideological paradigms on which it may be premised. They are often only loosely supervised by cen-tral government authorities, even if many of their participants are in theory accountable to elected officials. In an era when, after long struggles, both domestic regulatory processes and intergovernmental diplomatic arenas have been progressively opened up to public scrutiny and involvement by a wide range of non-governmental interests, transgovernmental networks represent a convenient escape from the new democratic disciplines and a regression to a more opaque, unaccountable style of governance.

Further concerns focus on the outcomes of some transgovernmental networks. There is evidence that the Basle Committee's capital adequacy re-quirements contributed to a global recession, although, as Slaughter (2004, 220) points out, this claim is disputed, and in any event networks such as the Basle Committee and IOSCO have had very limited success in convincing their members to adopt unified regulatory requirements. Some transgovern-mental interactions contribute to personal insecurity and human rights abuses. Given the secrecy that continues to shroud some events even in the wake of public inquiries, we may never know the full extent to which Can-adian law enforcement and intelligence officials communicated with US officials or facilitated their decisions to "render" Maher Arar and other Can-adian citizens to countries where they were tortured. Although transgovern-mental networks may be instruments of the United States and other powerful countries, we must remember that Canadian government officials may act as transnational agents in their own right, not always for the better. For these reasons numerous commentators have criticized transgovernmental networks as illegitimate and lacking in democratic transparency and accountability (Picciotto 1996-97).

For middle powers such as Canada, therefore, transgovernmental networks are a mixed blessing, enhancing their regulatory effectiveness in certain areas (law enforcement) and providing opportunities to help build governance capacity in developing countries, but also enabling the United States and other major powers to influence Canadian governance policies and practices and to expand the global reach of their own policies and laws. Consolidation of advantages already enjoyed by the people and corporations of these dominant countries is the main goal of these networks, even if it is accompanied by a secondary goal of improving security, stability, safety, and living standards elsewhere.

At a minimum, Canadian governments should ensure that the networks in which they participate are transparent and democratically accountable, and that they do not facilitate violations of human rights. A first step toward improving their transparency and accountability would be to subject such networks to the kinds of public scrutiny that are already applied to domestic regulatory processes (public notice of meetings, opportunities to comment on proposals, opportunities for direct participation by interested and affected parties, reporting to Parliament, application of freedom of information rules, and reviewability by auditors general). Such reforms might make these networks less effective as governance tools, but one thing we can conclude from the Arar case and other examples of transgovernmental interaction in the war against terrorism is that governments should not be allowed to sacrifice openness, democratic accountability, and civil liberties on the altar of effectiveness and national security.

GLOBALIZATION OF NATIONAL LAW

The globalization of national law refers to a range of processes by which domestic law shapes or is shaped by pressures from other national legal systems. National legal systems often reach beyond borders to affect laws, people, and conduct elsewhere in the world. When Canadian constitutional documents and doctrines are emulated by other jurisdictions, or when Ottawa attempts to regulate Spanish and Portuguese fishing fleets' behaviour on the high seas, we see the "export" side of legal globalization. On the other hand, the Canadian legal system more often imports and adapts to elements of other legal systems as, for instance, when Canada amends its telecommunications regulations under American pressure to bring its laws in line with US laws.

Globalization of state law is pervasive and has a long history (for example, legal unification projects such as those pursued through UNIDROIT – the International Institute for the Unification of Private Law – and UNCITRAL). The current phase is distinctive because of the unprecedented breadth and depth of change in the role of national law in governance and the asymmetry between the global North and South (Santos 2002, 194-95). The story of legal globalization in Canada follows a trajectory similar to the one we have traced in other areas: it is defined primarily by Canada's efforts to manage its relationship with the United States but is also characterized by the country's unusually prominent role as a model for imitation elsewhere. Although the categories are clumsy, we can reflect briefly on Canada's contemporary role as an "exporter" and "importer" of law.

Legal Exports

Canada's role as a legal globalizer takes two main forms. First, modelling, or legal transplantation, occurs when Canadian legal norms and experiences – the *Charter of Rights* and related jurisprudence being the most prominent example – are emulated or incorporated in other legal systems. Canada's liberal approach to constitutional rights and its approach to balancing individual rights against democratically determined collective limits ("Section 1" jurisprudence) have been copied in recent constitutional-rights-building exercises in South Africa and beyond. This modelling of Canadian law is at least in part inspired by efforts to shake off legacies of oppression, widen the social inclusivity of the importing legal systems, and improve the lot of the downtrodden and marginalized. To the extent that it contributes to these goals, Canadian judges, lawyers, and activists ought to encourage it.

Offering less cause for self-congratulation is Canada's own relation of dominance vis-à-vis weaker states, which has been accentuated through Ottawa's enthusiastic support for neo-conservative globalization. However much it has complained about NAFTA's Chapter 11 investor-state dispute settlement mechanism, Ottawa – at the behest of Canadian transnational companies – has imposed similar provisions on developing countries when negotiating bilateral investment treaties with them.

Second, extraterritoriality occurs when the Canadian legal system purports to regulate people or their conduct outside its territorial borders. Canadian governments and courts consider this prospect often but with varying degrees of enthusiasm. Examples include:

- Ottawa's aggressive regulation of ocean fishing through the *Coastal Waters Protection Act* in the 1990s, including the use of force against foreign fishing vessels on the high seas
- Ottawa's much less assertive procedures for environmental assessment of overseas projects under the *Canadian Environmental Assessment Act,* such as the proposed sale of a CANDU reactor to China
- Canadian courts' reluctance to entertain lawsuits seeking remedies for human rights abuses or environmental damage committed by Canadian corporations abroad
- Canadian prosecutors' uneven efforts to prosecute Canadian child-sex tourists for acts perpetrated abroad
- the largely failed endeavour to assert criminal jurisdiction over war crimes or genocide committed abroad
- several unsuccessful attempts to introduce legislation to govern the social and environmental conduct of Canadian corporations abroad.

Legislatures play a leading role in efforts to regulate extraterritorially, but courts are also highly significant. A huge body of largely judge-made law determines when courts will assert jurisdiction over disputes with a transnational element. Rules are developed and applied in commercial, family, personal injury, product liability, criminal, and other lawsuits to determine whether Canadian courts and Canadian laws will regulate transnational disputes. Examples include rules related to

- conflicts of laws, where the laws of one jurisdiction conflict with another
- comity, where the courts of one country show courtesy to another country by recognizing the validity of its laws
- *forum non conveniens,* where the courts of one country reject a lawsuit because another country would be a better forum for resolving a dispute
- cases where courts assert jurisdiction over a case on the basis that one of the parties is a *national* of that country, the *effects* of the disputed behaviour were felt in that country, or the conduct was such that the courts of any country have *universal* jurisdiction.

In the age of the Internet, new issues arise almost every day. Take, for example, the case of Cheickh Bangoura: born and raised in Guinea, he worked as a UN assistant regional director in Kenya but lost this job in 1997 after the *Washington Post* published reports of his misconduct at an earlier UN posting in the Ivory Coast. He subsequently immigrated to Canada and, in 2003, brought a damage suit against the *Post* in Ontario, where libel law is more plaintiff-friendly than in the US. The reporters who wrote the articles were all US residents and stationed in Africa or Washington at the time. The *Post*, which is owned and operated in the United States, had only seven paid subscribers in Ontario, although the articles were also published on its website, which was accessible from Ontario.

The *Post* moved to dismiss the action for lack of jurisdiction and *forum non conveniens*. In dismissing this motion, the trial court ruled that Ontario was as appropriate a forum as any to hear the dispute, observing among other things that the *Post* was "a major newspaper in the capital of the most powerful country in a world now made figuratively smaller by, *inter alia*, the Internet" and that "frankly, the defendants should have reasonably foreseen that the story would follow the plaintiff wherever he resided."[3] The Ontario Court of Appeal later reversed this decision and dismissed the action, noting that it was not reasonably foreseeable that Bangoura would end up living in Ontario years after the alleged defamation.[4] Foreign Internet publishers may, however, still find themselves liable in Canadian courts if it is foreseeable that a plaintiff might take up residence here and the allegedly defamatory statements are downloaded and read by someone in Canada.[5]

One variety of transnational litigation is of particular importance: transnational public-interest litigation, a broad term for lawsuits in pursuit of human rights, environmental protection, or corporate accountability, with at least some transnational elements. The classic example is where victims of alleged corporate environmental or human rights abuses in developing countries seek to sue corporate defendants in the corporation's home state. Plaintiffs from all over the world have used US courts, with some success, to seek redress for human rights abuses perpetrated outside the United States. This has been possible mainly because of a unique American federal statute, the *Alien Tort Claims Act*, which dates from the eighteenth century and makes violations of the "law of nations" against aliens actionable in the United States.

Attempts to try such cases have been made in Spain (where a magistrate endeavoured unsuccessfully to prosecute General Augusto Pinochet for crimes committed in Chile when he was its president), the United Kingdom (where the House of Lords ruled that Pinochet, who was temporarily in Britain for medical treatment, could be extradited to Spain to face charges of torture, but the home secretary refused to extradite him due to his poor health), and Belgium (where prosecutors sought to prosecute a "sitting" state official for crimes against humanity).[6] The targets of these cases range from heads of state allegedly responsible for large-scale torture and murder to private corporations allegedly responsible for environmental contamination. What links them is the attempt to seek justice in the courts of a state far removed from the jurisdiction in which the impugned acts took place.

Such efforts have had little success in Canada, since *forum non conveniens* and "real and substantial connection" tests typically favour the jurisdiction where the acts occurred (C.M. Scott 2001). This is especially the case where the plaintiffs were nationals or residents of the foreign country when the acts took place. Thus, Guyanese citizens were unable to sue a Quebec company in Quebec for damages arising from one of the worst environmental catastrophes in gold mining history, a tailings dam disaster at a Guyanese mine owned (via majority shareholding) by the Quebec company.[7] The court ruled that neither the victims nor their lawsuit had any real connection with Quebec and gave little weight to the plaintiffs' concerns that they could not get a fair trial in Guyana. More recently, foreign victims of Canadian corporate misconduct abroad have tried a different approach, suing not only corporate defendants directly but also Canadian stock exchanges for alleged negligence in listing a company despite warnings about its practices.[8] Time will tell if this approach meets with more success.

Where plaintiffs seek redress for abuses by foreign state officials, state immunity is another obstacle. An Iranian Canadian citizen attempted to sue Iran in Ontario for torture in Iran by agents of the Iranian state, but the suit was denied in 2004 on the basis of state immunity.[9] Maher Arar's effort to sue the Governments of Syria and Jordan in Ontario for torture by state agents in those countries met a similar fate.[10]

Canadian citizens and courts have a genuine interest in regulating and judging the conduct of Canadian corporations abroad and holding such corporations responsible in Canada for misconduct elsewhere. Canada and Canadians also have "universal" interests in preventing and punishing torture and other gross violations of human rights wherever they occur. But for a Canadian court to sit in judgment over events and actors, especially foreign state actors, in foreign countries may be perceived as presumptuous; further-more, if the situation were reversed, Canadians would probably not welcome it. This dilemma is lessened when it is the foreign victims themselves, or their chosen representatives (as in the case of the Guyanese mine disaster), who are seeking the intercession of Canadian courts, usually because there is no reasonable hope of obtaining justice in their home jurisdiction. Such lawsuits are in their nature progressive and emancipatory, and reforms to Canadian law should be considered to facilitate them. Not only have Canadian govern-ments not taken such steps, they have actively obstructed attempts by foreign victims of Canadian corporate abuses to seek justice in foreign courts. Ottawa has, for example, intervened in support of Talisman Energy's motions to dismiss actions brought against the company in New York state.

Another way in which Canadian law can reach beyond national borders is by the application of the *Charter of Rights and Freedoms* to actions of Can-adian government authorities abroad. The courts have held that the Charter generally does not apply outside the country, but in a welcome move, the Supreme Court of Canada held in 2008 that it did apply to Canadian govern-ment officials when they interrogated Canadian citizen Omar Khadr while he was in American detention at Guantanamo Bay.[11] The court ordered Ot-tawa to disclose to Khadr's lawyers the interview transcripts and the informa-tion provided to American authorities as a result of the interviews. The court found that comity, which might normally justify deference to foreign law prohibiting disclosure, had no application here since the US Supreme Court had held that the processes in place at Guantanamo when Khadr was inter-viewed violated American and international law. In doing so, it reiterated its statement from an earlier case that "comity cannot be invoked to allow Can-adian authorities to participate in activities that violate Canada's internation-al obligations," delivering a rebuke to Ottawa's long-standing policy of legitimizing Washington's illegal treatment of Khadr.[12]

An even more attenuated form of Canadian legal extraterritoriality is found in extradition law. The Supreme Court of Canada has held that Canada may not extradite accused persons who will face the death penalty if convicted. Canada's extradition treaty with the United States provides for compliance with American requests only if proper warranties are given that the death penalty will not be applied. Although the influence of this legal requirement on US law is hard to gauge, it does apply a subtle pressure on the US legal system.

More indirectly, some Canadian laws and policies – federal, provincial, territorial, or municipal – that are focused on domestic issues and the lives of Canadians can have an impact on the lives of people in other countries, particularly in the Third World. For example, seeking immigrants for their expertise and professional qualifications creates the same "brain drain" from other countries about which Canadians complain vis-à-vis the United States. Offering subsidies to Canadian industry to help its growth and exports makes it more difficult for producers elsewhere to compete, and in the case of the developing countries, to survive. Protecting Canadian farmers with tariffs, quotas, or subsidies helps them prosper at the expense of their destitute competitors in the global South, even if the situation of Canadian farmers is dire within their local context. Moreover, excluding migrant agricultural workers from the full protection of labour laws gives their Canadian employers easy access to cheap, compliant labour while perpetuating the existence of an underclass of Caribbean, Mexican, and Central American workers who return to their own countries year after year with a distinctly sour experience of Canadian law and society.[13]

The irony is that, even as the Canadian legal system negatively affects the global poor in some ways, our governments provide aid, support development projects, and organize trade missions to developing countries. In a number of areas, Canadian government departments and private institutions fund experts to work with officials in other countries. Examples of such technical assistance include training judges, setting up health care systems, bolstering law enforcement expertise, and giving technical aid to agricultural production. Expertise is also supplied when parties agree on contracts whose terms reflect Canadian norms. It is widely believed in the South that developing economies would gain much more from genuine free trade with Canada than from all the aid it offers them.

Legal Imports

The globalization of national law is a two-way street. As in other areas, Canada experiences legal globalization more as an importer than an exporter. Adjusting Canadian laws to incorporate or align with foreign laws has always been part of Canada's legal history. In recent times, this mainly takes the form of pressure to conform to US legal models, from informal demands for regulatory harmonization to unilateral American assertions of extraterritorial jurisdiction. This importation almost always involves local variation and adaptation at the receiving end, not uniform homogenization, because the receiving legal system exercises some form of agency even if limited.

The impetus to mould Canadian laws and regulations to American models does not come solely from the United States: it also arises internally from business interests, which consider regulatory harmonization to be critical to their economic future. Regulatory harmonization includes unilateral adjustment of Canadian regulatory requirements to match foreign ones (new US vehicle emission standards), mutual recognition of Canadian and foreign requirements as equivalent (Canada-EU mutual recognition agreements for drugs and medical devices), and negotiated changes to regulatory requirements so that these are identical in both jurisdictions.

One of the main priorities of the federal government's Smart Regulation initiative was greater harmonization of regulatory requirements and product approvals with the US. Among other things, the EACSR report called for more compatibility with US regulatory requirements in a wide range of policy areas, as well as integrated regulatory processes for industries that are continentally integrated, and a single review and approval of products and services for all of North America (External Advisory Committee on Smart Regulation 2004). The latter would comply with industry's frequently voiced demands for a "tested once, approved everywhere" system of product regulation.

Its proponents claim that harmonization will produce substantial economic gains for Canadian industry as well as gains for Canadian regulators, in that it would allow the smaller country with more limited resources for developing and applying regulations to "leverage" greater use of American and other foreign regulatory resources, especially by capitalizing on foreign research, testing, expertise, and best practices. It would also enable Canada to develop specialized regulatory expertise (in agricultural biotechnology) and use that leverage to attract investment (Policy Research Initiative 2004). Finally, proponents of regulatory harmonization also argue that it will increase the quality and effectiveness of Canadian regulation and the social welfare of Canadians (External Advisory Committee on Smart Regulation 2004).

The latter claim is hard to justify. As the West Coast Environmental Law Association (2004, 3-4) argued in its submission to the EACSR, pressure to align with foreign or international standards tends to exert a downward force on environmental, health, and safety standards, and to conflict with the transparency, accountability, timeliness, and effectiveness objectives proclaimed as desirable by the EACSR itself.

In addition to these concerns about substantive outcomes, regulatory harmonization with the United States raises issues of process legitimacy for Canadians. Smart Regulation proponents urge Canada not to wait for American regulators to come to the table but to pre-emptively synchronize Canadian regulatory requirements with American ones, presumably because this would be the outcome of bilateral negotiations anyway. Given North America's very small number of states with massive power disparities and high asymmetrical interdependence, harmonization necessarily means convergence on the preferred standards of the dominant party. Regulatory harmonization in effect means adopting standards that Canadians have little or no part in developing.

Again, we can distinguish between "imports," where external legal influences are incorporated or transplanted into Canadian law, and those where foreign legal systems regulate Canadians extraterritorially. Many measures adopted in Washington have such impacts on Canada. For example, US monetary policy so directly affects that of Canada – and with it, the value of the Canadian dollar – that the Bank of Canada has on occasion been referred to as the thirteenth of the US Federal Reserve Board's twelve districts. The US Federal Energy Regulatory Commission has promulgated directives intended to force Canada's provincial electricity utilities to privatize and deregulate if they want to export power to the US electricity grid (Cohen 2004).

Foreign governments are not alone in seeking to align the Canadian legal system with their legal systems. Private individuals and corporations are also key players in this game. US transnational corporations and the global law firms that serve them have been at the forefront of efforts to spread US approaches to and forms of business regulation around the world. American civil society organizations and lobby groups often try to influence Canadian legal developments. The fundamentalist US group Focus on the Family, for example, funded lobbying campaigns in Canada to oppose the legalization of same-sex marriage.

The federal justice minister, Irwin Cotler, acknowledged in 2005 that "we have free speech, but at the same time we want to protect the political equities in terms of the marketplace of ideas." He wished to "maintain the integrity of the Canadian political culture and the Canadian political debate" and not "see it skewered" by US-based lobbyists insensitive to the legal and cultural context of Canada. He concluded, however, that, from a legal standpoint, he could do nothing to stop foreign financing of the same-sex debate. "Ideas cross borders," he said, and the main way to protect the integrity of the Canadian debate was for Canadians to become aware of the source of particular lobbying campaigns (quoted in MacCharles 2005, A8).

This controversy was a reminder that the movement of ideas across national borders is often hastened or hindered by the material resources – especially money but also technology – that can be mobilized behind their promotion or opposition. Knowledge is power, and money has a powerful influence on determining which knowledge spreads and how far. From campaign finance to abortion rights to defamation lawsuits to telecom regulation, the question arises whether and how the law should regulate the role played by money, especially foreign money, in spreading knowledge and ideas.

The Focus on the Family episode also raises the question of how to delimit the community that has a legitimate stake in a political or legal debate. Do US religious groups have a legitimate stake and the right to voice their concerns in same-sex marriage disputes in Canada? Do Canadians have a stake and a right to express themselves during presidential elections in the United States or regarding female genital mutilation in Africa or human rights abuses in China? Canadian individuals, NGOs, aid agencies, and officials intervene regularly in such discussions. Should we simply concede that foreign individuals, groups, and governments have a similar right to be involved in Canadian political deliberation?

Extraterritorial regulation by foreign governments produces an involuntary form of legal import. Many laws – notably American (and on occasion European) ones – have extraterritorial application, in the sense that they apply to Canadian branches of American or European corporations and also to Canadian companies and citizens outside the United States. One example affecting Canadian business is the US *Helms-Burton Act*, which made it retroactively illegal for foreign individuals and companies to have acquired Cuban assets that were expropriated from Americans during Castro's revolution. A Saskatchewan-based mining company, Sherritt, operates a formerly US-owned bauxite mine nationalized by Fidel Castro's revolutionary government. As a result of *Helms-Burton*, any Sherritt employee who sets foot on American soil risks being arrested, fined, and incarcerated.

In the face of *Helms-Burton*'s impact on Canadian business, Ottawa took the position that corporate activities in Canada must defer to Canadian law. In order to reassure the United States that US goods would not be exported to Cuba through Canada, the *Export and Import Permit Act* requires that companies wishing to export goods of US origin to Cuba must seek a special permit from the American government.

When US law is applied extraterritorially to Canadian citizens (as opposed to Canadian corporations), it is harder for government to take protective action. British Columbia's privacy commissioner concluded that there is no way to prevent the long arm of US anti-terrorism legislation from extending into Canada and obtaining otherwise confidential information about individual citizens (figuratively, at least, since the information would actually be held in computers in the US). The *USA PATRIOT (Uniting and Strengthening America by Providing Appropriate Tools Required to Intercept and Obstruct Terrorism) Act* gives American law enforcement agents the right to obtain information from Canadian databases whose administration is contracted out to US companies – even if this violates privacy safeguards in Canada.

Canada's experience with the European Union concerning privacy matters was more straightforward. Brussels issued a directive blocking the cross-border transfer of personal data to companies from countries that did not have legislation protecting individuals in this regard. Canada had to amend its own policies to meet the EU's conditions lest there be a disruption of commercial relations.

These legal import/export processes highlight the contemporary disjuncture between the traditional model of democratic sovereignty (in which a national government is regarded to have the legitimate and exclusive authority to make laws for its territory and its nationals) and the complex cross-border and deterritorialized interactions that need to be governed under globalization. The problem is easy to see when Canadians are subjected to extraterritorial law or pushed to harmonize regulatory requirements with US ones, for this involves the imposition of rules that Canada and Canadians did not develop through their own democratic processes. The democratic deficit is less obvious when Canada exports its legal models, especially when other countries emulate our constitutional traditions. What, we might ask, could be wrong with that? But we should apply the same norms of legitimacy when we export law as when we import it. Otherwise, it is hypocritical to celebrate the adoption of Canadian legal models abroad while complaining about the imposition of American ones at home.

GOOD GOVERNANCE

Since the late 1980s, the World Bank, the IMF, the United States, other donor governments, and some developing-country elites have aggressively promoted "Good Governance" as a program for the reform of developing-country governments (World Bank 1992). This campaign epitomized the Washington

Consensus to make developing countries safe for transnational capital. It also represented the global exportation (with strong Canadian backing) of a specific US- and OECD-designed recipe for Third World governance.

The Good Governance campaign had two pillars: first, the adoption of and respect for the institutions of liberal democracy, individual rights, and the rule of law, and, second, efficient and accountable public administration. The first pillar of Good Governance required, *inter alia*, free and fair elections (often monitored by international observers), representative democratic institutions, an independent judiciary, a legal framework for impartial and effective enforcement of contracts and property rights without discrimination, respect for law and civil and political rights at all levels of government, and a free press. The second pillar demanded eradication of the corruption and inefficiency that were seen as endemic to public administration in the developing world. Good Governance called for an efficient, competent, and professional public service, openness and accountability in the administration of public funds and discharge of public functions, strong and effective anti-corruption rules, and oversight by an independent public auditor responsible to the legislature, all of which were to be achieved through capacity-building assistance from the rich Northern countries (Leftwich 1993; Rhodes 1996).

So far, this all sounds admirable, but let us continue. The main goal of the first pillar was to provide the legal and political conditions for the flourishing of capital, especially foreign, which was considered indispensable to national development. The focus was on the satisfaction of business requirements for stability. Such stability was to be guaranteed by the predictable and consistent enforcement of private property and contract rights, and a relatively contented civil society.

The second pillar called for public-sector efficiency to be achieved by aggressively adopting a range of market-oriented structural adjustments, including competitive provision of public services, the use of markets in the provision of public goods, privatization of public enterprise, fiscal restraint, reduction of bureaucratic staffs, decentralizing administration, and greater use of non-governmental institutions and resources to develop and administer public policy (Williams and Young 1994). Paradoxically, the very reforms intended to guarantee the stability of business expectations often produced increased instability resulting from worsening conditions for the populace and provoking economic and social crises even in countries, such as Argentina, that had once posed as success stories for neo-conservatism.

Good Governance was not just about reforming Third World governments. It was a project for complete societal transformation presented as an antidote to the allegedly failed experiment of post-colonial nationalist modernization. It encouraged submission to the global disciplines of market liberalization and privatization urged by international financial institutions, powerful states, banks, and transnational corporations. By calling for domestic capacity building, it required a strong state but only insofar as was needed to support an invigorated private marketplace, a pliant workforce, and integration into a world economy that many critics believe systematically reinforced a renewed version of neo-colonial subjugation (Gathii 1998-99, 2000; Leftwich 1993). The Good Governance agenda effectively perpetuated an image of developing-country governments as corrupt and predatory, and of their citizens as irrational and dependent, thus providing the self-fulfilling justification for intervention and rescue by a crusading, universalizing neo-conservatism that left no room for domestic democratic experimentation in pursuit of social solidarity and well-being (Gathii 1998-99, 2000).

Canada has been as vocal a champion of Good Governance as can be found, making it a centrepiece of its foreign policy, for instance, in the New Economic Partnership for African Development, for which Prime Minister Jean Chrétien campaigned vigorously among his G8 colleagues. Canada strongly supported the attachment of Good Governance conditions to multilateral development loans and bilateral aid. A hard look at this purportedly constructive agenda is long overdue because, no matter how well intentioned some of its supporters may have been, the legitimacy of the Good Governance project was compromised from the start of both process and outcomes.

Good Governance prescriptions emanated mainly from the IMF and the World Bank, whose decision-making structures reflected the economic power of the North, not representation by the population in the South, and they were pushed upon recipient countries as take-it-or-leave-it conditions for the receipt of desperately needed financial aid. The developing countries' publics had little or no say in the genesis or application of these prescriptions and often opposed them vocally.

These process concerns would perhaps have faded if Good Governance had had a palpably beneficial impact on the well-being of these countries' citizens. In some instances, it did. For example, Canadian law professors, lawyers, and judges have played positive roles in educating legal professionals about human rights in post-conflict situations and helping them to bring war criminals and perpetrators of genocide to justice. But the effects of Good Governance prescriptions upon ordinary people were overwhelmingly negative, especially for such already marginalized segments of the population as women and indigenous peoples (Rittich 1999, 36). The proposition that Good Governance was legitimate because Canada and other donor countries had a right to attach conditions to how their money was spent ("It's our money, after all"), is unpersuasive. Canadians – both citizens and government officials – should have asked themselves whether they would consider such prescriptions legitimate if they were developed and imposed on Canada by an external body in which Canadians had little or no voice and if their actual effect on ordinary Canadians' quality of life was negative or at best dubious. Canadians should consider whether they should support an agenda of governance reform abroad that results in changes (the entrenchment of private property rights and the elimination of basic social safety nets) that run counter to their own constitutional and political values.[14]

Although the first decade of this century witnessed a growing backlash by developing-country governments and populations against the neo-conservative aspects of Good Governance (especially in Latin America with the election of leftist governments in Bolivia, Brazil, Chile, and Venezuela), that agenda is not dead. The same menu of property rights and minimalist government is still found in UN-sponsored constitutional reform projects for developing countries. The major international financial institutions and donor countries still push the same policy prescriptions, albeit with less emphasis on privatization and more on counter-terrorism. Ottawa should reconsider its support for this paradigm, undertake a careful review of the package of state reforms proposed in its name with a view to distinguishing those that hinder social emancipation in developing countries from those that facilitate it, and recognize that local experimentation and self-determination, not imposition of a single legal and policy formula, are more promising avenues for effective creative and social development.

A Revitalized State

In important respects, states have been the "midwives of globalization" (Brodie 1996, 386) – both the masters of their own destiny and the leading architects of their own purported demise (Schneiderman 2000b, 758). For all their alleged weakness or irrelevance in a globalized world, they play a pivotal role. As Stephen McBride (2001, 15, 18) wrote,

States have had choices, and they have exercised that capacity for choice to construct [neo-conservative] globalization. States are unequal; clearly some of them, the United States in particular, have been in the forefront of recent developments. Still, this does not mean that other states such as Canada have been passive by-standers or victims of the globalization process. Canadian govern-ments have played an active role in shaping the global economy ... Canada, like other states, retained a distinct capacity to manage its continuing encounter with globalization.

Economic and political elites have had considerable success instrumen-talizing the Canadian state in the service of neo-conservative globalization. Most of the market-inspired and other contemporary transformations of the state we described above were driven by national political or economic elites. Canada's elites have mostly been enthusiastic handmaidens of the forces of globalized governance.

But Canadian state actors have the capacity, which they exercise on oc-casion, to resist the social, environmental, and economic damage done by neo-conservative globalization, align themselves with progressive social forces, and seek to restore some balance between the expansion of global trade and investment and the pursuit of health, safety, well-being, cultural diversity, peace, and ecological sustainability. Some elements of the globalized state have progressive possibilities, including the potential use of Canadian courts for transnational public-interest litigation, the influence of the Charter on the spread of a culture of human rights protection worldwide, and the role of Canadian government officials and judges in assisting post-conflict societies to pursue justice and reconciliation. But on the whole, Canadian state actors have asserted their capacity in ways that reinforce the prevailing orthodoxies of globalization. The discrepancies between Canadian governments' assertive-ness in fields such as security, counter-terrorism, and immigration, and their relative retreat from fields such as environmental and social regulation and provision of public goods have major consequences for human welfare and environmental quality. We need to call Canadian state actors to account for these discrepancies and press them to exercise their governance capacities in more progressive and emancipatory directions.

The present moment represents an opportunity for the re-emergence, albeit in new and unpredictable forms, of "compassionate states dedicated

to human well-being and the international practice of responsible sovereignty" (Falk 1999, 6). Liberal-democratic states such as Canada are particularly well positioned to take advantage of this opportunity, combining as they
do well-established governance institutions, access to significant material
resources, and substantial reservoirs of democratic legitimacy. However, they
are also vulnerable (and often openly receptive) to a more regressive politics
associated with neo-conservative globalization. The challenge, as Falk (*ibid.*,
7) recognizes,

> is to direct our energies toward this ongoing, yet seldom acknow-
> ledged, fight for "the soul of the state." In its essence, the question
> being posed ... is whether the state will function in the future
> mainly as an instrument useful for the promotion and protection
> of global trade and investment or whether, by contrast, the state
> can recover its sense of balance in this globalizing setting so that
> the success of markets will not be achieved at the expense of the
> well-being of peoples.

The goal of this struggle is not to turn back history and reinstate the post–
Second World War bargain between state, capital, labour, and society. It is
not to remake the Canadian state in the nostalgic image of a welfare state
that never fully existed. It is to reclaim for the state a central, albeit non-
exclusive role in the search for social emancipation in the changing and
unstable conditions of contemporary life. The Canadian state, with the support of Canadian citizens, should exercise its power to shape and govern
human affairs more confidently than it has in the recent past, and it should
do so in the service of hope rather than fear, of human rights and freedoms
rather than the suppression of dissent and difference, and of cosmopolitan
ideals of human solidarity and betterment rather than parochial economic
self-interest.

The state was a central player in the global system of Keynesian regulation,
and despite all the changes we collectively label as the supraconstitution, it
remains the most powerful actor, still able – especially in periods of crisis – to
bring transnational capital to heel. Given its record in transforming the world
on the basis of more ruthless, less generous principles, imagining it as a locus
for socially progressive governance strategies may be difficult. But states and

their laws can have just as big a role to play in opposing or moderating the negative impacts of neo-conservative globalization as they had in constructing it. They also have the potential – limited and always subject to the risk of subversion – to be used strategically to advance counter-hegemonic projects.

A revitalized role for the state must recognize that a whole array of governance relationships exists beyond the state, some of which we explore in the next chapter. The state plays, and will continue to play, a central role in enabling and regulating these complex governance relationships. Canadians must recognize that the character of the struggle for democracy and social justice has changed with the transformation of the state and the rise of private authority. As Santos (2002, 490) argues, "While before, the struggle was about democratizing the state's regulatory monopoly, today the struggle must be about democratizing the loss of such a monopoly."

In this context, one of the main challenges for government today is to coordinate the various organizations, interests, and networks that have emerged to fill the vacuum left by its retreat from social regulation. The Canadian state remains deeply involved in policy domains that affect the distribution of benefits and harms in society. Among its principal tasks should be to democratize and foster those aspects of non-state governance that support social emancipation, justice, health, welfare, and ecological integrity while reining in those that hinder them. For this reason, as we argue in the next chapter, it is imperative to evaluate the role of non-state actors and institutions in contemporary governance.

7
Global Law beyond the State: Governance by Business and Civil Society

To this point, our discussion of governance beyond borders has centred on the state and the interstate system, with Part 1 examining international organizations and regimes in order to sketch the contours of Canada's emerging supraconstitution, and Chapter 6 exploring the contemporary reconfiguration of the Canadian state. In this chapter, we consider governance arrangements beyond the state, from self-regulation by business to transnational governance initiatives of grassroots social movements and civil society organizations. Here we find ourselves in what is widely considered the domain of "private" authority: a multitude of spaces where non-state actors, whether transnational corporations and civil society organizations or illegal terrorist and organized-crime networks, successfully exert some degree of governance authority over certain issues (Hall and Biersteker 2002; Cutler, Haufler, and Porter 1999).

This chapter first examines the growing authority of transnational business actors and the increasing variety of initiatives – from voluntary corporate codes of conduct to the lex mercatoria – that they have deployed to regulate transnational enterprise and promote their own notions of global corporate social responsibility (CSR). Although these governance arrangements vary substantially in purpose and effect, they tend to entrench neo-conservative forms of globalization.

The next part of the chapter considers emergent forms of transnational governance by civil society, a broad category that includes individuals, informal grassroots social movements, flexible transnational advocacy networks, and NGOs. Although the governance arrangements constructed by civil society actors include both elite-led and grassroots-driven initiatives, they are more likely than their transnational-business-led counterparts to challenge neo-conservative globalization and to offer alternative models for global governance.[1]

The categories of state, market, and civil society are crude simplifications of messy social realities. They suggest autonomous, self-contained social systems, each with its own logic of action, whereas in practice, actors and social systems interpenetrate, pursuing multiple logics. It is difficult to tell where one ends and another begins, or whether particular entities fit better into one category or another. Yet these conventional distinctions retain meaning for social actors, even in today's world of blurred boundaries and shifting actor identities. However arbitrary and inadequate, they remain a useful starting point for our analysis.

The Rise of Transnational Business

The consolidation of a supraconstitution for economic globalization discussed in Chapter 3 and the contemporary transformations of the Canadian state discussed in Chapter 6 are closely linked to an increasing concentration of power in transnational business, notably transnational corporations (TNCs), banks, and credit-rating agencies. By the late 1990s, more than half of the world's hundred largest economies were corporations (Anderson and Cavanagh 2000, 3; Gabel and Bruner 2003, 2).[2] The majority of international trade takes the form of intra-firm transfers. Many important decisions affecting national societies and economies are made in corporate boardrooms that are outside the halls of government and often altogether beyond the political borders of the affected societies. This has always been true of developing countries and of semi-peripheral countries, like Canada, that are not only heavily dependent on natural resource industries, export markets, and imported manufactured and consumer goods but host few of the major corporations that determine their economic fates. In the colonial era, the imperial powers' corporations exercised profound influence over colonized societies, in many cases waging war, levying taxes, and otherwise exercising sovereign-like authority (Robins 2006).

Networks of production and consumption are increasingly global in nature, making foreign direct investment (FDI) and international trade more substantial, mobile, and sensitive to international competition than ever before. These changes in FDI and trade have been dwarfed by the increasingly volatile movement of transnational capital via portfolio investment and foreign currency transactions, whose hyper-mobility has brought entire economies to their knees in a matter of weeks. The higher the possibility of foreign capital taking flight, the greater the disciplinary power that TNCs wield over host economies, with profound implications for law and politics.

Business organizations have been among the most dedicated proponents of economic globalization, advocating a more integrated world economy and arguing that a free market can produce greater prosperity at optimal efficiency. In Canada, the Business Council on National Issues – now the Canadian Council of Chief Executives, the organization representing the major foreign and domestically owned TNCs operating in Canada – has lobbied for trade liberalization since the late 1970s. The Canadian Manufacturers Association (which, in 1996, merged with the Canadian Exporters Association to form Canadian Manufacturers and Exporters, the principal industry lobby group in Canada) abandoned protectionism during the same period and became a vocal supporter of economic liberalization. A big-business front, the Canadian Coalition for Job Opportunities, was set up as a vehicle to pour millions of dollars into promoting the *Canada-US Free Trade Agreement* (CUFTA) during the 1988 election campaign.

Satellite-based computer technologies have allowed businesses to link production systems with markets that operate twenty-four hours a day, seven days a week. International trade in goods has increased dramatically since the Second World War. Foreign direct investment has also mushroomed in recent years, especially among OECD countries, as corporations invest more and more capital in production facilities, subsidiaries, and joint ventures in foreign countries, or establish contractual relationships with foreign suppliers for the production of goods and services.

In Canada, both FDI and trade substantially intensified in the wake of CUFTA and NAFTA, and they continued their general upward trend until contracting sharply as a result of the US financial collapse and world economic downturn of 2008 (Organisation for Economic Co-operation and Development 2008a, 2008b). The most noticeable consequence has been an increase in the size, scope, autonomy, and transnational influence of business corporations. Within limits, TNCs can locate their head offices, manufacturing facilities, and sales divisions in a variety of places and so determine which region, country, or city gets the tax revenues, jobs, spin-off contracts, and philanthropic benefits their presence can generate. A TNC facing objectionable circumstances in one jurisdiction can shut down there and relocate to another. Some industries are more footloose than others: mobility is much higher for corporations in the apparel industry that work through local licencees and contractors than for those in the extractive sector that construct and operate their own production facilities.

Many corporations carry out operations in other countries, where they extract natural resources, engage in manufacturing, advertise their products, open branches, promote franchises of their business, or outsource functions such as customer service or accounting. In these cases, the local effects may be positive (increasing employment, transferring technology and know-how, expanding exports through opening a factory) or negative (endangering health through lax safety or environmental standards, exacerbating armed conflicts, depleting resources, or avoiding taxes through transfer pricing). Many TNCs apply standards abroad for labour practices, wages, human rights, and environmental impacts that are less stringent than those enshrined in the laws of their home countries and sometimes do not even comply with weaker host-country laws. Their economic muscle can provide them with a great deal of power over domestic politics and decisive influence over the lives of local residents. There is evidence that governments may in some cases be able to induce a regulatory race to the top in which companies in jurisdictions with higher regulatory standards become more competitive (Vogel 1995), but it is more typical for TNCs and domestic businesses affected by global markets to use their economic clout to exert downward pressure on government regulation in the name of international competitiveness. Although the evidence of a resulting regulatory race to the bottom, or "regulatory chill," is mixed (Esty 1995; Esty and Geradin 1997; Neumayer 2001), there is no doubt that TNCs and business elites in many places routinely invoke the spectre of global competition to urge reductions in government regulation and taxation, and that the corresponding fear of losing jobs, investment, or ground in a never-ending global economic race has a substantial influence on policy making in Canada and elsewhere.

Corporations also affect the transnational movement of people by recruiting workers or promoting tourism. Although they often provide local jobs, housing, education, cultural events, and community development, TNCs have generally been exempted by the newer international trade rules from performance requirements that, in exchange for permission to operate in a host economy, would oblige them to hire domestic workers, reinvest profits, transfer technology, source their inputs, and perform research and development locally, or contribute to building a developing country's educational or physical infrastructure.

The impacts of international trade and FDI are profound, but they are dwarfed in some respects by the effects of portfolio investment, currency trading, and other more volatile forms of transnational capital movement, which have accelerated dramatically in the last three decades. Massive increases in market capitalization of stock exchanges in both the developed and developing worlds, the rise of institutional investors, the growth of mutual funds, and the liberalization of investment regimes under the auspices of IMF structural adjustment programs and bilateral investment treaties have fuelled immense growth in transnational portfolio investment, in which investors buy and trade stocks listed on foreign stock exchanges. This form of investment is considerably more volatile than FDI, since investors may move their capital around instantly without sinking it into physical facilities or business relationships.

Even more volatile than portfolio investment is international currency trading. The liberalization of exchange rates and the development of twenty-four-hour-a-day computerized currency trading have made possible rapid, massive movements of capital in and out of national economies. Currency markets now respond instantaneously and sometimes catastrophically to the slightest signals of economic distress or to government policies perceived as unacceptable by global capital. When foreign capital flees an economy, as it has done on numerous occasions in recent memory (during the Asian, Mexican, Russian, and Argentine financial crises), it can spark or exacerbate economic chaos causing profound negative impacts on the security and well-being of ordinary people. For the countries that are most vulnerable to such effects, the constant threat of capital flight is at least as effective a discipline on government economic and social policy as are the demands of the international financial institutions or major trading partners. Indeed, this acceleration of hyper-volatile capital movement has been actively encouraged by the major international financial institutions, including the IMF, through their advocacy of open capital markets and their hostility – until very recently – to national capital controls. But focusing on the international financial institutions distracts attention from other power-brokers in this global game: the private American credit-rating agencies, such as Moody's and Standard and Poor's, which rate the quality of government bonds and other debt instruments. These ratings, which are determined in almost complete obscurity by private agencies that, up to now, have attracted almost no attention from students of governance, play a critical role in shaping transnational capital movements (T. Sinclair 2005).

TNCs, industry associations, governments, intergovernmental organizations, and civil society groups have devoted a great deal of energy over the last two decades to promoting corporate social responsibility (CSR), in which transnational businesses respect or promote social, economic, environmental, and cultural rights when engaged in foreign trade, direct investment, or in international securities or currency transactions. Many Canadian companies make concerted efforts to operate in a socially responsible manner or to promote norms of acceptable corporate behaviour (Dashwood 2005). Canadian business leaders are active in efforts to develop and implement transnational codes of good conduct in numerous economic sectors. Some Canadian firms are international leaders in sustainable business practices and green technology. Canada is also home to world-leading industry groups dedicated to sustainable business, including the World Green Building Council, which is responsible for promoting the LEED (Leadership in Energy and Environmental Design) green building-rating system worldwide.[3]

Even among Canadian companies that endorse the concept of social responsibility, there is a bewildering variety of views regarding what it entails. For many companies, it refers simply to engaging in philanthropic activities without examining, let alone changing, their business practices. Many others adopt a narrow instrumental attitude toward CSR, implementing discrete projects mainly to improve their public image or satisfy supply chain demands. A few integrate social responsibility into their core business, making a sustained strategic effort to transform their organizations from top to bottom. An increasing number of Canadian companies report publicly on their environmental or CSR performance, but the number and quality of reports are low in comparison with other jurisdictions (Canadian Business for Social Responsibility 2008). Many Canadian companies publicly claim that they or their products are socially responsible or environmentally friendly, but there are few external checks beyond basic false advertising laws to validate an almost infinite variation in these claims. Even genuine leaders committed to transparency and sustainability risk being conflated with the unscrupulous shills out to make a buck from public demand for socially responsible goods.

Other Canadian companies are less admirable. Irresponsible behaviour occurs when Canadian TNCs engage in corrupt dealings with foreign officials, adopt harmful labour practices that fail to respect workers' rights, exacerbate insecurity and violence in conflict zones, trample upon the rights of indigenous peoples, or violate environmental laws. Corporations that apply their home-state rules or transnational good governance norms in their overseas operations find it hard to compete against others that, in order to maximize their profits, refuse to comply even with voluntary industry standards.

Though the debate continues regarding which instruments constitute the most effective means of governing corporate behaviour, several egregious cases of misconduct by Canadian-based TNCs have moved observers to call for a concerted international effort on this front. Widespread outrage swept through Canada when it was revealed that Petro-Canada and Ivanhoe Mines, both operating in Myanmar, and Talisman Energy, operating in Sudan, provided substantial support to the repressive regimes in those countries. Although Ottawa's weak response to these instances of corporate misconduct has been attributed to a failure of political will, it can also be seen as reflecting a structural flaw in global governance mechanisms, which are insufficiently developed to regulate the activities of transnational capital. In the case of Talisman, concerns that it would lose out to other countries, notably China and Malaysia, which were willing to allow their own firms to operate in Sudan, muddled Canadian government priorities (Economist Intelligence Unit 2003; Cattaneo 2003). As we noted in Chapter 4, Ottawa sacrificed human security "on the altar of private sector profit" (Matthews 2004, 245). In the end, Talisman's withdrawal from Sudan did little to affect the regime, which continued to deal with TNCs based in other countries. The case of Sudan suggests the need for a coordinated international approach to preventing multinational corporations from doing business with highly repressive regimes (Simons 2004). Yet, currently, there exist no legal mechanisms of global governance capable of adequately regulating the conduct of transnational firms in failed or failing states.

UN special representative John Ruggie's 2008 report on TNCs and human rights took some of the heat off transnational corporations by insisting that states bear the primary responsibility to protect human rights.[4] The report retreated from earlier international efforts to define TNC obligations, such as the draft *United Nations Code of Conduct for Transnational Corporations*, which was scuttled by US opposition in the 1980s, and the *United Nations Draft Norms on the Responsibilities of Transnational Corporations and Other Business Enterprises with Regard to Human Rights*, which stalled after intense opposition from global business, powerful states, and Ruggie himself.[5] According to Ruggie, TNCs have an obligation to exercise due diligence to "respect" (rather than "protect") human rights, making them responsible only for human rights impacts they caused themselves or were complicit in and leaving them free of responsibility for human rights abuses by actors (such as security forces) they could have influenced but chose not to.[6]

The document did point a way forward by more clearly defining the parameters of corporations' independent responsibility to respect human rights. Whether and how this will develop remains to be seen, but the Ruggie report suggests that this responsibility should be operationalized primarily via national or non-state initiatives rather than in the form of enforceable international standards. Although emphasizing the importance of national state-based human rights mechanisms, it celebrates the emergence of a variety of multi-stakeholder and corporate self-regulatory mechanisms for improving corporate human rights practices.

The demand for the effective and humane regulation of transnational capital is understandably high. But governing global business is an extremely complicated proposition (Braithwaite and Drahos 2000). Some advocacy groups maintain that governments should force corporations to observe the same rules abroad that are required of them in their home jurisdiction or in the highest-standard jurisdiction in which they operate. Other groups assert that a single government's regulation of its own companies will fail to stop their foreign rivals from continuing their own harmful practices and will simply reduce the competitiveness of the regulating country's industry.

A number of questions arise regarding who should govern the behaviour of Canadian corporations, by what methods they can be held accountable, how they can be regulated outside the country, and whether international cooperation is preferable to unilateral Canadian action. Mendelsohn and Wolfe (2004, 279) found that 78 percent of Canadians believe that the government should withhold contracts from Canadian businesses operating abroad that do not respect their host countries' environmental or labour laws. In addition, 54 percent believe that Canadians boycotting these companies are doing the right thing.

This discrepancy between public preferences and corporate imperatives raises other issues. There may, for one, be no coordination among the players. Canada's corporate representatives may not be expressing the values espoused by most Canadians. Law firms build terms into transnational contracts without guidance from a central authority. Private-sector experts may provide advice to a foreign government favouring their own interests more than those of the host country or the Canadian government. The encroachment by non-state players, including transnational firms and industry associations, on the traditional functions of government is likely to keep increasing. This trend will generate multi-level, multi-actor governance relationships in which the nation-state either tries to mediate between international institutions, domestic business, and civil society or throws up its hands at the prospect of undertaking this task.

Global Governance by Business, for Business

Industry self-regulation has emerged as a preferred option for many firms, trade associations, and even some governments and NGOs. Examples range from business-led initiatives to promote environmentally friendly or socially responsible business, to the lex mercatoria – the growing body of private rules designed to facilitate transnational business transactions. We can only suggest the range and variety of initiatives here.

CSR INITIATIVES

Transnational trade associations and councils of business leaders have developed numerous sets of principles for socially or environmentally responsible business practices, such as the International Chamber of Commerce's *Business Charter for Sustainable Development*. Industry-dominated standards development bodies such as the International Organization for Standardization (ISO) have generated voluntary standards for corporate environmental management (the ISO 14000 series) and are now producing a guide on social responsibility (ISO 26000). Sector-specific principles and codes of conduct have also proliferated in sectors such as the chemical industry (Responsible Care), apparel (the business-led Fairtrade Labelling Organization), mining (the Canadian Mining Association's Towards Sustainable Mining initiative), the financial sector (the Equator Principles, developed by leading transnational banks to consider the social and environmental impacts of project finance), and forestry (the American Forest and Paper Association's Sustainable Forestry Initiative and the Canadian Standards Association's Sustainable Forest Management standard). Firm-specific voluntary initiatives have also proliferated beyond measure, including codes of conduct, environmental management systems, corporate environmental or sustainability reporting programs, and community advisory processes.

The proponents of these industry-led CSR schemes typically seek to establish their legitimacy by appealing either to a core constituency of business actors or to a wider audience of consumers, environmentalists, labour and human rights advocates, and policy makers (Cashore, Auld, and Newsom 2004). The former tactic typically implies emphasizing their responsiveness to the needs and demands of global business (ease of implementation, cost savings, return on investment, increased competitiveness) and characterizing them as merely "technical" rather than political or value-laden (Wood 2005). The latter typically involves emphasizing their ability to deliver substantial improvements of corporate social and environmental performance, their responsiveness to the wider public interest, and their ability to contribute to the realization of political goals such as sustainable development. The two tactics sometimes reinforce one another as, for instance, in the popular claim that CSR is simultaneously good for society and good for business (Schmidheiny 1992; Elkington 1998).

But they are more often in tension with each other, especially since the "social responsibility pays" argument often runs out of steam once the "low-hanging fruit" has been picked. What makes a governance initiative attractive to business managers often tends to decrease its appeal for labour unions, human rights activists, and environmentalists – and vice versa. Intriguingly, contending arguments are often deployed by the same actors in an effort to establish legitimacy with competing audiences. Thus, for example, ISO and its sister standardization body the International Electrotechnical Commission seek to establish their authority with global business by emphasizing that their standards are created "by industry, for industry," on the basis of market demand, to meet the needs of the industries that use them (International Electrotechnical Commission 2000; International Organization for Standardization 2002). These same bodies simultaneously seek to establish their bona fides with environmental, consumer, labour, and human rights NGOs, as well as governments, by claiming that their standards reflect a consensus of all interested parties, will improve environmental and social performance, and advance the agenda of sustainable development.

The proof of these often conflicting claims is in the pudding. In the long run, audiences other than business itself will need to be satisfied that governance by and for global business is legitimate and effective. These audiences often have concerns with the processes by which these governance arrangements are developed and the outcomes they produce. In terms of process, the proponents of self-regulation can at least say that the primary targets of these rules – business firms – have a direct say in their content. On the other hand, if many interested and affected parties – such as workers, consumers, citizens, governments, and human rights advocates – are excluded or marginalized from the rule-making process, these claims to legitimacy will ultimately collapse. Furthermore, if these initiatives ground their authority in claims that they are value-neutral technical standards, they are also bound to fail in the long run since everyone involved, including the industry participants, recognizes that determining the acceptable social and environmental impacts of business is a fundamentally political, value-laden exercise.

When it comes to outcomes, self-regulatory schemes will have to deliver environmental, labour, and social performance improvements that go substantially beyond "business as usual" if they are to be accepted as legitimate by external audiences. Industry-led CSR schemes may run into serious snags, since firms face incentives to free-ride on the efforts of others and to take the minimum action necessary to secure desired public image gains. No matter how well intentioned, initiatives that are designed primarily by and for business itself cannot ultimately produce outcomes that exceed expected business-as-usual technological improvements, let alone contribute substantially to human development or environmental protection (Wood 2006).

There is considerable evidence that many companies, having made forward-looking commitments to social responsibility in public, still lobby governments intensely in private for policies that contradict or undermine these commitments (SustainAbility and WWF-UK 2005). The US Chemical Manufacturers' Association lobbied Congress to remove more than 90 percent of the chemicals from the list of toxic releases that industry must report, in contrast with the commitment to public transparency found in the industry's voluntary Responsible Care program (Prakash 2000, 202). Thus, substantial gaps may exist between what firms say they stand for and how they actually behave.

Canadian firms and industry groups have played key roles in developing some environmental and CSR agendas. Responsible Care, the flagship environmental and social responsibility program of the global chemical industry, was pioneered by the Canadian chemical industry in the aftermath of the catastrophic Union Carbide factory explosion in Bhopal, India. Canadian chemical firms hoped to distance themselves from their American counterparts and forestall tougher regulation. Over time, this self-regulatory program became more stringent, making participation mandatory for chemical industry association members, toughening its standards, and requiring independent external verification. These changes were made mainly in response to pressure from civil society. Still, the program does not reach many small chemical companies that are not members of national trade associations.

Canadian industry executives and technical experts typically punch above their weight in ISO, an international industry-led NGO, which is the leading source of global technical standards for business. Canadians played key roles in launching the development of the ISO 26000 social responsibility guidance standard, and Canada holds the chair and secretariat of ISO Technical Committee 207 (responsible for the ISO 14000 family of environmental management standards) and Technical Committee 176 (which develops the flagship ISO 9000 quality management standards). In addition, the Canadian extractive industry has been active in the development of global CSR initiatives for mining, and the Canadian Standards Association is one of the main contenders in the market for voluntary sustainable forestry standards.

On the whole, however, Canadian business has been more of an object than an agent of these transnational self-regulatory efforts. With few major transnational corporations headquartered in Canada, Canadian businesses often find themselves pushed by external forces – commonly in the form of head offices and customers abroad – to adopt CSR standards designed for other markets. Canadian firms that want to do business with American, European, or Japanese TNCs must satisfy their growing demands for environmental management systems, CSR, fair trade, and the like. Canadian banks find themselves under pressure to apply such emerging global financial industry standards as the Equator Principles in their project finance activities. As nodes in global production and distribution networks, many Canadian companies are likewise under pressure to conform to such global environmental and sustainability standards as the Global Reporting Initiative and the UN Global Compact.

When it comes to transnational CSR and environmental initiatives, therefore, Canadian business finds itself in the same position that Canada occupies in the global economy generally: a satellite of the American economy with room for some agency in a limited number of fields.

THE LEX MERCATORIA

So far, we have been discussing examples in which business actors expressly seek to regulate themselves in the name of social or environmental responsibility. Global business has also devised a whole range of governance initiatives – including standardized international contracts, bills of lading, insurance terms, and credit ratings – that are aimed not at social or environmental responsibility but simply at facilitating and regularizing transnational business transactions. The most significant development from the point of view of legal globalization is the lex mercatoria, a stateless body of law built up by international commercial arbitrators to govern transnational business conflicts. To resolve their international disputes, many companies use private mediation and arbitration under processes perfected during the past century by the International Chamber of Commerce. International commercial arbitration is "globalization's favoured form of dispute resolution" (Watson Hamilton 2004, 127) and probably the fastest-spreading legal regime in the world.

It seems clear that a body of law developed almost exclusively by lawyers and arbitrators in closed proceedings with no participation by labour or civil society would face a legitimacy deficit. International commercial arbitration has been criticized for lawlessness because of the flexible, often arbitrary character of the rules applied to the dispute is basically no law at all, and because the dispute resolution processes and decisions are usually closed, secret, and highly discretionary (McConnaughay 1999; Scheuerman 1999). Whereas some scholars emphasize the role of national courts in giving concrete shape and meaning to the lex mercatoria (Wai 2002), others urge that the development of a private transnational legal system should be resisted because it marginalizes national judicial systems, undermining nation-state sovereignty (see Chibundu 1999).

On the other hand, the lex mercatoria can make a more credible claim to being neutral, technical, and private than can many of the CSR initiatives that explicitly address highly politicized issues. The lex mercatoria is not about redistribution, environmental protection, or social justice, at least ostensibly: it is simply about regulating international business transactions. But even here, it runs into difficulty. By privileging party autonomy and freedom of contract over other values and by presupposing symmetrical bargaining relationships, the lex mercatoria marginalizes competing values (such as consumer, labour, and environmental protection or social development) and masks the often huge disparities of knowledge and power that characterize dealings between transnational corporations and their much weaker contracting parties, especially in developing countries. Some Third World legal scholars argue that, for these reasons, international commercial arbitration subtly perpetuates a form of neo-colonialism (Shalakany 2000). Other scholars deplore similar power disparities in developed countries, pointing to the increasing use of compulsory arbitration in business-to-consumer contracts (Stipanowich 1997).

GLOBALIZATION OF THE LEGAL PROFESSION

The legal profession itself plays a very significant role in governing beyond borders since the lex mercatoria's principal architects are the legal experts who draft transnational business contracts and serve as arbitrators in transnational business disputes (Dezalay and Garth 1996). The lex mercatoria has spread hand in glove with the globalization of the legal profession, which has, in turn, been made possible by the globalization of business. Because the legal profession responds largely to the needs of business, and because globalized business is frequently led by American norms, the globalization of the profession mainly takes the form of the worldwide spread of American law firms and their ways of practising law (Dezalay and Garth 2002). For Canada, this has meant a marginalization of the Canadian legal profession as corporate Canada itself has been hollowed out by the increasing concentration of management functions in US headquarters rather than in Canadian subsidiaries (Arthurs 1998, 29-30). The more Canadian regulations are harmonized to US standards, the less TNCs require Canadian lawyers to deal with their branches' affairs in Canada. As a result of these trends, the Canadian legal profession is less and less able to compete in its own market for transnational legal services.

The globalization of law firms has been paralleled by the globalization of the practice of public-interest law, a development closely related to the rise of transnational public-interest litigation discussed in Chapter 6. Two transnational networks of public-interest lawyers, with similar names but very different approaches, exemplify the trend toward public-interest law's globalization. Avocats sans Frontières (AsF) was established by human rights lawyers in Belgium in 1992 to protect the rights of accused persons and to fight for human rights whenever and wherever circumstances demanded.[7] After an early focus on emergency criminal defence work, AsF expanded its mandate to include legal training, technical assistance, and criminal justice capacity building, with a strong emphasis on local needs, partners, assets, and constraints. Rather than imposing "Western" ideas and solutions, it emphasizes protecting human rights of the most vulnerable groups in countries in crisis and in developing countries more broadly. It often does so by shielding lawyers and judges against abuses by repressive governments. Independent national sections of AsF exist in Europe, West Africa, and (since 2002) Quebec.[8]

Lawyers Without Borders (LWOB) was established by a Connecticut lawyer in 2000 as a kind of pro bono legal service for NGOs around the world.

Its activities include volunteer legal support for projects aimed at advancing the rule of law in developing countries, neutral observation of closed trials, training and exchanges for lawyers and judges, provision of resources for developing-country law schools, and collaborative legal research opportunities for law students and law firms. Unlike AsF, LWOB characterizes itself as a neutral observer rather than an advocacy group. It works in partnership with governments, courts, and law enforcement agencies in host countries and with the World Bank and major global law firms. Much of its work is focused on training prosecutors, public defenders, private lawyers, and judges on such issues as corruption, mediation, and legal advocacy techniques.

LWOB advances a mainstream "rule of law" and "good governance" agenda in line with that described in Chapter 6, in which Western (and more pointedly, neo-conservative) legal values, institutions, and practices are exported to the developing world. In this relationship, the global South is a passive recipient soaking up the knowledge and adopting the expertise of Northern lawyers and legal systems. Some of LWOB's projects have been unabashedly wedded to US foreign policy priorities. After the 2003 Iraq invasion, for example, it was involved in a venture to provide Arabic translations of American law textbooks, *The Federalist Papers*, and the US constitution for courses taught by a US Army lawyer in Iraq. After a rough start (including a trademark challenge from Doctors Without Borders), LWOB has begun to build a profile in the United States, Canada, and the United Kingdom, and has supported legal projects in Africa, the Middle East, and elsewhere. It now claims to be the world's largest group of volunteer lawyers who stand ready to offer pro bono service to international projects and initiatives.[9]

Canada has its own transnational public-interest law organization in Canadian Lawyers Abroad–Avocats canadiens à l'étranger (CLA-ACE), a nonprofit group committed to serving the legal needs of developing countries by harnessing the experience and skills of Canadian lawyers in the areas of good governance, the rule of law, and human rights.[10] Similar transnational networks also exist in specific fields such as human rights (for example, US-based Human Rights First and Canadian Lawyers for International Human Rights) and the environment (for instance, Environmental Law Alliance Worldwide).[11]

Most of these groups are concentrated in the global North, but the involvement of Southern legal NGOs is increasing. In some cases, these networks have developed the capacity to establish and deploy integrated cross-national teams and multi-jurisdictional legal strategies in the service of peace, human rights, democracy, or environmental protection, but most remain far behind private law firms in organizational capacity and reach.

These bodies have an ambiguous and symbiotic relationship with the increasingly globalized private bar. Some – such as AsF – attract mainly career human rights lawyers, but most rely heavily on pro bono work by lawyers in private for-profit practice and on financial support from private law firms and bar associations. LWOB and Canada's CLA-ACE rely explicitly on this private bar pro bono model and actively cultivate closer relations with large private firms. They thus respond to, and rely upon, the increasingly globalized private bar's need for legitimacy by generating convenient outlets for pro bono work. Such outlets are critical for a profession that grounds its self-regulatory authority in an obligation to serve the public interest. Public-interest law groups that cultivate close symbiotic relationships with the predominantly Anglo-American global private bar are likely to have more material success and longevity than those that do not. If so, will their increasing dependence on and alliance with the global private bar ultimately compromise their pursuit of social justice and genuine change? Will they solidify the global dominance of Anglo-American legal culture at the expense of other legal traditions and local legal capacity? The answers remain unclear.

GOVERNANCE BY GLOBAL BUSINESS: AN ASSESSMENT

This section has sketched the materialization and growing authority of transnational governance by and for business, and the ambivalent supporting role played by lawyers in that process. Some of the self-regulatory transnational governance initiatives championed by Canadian businesses are innovative and transformative models for socially responsible businesses around the world. Others suffer from serious legitimacy deficits, exclude many interested and affected parties from meaningful participation, and make dubious contributions to the advancement of human rights and environmental protection. Many help to consolidate the neo-conservative model of globalization and global governance discussed in earlier chapters. Canadian governments, citizens, and some business leaders are actively exploring alternatives to this hegemonic model. Civil society actors have launched initiatives to hold businesses accountable for their adverse impacts on society and environment or to set best-practice standards for businesses to meet. Some business leaders have teamed up with civil society organizations to develop hybrid multistakeholder CSR initiatives. Some state and civil society actors have insisted on a greater role for democratically elected governments in business self-regulation, whether via incentives and preferences or via regulation and penalties. In short, government, business, and civil society actors interact in complicated ways in pursuit of sometimes overlapping, sometimes conflicting governance agendas. To appreciate this interaction, we turn now to the role of civil society in global governance.

Civil Society and Global Governance

The growth of international organizations and global business has been paralleled by a proliferation in the number and an expansion in the reach of international non-governmental organizations (INGOs), networks of public-interest activists, and transnational social movements (TSMs). The term "global civil society," while inadequate to capture their diversity and complexity, is useful because it distinguishes "a field of action and thought occupied by individual and collective citizen initiatives of a voluntary, nonprofit nature" (Falk 2004, 86) from those occupied by profit-oriented actors, government authorities, and international organizations. To identify civil society as a category is to recognize that the realms of social interaction that determine how humans govern and are governed are not exhausted by the formal apparatus of the state or the profit-seeking logic of the market.

Civil society encompasses individuals, unorganized social movements, informal social networks, formal civil society organizations (CSOs), and their interactions. By CSOs, we mean NGOs that are independent of both business and government, and are not substantially motivated by pursuit of profit for themselves or their members. CSOs might work on issues such as consumer protection, environment, human rights, humanitarian relief, and health. They include religious groups, labour unions, private foundations, policy think-tanks, and membership organizations. Like business actors, they vary greatly in size, scope, objectives, and effects. They range from local to global in their scope, and they vary from conservative to revolutionary in their ideology. They may be rights enhancing (advocating the extension of rights to new claimants) or rights limiting (opposing the claims of previously unrecognized rights claimants). They may preach tolerance or intolerance; they may advocate an exclusive, even divisive, politics of identity or an inclusive ethic of cosmopolitanism. They may be genuinely dedicated to eradicating a social evil, or they may be committed to defending the vested interests responsible for creating the problem (although, if they are simply fronts for commercial interests or governments, they would not meet our definition of a CSO). They may have broad membership bases and democratic decision processes, or they may be unaccountable and undemocratic. Although globally active CSOs are predominantly based in the global North and carry out many of their activities in the South, citizens in the global South are also organizing themselves wherever democratic rights have become more firmly established.

When thinking about global forces, many people – particularly those bombarded with images of chaos and reports of crises over which no one seems able to exert any control – feel battered by relentless tides of technological or social change. It is indeed understandable if, as victims of seemingly irresistible global forces, individuals feel powerless, whether they suffer as refugees, sweatshop workers, or victims of environmental disasters. Even beneficiaries of rising wages, high-tech jobs, and an increasing variety of consumer goods may feel they are vulnerable in the face of unpredictable external pressures. And yet it has never been more obvious – particularly to those who have come to consciousness with the Internet at their fingertips – that individuals can seek information from the most distant sources and interact with others anywhere in the world. If knowledge is power, never have the average man and woman had so much potential as agents to influence their surroundings, not just locally, but now globally.

Furthermore, simply in their role as individuals, citizens have global impacts when they buy something made in a developing-world factory, travel abroad, or send a message to a friend, relative, colleague, power holder, or institution outside their own national borders. Determining if the global reach of these individual citizens is for the better or for the worse is another matter and may depend on whether the factory in the South offers good working conditions or exploits under-age children, whether the tourist dollars are spent supporting a region's handicraft economy that employs local artisans or sustaining a local sex trade that enslaves young women, and whether the communications streaking over the Internet are organizing a campaign to impede the spread of malaria or to further a terrorist plot to kill innocent civilians halfway around the world.

Certain kinds of individuals can play globally influential roles, particularly when, in networks, their expertise persuades informed actors that a serious problem needs to be addressed. Transnational governance can be seen when the consensus generated by communities of experts induces governments to take the recommended action. Environmental policies related to ozone-layer depletion and global warming are a product of governments responding to advice received from the scientific community, sometimes mediated through environmental NGOs. The influence of these epistemic communities (Haas 1992) on governance varies greatly, however. Whereas ozone depletion is a policy domain in which a global scientific consensus prompted rapid action by governments, climate change is one marked by persistent foot dragging by most governments in the face of ever stronger global scientific agreement and increasingly urgent warnings.

Individuals can have a decisive impact on world affairs when they act in groups as moral entrepreneurs to catalyze social or legal change. In this regard, our concern is less with the disempowered or re-empowered person's relationship with globalizing forces than with how Canada's legal system should respond to the growing phenomenon of citizens who operate collectively to support a cause involving action outside their national borders. These collectivities include social movements with few or no formal organizational structures, as well as formal CSOs. When these collectivities mobilize in transnational advocacy groups, they can be seen as constituting "globalization from below" because they bring pressure to bear from the grassroots in order to urge economic and political elites to respond to their demands. Some CSOs, particularly those located in the global North, may also participate in "globalization from above" when they become part of policy elites themselves.[12]

CIVIL SOCIETY AND GLOBALIZATION FROM ABOVE

Some CSOs establish enough political and intellectual capital that they gain entry to elite policy-making circles, advising governments and international organizations, and dispensing prescriptions or delivering programs to recipient governments, organizations, or communities often located in the global South. These organizations typically offer technical expertise, specialized knowledge, and the legitimacy acquired by their independence from both government and business.

Just as business groups lobby to have their representatives included in government delegations to international negotiations, so have CSOs succeeded in winning a place on many government delegations. In the specialized transnational negotiations involved in working out multilateral environmental agreements on such issues as biodiversity or global warming, Canadian government delegations include CSO experts whose knowledge base is often superior to that of the diplomats whose job is to speak on behalf of Ottawa. Outside the context of government delegations, the emergence of certain kinds of CSOs could be seen when Ottawa mobilized foreign peace movements to press their own governments in support of its effort to achieve a treaty banning anti-personnel land mines. It can be seen when governments of developing countries retain the consulting services of Northern CSOs for advice on health issues, human development projects, nature conservation, or land reform. It occurs in the rare cases where governments delegate the administration of international agreements to CSOs, as in the case of the Lower Danube Green Corridor in which the WWF (World Wide Fund for Nature) plays a lead role on behalf of the participating states (Erens, Verschuuren, and Bastmeijer 2009). It also appears when intergovernmental organizations seek out and rely on advice from prominent CSOs in the North – such as Amnesty International – to monitor compliance with international treaties or to formulate policies and programs.

The CSOs that have succeeded in penetrating national and International policy elites are primarily known for their expertise and based in the North. Examples are the International Union for the Conservation of Nature, Consumers International, and the Winnipeg-based International Institute for Sustainable Development. Although there are exceptions where CSOs combine elite-oriented technical expertise with grassroots activism (such as Amnesty International, Médecins sans Frontières, WWF, and Greenpeace), this form of civil society involvement in global governance emphasizes incrementalist reform.

CSOs AND LEGITIMACY

As CSOs become more organized on various global stages, where they purport to speak in the name of international civil society, act on public opinion, and pursue a large number of political, economic, and social causes, questions of legitimacy inevitably arise. Their claims to speak for specific constituencies, or for "civil society" generally, are not easy to corroborate. Many CSOs have been criticized for inadequate transparency and accountability to their members or to external audiences – the same kind of democratic deficit they so often decry in governments and corporations. And there have been high-profile cases of abuse of donor funds and mismanagement in some. The problem is exacerbated when front groups for corporate interests or ideological extremists pose as responsible CSOs.

The now disbanded Global Climate Coalition was a case in point. The coalition was established by American industry in 1989 to oppose action to reduce greenhouse gas emissions. Although it did not actively conceal its connection to big business, it provided a veneer of independence and legitimacy under which its member companies and trade associations engaged in an aggressive lobbying, advertising, and disinformation campaign to discredit the science of global warming, tout the alleged benefits of climate change, and oppose any international agreement to reduce greenhouse gas emissions. It was ultimately disbanded after key members, including BP Amoco, Shell, Ford, and Chrysler, reconsidered their position on global warming in the face of mounting scientific evidence and worsening public relations (Brown 2000). Other CSOs may become fronts for government policy. Many American CSOs, for instance, are funded by US AID, which, in the George W. Bush era, required them to adopt an anti-abortion position as a condition for government funding.

Enforced transparency could be part of the solution. Just as Canadian political parties must submit formal accounts of their expenditures to the Canada Elections Office in order to qualify for the subsidies they receive from the public purse, CSOs could be brought under a regulatory regime whose purpose would be to assure the public that they are indeed genuine citizen-initiated not-for-profit organizations whose objectives are clearly stated, whose activities are adequately described, whose funding sources are credibly documented, and whose ultimate constituents are individuals rather than corporations. To be effective, such regulation would have to be transnational rather than national.

The non-profit sector itself developed a candidate scheme in 2006, when eleven leading international CSOs endorsed the *International Non-Governmental Organisations Accountability Charter*.[13] Signatories commit themselves to a series of principles for transparency and accountability including annual public reporting, compliance with applicable government accounting and reporting requirements, good governance, professional management, ethical fundraising, financial and political independence, and responsible advocacy.

The charter requires signatory organizations to have clearly defined missions, organizational structures, and decision-making procedures. Their governance structures must include an overall governing body; written procedures covering the appointment of members, responsibilities, and conflicts of interest; and a regular general meeting with authority to appoint and replace governing members. They must have internal financial controls, staff and program evaluation measures, safeguards against bribery and corruption, and protection for whistle-blowers. They must issue annual public reports describing their mission, values, objectives, outcomes, environmental impacts, governance structure and processes, audited financial performance, and compliance with the charter. They must disclose the details of major donations that might affect their independence, and their annual public report must break down their main sources of funding between corporations, foundations, governments, and individuals. Finally, they must engage in proactive dialogue with stakeholders, listening to their suggestions, encouraging input from directly affected parties, and making it easy for the public to comment on their programs and policies.

Observance of these principles would go a long way toward addressing the legitimacy challenge facing CSOs in global and domestic governance. Like many corporate self-regulatory codes and intergovernmental agreements, however, the charter is vague on how its laudable commitments are to be implemented and how their implementation is to be verified. Many of its principles are couched in general terms, requiring organizations to develop policies and procedures but saying nothing about how they are to be applied or monitored. Like many industry and intergovernmental codes, the charter relies on self-monitoring, self-assessment, and self-reporting of compliance by signatory CSOs. It makes no provision for external verification of compliance and says nothing about sanctions for non-compliance – ingredients that are widely viewed in the CSO community as essential for the credibility of voluntary codes (Wood 2006).

As experience with industry codes of conduct has shown, some form of independent verification of compliance and some genuine consequences for non-compliance are likely to be required if the *INGO Accountability Charter* is to gain lasting credibility. In some situations, it may be appropriate for governments or intergovernmental organizations to perform these functions, if, for instance, what is at stake is CSOs' receipt of government funding or their accreditation as participants in the work of international organizations. In other situations, governments and international organizations may not be the appropriate verifiers and enforcers, since they are often interested parties. It may be necessary for a global verification and enforcement capacity to evolve that is grounded in civil society yet independent of CSOs, business, and government. No clear prototype for such a capacity has yet emerged.[14]

Another weakness of the *INGO Accountability Charter* is that it provides little guidance on what counts as "responsible advocacy." It requires signatory CSOs to have clear processes for adopting public positions and explicit ethical policies to guide choice of advocacy strategies. They must adhere to "generally

accepted standards of technical accuracy and honesty in presenting and interpreting data and research" and ensure that any public criticism of individuals or organizations amounts to fair public comment, but the charter
does not go beyond these rather vague standards to specify concrete requirements for truth and accuracy in CSO statements.[15]

Furthermore, though the charter implicitly condemns illegal activities,
it includes no explicit statement that certain advocacy tactics are off limits.
Certainly, confrontation and civil disobedience must be within CSOs' acceptable strategic repertoire, but what about picketing the personal residences of
corporate executives or workers, demonstrating outside their children's
schools, or publicizing their home addresses and phone numbers and encouraging people to complain to them (Baker 2006)? Concerns about such
tactics are often exaggerated by CSOs' enemies, but they should not be ignored.
A CSO accountability code should clearly reject violence, intimidation, and
violation of human rights.

Although it may be vague on implementation, verification, and "responsible advocacy," the charter is clear about those to whom CSOs are accountable. It states that CSOs are answerable to

- the people and ecosystems they seek to protect, some of which cannot
  speak for themselves
- their members, supporters, staff, volunteers, and donors
- the partner organizations with whom they work
- the governments that regulate their establishment and operations
- those whose policies, programs, and behaviour they wish to influence,
  including businesses and governments
- the media
- the general public.[16]

This list is suitably broad and comprehensive, reflecting the range of parties
that have an interest in CSO activities. The views and interests of these various
stakeholders are bound to conflict with each other and, at times, with the
views and mission of the CSO. The charter gives little indication of how CSOs
are to resolve these inevitable tensions. But that is not the point. We cannot
expect CSOs to settle such disagreements, or always act in accordance with
the wishes of all their stakeholders, any more than we would expect the same
from corporations or elected governments. When confronted with incompatible demands, elected governments can rely on the principle of majority rule,

subject to certain protections for minorities. Corporations can rely on the principle of shareholder primacy, subject to certain protections for workers and minority shareholders.

What principle ought to apply to CSOs, which are not held accountable via the ballot box or stock market? When faced with conflicting demands, CSOs should be able to rely on the principle of fidelity to their publicly stated mission. Such fidelity, substantiated via transparency and good governance, is probably the best way for CSOs to maintain the trust of the broadest range of stakeholders. The *INGO Accountability Charter* recognizes this by noting that the main way in which CSOs should be held responsible for their actions is by having a clear mission, organizational structure, and decision-making machinery, acting in accordance with stated values and procedures, ensuring that programs achieve outcomes that are consistent with the mission, and reporting on these outcomes openly and accurately.[17]

This brings us to a larger point about CSO accountability. As Buchanan and Long (2002, 62) argue, the legitimacy of CSOs is determined far more by the ends they pursue and the results they achieve than by "the nature of their membership structures, funding sources, and decision-making processes." As the *INGO Accountability Charter* recognizes, CSOs' "right to act" is based on, among other things, "the values [they] seek to promote"; and their "first responsibility" is to achieve their stated missions effectively and transparently, in a manner consistent with their values.[18] The main function of the procedural transparency and accountability mechanisms emphasized by the charter is to give some credible assurance that a CSO has a clearly defined mission and pursues outcomes that are consistent with it. The legitimacy of CSOs in governance beyond borders will ultimately depend on the degree to which these missions and outcomes advance human rights, human security, ecosystem protection, sustainable development, and other public goods.

CIVIL SOCIETY AND GLOBALIZATION FROM BELOW

Alongside the various forms of CSO governance from above are myriad examples of civil-society-driven globalization from below. The potential for transnational civil society governance became obvious a few years after the power of transnational "market" governance had been dramatically demonstrated by the world's leading drug companies. During the Uruguay Round of trade negotiations in the early 1990s, the global pharmaceutical industry had pushed the European Union, Japan, and the United States to entrench strong intellectual property rights protection in the WTO TRIPS Agreement.

Once it became clear that these monopoly rights on privatized scientific knowledge were leading Big Pharma to charge extremely high prices for drugs to treat HIV/AIDS victims in the Third World, Médecins sans Frontières mobilized public opinion against this monopoly pricing and proceeded to negotiate directly both with governments and the industry. The result was to reduce the per capita price of drugs for HIV/AIDS patients in the South from several thousand dollars a year to a few hundred. Subsequently, an amendment to the WTO TRIPS Agreement extended the scope of compulsory licensing to facilitate the manufacture and distribution of generic drugs for HIV/AIDS patients in developing countries (as discussed in Chapter 4).

Transnational Social Movements

Distinct from the formal CSOs that profess to represent them but may not do so adequately, transnational social movements (TSMs) are informal and unorganized yet increasingly powerful. They include the angry environmentalists, human rights activists, and trade unionists who answered the call of diverse CSOs in the fall of 1999 by trekking from a number of countries to Seattle where they helped close down the biennial ministerial meeting of the World Trade Organization. Whether it springs from Islamic fundamentalists, adepts of the Christian Right, or globally dispersed ethnic diasporas such as the Jews or Tamils, the mobilized energy of TSMs can have powerful impacts on national and global governance. Here we focus briefly on the transnational movements for social justice that resist neo-conservative globalization (Armstrong, Farrell, and Maiguashca 2003; Dawkins 2003; Hayden and el-Ojeili 2005).

Although apparently united by what it opposes in market globalization, the broad movement for global social justice has deep divisions within its ranks. Inspired by nostalgia for the Keynesian welfare state, some members of the movement direct their efforts at domestic politics. The public's unease about current problems is related to awareness that not only has its quality of life not improved but there has been actual deterioration in countries such as Mexico, whose public had been assured that economic progress would follow in the wake of NAFTA's new continental free trade regime. The neo-conservative promise that freeing the marketplace from government control would lead to unprecedented prosperity has proven a chimera, given the decline in the level of public services, especially in health care and education, and in the quality of public goods such as bridges and roads, parks and clean air, sewers and water provision.

The consciousness of the state's deteriorating performance is directly linked to an understanding that it has been financially strangled by politicians who cut taxes in the belief that the imperatives of globalized competition required them to lighten the fiscal load on footloose corporations if investment was to flow into their economy. This is the paradigm laid out in the Washington Consensus, which promised a new era of economic progress provided that corporate initiative was liberated from public regulation. Citizens who lament the decline of the state also point out that shrinking budgets have cut back its administrative capacity by firing the civil servants needed even to enforce existing labour laws and environmental regulations let alone respond to new challenges that cry out for more public-sector intervention.

Bewailing the liberation of the marketplace from democratic control, others look toward a globalization of a different kind. To prevent the race to the bottom that jeopardizes the quality of citizens' lives by lowering domestic standards in order to attract investment, they are searching for a new global governance paradigm that would give priority to meeting social and human needs but would do this by bringing corporations under international control. In essence, this movement is projecting the Keynesian state upward in the hope of creating an effective governance that functions at the global level to fine-tune the world economy in the same way that governments once worked nationally to maintain a balance between economic growth and social welfare.

Future developments are likely to see progress along both paths. Citizens still expect their governments to maintain sustainable environments and an adequate standard of public services. But they also expect transnational governance to ameliorate the world disorder, not aggravate it. Though legal reforms are of some importance, sustaining Canadian citizens' transnational efforts to achieve global justice requires governments to provide financial support, both for traditional aid and for newer forms of CSO engagement in the South. With Canadian government expenditures on Third World aid having fallen to 0.27 percent of gross national product, any serious commitment to global justice must start with a citizenry that is willing to see more of its tax dollars spent on a vigorous national contribution to global human security.

With increasing access to information about what is taking place in remote corners of the world and in the daily lives of others, some citizen organizations are able to engage directly with burning global issues such as helping subsistence economies integrate into the global trading system or reconstructing societies devastated by armed conflict. The CSO Oxfam has long promoted

fair trade campaigns to help Third World farmers market their organic products in the North. With its Nobel Peace Prize for outstandingly courageous
work among the sick and wounded in wartorn societies and among the victims
of genocide, Brussels-based Médecins sans Frontières is but the most spectacular among hundreds of CSOs in which Canadians take an active, often
leading part (Orbinski 2008).

Canadian advocacy groups work with like-minded associations to influence their own and other governments' positions. They operate domestically
to get Canadian government policies changed, but they may also work in
foreign countries to support social or political action there by raising funds,
launching projects, and drawing media attention to situations requiring remedial action – which may include the local behaviour of Canadian TNCs.
A young Canadian, Craig Kielburger, generated tremendous popular support
for his campaign to eradicate child labour, sparking a worldwide youth movement that has influenced the practices of TNCs in developing countries and
at home."[19] Similarly, anti-sweatshop boycotts in Canada and elsewhere in-
duced such retail giants as Nike and Gap to give public assurances that their
suppliers would be required to accept certain labour standards for their workers. These global brands have followed through on these promises to varying
degrees by imposing labour codes of conduct on their suppliers and submitting to external scrutiny of the implementation of these codes.

Canadian grassroots social movements have also affected transnational
governance in other sectors. The Halifax Initiative was launched in 1994 by
a coalition of Canadian human rights, labour, development, environmental,
and religious groups to advocate a fundamental restructuring of the international financial system.[20] It is the principal voice of Canadian civil society
on the reform of the Bretton Woods institutions and it has had substantial
influence both nationally and internationally, being instrumental in Canada's
decision to cancel the debts of some of the least developed and most in-
debted countries and in the creation of the IMF's Independent Evaluation
Office (a mechanism for increasing IMF public accountability). In the extractive sector, MiningWatch Canada brings together environmental, social
justice, Aboriginal, and labour organizations from across the country to respond to threats to public health, environment, indigenous rights, and local
communities posed by irresponsible mineral policies and practices in Canada and around the world.[21] Established in 1974 as a coalition to help Canadian churches develop CSR policies, KAIROS: Canadian Ecumenical Justice

Initiatives was instrumental in the development of the *Principles for Global Corporate Responsibility: Bench Marks for Measuring Business Performance*, a set of criteria and indicators for measuring corporate social and environmental performance now in its third edition.[22] The Bench Marks program quickly went global and is now headquartered in South Africa. It is considered by many CSOs worldwide as the gold standard against which to measure corporate codes of conduct. Because of its stringency, it has not been widely adopted by businesses.

A Canadian doctor, Samantha Nutt, founded War Child Canada, a small organization that has gone on to play a leading role in a global non-governmental movement to assist children affected by war and to mobilize other children and youth to work for peace and children's rights everywhere. What War Child and many other CSOs do is a manifestation of governance, even if it does not revolve around lobbying governments for law reform or official policy initiatives. War Child involves itself in norm creation and promotion by advocating transnational norms of peace, security, and children's rights, and it engages in the creation or enhancement of governance institutions by working transnationally to re-establish or strengthen community institutions, legal systems, and human capacity in conflict zones. It does this in close collaboration with local groups in conflict-affected communities, working, for instance, with the Ugandan Law Society to provide legal education and advocacy services for indigent children in Northern Uganda whose lives have been disrupted by the ongoing armed conflict involving the Lord's Resistance Army. It also worked with the Afghanistan Women Council to educate vulnerable women and girls in literacy, health, parenting, conflict resolution, community leadership, women's rights, microcredit, and small-business management.[23]

No discussion of Canadian involvement in global civil society would be complete without mentioning the mother of all environmental activist organizations, Greenpeace, established in Vancouver in 1970 to protest US nuclear weapons testing in Alaska. It is a strikingly successful example of individual Canadians grouping together to raise popular consciousness of ecological issues, influence government policy, and change corporate behaviour. In generating these transnational movements and organizations, our compatriots may be thought to be acting more as global than as Canadian citizens. But the national regulatory and legal context in which even a globally active CSO establishes its domestic organization can affect both its effectiveness and its legitimacy, whether it originates in Canada (as Greenpeace did) or whether it is a Canadian branch of a foreign-based CSO (as is Médecins sans Frontières).

All over the world, individual citizens are organizing to challenge global arrangements that threaten their well-being. These movements seek to transform governance in order to promote rather than prejudice social and environmental goals. As they struggle to reveal and mobilize the emancipatory potential within established structures, engaged citizens become active participants in the governance of globalization. Consider the following examples:

- In 1994, a small number of determined Canadian activists formed the Global Campaign to Ban Landmines, beginning a process that would win the support of key governments and, only three years later, culminate in the establishment of an international treaty banning land mines.
- Advocates for affordable AIDS drugs in South Africa defeated a patent-infringement lawsuit filed by nineteen pharmaceutical TNCs. Buoyed by this victory, Brazilians then beat back a US threat to use the WTO dispute system to challenge their national health policy, which provided free or low-cost AIDS drugs to people in need, regardless of patent rights.
- The Jubilee 2000 network, building on decades of work by lay activists within the Roman Catholic Church, convinced the IMF, World Bank, and a number of governments to cancel nearly $100 billion of the debt owed by heavily burdened poor countries. The network continues to demand more cancellations, challenging the very legitimacy of the loans' terms in the first place.
- Farmers in India organized a seed satyagraha – a campaign of non-violent disobedience modelled on Gandhi's salt satyagraha in 1930, which led to India's independence from the British Empire. Declaring their non-cooperation with proposed new patent laws covering seeds and other genetic resources, this farmers' movement came to popularize an alternative conception of intellectual property ownership based on collective intellectual property rights.
- Defying resistance from China, Israel, and, in particular, the United States, proposals by NGOs helped Canada and its like-minded partners break through the intransigence of other governments to establish the International Criminal Court, a proposal that had languished in diplomatic limbo since the Holocaust. (Dawkins 2003, 100-4; Shiva 1993, 6)

The proliferation and increasing influence of social movements and CSOs prompt us to rethink the territorial and legal boundaries of activism. A relatively small investment of public funds in response to initiatives already taken or proposed by individuals can leverage very high levels of organized citizen engagement. Gaining charitable-donation status, for instance, dramatically improves a CSO's capacity to raise funds from well-wishing citizens. At present, advocacy groups face severe obstacles to getting official standing with Revenue Canada, which does not sanction organizations that engage in "political" activities. The Government of Canada should adapt the *INGO Accountability Charter* as the standard which, once achieved by a Canadian NGO, would qualify it for standing as a charitable organization and so encourage Canadians to support progressive citizen engagement where it is most needed.

The World Social Forum

The annual meetings of the World Social Forum (WSF) have brought together tens of thousands of CSO leaders and grassroots activists, and thereby helped spread a spirit of empowerment among the politically marginalized, including Aboriginal peoples, anti-poverty activists, environmentalists, and human rights advocates.

The WSF began in 2000 as an alternative to the World Economic Forum (WEF), an event held annually in Davos, Switzerland, and attended by the world's political and business leaders, along with selected journalists and intellectuals – the global elite that shapes the world we live in. Aiming to bring together hundreds of groups and CSOs that opposed neo-conservative globalization, the first assembly of the WSF was held in January 2001 at Pôrto Alegre, Brazil, a site with powerful symbolic value for globalization from below since the city's planning and decision making employ direct citizen participation such that an elected citizens' forum manages its policies (Barlow and Clarke 2001, 204; Santos 2005a, 2005b).

The WSF slogan – "another world is possible" – directly challenged former British prime minister Margaret Thatcher's famously arrogant claim that "there is no alternative" to neo-conservative prescriptions of free markets and pro-scriptions of government policies aimed at fostering social justice (Patomäki and Teivainen 2004, 145). The WSF invites diversity, within a broad anti-neo-conservative consensus: it "provides an amazingly open forum where any group from anywhere in the world can attend and organize their own events as part of the program. There is no filtering of political opinion beyond a broad, shared commitment to opposition to [neo-conservatism]. Here, participation is the key in the exploration of alternatives, not something to be contained or feared" (Conway 2003, 8).

From the beginning, the WSF's accommodation of this remarkable range of views made conflict inevitable. Although they share an opposition to neo-conservatism, the participants have very different ideas about power. From anarchist street protesters to political parties – with unions, NGOs, and agrarian reformers in between – there have been visible tensions among these "fragile coalitions" (Klein 2002, 205). More accurately represented as a worldwide, movement-based, multi-scale, and multi-sited cultural process that is evolving daily (Conway 2009), the WSF is "fulfilling the crucial role of being a point of coalescence, debate, and co-ordination" for the world's activists (Allahwala and Keil 2005, 409) and hence a crucial site for global governance from below (Santos 2005a).

The WSF is a forum in which political mobilization takes priority over legal mobilization; in which law, when resorted to, is understood to include local customary law, transnational law, or international law, not necessarily official state law; in which the legal knowledges susceptible to being mobilized are not limited to state-validated professional ones but include those of indigenous peoples, squatters, sweatshop workers, landless peasants, disadvantaged women, and minorities; in which the counter-hegemonic use of a hegemonic tool such as law is never taken for granted; and in which new politics, new legalities, and new experiments in emancipatory governance beyond borders are evolving (*ibid.*, 60-62).

One of the WSF's most visible achievements was its instrumentality in organizing NGOs and social movements in Brazil to support President Lula da Silva's election campaign (Byrd 2005, 153). The WSF also helped to build solidarities across national boundaries by disseminating local experiences through the creation of an open and diverse space (Allahwala and Keil 2005, 414). This solidarity building is especially critical for activists from the global South who do not have equal access to communications technology. The WSF is the first network of transnational networks that has been able to facilitate sustained cooperation across the southern continents. Although it is difficult to say whether the actions of the WSF have directly caused the major international economic organizations to modify their positions, it is clear that many themes, including Third World debt relief, responsible FDI practices, and the concept of a more equitable globalization process, have been steadily gaining legitimacy to the point that they have even been addressed directly at the WEF (Byrd 2005, 153). On a less conspicuous level, the very existence of the WSF is a reminder that the neo-conservative consensus has provoked global dissent – a remarkable achievement in itself.

A process of global diffusion began at the second WSF in 2002, when coordinators called on participants "to organize similar processes at whatever scale that made sense to them and to define their own priorities" (Conway 2004, 370). This resulted in a proliferation of social forums around the world, including regional forums such as the European Social Forum, the Asian Social Forum, and the Mediterranean Social Forum. As well, national forums have been held in Denmark, Germany, Guatemala, Italy, Kenya, Nigeria, and Uganda. Finally, local forums have also taken place in such cities as Boston, Chicago, Liverpool, and Sydney. These are just some indicators of the power and breadth of the WSF movement. The third and fifth WSFs were held in Pôrto Alegre; the fourth was in Mumbai, India. The sixth WSF was held simultaneously in Bamako (Mali), Caracas (Venezuela), and Karachi (Pakistan). The eighth was even more decentralized, taking place simultaneously in thousands of locales around the globe. The ninth, in 2009, was back in Brazil. The WSF has always aimed to be thoroughly international though still anchored in the global South.

Canadian activists and CSOs have been present from the first WSF, at which many participants resolved that large protests should be organized in opposition to the thirty-four-state Summit of the Americas to be held in Quebec City in April 2001, when the proposed Free Trade Area of the Americas (FTAA) was slated to be discussed by the hemisphere's political leaders. Informal polls suggest that the number of Canadian participants in Pôrto Alegre rose from approximately 250 in 2003 to about 750 in 2005 (Conway 2006, 80). Within Canada, autonomous organizing processes inspired by the WSF operate in Hamilton, Ottawa, Quebec City, Toronto, Vancouver, and Victoria, with others at varying stages of development (Conway 2003, 8). On 30 January 2005, activists gathered at the Toronto WSF and embraced a participatory model that included a wide spectrum of organizations of varying sizes. Groups that took part included Alternatives, the Canadian Labour Congress, the Confédération des Syndicats Nationaux, the Council of Canadians, World March of Women, and some Canadian church groups. An assortment of others also participated including youth active in the anti-globalization movement, people with strong links to centres where the polycentric WSFs were being held (particularly Latin America and South Asia), scholars studying social movements and left-wing politics, and activists who were connected to local social forums in Canada (Conway 2006, 81).

Peaceful Protest as an Instrument of Governance from Below

Peaceful protest is one of the principal instruments available for individuals and civil society groups to challenge existing governance arrangements and to imagine alternative ones. Since the 1997 Asia-Pacific Economic Cooperation (APEC) Summit in Vancouver, at which protesters were met with a sometimes brutal police crackdown, the possibility of citizen participation via peaceful protest has been in question in Canada.

Rather than reaffirming citizen protest's vital role in a democratic society, Canadian governments and law enforcement agencies have further restricted its availability. Animated by a collective sensibility of insecurity and fear, they have implemented legal regimes that collapse the distinction between protest-ers and terrorists, and demobilize citizen activism before it can start by establishing security perimeters – such as those for the G8 Summits in Kananaskis, Alberta (2002); Gleneagles, Scotland (2005); and Muskoka, Ontario (planned for 2010) – so tight and wide that they prevent protesters from getting anywhere near the objects of their concern. The lessons of the APEC Inquiry "have been swept off the radar screen by the irresistible wave of anti-terror initiatives and fear that have rolled over our collective political communities and consciousness" since 11 September 2001 (Farrow 2004, 214). Peaceful public protest – and the vast majority of anti-globalization protests have been peaceful – is an essential instrument of counter-hegemonic governance and a critical focal point for transnational networking among like-minded individuals and groups. It should be fostered, not silenced, by democratic governments and their legal systems.

During the Uruguay Round of negotiations, which transformed the *General Agreement on Tariffs and Trade* of 1947 into the World Trade Organ-ization of 1994, trade union leaders, environmentalists, cultural figures, and human rights activists had not realized that the global corporate community was writing new economic rules for itself that would have major repercus-sions not just on each country's economic order but on its environmental, social, and cultural systems. By the late 1990s, when they saw various do-mestic measures being struck down by the WTO dispute panels on the ground of being barriers to trade or investment, they woke up to comprehend that the transnational marketplace had stealthily prevailed over the nation-state.

Suddenly, market globalization became a synonym for local political disaster. There was nothing to be done but protest.

The practice of excluding civil society groups from the governments' trade-negotiating process had given corporations privileged access to the bargaining table but had created what many started to call a global "democratic deficit" – a giant legitimacy problem. The only way that CSOs felt they could hold this new global governance to account, which they deemed beyond their control, was to organize massive demonstrations when the WTO, the IMF, or the World Bank convened. We have already mentioned the 1999 WTO. meeting in Seattle. Protests followed in Washington for the annual meeting of the World Bank and the IMF (winter 2000), in Quebec City for the Summit of the Americas (spring 2001), and in Genoa for the G7/G8 Economic Summit (summer 2001). Global television coverage of the demonstrations brought the names of these cities into the public vocabulary as synonyms for popular protest. The 2002 G8 Summit in Kananaskis did not do likewise, only because protest was effectively prevented *ab initio*. For several years it seemed as if, wherever an international economic institution held its annual meeting, throngs of demonstrators convened to protest the imbalance that gave so much more weight to the economic rights of capital than to the labour, environmental, and human rights of citizens.

Because Canadian activists had been engaged in political battles against neo-conservative deregulation since the mid-1980s, organizations such as the Council of Canadians assumed international leadership when the issues they had been fighting domestically moved onto the global stage. In 1997, the Council of Canadians played a significant role in mobilizing support from CSOs in other countries to defeat the *Multilateral Agreement on Investment* (MAI), a code to enhance TNCs' freedom from state control, which was being negotiated at the OECD in Paris. Using networks they had developed during the fight against the MAI, these Canadian citizen activists were prominent in the subsequent protests against the WTO, the IMF, and the World Bank.

Several years after Seattle's protests, the social justice movement could claim some success. Supported outside Cancún's meeting halls by protesters representing globally networked social justice organizations, twenty Third World governments including those of Brazil, China, and India, which had come to believe that the WTO-based supraconstitution was working better for transnational corporations than for themselves, brought the September 2003 WTO ministerial meeting to a halt.

In response to these activist critics and, more immediately, to the complaints of Third World dissident governments, the WTO has made significant efforts to include the formerly excluded CSOs and recognize the weaker states' need for reinforcing, rather than undermining, the regulatory capacities of their governments. The momentum behind the neo-conservative model of market globalization has slowed – at least at the multilateral level, although much of the slack has been picked up by the governments of the United States, Canada, and other like-minded states in bilateral and regional trade negotiations. Global economic institutions still operate, of course. The IMF watches out for the stability of global currencies but is less inclined to impose as the condition for its loans the draconian belt tightening that helped ruin Argentina until president Kirchner defaulted on the country's debt. The World Bank maintains its focus on economic development but has recognized that governments need to enhance their capacity, not devolve state functions to the marketplace. And at the WTO, the Doha Round of negotiations continues but in a political context in which the Third World's demand for greater access to protected First World markets has become the prime issue.

Indigenous Peoples and Governance beyond Borders

Indigenous peoples occupy a unique position in the politics of globalization, having endured centuries of subjugation at the hands of colonial and post-colonial authorities. Often disproportionately affected by the adverse impacts of globalization, they nevertheless insist on their inherent right to determine their own cultures, values, and governance systems. They suffer the environmental damage of TNC operations, feel the economic pinch of privatization and structural adjustment programs, experience disproportionately high concentrations of toxic chemicals generated tens of thousands of kilometres away, and are sometimes forcibly displaced to accommodate corporate or government megaprojects. Yet indigenous peoples have also shown that they can operate as agents, starting with the creation at home of self-governance structures and extending this experience to innovative transnational and even global institutions. Canadian First Nations are world leaders in these efforts outside the formal regimes of global governance where, along with other social justice organizations, they have enhanced their autonomy by producing their own solidarities.

Forming transnational networks abroad and using the international system tactically to assert and defend their rights may increase indigenous peoples' political autonomy at home. If an Aboriginal group fails to achieve its local objectives through political negotiations, it can share its experience with other Aboriginal groups at global conclaves such as the World Social Forum or the Inuit Circumpolar Conference and bring its complaints to committees within the United Nations system. International confirmation that its rights are being violated can, in some cases, shame a provincial or federal government into making concessions. Indigenous peoples from Canada and elsewhere scored a significant victory in 2006 with the adoption of the UN *Declaration on the Rights of Indigenous Peoples*, a document that took a decade to negotiate. To its discredit, the Government of Canada eventually stood almost alone in opposing the declaration at the United Nations.[24]

Collaborative Governance

Some of the most innovative forms of non-state global governance involve collaboration between business and civil society. When these initiatives began to emerge in the 1990s, they were a departure for both parties, who had traditionally regarded each other as adversaries. Frustrated by government inaction on such problems as tropical deforestation, looking for alternatives to expensive advocacy campaigns and consumer boycotts, and intrigued by the idea of exploiting market dynamics to pursue social and environmental ends, some CSOs started to consider the idea of working with interested companies to develop best-practice standards. Wishing to avoid confrontational activist tactics, enticed by the "triple bottom line" thesis that environmental and social responsibility are good for business (Elkington 1998), and worried about securing their "social licence to operate" (Gunningham, Kagan, and Thornton 2004), some forward-looking companies embraced the notion of working with rather than against CSOs.[25] Governments were often unwelcome in these collaborations, being viewed as part of the problem, not the solution (Cashore, Auld, and Newsom 2004). Governments nevertheless took a keen interest, frequently encouraging these developments while also pursuing their own collaborative CSR initiatives with industry and CSOs – though more often with industry alone (Abbott and Snidal 2009). The result was the appearance of a range of two- and three-way alliances between business, civil society, and states.

These interactions constituted a transnational regulatory space that can be conceptualized as a triangle, with states at one apex, business firms at another, and CSOs at the third (see Figure 1). Collaborative transnational governance arrangements are not distributed evenly throughout this "governance triangle" *(ibid.)*.[26] Rather, they are concentrated mainly along two sides of the triangle: business–civil society initiatives and business-state initiatives. The former include the Global Reporting Initiative (a global multi-stakeholder standard for social and environmental reporting), the International Federation of Organic Agriculture Movements, the Fairtrade Labelling Organization, Social Accountability International (author of the SA 8000 labour practices standard), AccountAbility (author of the AA 1000 sustainability reporting and performance standard), the Forest Stewardship Council (FSC), and the Marine Stewardship Council.[27]

State-business collaborative initiatives include the UN Global Compact, the Equator Principles (a collaboration of leading commercial banks and the World Bank), and ISO 14001 (which comes closer to business self-regulation, although ISO is a federation of national standards bodies, many of which are government agencies).[28] A small but growing number of initiatives involving all three actor categories appears toward the centre of the triangle. These include the International Labour Organization's *Tripartite Declaration of Principles concerning Multinational Enterprises and Social Policy* first adopted in 1977 (International Labour Organization 2001), the *Voluntary Principles on Security and Human Rights* (which deal with the use of private-security forces in the energy and extractive sectors), the Kimberley Process on trade in conflict diamonds, and arguably the ISO 26000 social responsibility guide, for which ISO adopted an unprecedented multi-stakeholder approach.[29] All of these collaborative arrangements are vastly outnumbered by initiatives involving just one actor category (state laws, international treaties, business self-regulatory codes, and CSO initiatives), which cluster near the points of the triangle. They are nonetheless growing in number and significance.

What is most interesting about these hybrid multi-stakeholder initiatives is that many of them establish ongoing and innovative rule-making institutions. The leading example is the FSC, which was founded by a coalition of environmental, labour, human rights, indigenous, and business representatives in Toronto in October 1993 to create a global system for certification of sustainable forestry operations and forest products. The FSC's basic logic was that the growing market demand for sustainably harvested forest products could slow and ultimately reverse unsustainable forest management practices such as tropical deforestation if market actors had a clear and credible means to distinguish sustainably from unsustainably harvested products.

The FSC has been described as an example of "breakthrough rule innovation" (Webb 2004a, 16) because of several unique attributes that marked a major departure from established CSO strategy. Rather than (or in addition

FIGURE 1

The governance triangle

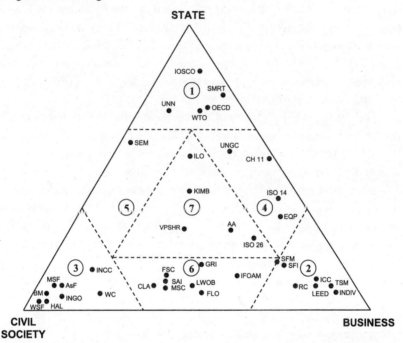

The triangle depicts the potential universe of governance initiatives in terms of direct participation by three actor categories: state, civil society, and business. Each vertex represents one category. The data points represent initiatives discussed in this book. A point's distance from the three vertices indicates the degree of involvement of the three actor categories. The numbered zones denote different combinations of actor participation. In the vertex zones (1, 2, and 3), actors of a single category adopt and implement governance initiatives on their own, with minimal participation from actors of other categories. Zone 1 covers situations in which states or interstate organs set and apply standards unilaterally. Zone 2 represents business self-regulation. Zone 3 contains initiatives promulgated and applied by CSOs on their own. Zones 4, 5, and 6 feature arrangements in which actors from two categories participate, whereas Zone 7 shows arrangements involving all three. The list below indicates the names of the initiatives, the year they were first adopted, and the chapter in which they are discussed.

ZONE 1: STATE AND INTERSTATE INITIATIVES

IOSCO International Organization of Securities Commissions (1983) (Ch. 6)
OECD *OECD Guidelines for Multinational Enterprises* (1976) (Ch. 5)
SMRT Smart Regulation initiative (Canada) (2004) (Ch. 6)
UNN *United Nations Draft Norms on the Responsibilities of Transnational Corporations and Other Business Enterprises with Regard to Human Rights* (2003) (Ch. 7)
WTO World Trade Organization agreements (1994) (Ch. 3)

Zone 2: Business initiatives

ICC   International Chamber of Commerce *Business Charter for Sustainable Development* (1991) (Ch. 7)
INDIV   Individual companies' codes of conduct (Ch. 7)
LEED   Leadership in Energy and Environmental Design green building standards (1998) (Ch. 7)
RC   Responsible Care (1987) (Ch. 7)
SFI   American Forest and Paper Association Sustainable Forestry Initiative (1994) (Ch. 7)
SFM   Canadian Standards Association Sustainable Forest Management standard (1996) (Ch. 7)
TSM   Towards Sustainable Mining (Canadian mining industry) (2004) (Ch. 7)

Zone 3: Civil society initiatives

AsF   Avocats sans Frontières (1992) (Ch. 7)
BM   Bench Marks Principles (1995) (Ch. 7)
HAL   Halifax Initiative (1994) (Ch. 7)
INCC   Inuit Circumpolar Conference (1977) (Ch. 7)
INGO   *International Non-Governmental Organisations Accountability Charter* (2006) (Ch. 7)
MSF   Médecins sans Frontières (1971) (Ch. 7)
WC   War Child (1999) (Ch. 7)
WSF   World Social Forum (2000) (Ch. 7)

Zone 4: State-business initiatives

CH 11   *North American Free Trade Agreement*, Chapter 11 (investor-state disputes) (1994) (Ch. 3)
EQP   Equator Principles (2003) (Ch. 7)
ISO 14   ISO 14001 environmental management systems standard (1996) (Ch. 7)
UNGC   United Nations Global Compact (2000) (Chs. 5, 7)

Zone 5: State–civil society initiatives

SEM   Submissions on Enforcement Matters under the *North American Agreement on Environmental Cooperation* (1994) (Ch. 5)

Zone 6: Civil society–business initiatives

CLA   Canadian Lawyers Abroad–Avocats canadiens à l'étranger (2005) (Ch. 7)
FLO   Fairtrade Labelling Organization (1997) (Ch. 7)
FSC   Forest Stewardship Council (1993) (Ch. 7)
GRI   *Global Reporting Initiative* (1997) (Ch. 7)
IFOAM   International Federation of Organic Agriculture Movements (1972) (Ch. 7)
LWOB   Lawyers Without Borders (2000) (Ch. 7)
MSC   Marine Stewardship Council (1997) (Ch. 7)
SAI   Social Accountability International SA 8000 labour practices standard (1997) (Ch. 7)

Zone 7: State–civil society–business initiatives

AA   AccountAbility AA 1000 sustainability reporting and performance standard (1999) (Ch. 7)
ILO   International Labour Organization *Tripartite Declaration of Principles concerning Multinational Enterprises and Social Policy* (1977) (Ch. 7)
ISO 26   ISO 26000 *Guidance on Social Responsibility* (Committee Draft, 2008) (Ch. 7)
KIMB   Kimberley Process on trade in conflict diamonds (2003) (Ch. 7)
VPSHR   *Voluntary Principles on Security and Human Rights* (2000) (Ch. 7)

SOURCE: Adapted from Abbott and Snidal (2009).

to) adopting the relatively blunt tools of boycotts, protests, and adverse publicity campaigns, the FSC generated an alliance between CSOs and companies to create ongoing rule-making institutions, agree upon transnational standards for desirable business conduct, and award firms and products that met those standards with a form of recognition that could be relied on in market transactions. This arrangement allowed CSOs to influence business behaviour in more subtle ways, and to reach a broader range of actors up and down the supply chain, than traditional advocacy tools permitted.

Another unique FSC feature is its organizational configuration. Its global membership, which is open to any individual, CSO, or company that supports its *Principles and Criteria of Forest Stewardship* and pays the applicable membership fee, is divided into three chambers – environmental, economic, and social – based on members' self-declared primary interest.[30] Although there is no limit to the number of members in each chamber, the FSC governing organs are structured to preclude domination by any one chamber. Each chamber holds one-third of the total vote in the FSC's main governing body, the General Assembly, and elects one-third of the members of the FSC's main executive body, the Board of Directors. The FSC governance structures are also designed to guarantee balance between the global South and global North by subdividing each chamber. The Northern subchambers consist of members based in high income countries, as defined by United Nations criteria, whereas the members of the Southern subchambers come from low-, middle-, and upper-middle-income countries. Each subchamber holds 50 percent of the chamber's total voting power. Moreover, the nine-member Board of Directors must have equal North-South representation over time. General Assembly decisions are normally adopted by consensus but if put to a vote, they require a simple majority of members of each subchamber and a 66.6 percent super-majority in the General Assembly as a whole. The FSC creates, in effect, a new political space in which policy decisions must reflect a compromise between industrial, environmental, indigenous, and community interests and between the global North and South (Tollefson, Gale, and Haley 2008, 242).

Yet another of the FSC's distinctive features is the manner in which it institutionalizes global-local interaction in the development and application of norms for sustainable forestry. It embraces substantial devolution of rule-making authority by promoting the grassroots, bottom-up development of specific forest stewardship standards by civil society and industry in particular localities, within an overarching global normative framework. This framework is supplied by the FSC's *Principles and Criteria of Forest Stewardship*, a set of ten generic principles and fifty-six associated criteria intended to ensure environmentally appropriate, socially beneficial, and economically viable forest management. The principles and criteria apply to all forest management operations. Because they are couched in general terms and do not take into account variations in environmental, social, or economic conditions, these global principles and criteria cannot by themselves provide a yardstick against which to measure any particular forest operations or products. Rather, they provide a framework within which on-the-ground, detailed forest stewardship standards are developed for specific local conditions.

These standards are generated by national and regional (subnational) working groups or, where such standards do not exist, by certification bodies themselves. National and regional FSC standards adapt the FSC principles and criteria to local conditions by adding specific indicators and verifiers for each criterion. Indicators are designed to stipulate as precisely as possible what the criteria require in the particular national or regional context. Verifiers identify information to be collected to determine whether a given indicator has been met. National and regional standards may contain extra criteria, so long as they are consistent with the FSC principles and criteria. The result is that the specific requirements for certification of sustainable forestry are developed not at the global level by the FSC itself but at the local level by national and regional working groups.

These working groups are self-organizing entities with substantial autonomy from the FSC itself. To a large extent, they determine their own membership, organizational structures, decision processes, and the details of their own FSC standards, although the FSC central organs have set down some basic rules for the development, structure, and content of these standards and have the ultimate authority to approve or disapprove them. For example, British Columbia's working group created a four-chamber structure in which indigenous peoples had a chamber of their own rather than being folded into the social chamber, thus recognizing the special status of First Nations in the Canadian constitutional order *(ibid.)*.

This considerable variation in both institutional arrangements and the requirements of different FSC national and regional standards means that FSC standards are both sensitive to local conditions and are likely to achieve local acceptance, or at least are more likely to do so than would externally imposed, globally uniform rules.

A major limitation of the FSC derives from the geographic inconsistency in its forest stewardship standards, which can lead to confusion and mistrust among relevant audiences. What is considered sustainable forestry manage-ment in one regional or national FSC standard may not be thought sustain-able in others. For instance, the recently approved FSC standard for British Columbia is far more stringent in terms of requirements for consultation with, and informed consent from, indigenous peoples than are comparable FSC standards in the United States, Sweden, or elsewhere in Canada (*ibid.*, 178-86). Thus, what is perceived as adequate to protect indigenous rights in some parts of Canada may not be considered adequate in others – even though the law on this issue is (in theory) uniform across the country.

Differences like these in the detail, prescriptiveness, and stringency of requirements have led to conflicts between and within regional working groups, national working groups, and FSC International, which has made a concerted but incomplete effort to harmonize all FSC standards. Given that the real teeth of FSC certification are found in these regional and national standards, and that the standards vary significantly in their requirements, one would expect that national and regional FSC standards-setting processes would have been subject to serious scrutiny in the scholarly and other litera-ture. But with a few exceptions (Tollefson, Gale, and Haley 2008 being the most notable), the literature tends to focus on FSC International or on high-level comparisons of FSC standards' development and content with those of competing, more industry-friendly forest certification schemes.

Another blemish on the FSC's record is its failure to penetrate the global South. Originally intended mainly to address unsustainable forest practices in the tropics, FSC certification is found predominantly in the advanced in-dustrialized nations and Eastern European countries in transition from social-ism to capitalism. In December 2008, there were 106.8 million hectares of FSC-certified forest areas in eighty-one countries. Only 19.2 million hectares, or 18 percent, were located in developing nations.[31] Canada and the United States held 35 percent of the total certified area, and Europe 46 percent (with countries in transition alone accounting for 33 percent of the worldwide total). The picture is similar if the total certified area is broken down by biome: whereas boreal and temperate forests account for 47 and 39 percent of the total area, respectively, tropical and subtropical forests account for only 14 percent. Developing countries' share of certified forest area has increased slightly in recent years, but the fastest-growing area is the boreal forest.

The FSC has achieved more success in attracting Southern individuals and organizations to join its membership. In the past, a majority of FSC members represented the North, but this gap has closed (*ibid.,* 28). Tollefson, Gale, and Haley (*ibid.,* 29) summarize the situation as follows:

> While the FSC is often perceived as being dominated by environ-mental interests, it is interesting to note that economic interests are strongly represented, constituting 43 percent of the total membership, with a dominant position in the North. Finally, the relative power of the North and the economic chamber may be somewhat understated by these raw membership numbers. Given that the FSC is now located in Bonn, Germany, as well as the rela-tive disparity in wealth between northern and southern members, the former tend to be over-represented at FSC General Assembly meetings and the latter are under-represented. Although the FSC does endeavour to subsidize the attendance of southern members, its ability to do so is constrained by somewhat limited finances.

The FSC's most important defect is not the inconsistency of its standards, the power of Northern interests in its governance, or the geographic concen-tration of FSC certificates in the North. It is its underlying assumption that market demand will eliminate unsustainable forest management practices. The FSC is the leading example of what has been dubbed "non-state, market-driven" (NSMD) governance (Cashore, Auld, and Newsom 2004), the defin-ing characteristic of which – aside from its claim to be purely non-state – is that it relies for its effectiveness on the decisions of self-interested commercial actors engaging in market transactions. For many, this is its key strength: by plugging into market dynamics, CSOs can achieve far greater success than they might otherwise. Admittedly, there is some market demand for FSC-certified products, and this demand appears to be growing. But the evidence so far does not support the conclusion that market demand for FSC-certified forest products is driving substantial changes in forest management practices. Retailers are generally unable to charge a price premium for certified forest products, and there is little evidence that consumers either care whether for-est products are certified or, if they do, can distinguish between the FSC and its more industry-friendly competitors.

In short, we can ultimately "forget about the market – or at least forget about relying on 'green' consumerism and similar devices to drive markets toward sustainability" (Wood 2006, 272). Market-driven governance is incapable of getting us where we need to go. Even if new opportunities for profitable environmental improvements continue to emerge with increasing resource scarcity and changing technology, and even if the market for "green" or "socially responsible" goods and services continues to expand rapidly, the effects on the global economy will be marginal. As Paul Hawken (1993, xiii) famously observed, "If every company on the planet were to adopt the best environmental practices of the 'leading companies,' the world would still be moving toward sure degradation and collapse." Industry will ultimately be driven toward sustainability "not by the promise of gain but by the grind of obligation," a grind that will be supplied not solely by official law but by the "sum total of aggravations from government authorities, financiers and insurers, neighbours, peers, non-governmental watchdogs, employees, customers, suppliers, and perhaps even investors" (Gibson 1999a, 251-52).

To maximize its market penetration and influence over business behaviour, NSMD governance must compromise its commitment to environmental protection and social transformation. It works only to the extent that it is accepted and implemented by the businesses it seeks to regulate. If it sets the environmental or social bar high enough to seriously threaten profitability or require a fundamental alteration in business practices, it will not be accepted by most of those businesses. This is what happened when the forest industry essentially walked away from the early drafts of the FSC-BC standard.

This perverse effect can be mitigated somewhat by direct action campaigns to pressure companies to improve their practices and/or accept an NSMD governance scheme, as was demonstrated by the effort to get Home Depot to sell only sustainably harvested forest products in its US stores. In Canada, similar drives have led a handful of major companies to commit to FSC certification, from catalogue industry giant Limited Brands (which owns Victoria's Secret) to Canadian home improvement retailer Rona and forest products company Tembec. In this way, old-style direct action can give NSMD governance schemes some teeth. But such pressure tactics typically work only against companies that have brands to protect and are sensitive to public opinion, and then only gradually. Moreover, they cannot change the fact that the need for market acceptance ultimately gives industry a critical say over the form and content of the scheme.

Throughout its short life, the FSC has struggled with what amounts to an identity crisis: is FSC certification the gold standard for ecologically and socially sustainable forestry that is intended to appeal only to the tiny eco-forestry segment of the forest products market, or is it a common-denominator standard intended for mainstream industrial forestry operators? Despite ongoing controversy, FSC International opted for the latter: it aspires to be a "general store" rather than a "boutique" standard, tailored to encompass industrial forestry, penetrate the entire forest products market, and attract the major forest industry TNCs. The result is a governance scheme that compromises environmental and social values in important ways so as to accommodate industrial forestry.

The FSC-BC standard is illustrative. On the one hand, it goes well beyond current forestry practice and existing legal requirements, being more ecologically and socially rigorous than any previously approved FSC national or regional standard. On the other hand, its final version embodied important compromises designed to make certification broadly achievable by a wide range of forest managers at relatively low cost, including "the elimination of all twenty-nine major failure provisions [violation of which would preclude certification], more flexible arrangements for negotiating with First Nations, more time for the phasing out of pesticides, and more flexibility in planning reserves and riparian management" (Tollefson, Gale; and Haley 2008, 99). Most other FSC standards go to even greater lengths to accommodate the desires of large industry.

Because it relies on the market as the driver of social change, and because it seeks to embrace mainstream industrial forestry rather than insist on a new model of eco-forestry, the FSC scheme does not pose a fundamental challenge to the status quo of the transnational forest economy. But by involving a substantial degree of bottom-up grassroots-driven civil society influence, it represents one of the most impressive models for non-state governance in the world today. It has very promising features of globalization from below, including its three-chamber structure in which social and environmental interests predominate over their business counterparts. By giving Southern members half the voting power in each chamber, it provides a real voice to the global majority – although the South of course holds much more than half of the world's population and so remains under-represented in this voting scheme.

As Webb (2004a, 16-20) argues, new governance institutions such as the FSC enrich and vitalize societal norm development and implementation, incubate new policy approaches, and operate as innovative voicing mechanisms for civil society actors. For this, they are to be applauded and encouraged, but their transformative potential is limited by the incrementalist, market-based logic to which the FSC and other NSMD governance schemes subscribe. Whether their promise as alternative governance structures will nonetheless be realized has yet to be seen.

From the lex mercatoria to the Forest Stewardship Council, from the World Economic Forum to the World Social Forum, business and civil society actors are constructing governance measures to promote, manage, resist, or reshape globalization. Those designed by and for transnational business interests tend on the whole to reinforce dominant forms of globalization. Those in which civil society organizations and transnational social movements have a leading role tend to challenge these dominant forms. Those involving business–civil society collaboration can establish innovative rule-making institutions that combine elite-led "globalization from above" and grassroots-driven "globalization from below." Bottom-up societal initiatives such as the World Social Forum are critical for envisioning alternatives to currently dominant approaches to globalization and governance, but they are unlikely to succeed on their own in effecting the desired transformation. They need to be accompanied by collaborative governance initiatives that reach across actor categories. The more these non-state initiatives succeed at bringing together civil society and progressive business actors in inventive partnerships, the greater the contribution they are likely to make to the search for viable alternatives to existing models of globalized governance.

8
Rethinking Canadian Governance and Law in a Globalized World

What does globalization mean for governance and law in Canada, and how are Canadians implicated in this phenomenon – both as agents and objects? This book has told a story of imbalances: between the priorities of economic expansion, on the one hand, and social and environmental integrity, on the other; between investors' rights and human rights; between the retreat of the nation-state in the social domain and its aggressive reassertion in the domain of security; between the war on terror and the wars on poverty and AIDS; between transnational corporations and transnational social movements; between Canadian autonomy and American hegemony; between the global North and global South. These imbalances are found not just between but within states, as globalization erases some distinctions yet exacerbates others. Many of these imbalances are manifestations of a global project to remake the world in a neo-conservative image, which has encountered resistance and setbacks but has proven remarkably adaptable and continues to provide the impetus for dominant forms of globalization, even despite the latest crisis in the world's financial and economic systems.

How might we begin to redress these imbalances and foster alternatives to this failed paradigm? Achieving a new balance will involve embracing a pluralist perspective that cultivates alternative forms of progressive governance and law to operate alongside those of the state, the interstate system, and the market. Canada plays an ambivalent role in these global dynamics, one of a problematic, heterogeneous entity fraught with tensions that complicate what progressive politics might mean and put into question the received wisdom about the country's role on the world stage.

The Hybridization of Governance
Chapter 6 traced some of the ways in which functions previously considered governmental have been privatized as part of the nation-state's contemporary

transformation, shifting from the public to the private sphere where they were assumed by non-state or quasi-state actors. States retreated from some domains of human activity, such as financial and industrial regulation, while aggressively reinserting themselves into others, such as immigration and counter-terrorism. Chapter 7 showed how the borders between public and private, state and non-state, were further eroded as business and civil society actors played increasingly prominent roles in transnational governance arrangements beyond the nation-state. It also hinted at the emergence of hybrid forms of governance involving collaboration between civil society, business, and state actors.

The examples of governance "beyond the state" canvassed in Chapter 7 involve not simply a privatization of governance but a complex hybridization of public and private authority, which takes many forms and has important implications. Governance beyond the state does not imply leaving the state behind, or making an all-or-nothing choice between state and non-state modes of governance, between public and private spheres, or between mandatory and voluntary regulation. Although these conventional dichotomies remain at the heart of most analyses of and programs for governance beyond the state, they break down under examination.

States and international organizations are deeply implicated in the constitution and operation of non-state authority at all levels and across all domains of human affairs. Non-state governance arrangements, whether developed by business or by civil society organizations, interact with and depend upon official governance systems in complicated ways. They frequently adopt the forms and trappings of official law, including legislatures, formal rules expressed in mandatory language, formal adjudication and dispute resolution processes, and monitoring and enforcement mechanisms (Meidinger 2001, discussing the Forest Stewardship Council). They are commonly designed as instruments for the enforcement of existing state or interstate legal requirements, such as when NGO-initiated corporate codes of conduct require apparel firms to demonstrate compliance with ILO conventions or domestic labour laws. The actors and organs of official state governance are entangled with non-state governance in numerous ways.

It is possible to identify at least eight ways in which state actors and organs engage with non-state governance initiatives (Wood 2002-03). In the first, *steering* occurs when state authorities attempt directly or indirectly to influence the development or operation of non-state governance. Such steering takes many forms. State authorities are often deeply involved in the constitution and operation of nominally non-state governance initiatives. Many professional self-governing groups, technical standardization bodies, and other private governance associations are officially constituted by governments, have their powers and purposes defined by statute, report to legislatures, receive operational funding from governments, and in some cases function as state enterprises or within government agencies. Many government officials make public statements intended to encourage, discourage, or influence the development or use of non-state governance initiatives. Some governments seek to exercise strategic leadership over non-state governance – for example, by developing national strategies for technical standardization (Standards Council of Canada 2000). Governments and intergovernmental organizations frequently participate actively in the development or implementation of non-state codes and standards. Some generate voluntary programs themselves, usually with the input or partnership of the target groups, such as the UN Global Compact, the *OECD Guidelines for Multinational Enterprises*, or the European Union Eco-Management and Audit Scheme.

Second, *self-discipline* takes place when state authorities subject themselves to the discipline of non-state codes of conduct. For instance, thousands of government bodies around the world, from municipalities to federal government departments to military bases to public utilities, have implemented the ISO quality or environmental management system (EMS) standards in their own operations. Many governments make this a requirement for certain of their departments and agencies. Most governments have also "lashed themselves to the mast" of non-state standards by enacting domestic laws or signing international agreements (for example, the WTO's *Technical Barriers to Trade Agreement*) that require them to use international standards developed by ISO or the Codex Alimentarius Commission as the basis for their own regulations.[1] They may then face trade sanctions if their laws depart significantly from these international standards.

Third, *knowledge production* occurs when state authorities generate or disseminate knowledge about the design, use, or value of non-state governance initiatives through public education, training programs, pilot projects, and research funding. In this way, governments play crucial roles in the construction of knowledge about and attitudes toward non-state governance initiatives, which can have substantial influence in the competition for legitimacy among these initiatives.

Fourth, *reward* takes place when state authorities provide material incentives to adhere to the terms of non-state governance schemes – for instance, through regulatory flexibility, fiscal incentives, or government procurement policies. Regulatory flexibility involves relaxation of existing regulatory requirements or forbearance from introducing new ones for firms that implement non-state governance programs such as codes of behaviour or environmental management systems. Such incentives may be incorporated in firm- or sector-specific agreements, generalized regulatory incentive programs, or relaxed enforcement policies. Fiscal inducements include grants, subsidies, preferential loan financing, and tax incentives to firms that implement non-state codes of conduct. Public procurement policies may favour or even require suppliers to comply with particular initiatives. All of these techniques feature prominently in Smart Regulation and other regulatory reform agendas.

Fifth, in a *command* situation, governments require firms to adhere to otherwise voluntary measures. Courts in a few countries, including Canada, have ordered firms to implement ISO 14001.[2] Most governments obligate firms to apply generally accepted accounting principles, and some have enacted legislation forcing them to adhere to the Forest Stewardship Council sustainable forestry scheme or to implement an industry-recognized EMS.[3] The International Maritime Organization requires member states to ensure that their shipping fleets implement safety management systems modelled on ISO standards. Another way in which non-state codes can be converted to legally binding commands is through private lawsuits. Supply contracts, trade association membership agreements, and other commercial arrangements increasingly require parties to implement such codes. Parties aggrieved by breaches of these agreements might sue in contract, tort, or intellectual property law. To the extent that courts allow such actions, the terms of these agreements become legally binding commands (Webb 1999; Meidinger 2001).

Sixth, in *borrowing*, governments incorporate non-state governance initiatives in legislation, permits, or international agreements. Governments may integrate non-governmental standards into official regulations, either by reproducing them verbatim, including them by reference, making their implementation a default basis for issuing an approval, making their violation the trigger for statutory duties, or authorizing their use for testing, inspecting, or measuring a regulated entity's activities or products (Hamilton 1978).

Seventh, *benchmarking* occurs when a court or administrative tribunal at the domestic or international level uses a non-state code of conduct as a benchmark for evaluating a party's behaviour and determining its legal liability. National courts may treat a defendant's failure to implement or comply with recognized industry standards or codes of practice as evidence of a lack of reasonable care or due diligence. The terms of non-state codes can thereby be imposed on firms that took no part in their development or use, giving these rule books a power they could not achieve on their own (Webb 1999).

Finally, government authorities may publicly *challenge* certain actors to adhere to voluntary governance programs. This has been popular with public authorities who wish industry to address health or environmental issues but who have no stomach for imposing new regulatory requirements. Such challenges may be addressed to business firms or individuals.

In sum, state and non-state governance are thoroughly interwoven. It has long been understood that almost all human choices and activities have both private and public dimensions, from marriage to child rearing to business management. As early feminists reminded us, the personal is political. Although all liberal democrats agree that the state has no business interfering in some matters – in other words, a sphere of private autonomy exists within which individuals and associations should be free to choose and pursue their own goals without official intrusion – the boundaries of this private zone and its relation to public authority are intensely political issues. To speak of non-state governance in terms of a dichotomy between public and private governance is therefore not very helpful. The absence of state authorities from the development or implementation of a governance program, for example, does not mean the program has no "public" dimension. On the contrary, nominally private authorities such as trade associations and CSOs regularly develop and promote norms with significant public policy stakes. This is reflected in the fact that countless groups explicitly devoted to the protection of public interests of various kinds (environmental protection, human rights, poverty alleviation) typically clamour to be heard in such non-state initiatives.

It is also misleading to think of non-state governance in terms of an opposition between mandatory and voluntary governance (Wood 2006). There is a tendency to identify mandatory regulation with the state and voluntary self-regulation with non-state initiatives. But virtually all voluntary action is undertaken because the relevant actors have been successfully pressured to act. The question, then, is not whether governance schemes are voluntary or mandatory but what effectively drives individuals and organizations to respect human rights, advance public interests, or improve their environmental performance. The drivers for business include cost savings; the threat of regulation; a desire to enhance or avoid damage to public image; anticipation of competitive advantage; demands or requirements of creditors, insurers, investors, industry associations, customers, suppliers, or consumers; pressure from employees or labour unions; pressure from environmental and community groups; and ethical commitments of top management.

Canadian government officials should recognize that they have the capacity to shape, steer, and regulate non-state governance in profound ways. They should exercise this faculty to ensure that non-state governance works to the benefit of Canadians' health, safety, and security. They should do so by, among other things, recognizing that a credible threat of regulation is an important impetus for voluntary action and then by stepping in with regulation should voluntary action fail to protect health, safety, and the environment. Getting the drivers right is crucial to the effectiveness of any system of governance, whether by or beyond the state. It is also crucial for a system's legitimacy.

Toward Credible and Effective Governance beyond Borders

What is the recipe for legitimacy in this complicated environment where state and non-state, public and private, domestic and international governance blur into each other? This question has received substantial attention within Canada (Government of Canada 1998; Gibson 1999b; Pollution Probe 1999; Webb 2004b; Cragg 2005; Government of Canada 2006; National Roundtables on CSR and the Canadian Extractive Industry Advisory Group 2007). In 1997, the New Directions Group, a gathering of Canadian industry leaders and environmental NGOs, agreed on a set of principles for the use of voluntary non-regulatory initiatives to achieve environmental policy objectives (New Directions Group 1999). In its view, to be credible and effective, an initiative should

- be developed and implemented in a participatory manner that enables the interested and affected parties to contribute equitably
- be transparent in its design and operation
- be performance-based, with specified goals, measurable objectives, and milestones
- clearly identify rewards for good performance and sanctions for non-compliance

- encourage flexibility and innovation in meeting specified goals and objectives
- clearly define roles and responsibilities of all participants
- require regular monitoring, verification, and reporting of performance
- encourage continual improvement of participants and the programs themselves
- be supported with adequate resources
- be positioned within a supportive public policy framework that includes appropriate legislative and regulatory tools. *(ibid.)*

These principles and criteria were directed at environmental issues but are nonetheless applicable across a wide variety of subject areas.

The New Directions Group report was aimed mainly at voluntary initiatives inside Canada. Its recommendations were echoed ten years later when another Canadian multi-stakeholder group generated CSR guidelines for Canadian extractive industries operating in developing countries. The National Roundtables on Corporate Social Responsibility and the Canadian Extractive Industry Advisory Group (2007) recommended the creation of a Canadian CSR Framework. Its report was the culmination of a nationwide consultation process undertaken by the federal government in 2006. Like the 1997 New Directions Group report, the framework was the product of an unusual accord among business and civil society groups, having been developed by representatives from the extractive industry, civil society organizations, labour, academics, and the ethical investment sector. The mere fact of consensus was remarkable given that relations among interested groups in the mining sector are normally characterized by deep animosity and mistrust.

The CSR framework proposed by the Advisory Group has four main components. The first is a set of *Canadian CSR Standards,* which extractive companies operating abroad would be expected to meet. The industry and civil society members of the Advisory Group rejected the idea that companies should voluntarily sign up to a CSR framework *(ibid.,* 8), favouring instead a clearly expressed government mandate that firms operating abroad must comply with specified national and international CSR standards. The Advisory Group agreed that such standards should include the *Voluntary Principles on Security and Human Rights,* an international initiative developed by government, business, and civil society representatives to regulate mining companies' relations with security forces, and the International Finance Corporation's (IFC) *Performance Standards on Social and Environmental Sustainability,* a set of mandatory requirements that companies must meet to receive funding from the IFC, the World Bank's private-sector finance organ. The group agreed that this list should be expanded later to possibly include international human rights treaties and the core ILO labour standards. The Advisory Group urged Ottawa to support multi-stakeholder initiatives to implement and expand the *Canadian CSR Standards*, and to provide international leadership in international CSR standards development.

The second element of the Advisory Group's proposed framework is transparency. Canadian extractive companies would report publicly on their CSR performance using the world's leading sustainability reporting system, the Global Reporting Initiative (GRI), or an equivalent framework. The Advisory Group also recommended that Ottawa incorporate GRI as the reporting component of the CSR framework, offer tax credits to companies using it, and collaborate with securities regulators to make its use a requirement for listing on stock exchanges. It also urged that extractive sector associations promote the use of GRI by their members and that financial institutions do the same by using GRI reports in assessing investment risk.

The proposed CSR framework's third component is compliance and enforcement. Both Canadian residents and foreign victims of corporate misconduct would be able to complain about Canadian extractive companies' operations in developing countries to an independent ombudsman who would perform advisory and investigative functions, publish the results of its fact-finding processes, and issue annual public reports. It would enjoy a level of independence and impartiality lacking in Canada's existing National Contact Point, which was established under the *OECD Guidelines for Multinational Enterprises*. Working with the ombudsman's findings, a tripartite Compliance Review Committee would determine cases of non-compliance with the *Canadian CSR Standards*. It would make recommendations about what measures the offending company should take to return to compliance, now to monitor those measures, and whether to refer the matter to external dispute resolution processes. The committee's decisions would be made public. Policies and guidelines would be developed for measuring serious failures to meet the *Canadian CSR Standards*. If efforts to remedy such failures were unsuccessful, the Canadian government would withdraw financial and political support from the offending company.

The final proposed element is a standing multi-stakeholder group drawn from government, industry, indigenous peoples, socially responsible investors, academics, labour, and civil society to advise the government on the implementation and further development of the framework.

The Advisory Group also had other recommendations, including a dedicated CSR unit within the federal government, a Centre of Excellence for research and education on CSR best practices, industry programs to support improved CSR performance in the Canadian extractive sector, government support for partnerships between Canadian and host-country CSOs, mandatory disclosure of corporate CSR policies and practices, extraterritorial application of criminal and anti-corruption laws, tax incentives to promote compliance with the *Canadian CSR Standards*, and Canadian government leadership to advance the rights of indigenous peoples and strengthen CSR standards in international forums.

The Canadian CSR Framework, in short, would combine the forces of business, government, and civil society to generate a hybrid form of transnational regulation that integrates state and non-state, voluntary and mandatory, domestic and international forms of regulation with an environmentally and socially progressive intent. The New Directions Group's 1997 principles and criteria represent a standard acceptable to civil society and industry alike for determining when multi-actor hybrid initiatives can be credible, effective, and legitimate governance tools. The Advisory Group's 2007 recommendations represented a momentous consensus on how such a hybrid approach might work in a particular sector. Yet Canadian governments have failed to heed the message.

There are rare exceptions. Ontario's Environmental Leaders program, a government-sponsored program for beyond-compliance environmental performance in industry, implements all the New Directions Group recommendations.[4] It is an example of transparency, accountability, stringency, and credibility not found in many voluntary programs, whether promulgated by industry or government. It requires participating firms to have clean compliance records, implement a robust environmental management system, set beyond-compliance environmental improvement goals for priority pollutants, engage in proactive public communication and outreach, monitor and report their performance to the government, and have their reports verified by an independent third party. It also provides incentives to participating firms in the form of flexible comprehensive pollution permits, technical assistance, one-window access to the Ministry of the Environment, favourable government publicity, use of a special logo, and enhanced regulatory certainty in the form of a promise of advance consultation with participants regarding the integration of new regulatory requirements with program requirements.

Despite these enticements, the program attracted only a handful of participants, mainly because it takes effectiveness so seriously that it is unpalatable to most of the firms it is intended to attract.[5] Consistent with the New Directions Group principles, it threatens sanctions in the form of adverse publicity for participants that violate program requirements and preserves the government's right to step in with new regulations at any time (Ontario Ministry of the Environment 2004). The program is intended for firms that are already at the top of their class environmentally and have made substantial investments in improving their environmental performance and achieving reputations for environmental excellence. The last thing such companies want is bad publicity from the government if they slip up in attaining voluntary goals that go beyond both what the law requires and what their competitors are doing. The threat of regulation is also unwelcome because firms typically want genuine assurances of regulatory stability if they are going to invest the resources necessary to implement a voluntary program.

The Advisory Group's 2007 report fared no better. Its historic consensus began to unravel as soon as it was achieved, as major extractive companies criticized the Advisory Group's report, notwithstanding the fact that the industry members of the Advisory Group had previously endorsed it unanimously. After a two-year silence in which it claimed to be conducting wider consultations, Ottawa's eventual response was a complete rejection of most of the Group's recommendations and a resounding victory for the narrow economic interests of extractive sector companies (Amnesty International Canada 2009). The title of the response – *Building the Canadian Advantage* – clearly signals the government's priority: to "improve the competitive advantage of Canadian international extractive sector companies" (Government of Canada 2009, 4).

Instead of mandating CSR standards for Canadian extractive companies, the policy promotes voluntary adherence to the IFC Performance Standards, the *Voluntary Principles on Security and Human Rights,* and the Global Reporting Initiative. There is no mention of filling gaps in these standards relating to internationally accepted human rights and labour norms, as the Advisory Group suggested. As for compliance and enforcement, there is no independent ombudsman or compliance review process leading to potential sanctions for non-compliant companies. Rather, the government appointed an extractive sector CSR counsellor, who reports directly to the Ministry of International

Trade. The counsellor may only review the CSR practices of Canadian companies operating internationally with their consent, practically guaranteeing that the most serious complaints will not be heard. Reviews may be initiated by an individual or group that "reasonably believes" (a threshold requirement absent from the Advisory Group recommendations) it is being or may be adversely affected by a Canadian extractive company's international activities (*ibid.*, 11).

In a cynical rebuff to the victims of mining abuses, Canadian extractive companies themselves may initiate a review if they believe they are the subject of unfounded allegations concerning their conduct abroad. The counsellor may engage in fact finding and informal mediation but may not act on his or her own initiative, make binding recommendations, suggest any changes to government policy or legislation, or create new performance standards. In short, the government opted for a lapdog rather than a watchdog.

Ottawa also rejected the Advisory Group's recommendation to condition government support on companies' compliance with CSR standards. Although it agreed to look into extraterritorial application of anti-corruption laws, Ottawa did not even try to sugar-coat its rejection of the multistakeholder Advisory Group recommendations or to disguise its crass support for the economic interests of the extractive sector.

In summary, there is considerable multi-stakeholder consensus on criteria for credible, effective, and legitimate "hybrid" forms of governance beyond borders but negligible governmental or corporate will to take a lead by translating these criteria into practice.

Righting the Imbalance

Having explored various hybrid forms of transnational governance that have arisen to challenge conventional distinctions between public and private, state and non-state, law and non-law, government and governance, and having speculated on their potential to advance an emancipatory global politics, we close the book with a brief recapitulation of the perilous imbalance in which globalized governance finds itself and the scale of the challenge facing Canadians and others working to right the balance.

We live in a world in which borders are increasingly in question, sometimes disappearing, sometimes shifting, sometimes being reinforced. In Canada and many other places, it seems that more and more of the critical decisions that affect people's lives are made outside national borders. As Kumm (2004, 913) says, "globalization has not led to a world in which borders are irrelevant. But it has led to a world in which decisions on how borders are relevant are increasingly made outside of the national democratic process." This prompts us to reconsider what we understand by law, government, sovereignty, and legitimacy, as well as the common dichotomies between domestic and international, public and private, state and non-state. More and more, governance and law involve questions of governing beyond existing conceptual and jurisdictional borders.

Canada's experience of, and role in, global governance is characterized by imbalances that imperil human rights, social inclusion, the environment, and the values many citizens associate with their country. From the growth of international trade and investment law to the reconfiguration of the domestic state, the dominant forms of globalized governance and law are informed by a neo-conservative program of liberating corporations from majoritarian politics, reining in the Interventionist state, shrinking the public sphere, aggressively disciplining nonconformity, and making the world a happy hunting ground for private enterprise.

These forms of globalized governance are largely experienced as hegemonic by the Canadian state and business elites, who adopt them consensually and even actively promote them. For other segments of Canadian society and many in the global South, they are experienced as coercive impositions. In either case, these dominant forms coexist with a great variety of alternatives – ranging from international human rights instruments, international environmental laws, the International Criminal Court, and other examples of globalization from above to such bottom-up initiatives as the World Social Forum, transnational indigenous peoples' networks, and CSO-led codes of conduct. These alternatives vary in the degree to which they challenge prevailing forms of globalization and contribute to social emancipation. The most promising examples involve the kinds of dynamic globalization from below that are rooted in civil society or in hybrid networks of civil society, business, and state actors. These initiatives hold out the most hope for combating the negative effects of globalization and improving its prospects for social emancipation.

The nation-state occupies a central, albeit ambivalent, position in the encounter between hegemonic and counter-hegemonic globalization. In many respects, it acts as an agent or instrument of globalization from above, but it also has a special, often underestimated, capacity to advance social emancipation and restore some balance between market supremacy and human and environmental well-being. One of the central tasks of the nation-state and the interstate system in achieving this new balance is to create and promote a safe space for the unfolding of alternatives. Although neo-conservativism's challengers will continue to craft their own forms of law and politics, the state and state legal systems remain the best guarantors of the space within which this experimentation can occur.

The first category of governance beyond borders examined in this book, the emerging supraconstitution, is characterized mainly by hegemonic forms of globalization from above that have questionable legitimacy and tend to aggravate social exclusion and ecological degradation. The second category, the globalized nation-state, has both regressive and progressive tendencies, although the latter have been repressed in Canada during recent years. The third category, governance beyond the state, also cuts both ways. Governance by civil society actors is the most promising in terms of emancipatory potential and the most marginal in terms of its relation to established power structures. It also has its own legitimacy challenges because of many leading NGOs' elitism, lack of transparency, and weak accountability and because of the deep power disparities between the global North and the global South.

There is ambiguity and thus room for contestation in all three arenas. Some types of globalized governance and some attempts at governing globalization enjoy a substantial degree of legitimacy and have the potential to contribute to liberating struggles, whereas others have severe legitimacy deficits and hinder social emancipation. The pursuit of social liberation rests in identifying and fostering governance strategies that constitute genuine alternatives to the neo-conservative agenda that enjoyed so much success in recent decades but culminated in a monumental global financial and economic disaster. Critical to this possibility is the realization that distinguishing sharply between agents and objects of globalization is not useful. Such commonly fingered agents of globalization as transnational corporations also feel its effects; and such objects of globalization as HIV/AIDS carriers may also be agents of globalization themselves as they organize locally and transnationally to secure affordable treatment. Globalization generates dynamic dialectical relationships in which Canadians are not simply passive objects but also active agents, often working at cross-purposes. Canada, as we have shown, has a problematic identity fraught with tensions and contradictions. The meaning of emancipation and progress is bound to be complicated in a country that, like the world at large, is subject to multiple and sometimes conflicting identities, allegiances, and interests.

The imbalances of globalized governance are evident not just within Canada but more importantly on a regional and global scale. We may differ regarding whether NAFTA and the WTO agreements have effected subtle transformations to Canada's constitutional order. For many developing countries there is no room for doubt: their constitutions have been revised, expressly or implicitly, to make way for the new constitutionalism of neo-conservative economic globalization. In the global South, it is not so simple to say that everyone is simultaneously an agent and an object of globalization. Although the reach of economic, cultural, and social norms and institutions might be global, participation in their creation and enjoyment is not. Just as globalized governance is experienced differently in developed and developing countries, the recipe for progressive politics in a developed country is generally very distinct from that for a developing country. And the recipe in a rapidly industrializing economy such as those of China, India, or South Korea may be very different from that of a sub-Saharan African country, a small island state, an emerging Latin American democracy, or a formerly communist East European country. As for North America, the experience of globalized governance and the possibilities for progressive politics are different than they are elsewhere because the fates of Mexico and Canada are tied so closely – and unequally – to the fortunes and whims of the superpower next door.

It would be a mistake to assume that neo-conservatism has run its course. Although it has suffered setbacks and undergone transformations, it has proven itself remarkably resilient, adapting to changing circumstances. It has crossed partisan lines and influenced the policies of social-democratic and other centre-left governments. When thwarted domestically, it has turned to the international sphere where it has enjoyed unprecedented successes. It is "a shape-shifter, forever changing its name and switching identities" (Klein 2007, 17). From its home base in the World Bank and OECD, it has permeated the major organs of the United Nations, especially those concerned with economic and social development. From post-Allende Chile in 1973 to post-Katrina New Orleans in 2005, it has exploited crises as opportunities for advancement (ibid.). The current global crisis is no exception. In the midst of a resurgence of state intervention and large-scale de facto nationalizations, the worldwide recession is being used as a cover to advance neo-conservative governance projects that would have made Maggie Thatcher proud. In Canada, for example, the federal Conservatives employed the crisis as an excuse to dismantle environmental impact assessment laws and support the reduction of the big Detroit automakers' assembly line wages to the level of their non-unionized Asian competitors. The Ontario Liberals introduced a proposal to eliminate two regulations for every new one introduced – a deregulatory agenda that would make Premier Mike Harris' Red Tape Reduction program of the mid-1990s seem modest.

True, today's neo-conservatism is not the same as yesterday's, as George W. Bush's was not the same as his father's. It differed in important respects, including its proselytizing right-wing Christian zeal and arrogant disregard for international law and human rights. In any case, the Bush administration has been replaced, and important aspects of its political doctrine have been repudiated. Despite President Obama's campaign statements discussed in Chapter 3, there is no appetite in Washington to reopen the continental trade and investment rule book. Even if NAFTA were amended to reflect recent changes to the expropriation-related language of Canadian and American bilateral investment treaties, this would not alter the general effect of Chapter 11. Nor would eliminating political interference with the citizen-complaint process under the environmental side agreement do much to alter the profound imbalance between continental economic and environmental governance. Nothing short of a fundamental renegotiation of the nascent continental governance regime would do the job, and there is no indication that this is in the offing.

Globalization's current governance system needs reordering. The global constitution is out of balance. Its muscular economic norms and institutions have strengthened the powerful and further impoverished the poor. Governance in defence of human, labour, and environmental rights is weak. Many countries' de facto supraconstitutions are in tension with their domestic constitutional values. In Canada's case, the supraconstitution has disturbing anti-democratic components that need to be challenged. Within nation-states, globalization's impact has exacerbated disparities between rich and poor, between have and have-not regions, and between economic and non-economic actors.

These imbalances can be improved, and perhaps ultimately corrected, by strengthening non-economic forms of global governance, by challenging and revising the supraconstitution – in particular NAFTA's Chapter 11 investor-state arbitration powers, and by disciplining corporate greed. If we need a watchword that can provide a unifying vision for emancipatory policy making under conditions of interdependence and interconnectedness, human cultural security may be a candidate. Human beings individually have a prime need for security against violence, disease, hunger, and poverty. Human beings collectively in their various social formations – nation-states, provinces, municipalities, communities, diasporas, First Nations – have a need for their cultures to be secure: not just protected against assimilation by dominant cultures but secure in their capacity for growth and self-realization. Security implies borders, a concept challenged by globalization but one that must not be discarded uncritically, especially when so much regulation is still the preserve of the state.

We began this study by acknowledging the contested nature of all understandings about globalization. Having developed an argument that proposes legitimacy and emancipation as the prime standards to use in deciding how to move forward, we must anticipate that this approach will be roundly dismissed by those who profit from these imbalances, proclaim the legitimacy of the resulting injustices, and exert a powerful influence on the public imagination through their control of major media entities. Still, the ideology of neo-conservatism has suffered many setbacks because the liberalization it has trumpeted has failed to produce the promised outcomes. A worldwide wave of resistance is deepening and broadening among publics skeptical of the neo-conservative panacea. Several Latin American countries have defied it by electing leaders who espouse social justice causes. President Obama was elected on the strength of a widespread hope that he represents a renewed American commitment to justice, equality, and peace. Such marginalized groups as Canadian First Nations are exploring ways to utilize the machinery of neo-conservative global governance to advance their own emancipation (Ladner and Dick 2008).

Canada and Canadians are far from alone in coping with the ramifications of globalization, most of which are experienced in all countries, though with varying intensity and diverse local applications. The Canadian state and its citizens are secondary but sometimes significant players on the world stage. As a result, their reactions matter. But their impact will be more substantial – whether they spring from government, business, or civil society – if they work in concert with like-minded associates. Given the widespread acceptance of liberal humanitarian values, Canadians' effectiveness at transforming global governance will be greater the more they work in transnational coalitions with like-minded governments, civil society organizations, businesses, and individuals. Turning globalization to emancipatory effect will be a more realizable project the more allies there are.

Notes

CHAPTER 1: INTRODUCTION

1   With apologies to Evans, Rueschemeyer, and Skocpol (1985) and Novkov (2008).
2   The Supreme Court of Canada endorsed the latter proposition, known as the subsidiarity principle, in *114957 Canada Ltée (Spraytech, Société d'arrosage) v. Hudson (Town)*, [2001] 2 S.C.R. 241 at 249. See also Bernstein (2004, 8).

CHAPTER 2: THE SUPRACONSTITUTION

1   It is usually true that the affected states gave their consent to the establishment of these decision-making bodies and processes, but that is not the same thing.
2   To be fair, this is something of an oversimplification. International lawyers' embrace of constitutionalism has always involved anxiety, from the perennial anxiety about the threat of war among separate self-regarding sovereigns to the more recent anxiety about the excessive fragmentation of traditional international law (Koskenniemi 2005; Dunoff 2006, 649).
3   Supremacy may not be the cardinal feature of European law it was once thought to be. Although Weiler (1999, 24) claims that national European courts actively promoted the doctrine of supremacy until recently, there is substantial evidence that they do not regard Community law as supreme over national law (Maduro 2003, 95; Kumm 2006, 523-24).

CHAPTER 3: MAKING THE WORLD SAFE FOR TRANSNATIONAL CAPITAL

1   *Free Trade Agreement between the Government of Canada and the Government of the United States of America*, 2 January 1988, Can. T.S. 1989 No. 3, 27 I.L.M. 293 (entered into force 1 January 1989) (CUFTA).
2   *North American Free Trade Agreement (Canada-Mexico-United States)*, 17 December 1992, Can. T.S. 1994 No. 2, 32 I.L.M. 289 (entered into force 1 January 1994) (NAFTA).
3   *General Agreement on Tariffs and Trade 1994*, done at Marrakesh (15 April 1994) (GATT), and *Agreement Establishing the World Trade Organization*, done at Marrakesh

(15 April 1994) (WTO Agreement), both reprinted in World Trade Organization 2007.

4   NAFTA, *supra* note 2 at arts. 301 (goods), 1102 (investors and investments), 1202 (services); GATT, *supra* note 3 at art. III (goods).

5   NAFTA, *supra* note 2 at arts. 308 (goods), 1103 (investors and investments), 1203 (services); GATT, *supra* note 3 at art. I (goods).

6   States are, however, permitted to impose *product-based* environmental trade restrictions – measures that relate to the products themselves as distinct from the processes and methods by which they were produced, provided that such measures are applied equally to like foreign and domestic products.

7   *Brazil–Export Financing Programme for Aircraft (Complaint by Canada)* (1999), WTO Doc. WT/DS46/AB/R (Appellate Body Report), http://www.wto.org/ *[Aircraft Complaint]*.

8   *European Communities–Measures Affecting Asbestos and Products Containing Asbestos (Complaint by Canada)* (2001), WTO Doc. WT/DS135/AB/R (Appellate Body Report), http://www.wto.org/.

9   *Aircraft Complaint, supra* note 7.

10 *Canada–Certain Measures concerning Periodicals (Complaint by the United States)* (1997), WTO Doc. WT/DS31/AB/R (Appellate Body Report), http://www.wto. org/.

11 WTO Agreement, *supra* note 3 at art. XV.

12 NAFTA, *supra* note 2 at art. 2205.

13 Another is the right, discussed below, of foreign investors to be free from expropriation of their investment or action tantamount to expropriation.

14 NAFTA, *supra* note 2 at art. 1106.

15 *Ibid.*, art. 1139.

16 *Canada (A.G.) v. S.D. Myers Inc.*, 2004 FC 38 (*S.D. Myers* (F.C.T.D.)); *Pope & Talbot Inc. v. Canada* (interim award) (26 June 2000) (NAFTA Chapter 11 investor-state arbitration) *(Pope & Talbot)*.

17 The takings clause provides that "nor shall private property be taken for public use, without just compensation." U.S. Const. amend. V.

18 In other words, courts will not interpret a statute to take away property without compensation unless the statutory language clearly demands otherwise. *Manitoba Fisheries Ltd. v. R.*, [1979] 1 S.C.R. 101 *(Manitoba Fisheries)*.

19 *Canadian Bill of Rights*, S.C. 1960, c. 44, s. 1, reprinted in R.S.C. 1985, App. III. For an example of a relevant provincial statute, see *Alberta Bill of Rights*, R.S.A. 2000, c. A-14, s. 1.

20 *Pennsylvania Coal Co. v. Mahon*, 260 U.S. 393 at 415, 43 S.Ct. 158 at 160 (1922) *(Pennsylvania Coal Co.)*.

21 US law also recognizes that a regulatory action that results in a permanent physical occupation of property is a taking per se (*Loretto v. Teleprompter Manhattan CATV*

Corp., 458 U.S. 419 (1982)), but we are more concerned here with public welfare regulation that restricts private property use without physically invading it.

22 *Lucas v. South Carolina Coastal Council*, 112 S.Ct. 2886 (1992).

23 *Lingle v. Chevron U.S.A. Inc.*, 544 U.S. 528 at 539 (2005) *(Lingle)*.

24 *Penn Central Transportation Co. v. New York City*, 438 U.S. 104 at 124 (1978) *(Penn Central)*.

25 *Armstrong v. United States*, 364 U.S. 40 at 49 (1960).

26 *Nollan v. California Coastal Comm'n*, 483 U.S. 825 (1987) *(Nollan); Dolan v. City of Tigard*, 512 U.S. 374 (1994) *(Dolan); First English Evangelical Lutheran Church v. County of Los Angeles*, 482 U.S. 304 (1987).

27 *Palazzolo v. Rhode Island*, 533 U.S. 606 (2001).

28 In *Lingle, supra* note 23, the court held that whether the government action substantially advanced a legitimate state interest was not an appropriate consideration in regulatory takings cases. The focus, rather, was on the action's impact on the private property.

29 *Ibid.; Hodel v. Indiana*, 452 U.S. 314 (1981); *Hodel v. Virginia Surface Mining & Reclamation Ass'n*, 452 U.S. 264 (1981); *Tahoe-Sierra Preservation Council, Inc. v. Tahoe Regional Planning Agency*, 535 U.S. 302 (2002); *Penn Central, supra* note 24.

30 Quotation from *Pennsylvania Coal Co., supra* note 20 at 413; see also *Penn Central, supra* note 24 at 125.

31 *Canadian Pacific Railway v. Vancouver (City)*, 2006 SCC 5, [2006] 1 S.C.R. 227 at para. 30, 262 D.L.R. (4th) 454 *(CPR)*.

32 *Mariner Real Estate Ltd. v. Nova Scotia (A.G.)* (1999), 26 R.P.R. (3d) 37, 177 D.L.R. (4th) 696, 68 L.C.R. 1, 178 N.S.R. (2d) 294, 549 A.P.R. 294, [1999] N.S.J. No. 283 (C.A.) *(Mariner Real Estate Ltd.)*.

33 *Beaches Act*, R.S.N.S. 1989, c. 32.

34 *Mariner Real Estate Ltd., supra* note 32 at para. 101.

35 *Ibid.* at paras. 38-39.

36 *Ibid.* at paras. 5, 50, 85.

37 *Ibid.* at para. 85.

38 *Ibid.* at paras. 93-101 (distinguishing *British Columbia v. Tener*, [1985] 1 S.C.R. 533, in which the Crown's prohibition of mining resulted in recovery of the mineral rights that had previously been granted to the plaintiff, and *Manitoba Fisheries, supra* note 18, in which the legislation that deprived a company of its goodwill also conferred that goodwill upon a Crown corporation).

39 *Nollan* and *Dolan, supra* note 26.

40 *CPR, supra* note 31 at para. 8.

41 *Ibid.* at para. 33.

42 *Ibid.* at para. 37.

43 *Constitución Politica de los Estados Unidos Mexicanos*, c. 1, art. 27.

44 *Ibid.*, quoted in Starner (2002, 414).

45 *Agreement on Trade-Related Aspects of Intellectual Property Rights*, 15 April 1994, 1869 U.N.T.S. 299, 33 I.L.M. 1197 (entered into force 1 January 1995), annex 1C to the *Marrakesh Agreement Establishing the World Trade Organization*, 15 April 1994, 1867 U.N.T.S. 154, 33 I.L.M. 1144 (TRIPS).

46 *Canada–Patent Protection of Pharmaceutical Products (Complaint by the European Communities)* (2000), WTO Doc. WT/DS114/R (Panel Report), http://www.wto.org/.

47 See Clarkson (2008b) for a detailed examination of North American institutionalization.

48 *Re Canada's Compliance with Article 701.3 with Respect to Durum Wheat Sales* (United States v. Canada) (1992), CDA-92-1807-01 (Ch. 18 Panel), NAFTA Secretariat, http://www.nafta-sec-alena.org.

49 Free Trade Commission, Interpretation of the Free Trade Commission of Certain Chapter 11 Provisions (31 July 2001), http://www.state.gov/.

50 Free Trade Commission, Statement of the Free Trade Commission on Non Disputing Party Participation (n.d.), http://www.state.gov/.

51 For the Canadian website, see Foreign Affairs and International Trade Canada, "Dispute Settlement: NAFTA – Chapter 11 – Investment," http://www.international.gc.ca/; for Mexico, see Ministry of the Economy, "Dispute Settlement," http://www.economia.gob.mx/; and for the United States, see US Department of State, "NAFTA Investor-State Arbitrations," http://www.state.gov/.

52 *Automatic Systems Inc. v. Bracknell Corp.*, 1994 CanLII 1871 at 13 (Ont. C.A.), 18 O.R. (3d) 257, 113 D.L.R. (4th) 449.

53 *Corporación Transnacional de Inversiones S.A. de C.V. v. STET International S.p.A.* (1999), 45 O.R. (3d) 183 (S.C.J.), aff'd (2000), 49 O.R. (3d) 414 (C.A.), leave to appeal refused (2001), [2000] S.C.C.A. No. 581, 271 N.R. 394 (note) (S.C.C.); *Waterside Ocean Navigation Co. v. International Navigation Ltd.*, 737 F.2d 150 at 152 (2d Cir. 1998).

54 *Quintette Coal Ltd. v. Nippon Steel Corp.* (1990), 50 B.C.L.R. (2d) 207 (C.A.), leave to appeal refused (1990), 50 B.C.L.R. (2d) xxviii (S.C.C.).

55 *S.D. Myers* (F.C.T.D), *supra* note 16 at para. 76.

56 *New York Convention on the Recognition and Enforcement of Foreign Arbitral Awards*, 10 June 1958, 330 U.N.T.S. 38, 21 U.S.T. 2517, UN Doc. E/Conf. 26/9/Rev. 1 (1958); *Model Law on International Commercial Arbitration*, adopted by the United Nations Commission on International Trade Law, 21 June 1985, UN Doc. A/40/17, Annex 1.

57 *United Mexican States v. Metalclad Corp.* (2001), 89 B.C.L.R. (3d) 359 (S.C.), additional reasons 95 B.C.L.R. (3d) 169 (S.C.) (*Metalclad* (B.C.S.C.)).

58 For a detailed account of the *Ethyl* case, see Michalos (2008).

59 The facts are drawn mainly from *Metalclad* (B.C.S.C.), *supra* note 57.

60 *Metalclad Corp. v. Mexico* (2000), 5 I.C.S.I.D. Rev. 230 at para. 103 (NAFTA Chapter 11 investor-state arbitration).

61 *Metalclad* (B.C.S.C.), *supra* note 57 at para. 99.

62 *Basel Convention on the Control of Transboundary Movements of Hazardous Wastes and Their Disposal*, 22 March 1989, 1673 U.N.T.S. 126, 26 I.L.M. 657 (entered into force 5 May 1992).

63 *S.D. Myers Inc. v. Canada* (partial award – merits) (13 November 2000) (NAFTA Chapter 11 investor-state arbitration).

64 *S.D. Myers* (F.C.T.D.), *supra* note 16.

65 *Methanex Corp. v. U.S.* (final award) (3 August 2005) (NAFTA Chapter 11 investor-state arbitration).

66 *Ibid.*, Part IV, c. D, at 4.

67 *Ibid.* at 5.

68 *Ibid.*, Part IV, c. E, at 9.

69 NAFTA, *supra* note 2 at art. 1101(1).

70 *Methanex, supra* note 65, Part IV, c. E, at 10.

71 *Pope & Talbot, supra* note 16 at 32.

72 *Stockholm Convention on Persistent Organic Pollutants*, 22 May 2001, 40 I.L.M. 532 (entered into force 17 May 2004).

73 As of December 2008, a total of fifty-five Chapter 11 claims had been filed with the three NAFTA parties, according to the NAFTA parties' official Chapter 11 investor-state arbitration webpages. Of these claims, sufficient information was available to classify the subject matter of forty-eight. The remaining seven could not be classified, due to insufficient information. See Foreign Affairs and International Trade Canada, "Dispute Settlement: NAFTA," *supra* note 51; Mexico, Ministry of the Economy, "Dispute Settlement," *supra* note 51; and US Department of State, "NAFTA Investor-State Arbitrations," *supra* note 51.

74 *Bipartisan Trade Promotion Authority Act of 2002*, 19 U.S.C. s. 3801 (2002).

75 *Agreement between Canada and the Republic of Peru for the Promotion and Protection of Investments* (2006), Annex B.13(1), Foreign Affairs and International Trade Canada, http://www.international.gc.ca/. Similar provisions are found in the current American and Canadian model BITs, which are used as the basis for new negotiations.

76 *Japan–Taxes on Alcoholic Beverages (Complaints by Canada, European Communities, and United States)* (1996), WTO Doc. WT/DS8/AB/R, WT/DS10/AB/R, WT/DS11/AB/R (Appellate Body Report), http://www.wto.org/.

77 *Canada–Certain Measures concerning Periodicals, supra* note 10.

78 The Council of Canadians launched a constitutional challenge against NAFTA Chapter 11 in 2001, but it was dismissed by the trial judge. *Council of Canadians v. Canada (A.-G.)*, Doc. No. 01-CV-208141 (Ont. Sup. Ct. J., 8 July 2005), 2005 CanLII 28426, aff'd (2006), 277 D.L.R. (4th) 527 (Ont. C.A.), 149 C.R.R. (2d) 290.

79 *Re Tariffs Applied by Canada to Certain U.S. Origin Agricultural Products (United States v. Canada)* (1996), CDA-95-2008-01 (Ch. 20 Panel).

80 *Montreal Protocol on Substances That Deplete the Ozone Layer,* 16 September 1987, 1522 U.N.T.S. 29, 26 I.L.M. 1550 (entered into force 1 January 1989).

81 *EC Measures concerning Meat and Meat Products (Hormones) (Complaints by Canada and the United States)* (1998), WTO Doc. WT/DS26/AB/R, WT/DS48/AB/R (Appellate Body Report), http://www.WTO.org/.

CHAPTER 4: GOOD CITIZENS OF PLANET EARTH?

1 *Trail Smelter Arbitration (United States – Canada)* (1931–41), 3 R.I.A.A. 1905, (1939) 33 A.J.I.L. 182, (1941) 35 A.J.I.L. 684.

2 *Ibid.,* 35 A.J.I.L. at 684, 3 R.I.A.A. at 1907.

3 Stockholm Declaration, in *Report of the United Nations Conference on the Human Environment,* Stockholm, 5–16 June 1972 (UN publication No E.73.IIA14 and corrigendum), Ch. 1, Principle 21.

4 *Lake Lanoux Arbitration (France v. Spain)* (1957), 12 R.I.A.A. 281, 24 I.L.R. 101; *Corfu Channel (UK v. Albania)* (Merits), [1949] I.C.J. Rep. 4.

5 See, for example, *Convention on Environmental Impact Assessment in a Transboundary Context* (1991), 30 I.L.M. 802.

6 Examples include *Basel Convention on the Control of Transboundary Movements of Hazardous Wastes and Their Disposal* (1989), 28 I.L.M. 657; *Rotterdam Convention on the Prior Informed Consent for Certain Hazardous Chemicals and Pesticides in International Trade* (1998), 38 I.L.M. 1. ˙

7 Rio Declaration, in *Report of the United Nations Conference on Environment and Development,* UN Doc. A/CONF.151/26, vol. 1 (1992), Principle 15.

8 *Vienna Convention for the Protection of the Ozone Layer,* 22 March 1985, 1513 U.N.T.S. 323, 26 I.L.M. 1529 (entered into force 22 September 1988) *(Ozone Convention); Montreal Protocol on Substances That Deplete the Ozone Layer,* 16 September 1987, 1522 U.N.T.S. 29, 26 I.L.M. 1550 (entered into force 1 January 1989).

9 *Southern Bluefin Tuna Cases (New Zealand v. Japan; Australia v. Japan) (Provisional Measures)* (1999), 38 I.L.M. 1624 (Order of 27 August 1999).

10 See, for example, *114957 Canada Ltée (Spraytech, Société d'arrosage) v. Hudson (Town),* [2001] 2 S.C.R. 241.

11 *Pest Control Products Act,* S.C. 2002, c. 28, s. 7(6).

12 *Canadian Environmental Protection Act, 1999,* S.C. 1999, c. 33, s. 2(1)(a). The government must also apply the precautionary approach when assessing substances for toxicity (s. 76.1), and the national advisory committee created by the statute must apply it when advising the government (s. 6).

13 *Great Lakes Water Quality Agreement,* 22 November 1978, 1153 U.N.T.S. 187 at art. II, Can. T.S. 1978 No. 20, 30 U.S.T. 1383 (entered into force 22 November 1978).

14 *Convention on Biological Diversity,* 5 June 1992, 1760 U.N.T.S. 79, 31 I.L.M. 818 (entered into force 29 December 1993) (CBD).

15   The Conference of the Parties to the *Convention on Biological Diversity,* Ecosystem
     Approach, COP 5 Decision V/6, http://www.cbd.int/.

16   See, for example, Rio Declaration, *supra* note 7, Principle 7.

17   *United Nations Framework Convention on Climate Change,* 9 May 1982, 1771 U.N.T.S.
     107, 31 I.L.M. 849 (entered into force 21 March 1994) (UNFCCC).

18   *Kyoto Protocol to the United Nations Framework Convention on Climate Change* (1997),
     37 I.L.M. 22.

19   See, for example, CBD, *supra* note 14 at art. 20(4); UNFCCC, *supra* note 17 at art.
     4(7).

20   *Oposa v. Factoran,* 33 I.L.M. 173 (Philippines Sup. Ct. 1993) (granting plaintiffs
     standing to sue the Philippine government on behalf of minor citizens and gen-
     erations of citizens yet unborn for the alleged violation of their constitutional
     right to a balanced and healthful ecology).

21   Rio Declaration, *supra* note 7, Principles 3, 4.

22   *Johannesburg Declaration on Sustainable Development,* adopted at the seventeenth
     plenary meeting of the World Summit on Sustainable Development, 4 September
     2002, UN Doc. A/CONF.199/20 (2002), 1 at para. 13.

23   Board of the Millennium Ecosystem Assessment, *Living beyond Our Means: Nat-
     ural Assets and Human Well-Being (Statement from the Board)* (prepublication draft,
     2005), 2.

24   *Cartagena Protocol on Biosafety to the Convention on Biological Diversity,* 29 January
     2000, 1760 U.N.T.S. 79, 39 I.L.M. 1027 (entered into force 11 September 2003).

25   The National Round Table on Environment and Economy (2007), for example,
     found that, by the government's own projections, Canada would exceed its Kyoto
     target by 34 percent.

26   Stockholm Declaration, *supra* note 3, Principle 1.

27   For example, *Convention on Access to Information, Public Participation in Decision
     Making and Access to Justice in Environmental Matters* (1999), 38 I.L.M. 515.

28   Canadian Consortium on Human Security (CCHS). Human Security Bulletin. 13
     July 2006. http://www.humansecurity.info/.

29   *Constitution of the World Health Organization* (1946), US Dept. State Bulletin (4
     August 1946), 211-19, at Preamble.

30   *Universal Declaration of Human Rights* (1948), UNGA Res. 217A (III), art. 25; *Inter-
     national Covenant on Economic, Social, and Cultural Rights* (1966), UNGA Res. 2200A
     (XXI), 993 U.N.T.S. 3, art. 12 (ICESCR).

31   *WHO Framework Convention on Tobacco Control* (2003), 42 I.L.M. 518.

32   *Patent Act,* R.S.C. 1985, c. P-4.

33   *Canada–Patent Protection of Pharmaceutical Products (Complaint by the European
     Communities and Their Member States)* (2000), WTO Doc. WT/DS114/R (Panel
     Report), http://www.WTO.org/.

34   *An Act to amend the Patent Act and the Food and Drugs Act (The Jean Chrétien Pledge
     to Africa),* S.C. 2004, c. 23.

35 Implementation of paragraph 6 of the *Doha Declaration on the TRIPS Agreement and Public Health*, Decision of the WTO General Council, 30 August 2003, Doc. No. WT/L/540 and Corr. 1.

36 Foreign Affairs and International Trade Canada, Glyn Berry Program for Peace and Security, http://www.international.gc.ca/.

37 *Convention on the Prohibition of the Use, Stockpiling, Production and Transfer of Anti-Personnel Mines and on Their Destruction* (1997), 36 I.L.M. 1507.

38 *Rome Statute of the International Criminal Court* (1998), 2187 U.N.T.S. 90.

39 For more information on the Human Security Network, visit http://www.humansecuritynetwork.org.

40 For more information about the Canadian Consortium on Human Security, visit http://www.humansecurity.info.

41 ICESCR, *supra* note 30 at art. 15(2); *Convention for the Safeguarding of Intangible Cultural Heritage*, 17 October 2003, UNESCO Doc. Misc./2003/CLT/CH/14 (entered into force 20 April 2006).

42 *Convention on the Protection and Promotion of the Diversity of Cultural Expressions*, 20 October 2005, UNESCO Doc. CLT-2005/Convention Diversite–Cult. Rev. (entered into force 18 March 2007).

43 *Ibid.* at arts. 4(1), 1(h).

44 *United States–Import Prohibition of Certain Shrimp and Shrimp Products* (1998), WTO Doc. WT/DS58/AB/R at para. 129 (Appellate Body Report) *(Shrimp-Turtle I)*, http://www.wto.org/.

CHAPTER 5: TAKING THE MEASURE OF THE SUPRACONSTITUTION

1 For more information on the United Nations Global Compact, visit http://www.unglobalcompact.org/.

2 *Convention on the Protection and Promotion of the Diversity of Cultural Expressions*, 20 October 2005, UNESCO Doc. CLT-2005/Convention Diversite–Cult. Rev. (entered into force 18 March 2007).

3 *International Covenant on Civil and Political Rights*, 16 December 1966, 999 U.N.T.S. 171, 6 I.L.M. 368 (entered into force 23 March 1976); *Convention on the Rights of the Child*, 20 November 1989, 1577 U.N.T.S. 3, 28 I.L.M. 1456 (entered into force 2 September 1990).

4 *Convention for the Protection of Human Rights and Fundamental Freedoms*, 4 November 1950, 213 U.N.T.S. 221 at 223, Eur. T.S. No. 5 (entered into force 3 September 1953).

5 We are grateful to an anonymous reviewer for helping us clarify this point.

6 *United States–Restrictions on Imports of Tuna from Mexico* (1991), GATT Doc. DS21/R, 30 I.L.M. 1598 *(Tuna-Dolphin I)*; *United States–Restrictions on Imports of Tuna* (1994), GATT Doc. DS29/R *(Tuna-Dolphin II)*.

7   *General Agreement on Tariffs and Trade 1994*, 15 April 1994, 1867 U.N.T.S. 187,
    33 I.L.M. 1153 (entered into force 1 January 1995), annex 1A to the *Marrakesh
    Agreement Establishing the World Trade Organization*, 15 April 1994, 1867 U.N.T.S.
    154, 33 I.L.M. 1144 at arts. XX(b) and (g) (GATT 1994).

8   *United States–Import Prohibition of Certain Shrimp and Shrimp Products (Recourse to
    Article 21.5 of the DSU by Malaysia)* (2001), WTO Doc. WT/DS58/AB/RW (Appel-
    late Body Report) *(Shrimp-Turtle II);* see also *United States–Import Prohibition of
    Certain Shrimp and Shrimp Products* (1998), WTO Doc. WT/DS58/AB/R (Appellate
    Body Report) *(Shrimp-Turtle I),* http://www.wto.org/.

9   GATT 1994, *supra* note 7 at art. XX.

10 *Shrimp-Turtle I, supra* note 8.

11 *Shrimp-Turtle II, supra* note 8 at para. 123.

12 *Ibid.* at para. 144 (emphasis in original).

13 *North American Free Trade Agreement (Canada-Mexico-United States)*, 17 December
    1992, Can. T.S. 1994 No. 2, 32 I.L.M. 289 at art. 104 (entered into force 1 January
    1994) (NAFTA).

14 *S.D. Myers Inc. v. Canada* (partial award – merits) (13 November 2000) at para.
    215 (NAFTA Chapter 11 investor-state arbitration); *Basel Convention on the Control
    of Transboundary Movements of Hazardous Wastes and Their Disposal* (1989), 28 I.L.M.
    657 at art. 11.

15 *North American Agreement on Environmental Cooperation (Canada-Mexico-United
    States)*, 8 September 1993, 32 I.L.M. 1480 at art. 14 (entered into force 1 January
    1994) (NAAEC).

16 NAFTA, *supra* note 13 at art. 1114(2).

17 *Ibid.* at art. 904.

18 NAAEC, *supra* note 15 at art. 3.

19 *Ibid.* at art. 4.

20 *Ibid.* at art. 6.

21 *Ibid.* at art. 7.

22 *Ibid.* at arts. 2, 4.

23 *Ibid.* at art. 5.

24 *Ibid.* at art. 14.

25 Ecojustice et al. to the Hon. John Baird, Administrator Stephen L. Johnson, and
    Secretario Juan Rafael Elvira Quesada (23 April 2008) (copy on file with authors);
    see also "Canada, U.S., Mexico Accused of Interference with NAFTA Watchdog,"
    Environment News Service (24 April 2008), http://www.ens-newswire.com/.

26 Commission for Environmental Cooperation, "Citizen Submissions on Enforce-
    ment Matters," http://www.cec.org/citizen/; for NAFTA, see Foreign Affairs and
    International Trade Canada, "Dispute Settlement: NAFTA – Chapter 11 – Invest-
    ment," http://www.international.gc.ca/; Mexico, Ministry of the Economy, "Dispute

Settlement," http://www.economia.gob.mx/; and US Department of State, "NAFTA Investor-State Arbitrations," http://www.state.gov/. The number fifty-five is approximate, since the three governments' Chapter 11 dispute webpages are inconsistent. In addition, one of the fifty-five actually represents more than a hundred individual Chapter 11 claims by Canadian cattlemen over the BSE-related closure of the US border to Canadian cattle. All of these claims are counted as a single case on the two governments' Chapter 11 dispute webpages.

27　*Devils Lake–Article 14(1) Determination* (2006), SEM-06-002, Secretariat for the Commission for Environmental Cooperation, Doc. Nos. A14/SEM/06-002/04/ 14(1) and A14/SEM/06-002/12/DETN.

28　*North American Agreement on Labor Cooperation (Canada-Mexico-United States)*, 14 September 1993, 32 I.L.M. 1499 at art. 16(3).

29　*Ibid.* For information about labour law complaints, see Commission for Labor Cooperation, "Public Communications," http://new.naalc.org/.

CHAPTER 6: FROM RETREAT TO REVITALIZATION

1　For commentary on the August 2008 propane explosion, see M. Winfield, "Public Safety in Private Hands: Rethinking the TSSA Model," *Toronto Star* (29 August 2008), http://www.thestar.com/.

2　Although rechristened as "performance-based regulation" by the current Conservative government elected in January 2006, the initiative retained substantially the same emphasis. For further information on the program, visit Government of Canada, "Regulation," http://www.regulation.gc.ca/.

3　*Bangoura v. Washington Post* (2004), 2004 CanLII 26633 at para. 22, 235 D.L.R. (4th) 564, 48 C.P.C. (5th) 318 (Ont. Sup. Ct. J.).

4　*Bangoura v. Washington Post* (2005), 258 D.L.R. (4th) 341, [2005] O.J. No. 3849 (Ont. C.A.), leave to appeal refused (2006), 221 O.A.C. 398 (note), 352 N.R. 197 (note) (S.C.C.).

5　See, for example, *Burke v. NYP Holdings Inc.*, 2005 BCSC 1287, (2005) 48 B.C.L.R. (4th) 363 (B.C.S.C.) (allowing an action by injured NHL player Brian Burke against the *New York Post* to proceed in British Columbia); *Crookes v. Holloway*, 2007 BCSC 1325, (2007) 75 B.C.L.R. (4th) 316 (B.C.S.C.), aff'd 2008 BCCA 165, (2008) 77 B.C.L.R. (4th) 201 (B.C.C.A.) (rejecting an action by a BC resident against Yahoo over allegedly defamatory statements hosted on Yahoo's servers outside Canada).

6　The House of Lords ruled that Pinochet could be extradited to face charges of torture and conspiracy to commit torture where the alleged acts took place after the relevant states (Chile, Spain, and the UK) ratified the 1984 *Convention against Torture*. *R. v. Bow Street Metropolitan Stipendiary Magistrate, ex parte Pinochet Ugarte (No. 3)*, [2000] 1 A.C. 147 (H.L. 1999). After the home secretary refused to extradite Pinochet, on the grounds that he was unfit for trial due to his poor health, he returned to Chile, where he died in 2006.

7 *Recherches Internationales Quebec v. Cambior Inc.*, [1998] Q.J. No. 2554 (Quicklaw) (Que. Sup. Ct.).

8 *Ramirez v. Copper Mesa Mining Corp.* (2009), No. CV09-37354 (Ont. Sup. Ct. J.) (Statement of Claim). For more information about the case, visit http://www. ramirezversuscoppermesa.com/.

9 *Bouzari v. Islamic Republic of Iran* (2004), 71 O.R. (3d) 675 (Ont. C.A.), leave to appeal refused, [2005] 1 S.C.R. vi (S.C.C).

10 *Arar v. Syria (Arab Republic)* (2005), 127 C.R.R. (2d) 252, 28 C.R. (6th) 187 (Ont. S.C.J.).

11 *Khadr v. Canada (Min. of Justice)*, [2008] 2 S.C.R. 125.

12 *R. v. Hape*, 2007 SCC 26 at para. 101 (per LeBel J.).

13 The twenty thousand or so seasonal agricultural workers who travel to Canada each year are excluded from collective bargaining legislation, and are covered instead by more restrictive statutes. In 2008, the Ontario Court of Appeal gave the Ontario government twelve months to draft new legislation respecting the workers' collective bargaining rights, but the government sought leave to appeal the decision to the Supreme Court of Canada. *Fraser v. Ontario (A.-G.)* (2008), 92 O.R. (3d) 481 (Ont. C.A.).

14 Canada, for example, supported the imposition of World Bank–prescribed user fees for health care in Tanzania, fees that reportedly made basic health care inaccessible to a huge segment of the Tanzanian population. Canada's support for the fees continued even after the World Bank began backing away from blanket demands for user fees in health care and education, and other donor countries, led by Britain, began to pressure the Tanzanian government to drop the fees. As a local Canadian International Development Agency official observed, there is a flagrant irony in the fact that the Canadian government supports health care user fees abroad even while it resists their introduction in Canada (Nolen 2005).

CHAPTER 7: GLOBAL LAW BEYOND THE STATE

1 This book cannot consider all expressions of non-state governance. It focuses on transnational business and civil society because they cover most of the ground. Transnational crime cartels and terrorist networks are beyond our scope and are dealt with in greater detail elsewhere (Naylor 2006).

2 This figure is based on a comparison of corporate revenues with national GDP. Critics who point out that revenues and GDP are not comparable nonetheless estimate that thirty-seven of the world's hundred largest economies are business corporations, a large proportion by any measure (Norberg 2003, 214).

3 For further information on the World Green Building Council, visit http://www. worldgbc.org.

4 Special Representative of the Secretary-General on the Issue of Human Rights and Transnational Corporations and Other Business Enterprises, *Protect, Respect and*

Remedy: A Framework for Business and Human Rights, UN Doc. A/HRC/8/5 (2008) (Ruggie Final Report).

5   Sub-Commission on the Promotion and Protection of Human Rights, *Norms on the Responsibilities of Transnational Corporations and Other Business Enterprises with Regard to Human Rights,* UN Doc. E/CN.4/Sub.2/2003/12/Rev.2 (2003). For Ruggie's reaction, see Special Representative of the Secretary-General on the Issue of Human Rights and Transnational Corporations and Other Business Enterprises, *Interim Report,* UN Doc. E/CN.4/2006/97 (2006) at paras. 56-69.

6   Ruggie Final Report, *supra* note 4; Special Representative of the Secretary-General on the Issue of Human Rights and Transnational Corporations and Other Business Enterprises, *Clarifying the Concepts of "Sphere of Influence" and "Complicity,"* UN Doc. A/HRC/8/16 (2008).

7   For further information on Avocats sans Frontières, visit http://www.asf.be.

8   For more details on the Quebec section of Avocats sans frontières, visit http://www.asfquebec.com.

9   For further information on Lawyers Without Borders, visit http://lawyerswithout-borders.org.

10 For more details on Canadian Lawyers Abroad–Avocats canadiens à l'étranger, visit http://www.cla-ace.ca.

11 For further information on Human Rights First, visit http://www.humanrightsfirst.org; for Canadian Lawyers for International Human Rights, visit http://www.claihr.ca; for Environmental Law Alliance Worldwide, visit http://www.elaw.org.

12 Some critics of neo-conservative globalization use the term "globalization from above" to denote the constitution by powerful states, transnational market actors, and other privileged elites of a new world order characterized by global corporations, global industrial and financial markets, instant global communications via the Internet, a radically transformed state, a neo-conservative ideology, a consumerist ethos, and a widening gap between rich and poor and between North and South. For them, "globalization from below," conversely, refers to the local and transnational politics of resistance and transformation emanating from society's grassroots, particularly from its marginalized and disadvantaged segments, in pursuit of environmental sustainability, human rights, equality, democratic control of states and markets, an end to poverty and oppression, and a human community that finds unity in diversity (Falk 1999, 127-36; 2004, 81-101; Likosky 2002, xxii). By contrast, we use the terms simply to denote the direction of governance efforts from the grassroots and margins "upward" toward state and economic elites, or vice versa. Although this distinction often corresponds to resistance to, rather than support for, neo-conservative globalization, this is not always the case. What Falk refers to as globalization from above and globalization from below correspond roughly to what Santos (2002) and his colleagues (Santos and Rodrí-

guez-Garavito 2005) call "hegemonic globalization," on the one hand, and "counter-hegemonic globalization" or "subaltern cosmopolitanism," on the other.

13 *International Non-Governmental Organisations Accountability Charter* (20 December 2005), http://www.ingoaccountabilitycharter.org/ *(INGO Accountability Charter)*. The founding signatories were ActionAid International, Amnesty International, CIVICUS World Alliance for Citizen Participation, Consumers International, Greenpeace International, International Save the Children Alliance, Oxfam International, Plan International, Survival International, Transparency International, and World YWCA.

14 The most obvious candidate to supply such verification and enforcement capacity would be the existing global network of professional auditing and certification firms, but this would be problematic for two reasons. First, such firms rely on continued business with audited or certified organizations for their income, thus creating an incentive for them not to be too stringent so as not to lose business to competitors. Second, many of these firms also provide consulting services to the same organizations they audit or certify, reinforcing the close symbiotic relationship between them and sometimes producing conflicts of interest where auditors audit their own work. All of this gives rise to the possibility that the verifiers and enforcers could be captured by the regulated organizations. The business model of the existing global auditing and certification network is inappropriate for ensuring the accountability not only of CSOs but of business actors as well.

15 *INGO Accountability Charter, supra* note 13 at 4.

16 *Ibid.* at 2.

17 *Ibid.* at 4.

18 *Ibid.* at 2.

19 For more information on Kielburger's organization Free the Children, visit http://www.freethechildren.com.

20 For further information on the Halifax Initiative, visit http://www.halifaxinitiative.org/.

21 For further information on MiningWatch Canada, visit http://www.miningwatch.ca/.

22 For further information on KAIROS: Canadian Ecumenical Justice Initiatives, visit http://www.kairoscanada.org; for the Bench Marks Principles, visit http://www.bench-marks.org.

23 For further information on War Child Canada, visit http://www.warchild.ca.

24 Only Russia joined Canada in voting against the declaration in the UN Human Rights Council (United Nations Human Rights Council 2006).

25 The "triple bottom line" thesis holds that corporations should simultaneously pursue, and their success should be measured against, the three "bottom lines" of economic, environmental, and social performance (Elkington 1998).

298

26 For an alternative conceptualization of this transnational regulatory space, see Wood (2006, 237).

27 For further information on the *Global Reporting Initiative*, visit http://www.globalreporting.org; for the International Federation of Organic Agriculture Movements, visit http://www.ifoam.org/; for the Fairtrade Labelling Organization, visit http://www.fairtrade.net/; for Social Accountability International, visit http://www.sa-intl.org/; for AccountAbility, visit http://www.accountability21.net/; for the Forest Stewardship Council, visit http://www.fsc.org/; for the Marine Stewardship Council, visit http://www.msc.org/.

27 For further information on the UN Global Compact, visit http://www.unglobalcompact.org/; for the Equator Principles, visit http://www.equator-principles.com/.

28 For further information on the Voluntary Principles on Security and Human Rights, visit http://www.voluntaryprinciples.org/; for the Kimberley Process, visit http://www.kimberleyprocess.com/, for ISO 26000, visit http://www.iso.org/sr.

29 Annual FSC membership fees range from US$38 for individuals from the global South to US$10,000 for very large companies from the global North. While some complain that this "pay to play" model compromises the FSC's legitimacy, the organization would not likely be able to function without these revenues since, unlike some standards development bodies, it earns nothing from the sale of standards.

30 Forest Stewardship Council, Global FSC Certificates: Type and Distribution (December 2008), http://www.fsc.org/facts-figures.html.

CHAPTER 8: RETHINKING CANADIAN GOVERNANCE AND LAW

1 See, for example, *National Technology Transfer and Advancement Act of 1995*, Pub. L. No. 104-113, s. 12(d), 110 Stat. 775 (7 March 1996) (US).

2 See, for example, *R. v. Calgary (City)* (2000), 272 A.R. 161, 35 C.E.L.R. (N.S.) 253 (Alta. Prov. Ct.); *R. v. Canada (Minister of Indian Affairs)*, [2000] O.J. No. 5076 (Quicklaw) (Ont. Sup. Ct. J. 2000); *R. v. Prospec Chemicals* (1996), 19 C.E.L.R. (N.S.) 178 (Alta. Prov. Ct.); *R. v. Van Waters and Rogers Ltd.* (1998), 220 A.R. 315 (Alta. Prov. Ct.). The *Canadian Environmental Protection Act, 1999*, S.C. 1999, c. 33, s. 291(1), authorizes a sentencing court to direct an offender to "implement an environmental management system that meets a recognized Canadian or international standard."

3 Nova Scotia and New Brunswick, for example, enacted regulations requiring gas pipeline operators to implement ISO 14000–based environmental management systems: see *Pipeline Regulations*, N.S. Reg. 66/98, s. 19(1); *Gas Pipeline Regulation*, N.B. Reg. 99-61, s. 46, and *Gas Distribution and Marketers' Filing Regulation*, N.B. Reg. 99-60, s. 7(12).

4   Ontario Ministry of the Environment, Ontario's Environmental Leaders, http://
    www.ene.gov.on.ca/.

5   As of April 2009, nine corporations and one industry association were members
    of the program. There were two big players in the group: General Motors Canada
    (including all of its Ontario facilities) and the Canadian Chemical Producers'
    Association. The rest were an assortment of chemical and manufacturing facilities,
    a meat-packing plant, a hospital, and a city-owned exhibition and entertainment
    facility. One major player, the Automotive Parts Manufacturing Association, joined
    the program in its early years but later dropped out.

References

Abbott, K.W., and D. Snidal. 2009. Strengthening International Regulation through Transnational New Governance: Overcoming the Orchestration Deficit. *Vanderbilt Journal of Transnational Law* 42: 501-78.

Afilalo, A. 2001. Constitutionalization through the Back Door: A European Perspective on NAFTA's Investment Chapter. *New York University Journal of International Law and Policy* 34: 1-55.

Aginam, O. 2005. *Global Health Governance: International Law and Public Health in a Divided World*. Toronto: University of Toronto Press.

Allahwala, A., and R. Keil. 2005. Introduction to a Debate on the World Social Forum. *International Journal of Urban and Regional Research* 29(2): 409-16.

Allum, J.R. 2006. "An Outcrop of Hell": History, Environment, and the Politics of the Trail Smelter Dispute. In *Transboundary Harm in International Law: Lessons from the Trail Smelter Arbitration*, ed. R.M. Bratspies and R.A. Miller, 13-26. New York: Cambridge University Press.

Amnesty International Canada. 2009. Government Squanders Opportunity to Hold Extractive Companies to Account. Media release, 29 March. http://www.amnesty.ca/.

Anand, R. 2004. *International Environmental Justice: A North-South Dimension*. Burlington, VT: Ashgate.

Anderson, S., and J. Cavanagh. 2000. *Top 200: The Rise of Corporate Global Power*. Washington, DC: Institute for Policy Studies.

Armstrong, D., T. Farrell, and B. Maiguashca. 2003. *Governance and Resistance in World Politics*. Cambridge: Cambridge University Press.

Arthurs, H.W. 1998. The Political Economy of Canadian Legal Education. *Journal of Law and Society* 25(1): 14-32.

–. 2000. The Hollowing Out of Corporate Canada? In *Globalizing Institutions: Case Studies in Social Regulation and Innovation*, ed. J. Jenson and B. Santos, 29-51. London: Ashgate.

Arts, B. 2006. Non-State Actors in Global Environmental Governance: New Arrangements beyond the State. In *New Modes of Governance in the Global System: Exploring Publicness, Delegation and Inclusiveness*, ed. M. Koenig-Archibugi and M. Zürn, 177-200. New York: Palgrave Macmillan.

Arup, C. 2000. *The New World Trade Organization Agreements: Globalizing Law through Services and Intellectual Property*. Cambridge: Cambridge University Press.

Avbelj, M. 2008. Questioning EU Constitutionalisms. *German Law Journal* 9: 1-26.

Axworthy, L. 2004. A New Scientific and Policy Lens. *Security Dialogue* 35(3): 348-49.

Ayres, I., and J. Braithwaite. 1992. *Responsive Regulation: Transcending the Deregulation Debate*. New York: Oxford University Press.

Baker, M. 2006. At Last: An Accountability Charter for NGOs. *Business Respect* 97 (18 June). http://www.mallenbaker.net/.

Bardach, E., and R.A. Kagan. 1982. *Going by the Book: The Problem of Regulatory Unreasonableness*. Philadelphia: Temple University Press.

Barlow, M., and T. Clarke. 2001. *Global Showdown*. Toronto: Stoddart.

Barnard, C.I. 1938. *The Functions of the Executive*. Cambridge, MA: Harvard University Press.

Been, V., and J. Beauvais. 2003. The Global Fifth Amendment? NAFTA's Investment Protections and the Misguided Quest for an International "Regulatory Takings" Doctrine. *New York University Law Review* 78: 30-143.

Belanger, L. 1999. Redefining Cultural Diplomacy: Cultural Security and Foreign Policy in Canada. *Political Psychology* 20(4): 677-99.

Bernstein, S. 2004. The Elusive Basis of Legitimacy in Global Governance: Three Conceptions. Working Paper Series GHC 04/2. Institute on Globalization and the Human Condition, McMaster University. http://www.humanities.mcmaster.ca/.

Bhagwati, J. 2004. *In Defense of Globalization*. New York: Oxford University Press.

Bhala, R. 1999. The Myth about Stare Decisis and International Trade Law. *American University International Law Review* 14: 845-956.

Bickerton, I., and N. Tait. 2006. World's Newest Court Prepares for Hague Debut. *Financial Times*, 24 June. http://www.ft.com/.

Birnie, P., and A.E. Boyle. 2002. *International Law and the Environment*. 2nd ed. Oxford: Oxford University Press.

Black, H.C. 1979. *Black's Law Dictionary*. 5th ed. St. Paul: West.

Blank, S., and S. Krajewski. 1995. U.S. Firms in North America: Redefining Structure and Strategy. *North American Outlook* 5(2): 9-72.

Bodansky, D. 1995. Customary (and Not so Customary) International Environmental Law. *Indiana Journal of Global Legal Studies* 3: 112-19.

Booth, K., ed. 2004. *Critical Security Studies and World Politics*. Boulder, CO: Lynne Rienner.

Boyd, D. 2003. *Unnatural Law: Rethinking Canadian Environmental Law and Policy*. Vancouver: UBC Press.

Brack, D. 1998. The *Shrimp-Turtle* Case: Implications for the Multilateral Environmental Agreement – World Trade Organization Debate. *Yearbook of International Environmental Law* 9: 13-19.

Braithwaite, J., and P. Drahos. 2000. *Global Business Regulation*. Cambridge: Cambridge University Press.

British Columbia Regulatory Reform Office. 2005. Message from John Les, Minister Responsible for Regulatory Reform. http://www.deregulation.gov.bc.ca/ (last updated 21 February 2005; archived at http://web.archive.org/).

Broadhead, L. 2002. *International Environmental Politics: The Limits of Green Diplomacy.* Boulder, CO: Lynne Rienner.

Brodie, J. 1996. New State Forms, New Political Spaces. In *States against Markets: The Limits of Globalization,* eds. R. Boyer and D. Drache, 383-98. New York: Routledge.

Brown, L.R. 2000. The Rise and Fall of the Global Climate Coalition. 25 July. Earth Policy Institute. http://www.earth-policy.org/.

Brunnée, J. 1993. Beyond Rio? The Evolution of International Environmental Law. *Alternatives* 20(1): 16-23.

Bubandt, N. 2005. Vernacular Security: The Politics of Feeling Safe in Global, National, Local Worlds. *Security Dialogue* 36(3): 275-96.

Buchanan, R., and R. Chaparro. 2008. International Institutions and Transnational Advocacy: The Case of the North American Agreement on Labor Cooperation. *UCLA Journal of International Law and Foreign Affairs* 13: 129-59.

Buchanan, R., and A. Long. 2002. Contested Global Governance: States, the World Trade Organization, and Global Civil Society. Report prepared for the Law Commission of Canada, December. Ottawa: Law Commission of Canada.

Byers, M. 2007. *Intent for a Nation: A Relentlessly Optimistic Manifesto for Canada's Role in the World.* Vancouver and Toronto: Douglas and McIntyre.

Byrd, S.C. 2005. The Pôrto Alegre Consensus: Theorizing the Forum Movement. *Globalizations* 2(1): 151-63.

Canadian Business for Social Responsibility (CBSR). 2008. *CSR Trends 2008.* Toronto: CBSR.

Canadian Environmental Law Association (CELA). 2004. Letter to Rt. Hon. Paul Martin regarding Report of the External Advisory Committee on Smart Regulation, 22 October. CELA Publication No. 487. http://www.cela.ca/.

–. 2008. Letter to Prime Minister Stephen Harper and President-Elect Barack Obama re Chapter 11 of NAFTA, 11 November. http://www.cela.ca/.

Canadian Environmental Law Association et al. 2004. Letter from CELA and 45 Other Organizations and Individuals to Members of External Advisory Committee on Smart Regulation regarding the Need to Give Regulatory Priority to Health, Safety and Environmental Protection, 16 August. http://www.cela.ca/.

Canadian Press. 2000. Trade Panel Rules Ottawa Violated NAFTA with PCB Export Ban. 13 November.

Cardwell, M. 2008. Exploring the New World. *Canadian Lawyer,* October, 31-37.

Cashore, B., G. Auld, and D. Newsom. 2004. *Governing through Markets: Forest Certification and the Emergence of Non-State Authority.* New Haven: Yale University Press.

Cass, D. 2001. The "Constitutionalization" of International Trade Law: Judicial Norm-Generation as the Engine of Constitutional Development in International Trade. *European Journal of International Law* 12(1): 39-75.

-. 2005. *The Constitutionalization of the World Trade Organization.* Oxford: Oxford University Press.

Cattaneo, C. 2003. Talisman Sudan Deal Dispute: Sale to India Delayed. *National Post,* 3 January, FP1.

Cerone, J.P. 2007. Dynamic Equilibrium: The Evolution of US Attitudes toward International Criminal Courts and Tribunals. *European Journal of International Law* 18(2): 277-315.

Chang, H. 1998. Transnational Corporations and Strategic Industrial Policy. In *Transnational Corporations and the Global Economy,* ed. R. Kozul-Wright and R. Rowthorn, 225-43. New York: Macmillan.

Chayes, A., and A. Handler Chayes. 1995. *The New Sovereignty: Compliance with International Regulatory Agreements.* Cambridge, MA: Harvard University Press.

Chayes, A., A. Handler Chayes, and R.B. Mitchell. 1995. Active Compliance Management in Environmental Treaties. In *Sustainable Development and International Law,* ed. Winfried Lang, 75-89. London: Kluwer.

Chibundu, M.O. 1999. Globalizing the Rule of Law: Some Thoughts at and on the Periphery. *Indiana Journal of Global Legal Studies* 7: 79-116.

Chimni, B.S. 2004. International Institutions Today: An Imperial Global State in the Making. *European Journal of International Law* 15(1): 1-37.

Clark, T. 1997. *Silent Coup: Confronting the Big Business Coup of Canada.* Toronto: James Lorimer.

Clarkson, S. 1985. *Canada and the Reagan Challenge: Crisis and Adjustment, 1981-85.* Rev. ed. Toronto: James Lorimer.

-. 2002. *Uncle Sam and Us: Globalization, Neoconservatism, and the Canadian State.* Toronto and Washington, DC: University of Toronto and Woodrow Wilson Center.

-. 2004. Canada's External Constitution under Global Trade Governance. In *Dessiner la société par le droit/Mapping Society through Law,* ed. Y. Gendreau, 1-31. Montreal: Université de Montréal.

-. 2008a. *Does North America Exist? Governing the Continent after NAFTA and 9/11.* Toronto and Washington, DC: University of Toronto and Woodrow Wilson Center.

-. 2008b. Manoeuvring within the Continental Constitution: Autonomy and Capacity within the Security and Prosperity Partnership of North America. In *Canada among Nations 2007,* ed. J. Daudelin and D. Schwanen, 248-67. Montreal and Kingston: McGill-Queen's University Press.

Clarkson, S., and S. Wood. 2006. Canada's External Constitution and Its Democratic Deficit. In *The Globalized Rule of Law: Relationships between International and Domestic Law,* ed. O.E. Fitzgerald, 97-124. Toronto: Irwin Law.

Cohen, M. 1974. Canada and the International Legal Order: An Inside Perspective. In *Canadian Perspectives on International Law and Organization,* ed. R. St. J. Macdonald, G.L. Morris, and D.M. Johnston, 3-32. Toronto: University of Toronto Press.

–. 2004. International Forces Driving Electricity Deregulation in the Semi-Periphery: The Case of Canada. In *Governing under Stress: Middle Powers and the Challenge of Globalization,* ed. S. Clarkson and M. Cohen, 175-96. London: Zed Books.

Cohn, T.H. 2003. *Global Political Economy: Theory and Practice.* 2nd ed. New York: Addison Wesley Longman.

Commission for Environmental Cooperation. 2004. Report of the Ten Year Review and Assessment Committee. Commission for Environmental Cooperation. http://www.cec.org/.

Commission on Human Security. 2003. *Human Security Now: Protecting and Empowering People (Final Report).* New York: United Nations.

Commissioner of the Environment and Sustainable Development. 2006. *Report of the Commissioner of the Environment and Sustainable Development to the House of Commons.* Ottawa: Office of the Auditor General of Canada.

Constitutional Law Group. 2003. *Canadian Constitutional Law.* 3rd ed. Toronto: Emond Montgomery.

Conway, J. 2003. Power of Social Forum Is its Global Diffusion. *Canadian Dimension* 37(2): 8.

–. 2004. Citizenship in Time of Empire: The World Social Forum as a New Public Space. *Citizenship Studies* 8(4): 367-81.

–. 2006. La Difusion Global del Foro Social Mundial: La Politica de Lugar y Escala Vista Desde Canada. In *El Foro Social Mundial: Camino a un Mundo Nuevo,* ed. F. Bracho, 77-89. Caracas, Venezuela: Fondo Editorial Question.

–. 2009. The Empire, the Movement, and the Politics of Scale: Considering the World Social Forum. In *Leviathan Undone? Towards a Political Economy of Scale,* ed. R. Keil and R. Mahon, 281-99. Vancouver: UBC Press.

Conzelmann, T., and K.D. Wolf. 2008. The Potential and Limits of Governance by Private Codes of Conduct. In *Transnational Private Governance and its Limits,* ed. J.-C. Graz and A. Nölke, 98-114. London and New York: Routledge.

Cox, R. 1996a. The Global Political Economy and Social Choice. In *App roaches to World Order,* ed. R.W. Cox and T.J. Sinclair, 191-208. Cambridge: Cambridge University Press.

–. 1996b. A Perspective on Globalization. In *Globalization: Critical Perspectives,* ed. J. Mittelman, 21-30. Boulder, CO: Lynne Rienner.

Cragg, W., ed. 2005. *Ethics Codes, Corporations and the Challenge of Globalization.* Cheltenham, UK: Edward Elgar.

Cullet, P. 1999. Differential Treatment in International Law: Towards a New Paradigm of Inter-State Relations. *European Journal of International Law* 10(3): 549-82.

Cutler, A.C., V. Haufler, and T. Porter, eds. 1999. *Private Authority and International Affairs.* Albany: State University of New York Press.

Daniels, R.J., P. Macklem, and K. Roach. 2001. *The Security of Freedom.* Toronto: University of Toronto Press.

Dashwood, H.S. 2005. Canadian Mining Companies and the Shaping of Global Norms of Corporate Social Responsibility. *International Journal* 60(4): 977-98.

Davey, W.J. 1996. *Pine and Swine*. Ottawa: Centre for Trade Policy and Law.

Dawkins, K. 2003. *Global Governance: The Battle over Planetary Power*. New York: Seven Stories Press.

De Beer, D. 2004. Speech on the Occasion of the Peace Art Project Cambodia, FCC Hotel, Phnom Penh, Cambodia, 16 February. Phnom Penh: European Union – Assistance on Curbing Small Arms and Light Weapons in Cambodia (EU-ASAC).

De Búrca, G., and J. Scott, eds. 2001. *The EU and the WTO: Legal and Constitutional Issues*. Oxford and Portland, OR: Hart.

de Wet, E. 2006. The International Constitutional Order. *International and Comparative Law Quarterly* 55: 51-76.

Dezalay, Y., and B. Garth. 1996. *Dealing in Virtue: International Commercial Arbitration and the Construction of a Transnational Legal Order*. Chicago: University of Chicago Press.

–. 2002. *Global Prescriptions: The Production, Exportation, and Importation of a New Legal Orthodoxy*. Ann Arbor: University of Michigan Press.

Doern, G.B., M. Hill, M. Prince, and R. Schultz, eds. 1999. *Changing the Rules: Canadian Regulatory Regimes and Institutions*. Toronto: University of Toronto Press.

Dunberry, P. 2001. The NAFTA Investment Dispute Settlement Mechanism: A Review of the Latest Case Law. *Journal of World Investment* 2: 151-95.

Dunoff, J.L. 2006. Constitutional Conceits: The WTO's "Constitution" and the Discipline of International Law. *European Journal of International Law* 17(3): 647-75.

Dunoff, J.L., and J.P. Trachtman, eds. 2009. *Ruling the World: Constitutionalism, International Law, and Global Governance*. Cambridge and New York: Cambridge University Press.

Echeverria, J.D. 2006. From a "Darkling Plain" to What? The Regulatory Takings Issue in U.S. Law and Policy. *Vermont Law Review* 30(4): 969-87.

Economist Intelligence Unit. 2003. What's New in Your Industry. *Business Middle East* 11(17): 7-9.

Elkington, J. 1998. *Cannibals with Forks: The Triple Bottom Line of 21st Century Business*. Gabriola Island, BC: New Society.

Ellis, J. 2006. Has International Law Outgrown *Trail Smelter*? In *Transboundary Harm in International Law: Lessons from the Trail Smelter Arbitration*, ed. R.M. Bratspies and R.A. Miller, 56-65. New York: Cambridge University Press.

Ellis, J., and S. Wood. 2006. International Environmental Law. In *Environmental Law for Sustainability*, ed. B.J. Richardson and S. Wood, 343-80. Oxford: Hart.

Epstein, R.A. 1985. *Takings: Private Property and the Power of Eminent Domain*. Cambridge, MA: Harvard University Press.

Erens, S., J. Verschuuren, and K. Bastmeijer. 2009. Adaptation to Climate Change to Save Biodiversity: Lessons Learned from African and European Experiences. In

Climate Law and Developing Countries: Legal and Policy Challenges for the World Community, ed. B. Richardson, H. McLeod-Kilmurray, Y. Le Bouthillier, and S. Wood, forthcoming. Cheltenham, UK, and Northampton, MA: Edward Elgar.

Esty, D.C. 1995. Private Sector Foreign Investment and the Environment. *Review of European Community and International Environmental Law* 4: 99-105.

Esty, D.C., and D. Geradin. 1997. Market Access, Competitiveness, and Harmonization: Environmental Protection in Regional Trade Agreements. *Harvard Environmental Law Review* 21: 265-336.

European Commission. 2005. Adoption of a UNESCO Convention on Cultural Diversity. Document No. MEMO/05/387, 20 October. Brussels: European Commission.

Evans, P.B., D. Rueschemeyer, and T. Skocpol, eds. 1985. *Bringing the State Back In.* Cambridge and New York: Cambridge University Press.

Ewald, F. 1990. Norms, Discipline and the Law. *Representations* 30: 138-61.

External Advisory Committee on Smart Regulation (EACSR). 2004. *Smart Regulation: A Regulatory Strategy for Canada.* Ottawa. EACSR.

Falk, R. 1999. *Predatory Globalization: A Critique.* Cambridge, UK: Polity Press.

–. 2004. *The Declining World Order: America's Imperial Geopolitics.* New York: Routledge.

Farrow, T.C.W. 2004. Citizen Participation and Peaceful Protest: Let's Not Forget APEC. In *Participatory Justice in a Global Economy: The New Rule of Law*, ed. P. Hughes and P.A. Molinari, 205-32. Montreal: Thémis.

Fassbender, B. 1998. The United Nations Charter as Constitution of the International Community. *Columbia Journal of Transnational Law* 36: 529-619.

–. 2005. The Meaning of International Constitutional Law. In *Towards World Constitutionalism: Issues in the Legal Ordering of the World Community*, ed. R. St. J. Macdonald and D.M. Johnston, 837-51. Leiden: Martinus Nijhoff.

Fidler, D.P. 2003. SARS: Political Pathology of the First Post-Westphalian Pathogen. *Journal of Law, Medicine and Ethics* 31(4): 484-505.

–. 2004. Germs, Governance, and Global Public Health in the Wake of SARS. *Journal of Clinical Investigation* 113(6): 799-804.

Flores, I.B. 2005. Reconstituting Constitutions – Institutions and Culture: The Mexican Constitution and NAFTA: Human Rights vis-à-vis Commerce. *Florida Journal of International Law* 17: 693-717.

Folson, R.B. 2004. *Calculated Kindness: Globalization, Immigration and Settlement in Canada.* Halifax: Fernwood.

Franck, T.M. 1990. *The Power of Legitimacy among Nations.* New York: Oxford University Press.

French, D. 2000. Developing States and International Environmental Law: The Importance of Common but Differentiated Responsibilities. *International and Comparative Law Quarterly* 49: 35-60.

Gabel, M., and H. Bruner. 2003. *GlobalInc.: An Atlas of the Multinational Corporation.* New York: New Press.

Gabriel, C., and L. MacDonald. 2003. Beyond the Continentalist/Nationalist Divide: Politics in a North America "without Borders." In *Changing Canada: Political Economy as Transformation*, ed. W. Clement and L.F. Vosko, 213-40. Montreal and Kingston: McGill-Queen's University Press.

Garmaise, D., ed. 2001. Human Rights, Global Responsibility and Access to Treatments in the Developing World: Presentations Made on Occasion of the Canadian HIV/AIDS Legal Network Annual General Meeting and Skills Building Workshops, 21-23 September 2001, Montreal. Montreal: Canadian HIV/AIDS Legal Network. http://www.aidslaw.ca/.

Gathii, J. 1998-99. Representations of Africa in Good Governance Discourse: Policing and Containing Dissidence to Neo-Liberalism. *Third World Legal Studies* 18: 65-108.

–. 2000. Retelling Good Governance Narratives about Africa's Economic and Political Predicaments: Continuities and Discontinuities in Legal Outcomes between Markets and States. *Villanova Law Review* 45: 971-1035.

Gibson, R.B. 1999a. Voluntary Initiatives, Regulations, and Beyond. In *Voluntary Initiatives: The New Politics of Corporate Greening*, ed. R.B. Gibson, 239-57. Peterborough, ON: Broadview.

–, ed. 1999b. *Voluntary Initiatives: The New Politics of Corporate Greening*. Peterborough, ON: Broadview.

Giddens, A. 2000. *The Third Way and its Critics*. Cambridge, UK: Polity Press.

Gill, S., ed. 1993. *Gramsci, Historical Materialism and International Relations*. Cambridge: Cambridge University Press.

–. 1995. Globalisation, Market Civilisation, and Disciplinary Neoliberalism. *Millennium* 24(3): 399-423.

Gore, A., Jr. 1993. *From Red Tape to Results: Creating a Government that Works Better and Costs Less*. Washington, DC: US Government Printing Office.

Government of Canada. 1998. *Voluntary Codes: A Guide for Their Development and Use*. Ottawa: Government of Canada.

–. 2005. *Canada's International Policy Statement: A Role of Pride and Influence in the World*. Ottawa: Department of Foreign Affairs and International Trade.

–. 2006. *Corporate Social Responsibility: An Implementation Guide for Canadian Business*. Ottawa: Government of Canada.

–. 2007. *Regulatory Framework for Air Emissions*. Ottawa: Minister of Environment.

–. 2008. *Turning the Corner: Regulatory Framework for Industrial Greenhouse Gas Emissions*. Ottawa: Minister of Environment.

–. 2009. *Building the Canadian Advantage: A Corporate Social Responsibility (CSR) Strategy for the Canadian International Extractive Sector*. Ottawa: Department of Foreign Affairs and International Trade.

Gunningham, N., and P. Grabosky. 1998. *Smart Regulation: Designing Environmental Policy*. Oxford: Clarendon.

Gunningham, N., R. Kagan, and D. Thornton. 2004. Social License and Environmental Protection: Why Businesses Go beyond Compliance. *Law and Social Inquiry* 29(2): 307-41.

Gwodecky, M., and J. Sinclair. 2001. Case Study: Landmines and Human Security. In *Human Security and the New Diplomacy: Protecting People, Promoting Peace*, ed. R. McRae and D. Hubert, 28-40. Montreal and Kingston: McGill-Queen's University Press.

Haas, P.M., ed. 1992. Knowledge, Power, and International Policy Coordination. Special issue, *International Organization* 46.

Habermas, J. 1975. *Legitimation Crisis.* Trans. Thomas McCarthy. Boston: Beacon.

Hall, R.B., and T.J. Biersteker, eds. 2002. *The Emergence of Private Authority in Global Governance.* Cambridge: Cambridge University Press.

Hamilton, R.W. 1978. The Role of Nongovernmental Standards in the Development of Mandatory Federal Standards Affecting Safety or Health. *Texas Law Review* 56: 1329-484.

Hampson, F.O. 2004. A Concept in Need of a Global Policy Response. *Security Dialogue* 35(3): 349-50.

Handl, G. 1997. Compliance Control Mechanisms and International Environmental Obligations. *Tulane Journal of International and Comparative Law* 5: 29-49.

Hansen, J., M. Sato, P. Kharecha, D. Beerling, R. Berner, V. Masson-Delmotte, M. Pagani, M. Raymo, D.L. Royer, and J.C. Zachos. 2008. Target Atmospheric CO_2: Where Should Humanity Aim? *Open Atmospheric Science Journal* 2: 217-31.

Hawken, P. 1993. *The Ecology of Commerce.* New York: Harper Collins.

Hayden, P., and C. el-Ojeili. 2005. *Confronting Globalization: Humanity, Justice and the Renewal of Politics.* New York: Palgrave Macmillan.

Hazell, S. 1999. *Canada v. the Environment: Federal Environmental Assessment 1984-1998.* Toronto: Canadian Environmental Defence Fund.

Held, D., A. McGrew, D. Goldblatt, and J. Perraton. 1999. *Global Transformations.* Stanford: Stanford University Press.

Hogg, P.W. 2004. *Constitutional Law of Canada.* Student ed. Scarborough, ON: Carswell.

Horlick, G., and F.A. DeBusk. 1993. Dispute Resolution under NAFTA: Building on the U.S.-Canada FTA, GATT and ICSID. *Journal of World Trade* 27(1): 21-41.

Howse, R. 1998. Settling Trade Remedy Disputes: When the WTO Forum Is Better than the NAFTA. *C.D. Howe Institute Commentary* 111 (June).

–. 2000. The Canadian Generic Medicines Panel – A Dangerous Precedent in Dangerous Times. *Journal of World Intellectual Property* 3(4): 493-508.

–. 2007. *The WTO System: Law, Politics and Legitimacy.* London: Cameron May.

Howse, R., and K. Nicolaidis. 2001. Legitimacy and Global Governance: Why Constitutionalizing the WTO Is a Step Too Far. In *Efficiency, Equity, and Legitimacy: The Multilateral Trading System at the Millennium*, ed. R.B. Porter, P. Sauve, A. Subramanian, and A.B. Zampetti, 227-52. Washington, DC: Brookings Institution Press.

Howse, R., and D. Regan. 2000. The Product/Process Distinction – An Illusory Basis for Disciplining Unilateralism in Trade Policy. *European Journal of International Law* 11(2): 249-89.

Hubert, D. 2004. An Idea That Works in Practice. *Security Dialogue* 35(3): 351-52.

Hughes, P. 2004. The Rule of Law: Challenges in a Global Economy. In *Participatory Justice in a Global Economy: The New Rule of Law*, ed. P. Hughes and P.A. Molinari, 29-63. Montreal: Thémis.

Human Security Centre. 2005. *Human Security Report 2005*. New York and Oxford: Oxford University Press.

International Commission on Intervention and State Sovereignty (ICISS). 2001. *Responsibility to Protect: Report of the International Commission on Intervention and State Sovereignty*. Ottawa: International Development Research Centre.

International Electrotechnical Commission. 2000. IEC President in Australia. *IEC E-Tech Online News* (January-April). http://www.iec.ch/.

International Joint Commission (IJC). 1998. *Ninth Biennial Report on Great Lakes Water Quality*. Washington, DC: IJC.

International Labour Organization (ILO). 2001. *Tripartite Declaration of Principles concerning Multinational Enterprises and Social Policy*. 3rd ed. Geneva: ILO.

International Organization for Standardization (ISO). 2002. *ISO in the 21st Century: Strategies for 2002-2004*. Geneva: ISO.

Jaccard, M., N. Rivers, C. Bataille, R. Murphy, J. Nyboer, and B. Sadownik. 2006. Burning Our Money to Warm the Planet: Canada's Ineffective Efforts to Reduce Greenhouse Gas Emissions. *C.D. Howe Institute Commentary* 234 (May).

Jackson, J. 1969. *World Trade and the Law of GATT*. Indianapolis: Bobbs-Merrill.

–. 1980. The Birth of the GATT-MTN System: A Constitutional Appraisal. *Law and Policy in International Business* 12: 21-58.

Joerges, C., and E. Petersmann, eds. 2006. *Constitutionalism, Multilevel Trade Governance and Social Regulation*. Oxford and Portland, OR: Hart.

Joerges, C., I. Sand, and G. Teubner, eds. 2004. *Transnational Governance and Constitutionalism: International Studies in the Theory of Private Law*. Oxford and Portland, OR: Hart.

Johnston, D.M. 2005. World Constitutionalism in the Theory of International Law. In *Towards World Constitutionalism: Issues in the Legal Ordering of the World Community*, ed. R. St. J. Macdonald and D.M. Johnston, 3-30. Leiden: Martinus Nijhoff.

Jordana, J., and D. Levi-Faur. 2004. The Politics of Regulation in the Age of Governance. In *The Politics of Regulation: Institutions and Regulatory Reforms for the Age of Governance*, eds. J. Jordana and D. Levi-Faur, 1-28. Cheltenham, UK, and Northampton, MA: Edward Elgar.

Kanji, N., N. Kanji, and M. Froze. 1991. From Development to Sustained Crisis: Structural Adjustment, Equity and Health. *Social Science and Medicine* 33(9): 985-93.

Kent, C. 1994. The Uruguay Round GATT, TRIPS Agreement and Chapter 17 of the NAFTA: A New Era in International Patent Protection. *Canadian Intellectual Property Review* 10(3): 711-33.

Kent, M.B., Jr. 2008. Construing the Canon: An Exegesis of Regulatory Takings Jurisprudence after *Lingle v. Chevron*. *New York University Environmental Law Journal* 16: 63-109.

Keohane, R.O. 1984. *After Hegemony: Cooperation and Discord in the World Political Economy*. Princeton: Princeton University Press.

Kindred, H.M. 2006. The Use and Abuse of International Legal Sources by Canadian Courts: Searching for a Principled Approach. In *The Globalized Rule of Law: Relationships between International and Domestic Law*, ed. O.E. Fitzgerald, 5-30. Toronto: Irwin Law.

Kirton, J.J., and M.J. Trebilcock. 2004. Introduction: Hard Choices and Soft Law in Sustainable Global Governance. In *Hard Choices, Soft Law: Voluntary Standards in Global Trade, Environment and Social Governance*, ed. J.J. Kirton and M.J. Trebilcock, 1-33. Burlington, VT: Ashgate.

Kissinger, H. 1999. Globalization and World Order. Public lecture, Trinity College Dublin, 12 October.

Klein, N. 2002. *Fences and Windows: Dispatches from the Front Lines of the Globalization Debate*. Toronto: Vintage Canada.

–. 2007. *The Shock Doctrine: The Rise of Disaster Capitalism*. Toronto: Knopf Canada.

Koenig-Archibugi, M. 2006. Introduction: Institutional Diversity in Global Governance. In *New Modes of Governance in the Global System: Exploring Publicness, Delegation and Inclusiveness*, ed. M. Koenig-Archibugi and M. Zürn, 1-30. New York: Palgrave Macmillan.

Koskenniemi, M. 2001. *The Gentle Civilizer of Nations: The Rise and Fall of International Law 1870-1960*. Cambridge: Cambridge University Press.

–. 2004. International Law and Hegemony: A Reconfiguration. *Cambridge Review of International Affairs* 17: 197-218.

–. 2005. Global Legal Pluralism: Multiple Regimes and Multiple Modes of Thought. Paper presented at "Comparative Visions of Global Public Order," Harvard Law School, Cambridge, MA, 5 March.

–. 2007. Constitutionalism as Mindset: Reflections on Kantian Themes about International Law and Globalization. *Theoretical Inquiries in Law* 8: 9-36.

Kumm, M. 2004. The Legitimacy of International Law: A Constitutionalist Framework of Analysis. *European Journal of International Law* 15(5): 907-31.

–. 2006. Beyond Golf Clubs and the Judicialization of Politics: Why Europe Has a Constitution Properly so Called. *American Journal of Comparative Law* 54: 505-30.

Ladner, K.L., and C. Dick. 2008. Out of the Fires of Hell: Globalization as a Solution to Globalization – An Indigenist Perspective. *Canadian Journal of Law and Society* 23(1-2): 63-91.

Lang, A. 2006. Review of Deborah Cass, *The Constitutionalization of the World Trade Organization*. Oxford: Oxford University Press, 2005. *European Journal of International Law* 17(1): 309-12.

Latham, R. 1999. Politics in a Floating World. In *Approaches to Global Governance Theory*, ed. M. Hewson and T.J. Sinclair, 23-54. Albany: State University of New York Press.

Lauterpacht, H. 1950. *International Law and Human Rights*. Hamden, CN: Archon Books.

Leaning, J. 2004. Psychosocial Well-Being over Time. *Security Dialogue* 35(3): 354-55.

Leftwich, A. 1993. Governance, Democracy and Development in the Third World. *Third World Quarterly* 14(3): 605-24.

Lenaerts, K. 1990. Constitutionalism and the Many Faces of Federalism. *American Journal of Comparative Law* 38: 205-63.

Levin, R.C., and S.E. Marin. 1996. NAFTA Chapter 11: Investment and Investment Disputes. *NAFTA: Law and Business Review of the Americas* 2(3): 82-115.

Lewis, S. 2003. Statement by Stephen Lewis: The Politics of Resource Allocation. Speech delivered at the Thirteenth International Conference on AIDS and STIs in Africa, Nairobi, 25 September. The Stephen Lewis Foundation. http://www.stephenlewisfoundation.org/.

–. 2005. *Race against Time*. Toronto: House of Anansi.

Likosky, M. 2002. Editor's Introduction: Transnational Law in the Context of Power Disparities. In *Transnational Legal Processes*, ed. M. Likosky, xvii-xxxiv. London: Butterworths.

Loungnarath, V., and C. Stehly. 2000. The General Dispute Settlement Mechanism in the North American Free Trade Agreement and the World Trade Organization System: Is North American Regionalism Really Preferable to Multilateralism? *Journal of World Trade Law* 34(1): 39-71.

MacCharles, T. 2005. Cotler: "Ideas Cross Borders." *Toronto Star*, 10 February, A8.

Macdonald, R. St. J. 2005. The International Community as a Legal Community. In *Towards World Constitutionalism: Issues in the Legal Ordering of the World Community*, ed. R. St. J. Macdonald and D.M. Johnston, 853-909. Leiden: Martinus Nijhoff.

Macdonald, R. St. J., and D.M. Johnston, eds. 2005. *Towards World Constitutionalism: Issues in the Legal Ordering of the World Community*. Leiden: Martinus Nijhoff.

Maduro, M.P. 2003. Europe and the Constitution: What if This Is as Good as it Gets? In *European Constitutionalism beyond the State*, eds. J.H.H. Weiler and M. Wind, 74-102. Cambridge: Cambridge University Press.

Majone, G., ed. 1990. *Deregulation or Re-Regulation: Regulatory Reform in Europe and the United States*. London: Pinter; New York: St. Martin's.

–. 1997. From the Positive to the Regulatory State: Causes and Consequences of Change in the Mode of Governance. *Journal of Public Policy* 17(2): 139-67.

Mani, Devyani. 2001. Culture as a Key Element of Human Security. United Nations Centre for Regional Development (UNCRD), Second Thematic Training Course:

Human Security and Regional Development, 1-30 November. Nagoya, Japan: UNCRD.

Mann, H., and K. Von Moltke. 2001. *Private Rights, Public Problems: A Guide to NAFTA's Controversial Chapter on Investor Rights.* Winnipeg: International Institute for Sustainable Development. http://www.iisd.org/.

Matsui, Y. 2002. Some Aspects of the Principle of "Common but Differentiated Responsibilities." *International Environmental Agreements: Politics, Law and Economics* 2: 151-71.

Matthews, R.O. 2004. Canadian Corporate Responsibility in Sudan: Why Canada Backed Down. In *Hard Choices, Soft Law: Voluntary Standards in Global Trade, Environment and Social Governance,* ed. J.J. Kirton and Michael J. Trebilcock, 228-49. Burlington, VT: Ashgate.

McBride, S. 2001. *Paradigm Shift: Globalization and the Canadian State.* Halifax: Fernwood.

–. 2005. *Paradigm Shift: Globalization and the Canadian State.* 2nd ed. Halifax: Fernwood.

McBride, S, and J. Shields. 1997. *Dismantling a Nation: The Transition to Corporate Rule in Canada.* 2nd ed. Halifax: Fernwood.

McConkey, M. 2003. Thinking Regulation: A Roadmap to the Recent Periodical Literature. Report prepared for the Privy Council Office of the Government of Canada, September. Toronto: Institute of Public Administration of Canada.

McConnaughay, P.J. 1999. The Risks and Virtues of Lawlessness: A "Second Look" at International Commercial Arbitration. *Northwestern University Law Review* 93: 453-523.

McRae, R. 2001a. Conclusion: International Relations and the New Diplomacy. In *Human Security and the New Diplomacy: Protecting People, Promoting Peace,* ed. R. McRae and D. Hubert, 250-59. Montreal and Kingston: McGill-Queen's University Press.

–. 2001b. Human Security in a Globalized World. In *Human Security and the New Diplomacy: Protecting People, Promoting Peace,* ed. R. McRae and D. Hubert, 14-27. Montreal and Kingston: McGill-Queen's University Press.

Meidinger, E. 2001. Environmental Certification Programs and U.S. Environmental Law: Closer than You May Think. *Environmental Law Reporter* 31: 10162-79.

Meltz, R. 2007. Takings Law Today: A Primer for the Perplexed. *Ecology Law Quarterly* 34: 307-71.

Mendelsohn, M., and R. Wolfe. 2004. Embedded Liberalism in the Global Era: Would Citizens Support a New Grand Compromise? *International Journal* 59(2): 261-80.

Merchant, L.T., and A.D.P. Heeney. 1965. Canada and the United States – Principles of Partnership. *Department of State Bulletin* 53(1362): 193-208.

Merry, S.E. 1988. Legal Pluralism. *Law and Society Review* 22(5): 869-96.

Michalos, A.C. 2008. *Trade Barriers to the Public Good.* Montreal and Kingston: McGill-Queen's University Press.

Mickelson, K. 1996. Seeing the Forest, the Trees and the People: Coming to Terms with Developing Country Perspectives on the Proposed Global Forests Convention. In

Global Forests and International Environmental Law, ed. Canadian Council of International Law, 239-64. London: Kluwer Law International.

Monahan, P. 2002. *Constitutional Law*. 2nd ed. Toronto: Irwin Law.

National Round Table on Environment and Economy (NRTEE). 2007. *Report on Canada's Greenhouse Gas Plan*. Ottawa: NRTEE.

National Roundtables on CSR and the Canadian Extractive Industry Advisory Group. 2007. *National Roundtables on Corporate Social Responsibility (CSR) and the Canadian Extractive Industry in Developing Countries: Advisory Group Report*. Mining.ca. http://www.mining.ca/.

Naylor, R.T. 2006. *Satanic Purses: Money, Myth, and Misinformation in the War on Terror*. Montreal and Kingston: McGill-Queen's University Press.

Neilson, W.A.W. 2004. Some Legal Badges of Economic Globalization from Rome to the WTO and Regional Trade Agreements. In *Participatory Justice in a Global Economy: The New Rule of Law*, ed. P. Hughes and P.A. Molinari, 1-27. Montreal: Thémis.

Neumayer, E. 2001. *Greening Trade and Investment*. London: Earthscan.

New Directions Group. 1999. The New Directions Group Position. In *Voluntary Initiatives: The New Politics of Corporate Greening*, ed. R.B. Gibson, 229-38. Peterborough, ON: Broadview.

Newman, E. 2001. Human Security and Constructivism. *International Studies Perspectives* 2: 239-51.

Nolen, S. 2005. In Tanzania, "Death Doesn't Wait" for the Poor to Raise Money. *Globe and Mail*, 19 February, A17.

Nonet, P., and Selznick, P. 1978. *Law and Society in Transition: Toward Responsive Law*. New York: Harper Colophon.

Norberg, J. 2003. *In Defense of Global Capitalism*. Washington, DC: Cato Institute.

Novkov, J. 2008. Bringing the States Back In: Understanding Legal Subordination and Identity through Political Development. *Polity* 40(1): 24-48.

Ó Tuathail, G., A. Herod, and S.M. Roberts. 1998. Negotiating Unruly Problematics. In *An Unruly World? Globalization, Governance and Geography*, ed. A. Herod, G. Ó Tuathail, and S.M. Roberts, 1-24. London: Routledge.

O'Connor, D.R. 2002a. *Report of the Walkerton Inquiry: A Strategy for Safe Drinking Water, Part Two*. Toronto: Publications Ontario.

–. 2002b. *Report of the Walkerton Inquiry: The Events of May 2000 and Related Issues, Part One*. Toronto: Publications Ontario.

O'Connor, D., and S. Ilcan. 2005. The Folding of Liberal Government: Contract Governance and the Transformation of the Public Service in Canada. *Alternatives* 30: 1-23.

Ontario Ministry of the Environment. 2004. *A Framework for Ontario's Environmental Leaders Program*. Toronto: Ministry of the Environment.

Opsahl, T. 1961. An "International Constitutional Law"? *International and Comparative Law Quarterly* 10: 760-84.

Orbinski, James. 2008. *An Imperfect Offering: Humanitarian Action for the 21st Century.* Toronto: Doubleday Canada.

Organisation for Economic Co-operation and Development (OECD). 2000. *The OECD Guidelines for Multinational Enterprises (Revision 2000).* Paris: OECD.

–. 2008a. *OECD Economic Outlook 2008/2 (No. 84).* Paris: OECD.

–. 2008b. *OECD Economic Surveys 2008: Canada.* Paris: OECD.

Orrego Vicuña, F. 2004. *International Dispute Settlement in an Evolving Global Society: Constitutionalization, Accessibility, Privatization.* Cambridge: Cambridge University Press.

Orts, E.W. Reflexive Environmental Law. *Northwestern University Law Review* 89: 1227-1340.

Osborne, D., and T. Gaebler. 1992. *Reinventing Government: How the Entrepreneurial Spirit is Transforming the Public Sector.* Boston: Addison-Wesley.

Ostry, S. 2001. Global Integration: Currents and Counter-Currents. Walter Gordon Lecture Massey College, University of Toronto, Toronto, 23 May.

Owen, T. 2004. Human Security – Conflict, Critique and Consensus: Colloquium Remarks and a Proposal for a Threshold-Based Definition. *Security Dialogue* 35(3): 373-87.

Palmeter, D., and P.C. Mavroidis. 1998. The WTO Legal System: Sources of Law. *American Journal of International Law* 92: 398-413.

Paris, R. 2001. Human Security: Paradigm Shift or Hot Air? *International Security* 26(2): 87-102.

–. 2004. Still an Inscrutable Concept. *Security Dialogue* 35(3): 370-72.

Patomäki, H., and T. Teivainen. 2004. The World Social Forum: An Open Space or a Movement of Movements? *Theory, Culture and Society* 21(6): 145-54.

Pauly, L.W. 2002. Global Finance, Political Authority, and the Problem of Legitimation. In *The Emergence of Private Authority in Global Governance*, ed. R.B. Hall and T.J. Biersteker, 76-90. Cambridge: Cambridge University Press.

Pauwelyn, J. 2005. The UNESCO Convention on Cultural Diversity, and the WTO: Diversity in International Law-Making? American Society of International Law. http://www.asil.org/.

Peabody, J.W. 1996. Economic Reform and Health Sector Policy: Lessons from Structural Adjustment Programs. *Social Science and Medicine* 43(5): 823-35.

Peters, B.G. 2003. Democracy and Political Power in Contemporary Western Governments: Challenges and Reforms. In *The Art of the State: Governance in a World without Frontiers*, ed. T.J. Courchene and D.J. Savoie, 81-108. Montreal: Institute for Research on Public Policy.

Picciotto, S. 1996-97. Networks in International Economic Integration: Fragmented States and the Dilemmas of Neo-liberalism. *Northwestern Journal of International Law and Business* 17: 1014-56.

Plato. 1952. Statesman. In *Great Books of the Western World*. Vol. 7, *Plato*, ed. R.M. Hutchins. Trans. Benjamin Jowett, 580-608. Chicago: Encyclopedia Brittanica.

Poku, N.K. 2002. Global Pandemics: HIV/AIDS. In *Governing Globalization: Power, Authority and Global Governance*, ed. D. Held and A. McGrew, 111-26. Malden, MA: Polity Press.

Polanyi, K. 1944/1957. *The Great Transformation: The Political and Economic Origins of Our Time*. Boston: Beacon Press.

Policy Research Initiative (PRI). 2004. North American Linkages. Special issue, *Horizons* 7.

Pollution Probe. 1999. *Towards Credible and Effective Environmental Voluntary Initiatives: Lessons Learned.* Toronto: Pollution Probe.

Prakash, A. 2000. Responsible Care: An Assessment. *Business and Society* 39: 183-209.

Rhodes, R.A.W. 1996. The New Governance: Governing Without Government. *Political Studies* 44: 652-67.

Richardson, B., and J. Razzaque. 2006. Public Participation in Environmental Decision-Making. In *Environmental Law for Sustainability*, ed. B.J. Richardson and S. Wood, 165-94. Oxford and Portland, OR: Hart.

Rittich, K. 1999. Law and Social Justice. *UNESCO Courier* (November): 36.

Robins, N. 2006. *The Corporation That Changed the World: How the East India Company Shaped the Modern Multinational*. London: Pluto.

Rose, N. 1999. *Powers of Freedom: Reframing Political Thought*. Cambridge: Cambridge University Press.

Rose, N., and M. Valverde. 1998. Governed by Law? *Social and Legal Studies* 7: 541-51.

Ross, A. 1950. *The Constitution of the United Nations: Analysis of Structure and Function*. New York: Rinehart.

Rubinstein, R.A. 2005. Intervention and Culture: An Anthropological Approach to Peace Operations. *Security Dialogue* 36(4): 527-44.

Ruggie, J.G. 1982. International Regimes, Transactions, and Change: Embedded Liberalism in the Postwar Economic Order. *International Organization* 36: 379-415.

–. 1998. *Constructing the World Polity: Essays on International Institutionalization*. London and New York: Routledge.

Salter, L. 1993-94. The Housework of Capitalism: Standardization in the Communications and Information Technology Sectors. *International Journal of Political Economy* 23: 105-33.

Salter, L., and R. Salter. 1997. The New Infrastructure. *Studies in Political Economy* 53: 67-102.

Salskov-Iversen, D., H.K. Hansen, and S. Bislev. 2000. Governmentality, Globalization, and Local Practice: Transformations of a Hegemonic Discourse. *Alternatives* 25: 183-222.

Santos, B.S. 2002. *Toward a New Legal Common Sense: Law, Globalization and Emancipation*. London: Butterworths.

–. 2005a. Beyond Neoliberal Governance: The World Social Forum as Subaltern Cosmopolitan Politics and Legality. In *Law and Globalization from Below: Towards a Cosmopolitan Legality,* ed. B.S. Santos and C.A. Rodríguez-Garavito, 29-63. Cambridge:
Cambridge University Press.

–. 2005b. Two Democracies, Two Legalities: Participatory Budgeting in Pôrto Alegre,
Brazil. In *Law and Globalization from Below: Towards a Cosmopolitan Legality,* ed. B.S.
Santos and C.A. Rodríguez-Garavito, 310-38. Cambridge: Cambridge University
Press.

Santos, B.S., and C.A. Rodríguez-Garavito, eds. 2005. *Law and Globalization from Below:
Towards a Cosmopolitan Legality.* Cambridge: Cambridge University Press.

Saunders, P. 1996. Development Assistance Issues Related to a Convention on Forests.
In *Global Forests and International Environmental Law,* ed. Canadian Council of
International Law, 265-313. London: Kluwer Law International.

Sax, J.L. 1971. *Defending the Environment: A Strategy for Citizen Action.* New York: Knopf.

Schepel, H. 2005. *The Constitution of Private Governance.* Oxford and Portland, OR: Hart.

Scheuerman, W.E. 1999. Economic Globalization and the Rule of Law. *Constellations*
6(3): 3-25.

Schmidheiny, S. 1992. *Changing Course: A Global Business Perspective on Development and
the Environment.* Cambridge, MA: MIT Press.

Schneiderman, D. 1996. NAFTA's Takings Rule: American Constitutionalism Comes to
Canada. *University of Toronto Law Journal* 46: 499-538.

–. 2000a. Constitutional Approaches to Privatization: An Inquiry into the Magnitude
of Neo-Liberal Constitutionalism. *Law and Contemporary Problems* 63: 83-109.

–. 2000b. Investment Rules and the New Constitutionalism. *Law and Social Inquiry* 25(3):
757-87.

–. 2004. Canadian Constitutionalism, the Rule of Law, and Economic Globalization.
In *Participatory Justice in a Global Economy: The New Rule of Law,* ed. P. Hughes and
P.A. Molinari, 65-86. Montreal: Thémis.

–. 2008. *Constitutionalizing Economic Globalization: Investment Rules and Democracy's
Promise.* Cambridge: Cambridge University Press.

Schoenbaum, T.J. 1998. The Decision in the *Shrimp-Turtle* Case. *Yearbook of International Environmental Law* 9: 36-39.

Schwanen, D. 1998. The Summer of Our (Canadian) Content: Thinking about Canada's
Response to the WTO Magazine Decision. *C.D. Howe Institute Backgrounder* (29
June).

Schwartz, B.P., and M.R. Bueckert. 2006. Regulatory Takings in Canada. *Washington
University Global Studies Law Review* 5: 477-91.

Scott, C. 2002. Private Regulation of the Public Sector: A Neglected Facet of Contemporary Governance. *Journal of Law and Society* 29(1): 56-76.

–. 2004. Regulation in the Age of Governance: The Rise of the Post-Regulatory State. In
The Politics of Regulation: Institutions and Regulatory Reforms for the Age of Governance,

eds. J. Jordana and D. Levi-Faur, 145-74. Cheltenham, UK, and Northampton, MA: Edward Elgar.

Scott, C.M., ed. 2001. *Torture as Tort*. Oxford and Portland, OR: Hart.

Shalakany, A. 2000. Arbitration and the Third World: A Plea for Reassessing Bias under the Specter of Neoliberalism. *Harvard International Law Journal* 41(2): 419-68.

Shiva, V. 1993. Understanding the Threats to Biological and Cultural Diversity. First Annual Hopper Lecture in International Development. University of Guelph, Guelph, ON, 21 September.

Shrybman, Steven. 2002. The Impact of International Services and Investment Agreements on Public Policy and Law Concerning Water. Paper presented at "From Doha to Kananaskis: The Future of the World Trading System and the Crisis of Governance," organized by Robarts Centre for Canadian Studies, York University, and Munk Centre for International Studies, University of Toronto, Toronto, 1-3 March.

Simons, P. 2004. Corporate Voluntarism and Human Rights: The Adequacy and Effectiveness of Voluntary Self-Regulation Regimes. *Relations Industrielles* 59(1): 101-41.

Simpson, J., M. Jaccard, and N. Rivers. 2007. *Hot Air: Meeting Canada's Climate Change Challenge*. Toronto: McClelland and Stewart.

Sinclair, S. 2000. *GATS: How The World Trade Organization's New Services Negotiations Threaten Democracy*. Ottawa: Canadian Centre for Policy Alternatives.

Sinclair, T. 2005. *The New Masters of Capital: American Bond Rating Agencies and the Politics of Creditworthiness*. Ithaca, NY: Cornell University Press.

Sinha, S.P. 1995. Legal Polycentricity. In *Legal Polycentricity: Consequences of Pluralism in Law*, ed. H. Petersen and H. Zahle, 31-69. Aldershot, UK, and Brookfield, VT: Dartmouth University Press.

Slaughter, A.-M. 2004. *A New World Order*. Princeton: Princeton University Press.

Small, M. 2001. Case Study: The Human Security Network. In *Human Security and the New Diplomacy: Protecting People, Promoting Peace*, ed. R. McRae and D. Hubert, 231-35. Montreal and Kingston: McGill-Queen's University Press.

Smith, G., and G. Galloway. 2006. Chrétien's Drug Program Ineffective, Clement Says; Poor Countries Haven't Taken Advantage of Cheap Medicine, Health Minister Notes. *Toronto Globe and Mail*, 28 April, A12.

Snyder, F. 2003. The Unfinished Constitution of the European Union: Principles, Processes and Culture. In *European Constitutionalism beyond the State*, ed. J.H.H. Weiler and M. Wind, 55-73. Cambridge: Cambridge University Press.

Standards Council of Canada. 2000. *Canadian Standards Strategy and Implementation Proposals*. Ottawa: Standards Council of Canada.

Starner, G.M. 2002. Taking a Constitutional Look: NAFTA Chapter 11 as an Extension of Member States' Constitutional Protection of Property. *Law and Policy in International Business* 33: 405-36.

Steger, M.B. 2005. American Globalism "Madison Avenue–Style": A Critique of US Public Diplomacy after 9/11. In *Confronting Globalization: Humanity, Justice and the*

Renewal of Politics, ed. P. Hayden and C. el-Ojeili, 227-41. New York: Palgrave Macmillan.

Stein, E. 1981. Lawyers, Judges, and the Making of a Transnational Constitution. *American Journal of International Law* 75: 1-27.

Stiglitz, J. 2002. *Globalization and Its Discontents.* New York: W.W. Norton.

Stipanowich, T.J. 1997. The Growing Debate over "Consumerized" Arbitration: Adding Cole to the Fire. *Dispute Resolution Magazine* 3(4): 20.

Stone, C.D. 1975. *Where the Law Ends: The Social Control of Corporate Behavior.* New York: Harper and Row.

Strange, S. 1996. *The Retreat of the State.* Cambridge: Cambridge University Press.

SustainAbility and WWF-UK. 2005. Influencing Power: Reviewing the Conduct and Content of Corporate Lobbying. Corporate Accountability. http://www.sustainability. com.

Swenarchuk, M. 2003. The NAFTA Investment Chapter: Extreme Corporate Rights. Publication No. 451, 11 June. Canadian Environmental Law Association. http:// www.cela.ca/.

Szablowski, D. 2004. Legitimation and Regulation in the Global Economy. PhD diss., Osgoode Hall Law School, Toronto.

–. 2007. *Transnational Law and Local Struggles: Mining, Communities and the World Bank.* Oxford and Portland, OR: Hart.

Taylor, A.L. 2004. Governing the Globalization of Public Health. *Journal of Law, Medicine and Ethics* 32(3): 500-8.

Teubner, G. 1983. Substantive and Reflexive Elements in Modern Law. *Law and Society Review* 17: 239-86.

–, ed. 1993. *Law as an Autopoietic System.* Trans. A. Bankowska and R. Adler. Oxford: Blackwell.

–. 1997. "Global Bukowina": Legal Pluralism in the World Society. In *Global Law without a State,* ed. G. Teubner, 3-28. Aldershot, UK: Dartmouth.

–. 2004. Societal Constitutionalism: Alternatives to State-Centred Constitutional Theory? In *Transnational Governance and Constitutionalism: International Studies in the Theory of Private Law,* ed. C. Joerges, I. Sand, and G. Teubner, 3-28. Oxford and Portland, OR: Hart.

Thomas, Caroline. 2002. Trade Policy and the Politics of Access to Drugs. *Third World Quarterly* 23(2): 251-64.

Thomas, Caroline, and M. Weber. 2004. The Politics of Global Health Governance: Whatever Happened to "Health for All by the Year 2000"? *Global Governance* 10(2): 187-205.

Thomas, Chantal. 2000. Constitutional Change and International Government. *Hastings Law Journal* 52: 1-46.

Tie, W. 1999. *Legal Pluralism: Toward a Multicultural Conception of Law.* Aldershot, UK: Ashgate.

Tollefson, C., F. Gale, and D. Haley. 2008. *Setting the Standard: Certification, Governance and the Forest Stewardship Council.* Vancouver: UBC Press.

Tomuschat, C. 1999. International Law: Ensuring the Survival of Mankind on the Eve of a New Century. *Recueil Des Cours* 281: 9-438.

Trachtman, J.P. 2006. The Constitutions of the WTO. *European Journal of International Law* 17(3): 623-46.

Trakman, L. 1997. *Dispute Settlement under the NAFTA.* New York: Transnational.

Trebilcock, M., and R. Howse. 1999. *The Regulation of International Trade.* 2nd ed. New York: Routledge.

Trickey, M. 2002. U.S. to Ease Canadians' Entry Ordeal: Foreign-born Citizens Won't Be Booked, Printed; Commentator Pat Buchanan Calls Canada "Soviet Canuckistan" for Stand on Targeting. *Ottawa Citizen,* 1 November, A1.

Underkuffler-Freund, L.S. 1996. Takings and the Nature of Private Property. *Canadian Journal of Law and Jurisprudence* 9: 161-206.

Unger, R. 1998. *Democracy Realized.* London: Verso.

United Nations Commission on Human Rights (UNCHR). 2001. Economic, Social and Cultural Rights: The Impact of the Agreement on Trade-Related Aspects of Intellectual Property on Human Rights. Report of the High Commissioner. Geneva: UNCHR. http://www.ohchr.org/.

United Nations Development Program (UNDP). 1994. *Human Development Report 1994: New Dimensions of Human Security.* New York and Oxford: Oxford University Press.

–. 2002. *Human Development Report 2002: Deepening Democracy in a Fragmented World.* New York and Oxford: Oxford University Press.

United Nations Environment Programme (UNEP). 2007. *Global Environmental Outlook, GEO4: Environment for Development.* Nairobi: UNEP.

United Nations Environment Programme, and International Institute for Sustainable Development (IISD). 2005. *Environment and Trade: A Handbook.* 2nd ed. Winnipeg: IISD.

United Nations Human Rights Council (UNHRC). 2006. Resolution 2006/2 on a United Nations Declaration on the Rights of Indigenous Peoples. UN Doc. No. A/HRC/RES/1/2/Annex (29 June).

United States White House. 1995. *Reinventing Environmental Regulation.* Washington, DC: The White House.

Uvin, P. 2004. A Field of Overlaps and Interactions. *Security Dialogue* 35(3): 352-53.

Van Ert, G. 2002. *Using International Law in Canadian Courts.* The Hague: Kluwer Law International.

Van Harten, G., and M. Loughlin. 2006. Investment Treaty Arbitration as a Species of Global Administrative Law. *European Journal of International Law* 17(1): 121-50.

Verdross, A. 1926. *Die Verfassung der Volkerrechtsgemeinschaft.* Vienna and Berlin: Julius Springer.

Vogel, D. 1995. *Trading Up: Consumer and Environmental Regulation in the Global Economy.* Cambridge, MA: Harvard University Press.

von Bogdandy, A. 2006. Constitutionalism in International Law: Comment on a Proposal from Germany. *Harvard International Law Journal* 47: 223-42.

Wai, R. 2002. Transnational Liftoff and Juridical Touchdown: The Regulatory Function of Private International Law in an Era of Globalization. *Columbia Journal of Transnational Law* 40: 209-74.

Walker, N. 2003. Postnational Constitutionalism and the Problem of Translation. In *European Constitutionalism beyond the State,* ed. J.H.H. Weiler and M. Wind, 27-54. Cambridge: Cambridge University Press.

Watson Hamilton, J. 2004. The Impact of International Commercial Arbitration on Canadian Law and Courts. In *Participatory Justice in a Global Economy: The New Rule of Law,* ed. P. Hughes and P.A. Molinari, 125-72. Montreal: Thémis.

Webb, K. 1999. Voluntary Initiatives and the Law. In *Voluntary Initiatives: The New Politics of Corporate Greening,* ed. R. Gibson, 32-50. Peterborough, ON: Broadview.

–. 2004a. Understanding the Voluntary Codes Phenomenon. In *Voluntary Codes: Private Governance, the Public Interest and Innovation,* ed. K. Webb, 3-34. Ottawa: Carleton University Research Unit for Innovation, Science and the Environment.

–, ed. 2004b. *Voluntary Codes: Private Governance, the Public Interest and Innovation.* Ottawa: Carleton University Research Unit for Innovation, Science and the Environment.

Weber, M. 1947. *The Theory of Social and Economic Organization.* New York: Free Press.

–. 1968. *Economy and Society: An Outline of Interpretive Sociology.* Translation edited by G. Roth and C. Wittich. New York: Bedminster Press.

Weiler, J.H.H. 1999. *The Constitution of Europe: "Do the New Clothes Have an Emperor?" and Other Essays on European Integration.* Cambridge: Cambridge University Press.

–. 2001. The Rule of Lawyers and the Ethos of Diplomats' Reflections on the Internal and External Legitimacy of WTO Dispute Settlement. *Journal of World Trade* 35(2): 191-207.

–. 2003. In Defence of the Status Quo: Europe's *Sonderweg.* In *European Constitutionalism beyond the State,* ed. J.H.H. Weiler and M. Wind, 7-23. Cambridge: Cambridge University Press.

Weiler, J.H.H., and M. Wind, eds. 2003. *European Constitutionalism beyond the State.* Cambridge: Cambridge University Press.

Welsh, J. 2004. *At Home in the World: Canada's Global Vision for the 21st Century.* Toronto: Harper Collins.

West Coast Environmental Law Association (WCEL). 2004. West Coast Environmental Law's Comments on Smart Regulation for Canada. Submission to External Advisory Committee on Smart Regulation. Vancouver: WCEL. http://www.wcel.org/.

Whitaker, R. 2006. Drifting Away from the Edge of Empire: Canada in the Era of George W. Bush. In *Empire's Law: The American Imperial Project and the "War to Remake the World,"* ed. A. Bartholomew, 265-81. London and Ann Arbor, MI: Pluto.

Wiener, A. 2003. Finality vs. Enlargement: Constitutive Practices and Opposing Ration-
ales in the Reconstruction of Europe. In *European Constitutionalism beyond the State*,
ed. J.H.H. Weiler and M. Wind, 157-201. Cambridge: Cambridge University Press.

Williams, D., and T. Young. 1994. Governance, the World Bank and Liberal Theory.
Political Studies 42: 84-100.

Wind, M. 2003. The European Union as a Polycentric Polity: Returning to a Neo-
medieval Europe? In *European Constitutionalism beyond the State*, ed. J.H.H. Weiler
and M. Wind, 103-31. Cambridge: Cambridge University Press.

Winfield, M.S., D. Whorley, and S.B. Kaufman. 2002. Public Safety in Private Hands: A
Study of Ontario's Technical Standards and Safety Authority. *Canadian Public Administration* 45: 24-51.

Wood, S. 1997. Renegades and Vigilantes in Multilateral Environmental Regimes: Lessons of the 1995 "Turbot War." In *Innovations in International Environmental Negotiation*, ed. L. Susskind, W. Moomaw, and T.L. Hill, 184-200. Cambridge, MA:
Harvard Program on Negotiation.

–. 2001. The High Price of Habitat Protection. *Alternatives: Environmental Thought, Policy
and Action* 27(3): 9-11.

–. 2002-03. Environmental Management Systems and Public Authority in Canada:
Rethinking Environmental Governance. *Buffalo Environmental Law Journal* 10: 129-
210.

–. 2003a. Green Revolution or Greenwash? Voluntary Environmental Standards, Public
Law and Private Authority in Canada. In *New Perspectives on the Public-Private
Divide*, ed. Law Commission of Canada, 123-65. Vancouver: UBC Press.

–. 2003b. Sustainability in International Law. *UNESCO Encyclopedia of Life Support Systems*, Article No. 1.45.4.10. Oxford: EOLSS. http://www.eolss.net.

–. 2005. Three Questions about Corporate Codes: Problematizations, Authorizations
and the Public/Private Divide. In *Ethics Codes, Corporations and the Challenge of
Globalization*, ed. W. Cragg, 245-88. Cheltenham, UK: Edward Elgar.

–. 2006. Voluntary Environmental Codes and Sustainability. In *Environmental Law for
Sustainability*, ed. B.J. Richardson and S. Wood, 229-76. Oxford and Portland, OR:
Hart.

Wood, S., and L. Johannson. 2008. Six Principles for Integrating Non-Governmental
Environmental Standards into Smart Regulation. *Osgoode Hall Law Journal* 46:
345-96.

Woods, A. 2009. Ottawa Waiting to See U.S. Green Plan. *Toronto Star*, 12 February. http://
www.thestar.com/.

World Bank. 1992. *Governance and Development*. Washington, DC: World Bank.

World Commission on Environment and Development. 1987. *Our Common Future*.
Oxford: Oxford University Press.

World Trade Organization. 2007. *The Legal Texts: The Results of the Uruguay Round of
Multilateral Trade Negotiations*. Cambridge: Cambridge University Press.

Wyn Jones, R. 1999. *Security, Strategy, and Critical Theory.* Boulder, CO: Lynne Rienner.

Yeager, P.C. 1991. *The Limits of Law: The Public Regulation of Private Pollution.* Cambridge: Cambridge University Press.

Acknowledgments

This collaborative enterprise began when we were both working as Virtual Scholars in Residence with the now-defunct Law Commission of Canada, which asked us to prepare a background report on the relationship between globalization and Canadian law. The project aimed to examine how global forces shape Canadian legal systems and how Canadians shape law and governance beyond our national borders, with an emphasis on how these complex phenomena are experienced by ordinary Canadians and how they might be made to serve collective goals of justice, democracy, and progress. Like many other questions addressed by the Law Commission, these were among the most challenging puzzles facing contemporary societies.

This "Governance Beyond Borders" project was one of the last undertaken by the Commission before its untimely termination by the federal government in 2006. The Commission's demise was a great loss not just to Canada but to the many nations for whom it represented a model of best practice. It took the function of law reform directly to the people, giving them substantial influence over the Commission's agenda and striving toward a legal system that would respond to their needs and aspirations. It was not just a talk shop for privileged legal elites. It gathered the best scholars from a range of academic disciplines to conduct comprehensive research into, and propose imaginative solutions to, the toughest questions – questions that had immediate relevance for ordinary Canadians and that were not just of esoteric interest to a few law professors.

The Commission performed an invaluable service for the federal government by providing independent and non-partisan advice about how to ensure that law is effective, accessible, and responsive to the changing needs of Canadian society. It also helped stimulate broader debates about the role of law in achieving justice, equality, fairness, and accountability.

The decision to discontinue the Commission showed a striking disregard for the lessons learned from the termination of the earlier Law Reform Commission of Canada, which was established in 1971 and became a path-breaking institution in the world of law reform. Prime Minister Brian Mulroney's neo-conservative government abolished it in 1992 in a round of budget cuts that deprived Ottawa of several important sources of independent research and advice. Five years later, realizing the false economy of this short-sighted move, the government led by Prime Minister Jean Chrétien established the Law Commission of Canada, giving it a unique mandate to engage Canadians in the continual renewal of their laws and legal system. The decision by Prime Minister Stephen Harper's government to shut down the Commission betrayed a crass disdain for the benefits this institution conferred upon the federal government and Canadians. The amount saved for the federal coffers was a mere pittance in relative terms: the Commission accomplished its important work on a budget of just over $4 million per year.

This book is offered in the hope that the federal government will once again see the value of this modest investment in the future of our legal system.

Two Law Commission of Canada/Social Sciences and Humanities Research Council of Canada Virtual Scholar in Residence grants made the initial phase of research for this book possible by providing each of us with research funding and a year-long teaching release.

We are particularly grateful to Nathalie Des Rosiers, President of the Law Commission when we began the project, for her tireless dedication to the Commission's mandate and her keen interest in the challenge of governance beyond borders; Lorraine Pelot, erstwhile Senior Research Officer with the Law Commission, who brought great enthusiasm and insight to the project; and Bernard Colas, Acting President of the Commission during the latter part of our work, who provided valuable input at critical junctures.

One or the other of us presented portions of the work in progress at several academic venues, including the Law and Society Association, the Centre de recherche en droit public at the Université de Montréal, the Canadian Centre for Policy Alternatives, Osgoode Hall Law School, and the University of Toronto Faculty of Law. We benefited in particular from the advice of Harry Arthurs and Ruth Buchanan, whose challenging yet encouraging feedback stimulated us to turn our Law Commission background report into a book. We thank Harry, Ruth, Rod MacDonald, and other scholars who attended a roundtable at the combined 2005 Annual Meetings of the Law and Society Association and the Canadian Law and Society Association in Harrison Hot Springs, British Columbia. We also thank Daniel Drache, Stephen McBride, Scott Prudham, and other participants in a joint session of the Canadian Political Science Association and Canadian Association of Geographers at the 2005 Congress of the Social Sciences and Humanities in London, Ontario.

We are grateful to Oonagh Fitzgerald and the excellent international law scholars and practitioners who participated in the federal Department of Justice's research project on the Globalized Rule of Law for helping us to refine our thinking about Canada's supraconstitution. We also acknowledge the three anonymous reviewers whose comments were very helpful in finalizing the manuscript for this book.

We could not have completed the project without the assistance of several capable students at Osgoode Hall Law School and the University of Toronto, including Ren Bucholz, Jennifer Kirton, Alanna Krolikowski, Kim Lawton, Heather Hui-Litwin, Tim Phillips, and Ugo Ukpabi. Michael Lawrence did outstanding research on the evolution of human security norms and the notion of human *cultural* security.

Finally, what can be said to thank the family members and loved ones, both present and departed, to whom we owe so much?

Index

Amanda Glasbeek
  Feminized Justice: The Toronto Women's Court, 1913-34 (2009)

Kimberley Brooks (ed.)
  Justice Bertha Wilson: One Woman's Difference (2009)

Wayne V. McIntosh and Cynthia L. Cates
  Multi-Party Litigation: The Strategic Context (2009)

Renisa Mawani
  Colonial Proximities: Crossracial Encounters and Juridical Truths in British Columbia, 1871-1921 (2009)

James B. Kelly and Christopher P. Manfredi (eds.)
  Contested Constitutionalism: Reflections on the Canadian Charter of Rights and Freedoms (2009)

Catherine E. Bell and Robert K. Paterson (eds.)
  Protection of First Nations Cultural Heritage: Laws, Policy, and Reform (2008)

Hamar Foster, Benjamin L. Berger, and A.R. Buck (eds.)
  The Grand Experiment: Law and Legal Culture in British Settler Societies (2008)

Richard J. Moon (ed.)
  Law and Religious Pluralism in Canada (2008)

Catherine E. Bell and Val Napoleon (eds.)
  First Nations Cultural Heritage and Law: Case Studies, Voices, and Perspectives (2008)

Douglas C. Harris
  Landing Native Fisheries: Indian Reserves and Fishing Rights in British Columbia, 1849-1925 (2008)

Peggy J. Blair
  Lament for a First Nation: The Williams Treaties in Southern Ontario (2008)

Lori G. Beaman
  Defining Harm: Religious Freedom and the Limits of the Law (2007)

Stephen Tierney (ed.)
  Multiculturalism and the Canadian Constitution (2007)

Julie Macfarlane
  The New Lawyer: How Settlement Is Transforming the Practice of Law (2007)

Kimberley White
  Negotiating Responsibility: Law, Murder, and States of Mind (2007)

Dawn Moore
  Criminal Artefacts: Governing Drugs and Users (2007)

Hamar Foster, Heather Raven, and Jeremy Webber (eds.)
  Let Right Be Done: Aboriginal Title, the Calder Case, and the Future of Indigenous Rights (2007)

Dorothy E. Chunn, Susan B. Boyd, and Hester Lessard (eds.)
  Reaction and Resistance: Feminism, Law, and Social Change (2007)

Margot Young, Susan B. Boyd, Gwen Brodsky, and Shelagh Day (eds.)
  Poverty: Rights, Social Citizenship, and Legal Activism (2007)

Rosanna L. Langer
  Defining Rights and Wrongs: Bureaucracy, Human Rights, and Public Accountability (2007)

C.L. Ostberg and Matthew E. Wetstein
  Attitudinal Decision Making in the Supreme Court of Canada (2007)

Chris Clarkson
  Domestic Reforms: Political Visions and Family Regulation in British Columbia, 1862-1940 (2007)

Jean McKenzie Leiper
  Bar Codes: Women in the Legal Profession (2006)

Gerald Baier
  Courts and Federalism: Judicial Doctrine in the United States, Australia, and Canada (2006)

Avigail Eisenberg (ed.)
  Diversity and Equality: The Changing Framework of Freedom in Canada (2006)

Randy K. Lippert
  Sanctuary, Sovereignty, Sacrifice: Canadian Sanctuary Incidents, Power, and Law (2005)

James B. Kelly
  Governing with the Charter: Legislative and Judicial Activism and Framers' Intent (2005)

Dianne Pothier and Richard Devlin (eds.)
  Critical Disability Theory: Essays in Philosophy, Politics, Policy, and Law (2005)

Susan G. Drummond
  Mapping Marriage Law in Spanish Gitano Communities (2005)

Louis A. Knafla and Jonathan Swainger (eds.)
  Laws and Societies in the Canadian Prairie West, 1670-1940 (2005)

Ikechi Mgbeoji
  Global Biopiracy: Patents, Plants, and Indigenous Knowledge (2005)

Florian Sauvageau, David Schneiderman, and David Taras, with Ruth Klinkhammer and Pierre Trudel
  The Last Word: Media Coverage of the Supreme Court of Canada (2005)

Gerald Kernerman
  Multicultural Nationalism: Civilizing Difference, Constituting Community (2005)

Pamela A. Jordan
  Defending Rights in Russia: Lawyers, the State, and Legal Reform in the Post-Soviet Era (2005)

Anna Pratt
  Securing Borders: Detention and Deportation in Canada (2005)

Kirsten Johnson Kramar
  Unwilling Mothers, Unwanted Babies:
  Infanticide in Canada (2005)

W.A. Bogart
  Good Government? Good Citizens?
  Courts, Politics, and Markets in a
  Changing Canada (2005)

Catherine Dauvergne
  Humanitarianism, Identity, and
  Nation: Migration Laws in Canada
  and Australia (2005)

Michael Lee Ross
  First Nations Sacred Sites in Canada's
  Courts (2005)

Andrew Woolford
  Between Justice and Certainty: Treaty
  Making in British Columbia (2005)

John McLaren, Andrew Buck, and Nancy
Wright (eds.)
  Despotic Dominion: Property Rights in
  British Settler Societies (2004)

Georges Campeau
  From UI to EI: Waging War on the
  Welfare State (2004)

Alvin J. Esau
  The Courts and the Colonies:
  The Litigation of Hutterite Church Dis-
  putes (2004)

Christopher N. Kendall
  Gay Male Pornography: An Issue of Sex
  Discrimination (2004)

Roy B. Flemming
  Tournament of Appeals: Granting
  Judicial Review in Canada (2004)

Constance Backhouse and Nancy L.
Backhouse
  The Heiress vs the Establishment:
  Mrs. Campbell's Campaign for Legal
  Justice (2004)

Christopher P. Manfredi
  Feminist Activism in the Supreme
  Court: Legal Mobilization and the
  Women's Legal Education and Action
  Fund (2004)

Annalise Acorn
  Compulsory Compassion: A Critique of
  Restorative Justice (2004)

Jonathan Swainger and Constance
Backhouse (eds.)
  People and Place: Historical Influences
  on Legal Culture (2003)

Jim Phillips and Rosemary Gartner
  Murdering Holiness: The Trials of
  Franz Creffield and George Mitchell
  (2003)

David R. Boyd
  Unnatural Law: Rethinking Canadian
  Environmental Law and Policy (2003)

Ikechi Mgbeoji
  Collective Insecurity: The Liberian
  Crisis, Unilateralism, and Global
  Order (2003)

Rebecca Johnson
  Taxing Choices: The Intersection of
  Class, Gender, Parenthood, and the
  Law (2002)

John McLaren, Robert Menzies, and
Dorothy E. Chunn (eds.)
  Regulating Lives: Historical Essays on
  the State, Society, the Individual, and
  the Law (2002)

Joan Brockman
  Gender in the Legal Profession: Fitting
  or Breaking the Mould (2001)

Printed and bound in Canada by Friesens

Set in Giovanni and Scala Sans by Artegraphica Design Co. Ltd.

Copy editor: Deborah Kerr

Proofreader: Danielle Arbuckle

Indexer: Margaret Manery